ARCHAEOLOGY AS CULTURAL HISTORY

Social Archaeology

General Editor: Ian Hodder, Stanford University

Advisory Editors
Margaret Conkey, University of California at Berkeley
Mark Leone, University of Maryland
Alain Schnapp, U.E.R. d'Art et d'Archéologie, Paris
Stephen Shennan, University of Southampton
Bruce Trigger, McGill University, Montreal

Titles in Print

In preparation

Archaeology as Cultural History

Words and Things in Iron Age Greece

Ian Morris

BLACKWELL
Publishers

First published 2000

2 4 6 8 10 9 7 5 3 1

Blackwell Publishers Inc.
350 Main Street
Malden, Massachusetts 02148
USA

Blackwell Publishers Ltd
108 Cowley Road
Oxford OX4 1JF
UK

Library of Congress Cataloging-in-Publication Data
Morris, Ian, 1960–
    Archaeology as cultural history : words and things in Iron Age
Greece / Ian Morris.
        p.   cm. – (Social archaeology)
    Includes bibliographical references.
    ISBN 0-631-17409-5 (alk. paper). – ISBN 0-631-19602-1 (pbk : alk. paper)
    1. Iron age – Greece.   2. Greece – Civilization.   3. Greece – Antiquities.
4. Archaeology – Social aspects – Greece.   I. Title.   II. Series.
DF78.M635   1999
938 – dc21   99-19855
                                                                              CIP

British Library Cataloguing in Publication Data

A CIP catalogue record for this book is available from the British Library.

Typeset in 10½ on 12 pt Stemple Garamond
by Best-set Typesetter Ltd, Hong Kong
Printed in Great Britain by MPG Books Ltd, Bodmin, Cornwall
This book is printed on acid-free paper.

In memory of
Braxton Ross

Contents

Illustrations

Preface and Acknowledgments

In 1997 Mads Ravn, an old digging friend, asked me to write an essay for a volume of the *Archaeological Review from Cambridge* he was editing on archaeology and history. I produced a short paper called "Archaeology as Cultural History." Brevity focuses the mind; as I wrote, I realized how much my work in the 1990s had been driven by seeing archaeology as a kind of cultural history, and I decided to explore this at more length.

Like most historians, I make my arguments not through high-level theorizing but through empirical study of a specific case, Iron Age Greece (roughly 1100–600 BC). In Part I, I clarify my terms. Part II is a historiographical study, locating Iron Age Greek archaeology within the larger field of archaeology and explaining why so few archaeologists have seen it as cultural history. In Part III I set out my reasons for studying this period, trying to address big questions about the nature of equality; and in Part IV I explore in detail the archaeology.

This book does not look like most archaeology books (or most history books for that matter), but I see that as its main strength. I devote roughly equal space to words and things. This courts the danger of falling between several stools – not saying enough about questions of detail to satisfy specialists, but dwelling on them too much for comparativists; and of spending too much time on texts for archaeologists, and too much on artifacts for historians. But the risks are worth taking. I argue that we are entering a new phase in archaeological scholarship, when historical archaeology, in the traditional sense of the archaeology of textually documented periods, should displace prehistory as the central arena for generating and debating new concepts. As this happens, archaeology as a whole will become more historical, in the broader sense of thinking historically about people in the past. I try to treat words and things equally seriously, bringing together the details of the primary written sources and the analysis of large numbers of material data.

I want to thank everyone who has read and commented on parts of the manuscript at various stages (David Aftandilian, Anders Andrén, Martin Bernal, Margot Browning, Joseph Bryant, Paul Cartledge, Robert Cook, Eric Csapo, Jack Davis, Carol Dougherty, Kenneth Dover, Steve Dyson, Mihalis Fotiadis, Charles Hedrick, Michael Herzfeld, Herbert Hoffmann, Sanne Houby-Nielsen, Nick Kardulias, Leslie Kurke, Hilary Mackie, Lisa Maurizio, Joe Manning, Margaret Miller, Sarah Morris, Greg Nagy, Martin Ostwald, John Papadopoulos, Kurt Raaflaub, Eric Robinson, Kathy St. John, Richard Saller, Chester Starr, George Stocking, Bruce Trigger, Hans van Wees, Peter White, and James Whitley) – without, of course, implicating them in the results. And I particularly want to thank Ian Hodder, Josh Ober, Michael Shanks, and Anthony Snodgrass for giving me extremely helpful suggestions on a longer and more convoluted version of the whole book.

I have presented some of my arguments in papers at Austin, Berkeley, Brussels, Cardiff, Chicago, Cincinnati, Columbia, Evanston, Houston, London (Ontario), Los Angeles, Naples, San Jose, Stanford, Toronto, and Washington, and I benefited greatly from the discussions that followed. Part of this book is about the institutional history of academia, and I must also thank those institutions which shaped my work: the Center for Hellenic Studies, where I held a fellowship in 1989/90 and thought through some of the ideas in chapter 2; the Institute for the Humanities at the University of Wisconsin, where I held a fellowship in 1992/3 and worked on what eventually became Part III; and particularly Stanford University and the University of Chicago. At Stanford the meetings of the Social Science History Institute and of the "Early Greece" seminar in autumn 1998 made me think harder about my assumptions. Chairing the Classics department in 1996–8 inevitably slowed down this book, but also helped me to see many issues differently.

I have been thinking about the issues in this book all through the 1990s, and some chapters return to problems I have written about elsewhere. I based chapter 2 on "Archaeologies of Greece," in Ian Morris, ed., *Classical Greece: Ancient Histories and Modern Archaeologies* (Cambridge, 1994), pp. 8–47, and chapter 3 on "Periodization and the Heroes," in Mark Golden and Peter Toohey, eds., *Inventing Classical Culture: Historicism, Periodization, and the Ancient World* (New York, 1997), pp. 96–131. I have extensively rewritten both. Part III expands the arguments of "The Strong Principle of Equality and the Archaic Origins of Greek Democracy," in Josh Ober and Charles

Hedrick, eds., *Demokratia: A Conversation on Democracies, Ancient and Modern* (Princeton, 1996), pp. 19–48. I sketched out some of the ideas in chapter 6 in "Negotiated Peripherality in Iron Age Greece," in P. Nick Kardulias, ed., *World-Systems Theory in Practice* (Lanham, MD, 1999), pp. 63–84, and some of those in chapter 7 in "Burning the Dead in Archaic Athens," in Annie Verbanck-Piérard and Didier Viviers, eds., *Culture et cité: l'avènement de l'Athènes archaïque* (Brussels, 1995), pp. 45–74. I thank the Cambridge University Press, Duckworth, Princeton University Press, Rowman and Littlefield, and the Free University of Brussels for permission to rework this material.

When quoting long passages from ancient authors, I use the following easily available translations: Aristophanes: Parker 1969; Aristotle: Rhodes 1984; Herodotus: Grene 1986; Homer: Lattimore 1951, 1965; the Old Oligarch: Gray 1986; Plato: Adkins 1986 (*Apology*), Guthrie 1956 (*Protagoras*); Thucydides: Warner 1954; Xenophon: Pomeroy 1994. The translations of shorter passages are my own, unless noted otherwise. When citing the fragments of archaic poets, I use the following editions, unless noted otherwise: Alcaeus, Sappho: Lobel and Page 1955. Alcman, Anacreon, Simonides, Stesichorus: Page 1962. Archilochus, Callinus, Hipponax, Mimnermus, Semonides, Simonides (elegiac fragments), Solon, Tyrtaeus: West 1991/2. Bacchylides: Snell and Maehler 1970. Hesiod fragments: Merkelbach and West 1967. Pindar fragments: Maehler 1989. Xenophanes: Diels and Kranz 1956.

Generally, I follow the conventions of other books in the *Social Archaeology* series, but one of the pecularities of Iron Age Greek archaeology is that a lot of evidence is known only from brief preliminary reports in journals. To avoid making the bibliography even longer, I depart from the normal referencing style and limit citations of these journal reports to the footnotes. I list the abbreviations for the journals in the section which follows.

Finally, Ian Hodder, Tessa Harvey, Louise Spencely, Cameron Laux, and John Davey have provided timely help, and put up with delays, surprises, and abrupt changes in direction. I thank them for their skill, wisdom, and patience in seeing the book into print.

Boulder Creek, California

Journal Abbreviations

AA	*Archäologischer Anzeiger*
AAA	*Athens Annals of Archaeology*
AArch	*Acta Archaeologica*
AD	*Archaiologikon Deltion*
AE	*Archaiologiki Ephemeris*
AEMTh	*To Archaiologiko Ergo sti Makedonia kai Thraki*
AJ	*Antiquaries Journal*
AJA	*American Journal of Archaeology*
Anat St	*Anatolian Studies*
Annales ESC	*Annales: économies, sociétés, civilisations*
Ann Rev Anth	*Annual Review of Anthropology*
AION	*Annali di Archeologia e Storia Antica, Istituto Universitario Orientale di Napoli*
Ant K	*Antike Kunst*
ASAA	*Annuario di Scuola Archeologica di Atene*
AM	*Athenische Mitteilungen*
BAR	*British Archaeological Reports*
BCH	*Bulletin de correspondance hellénique*
BICS	*Bulletin of the Institute of Classical Studies*
BSA	*Annual of the British School at Athens*
CA	*Classical Antiquity*
CAH	*Cambridge Ancient History*
CJ	*Classical Journal*
ClR	*Clara Rhodos*
CM	*Classica et Medievalia*
CP	*Classical Philology*
CQ	*Classical Quarterly*
EA	*Ephemeris Archaiologiki*
HWJ	*History Workshop Journal*
IM	*Istanbuler Mitteilungen*

JdI	Jahrbuch des deutschen archäologisches Instituts
JHS	Journal of Hellenic Studies
JMA	Journal of Mediterranean Archaeology
JMH	Journal of Modern History
JRS	Journal of Roman Studies
NAR	Norwegian Archaeological Review
ÖJh	Jahreshefte des österreichisches archäologisches Instituts
QUCC	Quaderni Urbinati di Cultura Classica
RDAC	Report of the Department of Antquities, Cyprus
TAPA	Transactions of the American Philological Association
WA	World Archaeology

Part I

1

Archaeology as Cultural History

The Argument

Archaeology is cultural history or it is nothing.

I hold this truth to be self-evident, but like most such truths, the problems begin when we try to say exactly what it means. I start with a simple proposition, then spend most of this chapter elaborating on it. Archaeology is the study of what survives of the material culture of people who lived in the past. Insofar as archaeology is about people who lived in the past, it is historical; and insofar as it is about material culture, it is cultural. Therefore archaeology is cultural history.

This sounds like common sense, but surprisingly few archaeologists seem to agree. Fifty years ago, it was a truism in Europe (though less so in America) that archaeology was the handmaiden to history. That perspective now seems distinctly limited. Some people would see archaeology as a natural science; others, as a social science, probably anthropology. Others still hold that archaeology is simply itself: archaeology is archaeology is archaeology. Or maybe it is like literary criticism, or even a form of political activism. Some postprocessual archaeologists call themselves historians of the long term (e.g., Hodder 1987a); others look for ways to bring texts and artifacts together (e.g., Kepecs and Kolb 1997; Ravn and Britton 1997). But overall, the one group that archaeologists hardly ever hold up as a model is the tribe of historians, the only other scholars to devote themselves systematically to the human past.

Yet saying that archaeology is cultural history is rather a quiet revolution, because cultural history is already to a considerable extent anthropology, sociology, literary criticism, and a whole string of other things. We live in an age of what Clifford Geertz (1983: 19–35) calls blurred genres, and one of its most striking developments is a "historical turn" all across the social sciences (e.g., Cohen and Roth 1995; McDonald 1996). Anthony Giddens (1979: 230) bluntly claims that "There simply are no logical or even methodological distinctions between the social sciences and history – appropriately conceived." William Sewell (1996: 272) spells out the implications of this: history is not the past tense of sociology, increasing the number of comparisons available. Rather, thinking historically requires an "eventful sociology," in which "temporalities . . . are path dependent, causally heterogeneous, and contingent, and reconfiguration of structures by social action is at the core of explanatory models."

If this is so, what does it mean to say that archaeology is cultural history? I explain what I mean by "cultural history" in the next section, but for now I emphasize just two features of what historians of all stripes do. First, they study how people construct and contest culture and meaning *through time*; and second, they explore these issues empirically, through concrete analyses of real people in the past. Despite the obvious relevance of such work, archaeologists seem to understand what historians do less well than many other groups of social scientists.

To clarify what I mean by thinking "through time," I draw on Fernand Braudel's well-known proposal "to dissect history into various planes, or, to put it another way, to divide historical time into geographical time, social time, and individual time" (1972 [1949]: 21). He criticized his predecessors for concentrating on *l'histoire événementielle*, the doings of kings and diplomats, measured in individual time. He suggested that the fundamental temporal level was geographical, the barely perceptible rhythms of *la longue durée*, measured in centuries, which could even be *l'histoire immobile*. Political events were no more than "surface disturbances, crests of foam that the tides of history carry on their strong backs" (Braudel 1980 [1958]: 21). Between these levels lay the time of *conjonctures*, social time, measured in periods of anywhere from five to fifty years. This was the scale on which economic cycles and institutions worked.

This layering of time is central to the historical turn in the social sciences. For Giddens, tracing Braudel's terminology back to Henri Bergson's,

> there are three intersecting planes of temporality involved in every moment of social reproduction. There is the temporality of immediate experience, the continuous flow of day-to-day life: what Schutz, following Bergson, calls the *durée* of activity. Second, there is the temporality of *Dasein*, the life-cycle of the organism. Third, there is what Braudel calls the *longue durée*. (Giddens 1981: 19–20)

ARCHAEOLOGY AS CULTURAL HISTORY 5

Archaeologists now regularly draw on the ideas of the Annaliste school of historians which Braudel led for twenty years (e.g., Bintliff 1991; Knapp 1992), following his emphasis on the *longue durée*. But they have taken little notice of the Annalistes' subsequent reaction against the "tyranny of the long-term" (*Annales* 1988; 1989). Jean-Yves Grenier (1995) and André Burguière (1995), for example, would deconstruct the very notion of a *longue durée*. I propose less drastic steps in this book; but the core of the approaches pioneered by social scientists like Bourdieu (1977), Sahlins (1985), and Giddens (1979) lies in linking microanalysis of social interactions via institutional analysis to long-term processes, working at all three temporal levels. Yet archaeologists have virtually ignored human time.

Empirical constraints have a lot to do with this. Much of the most ambitious postprocessual archaeology focuses on neolithic Europe, where the data rarely allow us to think in human time. John Barrett's important study of southern England between 2900 and 1200 BC illustrates the issues. Although noting that "we are obviously dealing with a high degree of chronological uncertainty" (1994: 47), he suggests that the real problem lies in the way we think of "individuals . . . as given, pre-existing the material consequences of their actions." This reduces discussion to "the methodological question of how we might recognize an individual's life." In the neolithic we cannot do so, leading some to conclude that "the individual is not an analytically useful unit of study." But Barrett proposes "that we should abandon this whole approach and begin instead to investigate the more interesting questions concerning the ways in which lives were constituted as knowledgeable and motivated." This requires that "we move away from asking 'what kinds of people made these conditions?', to an understanding of what the possibilities were of being human within those material and historical conditions" (Barrett 1994: 4–5).

I single out Barrett's book because he faces the issues so directly. But in doing so he redefines the terms more than he engages with human time. The same problems arise in other postprocessual work dealing with such vast sweeps of time. Their strengths are great but they remain *unhistorical*, because they cannot relate structure and conjuncture to human time. They leave us with what Lynn Meskell (1996: 7) calls "uninhabited histories and non-peopled pasts." Most prehistorians evade individual time by taking refuge in evolutionism or burying it in abstract theorizing.

In this book I want to offer a more properly historical archaeology, taking all three temporal levels equally seriously. Following historians' normal practice, I do this through empirical analysis of a particular time and place, Iron Age Greece (roughly the half-millennium

1100–600 BC). I want to make two points about this period at the
outset. First, in certain places and certain contexts, its archaeological
chronology is exceptionally precise. It has its problems, and I have set
out my views on these elsewhere (I. Morris 1987: 10–18, 158–67;
1993a; 1996), but from about 750 BC on, we can date some kinds of
deposits within a margin of plus or minus 25 years. In practical terms,
this is about as tight a margin as archaeologists are ever likely to get.
It is not what Braudel had in mind when he spoke of individual time,
and modern historians might think a quarter-century chronology
absurdly crude. But as Anthony Snodgrass (1987: 36–66) shows, classical archaeologists' attempts to write narrative political history have
been unsuccessful. This chronological framework leaves us on the cusp
between social and individual time, but it is nonetheless a timescale
which makes sense in human terms (cf. Manning 1998: 321). Before
750 there is more debate, although dendrochronology now supports
the traditional dates (Kuniholm 1996).

Andrén suggests that archaeologists think of texts as "contemporary analogies." Texts are not a different order of evidence, telling us
what artifacts mean. Nor should we expect the material record to
prove written accounts right or wrong. All archaeological interpretation is analogical. The best analogies will be those that Ian Hodder
(1982: 11–27) calls "relational," where there are so many similarities
between the overall contexts being compared, or between the archaeological data and a general ethnological model, that we can plausibly
extrapolate from an ethnographic or historical comparison to an
archaeological case. Andrén argues that

> Closeness in time, space, and form (such as technological similarity) is
> always held up as a criterion of a good analogy. The field of historical
> archaeology can thus be seen as a special case in archaeology as a whole,
> since the analogies are particularly close because artifact and text are
> "contemporary analogies." (Andrén 1998: 156)

Whether interpreting a mesolithic site through an Eskimo ethnography or a classical site through contemporary literature, we are making
analogical arguments. But when we read primary texts alongside the
artifacts, our analogies are far stronger than when we rely on
information from other times and places.

Geertz (1973: 28) suggests that the goal of cultural anthropology is
"to draw large conclusions from small, but very densely textured facts;
to support broad assertions about the role of culture in the construction of collective life by engaging them exactly with complex
specifics." The problem is that for prehistorians, the facts rarely seem

Table 1.1   Standard periodization for central Greece

Late Bronze Age/Mycenaean	*c.* 1600–1200 BC
Late Helladic IIIC	*c.* 1200–1075 BC
Early Iron Age/Dark Age	*c.* 1075–700 BC
Archaic	*c.* 700–480 BC
Classical	480–323 BC
Hellenistic	323–31 BC

The Early Iron Age is usually subdivided by pottery styles. The dates of these vary locally, but the Athenian sequence is normally dated as follows:

Submycenaean	*c.* 1075–1025 BC
Protogeometric	*c.* 1025–900 BC
Early Geometric	*c.* 900–850 BC
Middle Geometric	*c.* 850–760 BC
Late Geometric	*c.* 760–700 BC

densely textured enough, and the appraisals (the word Geertz (1973: 16) prefers to verification) not rigorous enough.

The more varied and detailed our evidence, the thicker and better our descriptions will be. That much is obvious. Written evidence makes our accounts more specific and our analogies much closer. We can play categories of evidence against each other more confidently and subtly than if we had to rely entirely on analogy with other societies. But that does not mean that archaeology can *only* be cultural history when we have texts. As Barrett (1994: 71) points out, "we must allow for non-linguistic and pre-linguistic knowledges, as practical ways of knowing the world, but which informants would have considerable difficulty in ever expressing verbally." The crucial issue is not the presence or absence of writing but the density, quality, and variety of data points. When we study fifth- or fourth-century BC Athens, for example, there is a rich literary record. This is a fully historical period, even though certain genres – private letters, diaries, household accounts – are largely lacking. When we move back into the archaic period (table 1.1), the range of sources narrows, to poetry, then in the eighth century to epic poetry, until by the ninth century there is nothing at all. But even when we think about the tenth century, as I do in chapter 6, we gain much by looking back in the light of archaic poetry. It does not make much sense to say that there is a threshold defined by the quantity, the range, or even the presence of written sources, which a period must meet to be dignified as "historical." Rather, as we move back in time from the fourth century, or out in space from Athens, it gradually gets harder to write accounts which meet the challenges I discuss in this chapter. As the quantity of finds from the Greek Dark Age has increased, our accounts have become more historical, although we have not found written sources older than Homer (and probably never will).

In a few cases, the texture of prehistoric facts is dense enough for thinking on something like a human timescale. The rebuilding of neolithic long houses on some central European sites can be broken down into phases of just twenty years (Bradley 1998: 43–8), and at Çatalhöyük the replastering of houses and the burials beneath their floors offer even finer chronologies. Matthews *et al.* (1997: 304) argue that "These discrete lenses perhaps allow us to come close to attaining the required degrees of precision for tracing remains of individual actions or sets of activities which are central to current methodological and theoretical objectives in archaeology." These are exceptional cases, but dendrochronology holds out the possibility of extending historical approaches, combining all temporal levels, back to the third millennium (Baillie 1995; Manning 1998: 322–5).

Cultural history is not, then, solely the concern of text-aided archaeologists. But taking history seriously will change the relationships between text-aided and prehistoric archaeology. Kathleen Deagan (1988: 10) notes that as Americanist historical archaeology became more theory-conscious in the 1980s, it moved from being the "handmaiden to history" to being a "handmaiden to prehistoric archaeology," a testing ground for models developed in prehistory, where the real action was. Incorporating human time means that text-aided archaeology, which has the thickest and richest evidence, should move to the forefront of theoretical and methodological debates. Some historical archaeologists are already claiming this place (e.g., Johnson 1996; Orser 1996a,b).

In the next section, I define more fully what I mean by cultural history. I stress (1) a shift from materialist causation toward studying representations; (2) interest in the construction and contestation of meaning; and (3) a focus on voluntarism. I then turn to cultural analysis in archaeology, asking why archaeologists show so little interest in cultural history. I explain this historically, focusing on the effects of institutional confinements. In the fourth section I discuss the methods of this book, and set out its arguments.

I hope to reach several audiences. The first is that which I think the editorial board of the *Social Archaeology* series imagines: a broad archaeological community including workers in the new and old worlds, from the palaeolithic through the twentieth century. I want to say something of interest to archaeologists of all times and places. But since my argument is that archaeology is cultural history, I set about my task like a historian. As I explain in the final section of this chapter, Parts III and IV of this book are a detailed study of changing notions of time, place, and space in Iron Age Greece. I therefore want classical archaeologists and ancient historians to read this book too: the methods of cultural history and arguments within nonclassical archaeologies have still had only limited impact in these fields. Finally, saying that archaeology is cultural history should be as significant for cultural historians as for archaeologists. Some of the best work in modern cultural history is being done on material culture, but few of the scholars engaged in it seem to care about how archaeologists approach the world of things. As so often, promising lines of inquiry coincide with institutional and disciplinary boundaries, and I hope to do something to bridge these.

Cultural History

If anything unites cultural history, it is polemic. The "new cultural history" of the last fifteen years comes in several national schools (the French, drawing on Foucault and Parisian re-readings of Marx; the British, influenced heavily by E. P. Thompson, and often focusing on political language; the American, sometimes leaning on Geertz and Sahlins as well as Foucault, other times more influenced by deconstruction; and Italian microhistory, borrowing from postmodern ethnography), divided by misunderstandings and controversies (e.g., Cerutti 1997; Joyce 1998; Stedman Jones 1998). But two main themes recur. The first is a rejection of material causation. Introducing a volume of essays called simply *The New Cultural History*, Lynn Hunt (1989: 7) suggests that "Economic and social relations are not prior to or determining cultural ones; they are themselves fields of cultural practice and cultural determination – which cannot be explained deductively by reference to an extracultural dimension of meaning." The second theme follows from the first. For older social histories, with their "almost tyrannical pre-eminence of the social dimension, which predefines the cultural cleavages that are to be described" (Chartier 1988: 30), we should substitute what Chartier calls "a cultural history of society." This focuses on how people *represent* their worlds, the social categories they create, and the conflicts these generate:

The definition of cultural history . . . must be conceived as the analysis of the process of representation – that is, of the production of classifications and exclusions that constitute the social and conceptual configurations proper to one time or one place . . . [but t]his history must also be understood as the study of the processes by which meaning is constructed. Breaking with the old idea that endowed texts and works with an intrinsic, absolute and unique meaning which it was the critic's task to identify, history is turning to practices that give meaning to the world in plural and even contradictory ways. (Chartier 1988: 13–14)

But beyond a shared commitment to extending cultural analysis to all dimensions of life, and shifting from digging out social facts to enjoying the play of representations, there is little agreement. I divide the debates into three groups.

1. Cultural History as Community

The first line of thought is that cultural history is about widely shared dispositions, which unite the inhabitants of a village, city, or nation at a given time. This concept is familiar in most human sciences. In the heyday of functionalism, scholars tended to imagine the world as made up of discrete, spatially bounded cultures. Any ethnographic yarn could begin "among the so-and-so," and listeners would immediately understand the frame of reference. For most of us, expressions like "Old Regime France" or "Jacksonian America" conjure up particular (if vague) images of "what it was like" back then. And with good reason; cultural historians and ethnographers regularly find that even in the most conflict-ridden societies, certain mentalities cross-cut most or all boundaries, allowing them to define the group in question as a "society."

Kroeber and Kluckhohn (1952) traced this idea of culture back to the eighteenth-century Göttingen school of historians, whose approach was marginalized in the nineteenth century by the Rankean model of document-driven political history. Robert Darnton, who has worked closely with Geertz, is the best-known exponent of what he calls "the anthropological approach." Darnton (1984: 4–5) argues that the key to cultural history is the fact that "What was proverbial wisdom for our ancestors is completely opaque to us . . . When we cannot get a proverb, or a joke, or a ritual, or a poem, we know we are on to something. By picking at the document where it is most opaque, we may be able to unravel an alien system of meaning. The thread might even lead into a strange and wonderful world view." Such a world view, the ability to get a joke, belongs to the whole community:

All of us, French and "Anglo-Saxons," pedants as well as peasants, operate within cultural constraints, just as we all share conventions of speech. So historians should be able to see how cultures shape ways of thinking, even for the greatest thinkers. A poet or philosopher may push a language to its limits, but at some point he will hit against the outer frame of meaning. Beyond it, madness lies – the fate of Hölderlin or Nietzsche. But within it, great men can test and shape the boundaries of meaning. Thus there should be room for Diderot and Rousseau in a book about *mentalités* in eighteenth-century France. By including them along with the peasant tellers of tales and the plebian killers of cats, I have abandoned the usual distinction between elite and popular culture, and have tried to show how intellectuals and common people coped with the same sort of problems. (Darnton 1984: 6–7)

2. Cultural History as Conflict

But there were jokes at the court of Louis XVI which peasants in Languedoc did not get, and vice versa, and some of Darnton's best essays highlight just such failures of comprehension. Cultural history is about divisions and conflicts as much as agreements and shared understandings. Returning to the example of Jacksonian America, our feel for "what it was like" fragments on closer inspection. We see distinctions between the worlds of European colonists, native Americans, and African slaves. Even among whites, we find remarkable differences between subcultures of men and women, rich and poor, urban and rural, not to mention immigrants from different nations and members of different churches. Even, say, among rich, male, white Anglo-Saxon Protestants, we find profound disagreements over that most fundamental question, the nature of the good society. Some clung to an ideal of a republic of yeoman farmers; others vigorously promoted urbanization, industry, and modern financial institutions. Culture breaks down; one man's shared disposition is another's ideology, a false consciousness. Where Geertzian/Darntonian cultural historians find meaning and complexity, Marxists and feminists may see mystification and oppression.

1820s north America was a complex society going through rapid changes, but even in the most isolated groups ethnographers find similar distinctions. However much people have in common, they still have to reproduce their attitudes through time. Try as we might to remain faithful to what we take to be the wisdom of the ancestors, we always encounter new situations, and must adapt it to them. What is more, we regularly find that other people have different ideas about how to do this (and different ideas about what the traditions are). We can hardly doubt that the culture of the !Kung San is more homogeneous than was that of Jacksonian America, but the contrast between the two affects the answers we come up with more than the questions we have to ask. Criticizing Darnton, Chartier (1988: 102) suggests that it is to deal with this that "a definition of history primarily sensitive to inequalities in the appropriation of common materials or practice has come into being . . . it is indisputable that the most pressing question inherent in cultural history today . . . is that of the different ways in which groups or individuals make use of, interpret and appropriate the intellectual motifs or cultural forms they share with others."

3. The Cultural History of Society

Some cultural historians suggest that whatever kinds of documents we deal with, the fact of their textuality always traps analysis at the level of competing language games. "It is clear from the outset," Chartier argues, "that no text, even the most apparently documentary, even the most 'objective' (for example, a statistical table drawn up by a government agency), maintains a transparent relationship with the reality that it apprehends" (1988: 43). There can never be a neutral reflection of unmediated social realities. We cannot move from how our sources present the world to how the world really is; every presentation is a re-presentation. All we can do is play off one (mis)re-presentation against another.

For a century, most historians have distinguished between how people in the past saw the world and how that world really was, explaining the former (culture) in terms of the latter (economy and society). In the *locus classicus*, we read that "Just as our opinion of an individual is not based on what he thinks of himself, so can we not judge of a period of transformation by its own consciousness; on the contrary, this consciousness must be explained rather from the contradictions of material life" (Marx 1977a [1859]: 390). Cultural historians now question the materialist consensus.

Gareth Stedman Jones, for example, concludes about the British industrial revolution that "We cannot therefore decode political language to reach a primal and material expression of interest since it is the discursive structure of political language which conceives and defines interest in the first place" (1983: 22). For Stedman Jones, confronting textuality not only drives a wedge between representations of social structures and the reality of such structures; it also breaks down the distinctions between such structures and the ways people construct them. Class exists not in Marx's objective sense of relations to the means of production, but only insofar as people interpret the productive relations into which they are born or enter as class relationships. Moving from representations to realities is not just tricky; it is a mistake even to try, since economy and society are themselves constituted in discourse.

Some cultural historians now attack all forms of structural analysis. Where Giddens and Bourdieu move from social structures to ongoing processes of structuration, Bernard Lepetit rejects the long term altogether:

> To Saussurian linguistics, we oppose situational semantics; against determination by *habitus*, we insist on the plurality of the worlds of action; the substantive rationality of economic actors is challenged in the name of the conventions of procedural rationality; structural anthropology is contested by the study of the modalities and effects of historicizing cultures. (Lepetit 1995a: 14)

For Simona Cerutti (1995: 131), history becomes "the explication of the strategies of manipulation of social subjects in the face of a plurality of normative fields, whose principal characteristic is that they are mutually contradictory." The historian's job is to share the experiences of past actors, grasping their meanings, even in the absence of direct evidence. Historians move, in Raphael Samuel's (1992) telling phrase, from being "fact grubbers" to being "mind readers."

This undermines historians' traditional realist, empiricist, and documentarist assumptions. Some critics even question the distinction between primary and secondary sources, the bedrock of historical science, suggesting that claims to ground historical narratives factually in primary sources are no different from the intertextual methods of other literary genres:

> "History" refers in actual practice only to other "histories," in the eyes of these critics. Thus they fail to see much, if anything, in the distinction drawn by normal historians between fact and fiction, for factual reconstruction is really nothing but construction according to the working "fictions" of normal historical practice, which, in turn, are the premises of both historical realism and realistic mimesis . . . Normal, that is, traditional history is shown to be but a conventional, hence arbitrary, mode of coding communication as factuality by presenting the representation as if it were entirely referential and realistic. (Berkhofer 1988: 445–6)

A postmodern cultural history celebrates the inventiveness of agents cut free from structural constraints, and gives more leeway for the inventiveness of historians, to the point that boundaries between history and literary criticism rapidly lose their meaning.

It often builds on Hayden White's classic *Metahistory*. White (1973: 13, 432–3) argues that "History remains in the state of conceptual anarchy in which the natural sciences existed during the sixteenth century, when there were as many different conceptions of 'the scientific enterprise' as there were metaphysical positions." He identifies four strategies of explanation through narrative emplotment, each with specific modes of argument, ideological implication, and literary trope. White concluded that *"on historical grounds alone* I have no basis for preferring one conception of the 'science' of history over the other. Such a judgment would merely reflect a logically prior preference, either for the linguistic mode in which Tocqueville and Marx prefigured the historical field or for the ideological implications of their specific figurations of the historical process."

Not surprisingly, there have been heated arguments over these claims. There have been explicitly theoretical contributions (Jenkins 1997), but most debates nestle into substantive disputes, such as those over the history of science and the Holocaust. In the early 1980s, advocates of a "strong programme" (British spelling) of constructivism argued that there was nothing special about scientific knowledge (Barnes and Bloor 1982). Poring over scientists' less-studied writings, they showed how nonscientific factors – Newton's obsession with alchemy (Dobbs 1991), or Darwin's with the inferiority of the poor (Oldroyd 1984) – drove research agendas. But by the early 1990s, there was growing concern about how much the strong programme could *not* explain, particularly how discoveries withstand empirical testing outside their immediate cultural context. We do not care about the same things as seventeenth-century Englishmen, but gravity still works. A new school advocated a "hard program" (American spelling), insisting that radical constructivism had failed (Schmaus *et al.* 1992). They called for modified objectivism. Hard programmers recognized that constructivism had overthrown the heroic model of science, and that no one can go back to models of value-free scientific facts and laboratories driven purely by internalist, rational forces. But, they added, historians must now explain how the cultural and the natural coexist, and how, for all the power of the discursive formations within which we make sense of the world, scientific creations can outlast their creators' worldviews. After all, the Nazi scientists' rockets still worked after 1945 (Beyerchen 1992).

The Holocaust raises even tougher questions: if there truly are no historical grounds for preferring one form of emplotment to another, can we only evaluate accounts of this horror according to how they conform to our aesthetic and ideological preferences? White (1992) concedes that here the events themselves rule out comic and romantic plots, and proposed that historians need a new language of representation, something like the middle voice of ancient Greek, allowing the facts to speak through them. Some historians conclude that the Holocaust is unrepresentable; others, that it was a singular event calling for a special language; others still, that it exposes the limits of postmodern historiography, and the need to ground analysis in traditional conceptions of evidence, temporal layers, and structures.[1]

Cultural historians have moved with the times. Modifying his earlier claims, Chartier now insists on

> the exteriority and the specificity of practices that are not in themselves of a discursive nature in relation to the discourses that, in many ways, are articulated on the basis of these practices. Recognizing that access to such non-discursive practices is possible only by deciphering the texts that describe them, prescribe them, prohibit them, and so on, does not in itself imply equating the logic that commands them or the "rationality" that informs them with the practices governing the production of discourses. Discursive practice is thus a specific practice . . . that does not reduce all other "rules of practice" to its own strategies, regularities, and reasons. (Chartier 1994: 174–5)

There could be no greater error, he goes on, than to "constitut[e] ideology as the determining instance of social operations, whereas all regimes of practices are endowed with a regularity, logic, and reason of their own, irreducible to the discourses that justify them" (1994: 177). Stedman Jones defends the "linguistic turn" in British cultural history against Chartier, but concedes that

> It would be foolish to deny that there are processes in the past which are not encompassed – or at least not sufficiently or adequately encompassed – by the languages and discourses of the past. Urbanisation and population change would be good examples . . . In all these instances, it is possible to refer to social practices which were not governed by the rationality of individual agents, or whose macro-social effects bore only a paradoxical relationship with individual intentions. (Stedman Jones 1996: 27–8)

Marx famously observed (1977b [1852]: 300) that "Men make their own history, but they do not make it just as they please; they do not make it under circumstances chosen by themselves, but under circumstances directly encountered, given, and transmitted from the past." The great contribution of cultural historians like Stedman Jones lies in showing how often people *have* made history as they pleased, with discursive forces – Marx's superstructure – dominating supposedly nondiscursive infrastructures to the point that Marx's categories need redefinition. But like the strong programmers, they have to recognize that this is only part of the story, and that the 1980s emphasis on self-fashioning and language can be as misleading as the 1970s obsession with class and production.

Stedman Jones points out that Chartier cannot specify where to draw lines between the cultural and the social, given the textuality of all evidence. But we might respond with some of historiography's most traditional methods, setting up a hierarchy of sources. Returning to Chartier's example of a government statistical table (p. 12 above), such a document may well have contributed to and been constructed within new concepts of state surveillance, requiring it to be read as part of an argument about what the community should be like. But that does not necessarily invalidate readings which move past form to content. There will always be problems in this, but these are problems of well-known types, and historians have tools to tackle them. In some cases the discourse of state control operates in such a way as to rule out attempts to go beyond form, but that must be demonstrated empirically, not assumed.

When we read texts by authors engaged in different language games, and find that they nonetheless represent an external social/economic reality in similar ways, we are on to something. At the very least we are uncovering shared dispositions, culture in the Geertzian sense, cutting across lines which in other contexts act as boundaries; and if the contexts are different enough and numerous enough, we may conclude that for all the complexities of the exercise, we have reached a nondiscursive reality apprehended by past actors. Thus when Emmanuel Le Roy Ladurie (1974: 23–9) found that all the sources relating to land distribution in Languedoc from 1400 through 1800 pointed to a cyclical pattern of concentration and dispersal, despite the differences in the motives and cultural worlds of their producers, he was surely right to conclude that there was an increase in the number of middle-sized farms at the expense of very small and very big holdings in the fifteenth century, and that many of these middling properties disappeared in the sixteenth and seventeenth centuries, some breaking into several smaller farms, others being absorbed into larger estates.

What this meant (an interpretive question) and why it happened (a causal question) are different matters. But the important points are that there *are* ways to move outside a world of competing representations, and that this *is* necessary if we want a cultural history of society rather than a bloodless, aestheticized literary exercise. It is one thing to reconstitute Old Regime folk tales, as Darnton does with great skill (1984: 9–72); it is another (fuller and more complex) thing to read them against the background of a population growing as fast as mice breeding in a barn, as one sixteenth-century observer put it (Le Roy Ladurie 1974: 53), and rapidly outrunning resources. Refusing to set cultural constructions of reality into their material contexts fulfills Geertz's fear (1973: 30) that culturalism might lose contact with the hard surfaces of life. For most people in seventeenth-century Languedoc these surfaces were hard indeed. To overlook that is to write just the kind of idealist history that Marx tried to end.

Conclusion

Archaeologists study material culture in the past. They therefore need to take cultural historians' debates seriously. The linguistic turn within cultural history has undermined older social histories of culture, and in this book I try to write something more like the cultural history of society that Chartier advocates, recognizing both individual agency and the limits of self-fashioning. Cultural history is, as Chartier indicates in the subtitle to his 1988 collection of essays, a matter of moving between practices and representations.

E. P. Thompson, who pioneered many of the cultural historians' concerns, explained that

> Historical and cultural materialism cannot explain "morality" away as class interests in fancy dress, since the notion that all "interests" can be subsumed in scientifically-determinable material objectives is nothing more than utilitarianism's bad breath. Interests are what interest people, including what interests them nearest to the heart. A materialist examination of values must situate itself, not by idealist propositions, but in the face of culture's material abode: the people's way of life, and, above all, their productive and familial relationships. (Thompson 1978: 176)

We must recognize different kinds of historical time. No structural, long-term history gets to the heart of experience unless we interweave it with short-term, event-oriented, cultural histories. Events are a primary category of analysis. But the other side of the coin is that they only really make sense when set into grander flows of conjunctural and structural time.

Cultural Archaeology

Archaeologists largely ignore what historians are saying. In part this is because historians often decline to draw the implications of their work to the attention of anyone not specifically interested in the Investiture Conflict, the Corn Laws, etc. Yet anthropologists and literary critics find plenty to read on the history bookshelves. Archaeologists seem uniquely insulated from historical thought, despite being the only other academic group defined by an obsessive focus on the human past. Why so?

This is really a historical question. It seems to me that a kind of institutional inertia – the dull compulsion of situated, routinized patterns of communication – has made it difficult for archaeologists and historians to talk to each other. A hundred years ago, administrators generally grouped prehistoric archaeology with ethnology as part of the study of primitives. Prehistoric artifacts found their way to Museums of Ethnology, and when universities wanted to hire prehistorians (which, in most countries, was not often), they attached them to Anthropology departments or, in Europe, carved out separate Archaeology departments. Those who worked in the Mediterranean, on the other hand, were placed in higher-status Classics departments or Divinity schools, and had famous museums of art chasing their discoveries. Yet neither group had strong professional contacts with historians.[2]

Alain Schnapp (1996) has skillfully described the slow emergence of cultural approaches to artifacts up to the 1850s, and I will look back only as far as the early twentieth century, when Europeanists began a series of great syntheses of the evidence. They looked chiefly to ethnology for frameworks, often consciously reacting against earlier antiquarian extrapolations from Mediterranean history. Gustav Kossinna, rejected by the German academic establishment (particularly its classicists), insisted in his wildly successful 1912 booklet *Die deutsche Vorgeschichte* that archaeologists could answer ethnologists' questions about the origins of the German people better than philologists. Contemporary ethnologists held that each *Volk* had its own *Kultur* (see Stocking 1996). Kossinna suggested that by following a "siedlungsarchäologische Methode," archaeologists could treat what they excavated as ethnic markers. When they consistently found certain types of artifacts together, they could equate the *Kultur* with the *Volk*, documenting the prehistory of the German race.

Already in the early 1920s British archaeologists were using the word "culture" in much the same ways as the Germans (S. Jones 1997: 16–17).

Gordon Childe's celebrated proposition – "We find certain types of remains – pots, implements, ornaments, burial sites, house forms – constantly recurring together. Such a complex of regularly associated traits we shall term a 'cultural group' or just a 'culture.' We assume that such a complex is the material expression of what today would be called a 'people' (1929: v–vi) – formalized what many archaeologists were already thinking. What made Childe stand out was his combination of this model with extraordinary empirical knowledge and Marxism. He went beyond (though without abandoning) migration and diffusion to emphasize internal developments and revolutions.

By 1950, Childe's methods had entered mainstream British archaeology. But his historical/political agendas fell on stony ground. This is a recurring theme: archaeology's institutional confinements separated it from historical practice, and when mavericks like Childe tried to cross the barriers, other archaeologists took over those ideas which worked well within existing frameworks, and ignored those which did not. Childe's culture history was useful; his Marxist history was not.

Americanists followed similar paths. North American data were poorer than those in central Europe, and synthesizers relied more on seriation than on stratigraphy, but by the 1920s they had enough evidence to conclude that the natives did have some kind of history before Europeans arrived. Archaeologists began using "culture" in a sense like Childe's, and fixed relative chronologies for their cultures, describing what they did as "culture history." In a programatic essay on "The Strategy of Culture History," Irving Rouse listed archaeology's "historic objectives": the diffusion and persistence of cultures, independent invention of culture traits, migration and other mechanisms of spread, participation in culture, acculturation, ecological adaptation, biological models of phylogeny, parallel development, evolution, and assorted "other processes" (Rouse 1953: 98–100).

Given the empirical situation they faced, it made sense for 1930s archaeologists to concentrate on chronology. But as Rouse's essay shows, what they called "culture history" had little to do with history as practiced by historians. This was an age of ferment in American historiography. As archaeologists created culture history, James Harvey Robinson and Charles Beard established the "New History," raising profound epistemological questions and insisting on economic and social causation. By the 1950s, when culture history was virtually unchallenged among archaeologists, historians like Kenneth Stampp and Stanley Elkins were tearing down the old consensus models of American slavery and moving historical scholarship into the center of the political uproar over racism (see Novick 1988: 86–108, 250–64, 348–60).

Even more than Europeanists, American culture historians reacted
against the low status of nineteenth-century archaeology, trying to
show that natives had history, and that archaeology – as the only
discipline with direct access to it – was not just an appendage to ethnology. But as often happens, the debate took place within frameworks
established in earlier periods. Archaeologists did not move beyond
the ideas about culture they inherited from late nineteenth-century
ethnology, even in years when historians were energized by economic
questions that archaeologists might under other circumstances have
felt able to address. The institutional and intellectual gap was already
wide. Culture history grew up without much interchange with other
fields. Its foundations were, as the authors of the only systematic study
of it say, "an ad hoc consensus concerning some empirical generaliza-
tions that, in the absence of theory, were incapable of serving as
explanations" (Lyman *et al.* 1997: 11).

The exception that proves the rule is Walter Taylor's extraordinary
A Study of Archaeology (1948). Taylor identified a contradiction in
Americanist archaeology: archaeologists taught in Anthropology
departments, yet said their goal was to recreate culture history. He
attacked the field's leaders for confusion and intellectual sloppiness,
concluding that they were writing

> mere chronicle, the ordering of cultural materials in temporal sequence
> together with an attempt to demonstrate their derivations and cross-
> cultural relationships . . . They have categorized events and items,
> tagged them, but not investigated them in their contexts or in their
> dynamic aspects. As a result of these conditions, Americanist archeol-
> ogy is not in a healthy state. Its metabolism has gone awry. It is wasting
> and not assimilating its foodstuffs. (Taylor 1948: 94)

Taylor urged that archaeologists think of material culture as the
residues of functioning societies, produced by real people, rather
than reducing cultures to abstract entities interesting only for their
"influences" upon one another. He understood trends in 1930s
historiography and cultural anthropology, and insisted that the only
difference between the two was that the former aimed at understanding specific contexts while the latter moved on to generalize. This
meant that "ethnography is really a branch of historiography and not
of anthropology" (Taylor 1948: 41), since it was about cultural details
in their context. To do archaeology was to do history:

> One may "do" historiography by interpreting the written record
> (archives, letters, cuneiform tablets, Maya hieroglyphs, inscriptions
> on seals and coins and monuments), by interpreting the oral record

(informants of non-literate or illiterate peoples, oral tradition of literate peoples), or by interpreting "non-verbal documents" (stone axes, Greek temples, Toltec pyramids, Hohokam pottery, Magdalenian cave art). The important fact is that the moment cultural data are synthesized into a context representing past actuality, the result is historiography. (Taylor 1948: 43)

Archaeologists generally ignored Taylor through the 1950s, but Lewis Binford (1972: 2, 6, 8–9) identified *A Study in Archaeology* as a stimulus in his own revolt against culture history. Like Taylor, Binford thought that culture historians treated archaeological cultures simplistically, as units in which artifacts, regardless of function, were interchangeable traits which could be compared with artifacts from other cultures to document blending or influence. Instead, Binford suggested, "artifacts having their primary functional context in different operational sub-systems of the total cultural system will exhibit differences and similarities differentially, in terms of the structure of the cultural system of which they were a part." He recommended dividing artifacts into three classes, according to whether they functioned primarily (a) to deal directly with the physical environment (what he called "technomic"), (b) to signal status and group membership (his "socio-technic"), or (c) to communicate ideology ("idio-technic"). Developments within each class would be different. Instead of comparing artifacts between cultures, archaeologists should look at the structure of subsystems within cultures, above all those which "function to adapt the human organism, conceived generically, to its total environment both physical and social," because "Culture is viewed as the extra-somatic means of adaptation for the human organism" (Binford 1972 [1962]: 22).

Despite his admiration for Taylor, Binford took no more from his discussion of historical method than had 1950s culture historians. Taylor's lone voice could not overcome three generations of institutional divisions and anthropological hostility to historicism, any more than Childe's had overcome British empiricism. Binford took for granted culture historians' definitions of anthropology, archaeology, and history. He merged the methods of contemporary Americanist archaeologists and Boasian particularists in anthropology into a single category of "historical" thought, and distinguished his own approach as "processual." These categories were canonized in debates over the new archaeology, and Taylor's historical perspective disappeared.

In an influential confrontation, Jeremy Sabloff and Gordon Willey (1967) defended a "historical" explanation for the collapse of the

Classic Maya, by which they meant that an invasion had been the prime mover, rather than long-term social and economic trends. Binford (1972 [1968]: 114–21) rightly responded that even if there had been an invasion around AD 900, this would only have led to collapse if it fed into ongoing processes within Maya society. This was the kind of argument social historians had been making for forty years, but to culture historians and new archaeologists alike, the issue was one of "process" versus "history" *tout court*. "History" lost. A decade later Binford described himself as feeling "uncomfortable" even thinking about addressing a conference on historical archaeology, because "I felt that persons doing 'historical' archaeology were different from myself with different interests . . . Why? That word 'historical' again!" (1977: 13). He got over his discomfort, however, suggesting that historical archaeologists did have a part to play: they could test his hypotheses against textual data, making them almost as useful as ethnoarchaeologists'.

In the 1970s, academic archaeology developed similarly in western Europe and the United States, with a culture-historical mainstream and a processual critique, albeit stronger in America than in Britain, and stronger there than on the continent. Cultural and social anthropologists were by now in full revolt against the functionalist verities which underpinned the new archaeology; and at the end of the decade, Ian Hodder and his students at Cambridge began to engage with Giddens' and Bourdieu's work.[3] They concluded that material culture, like all culture, was actively manipulated by thinking people in pursuit of their own ends. People used it to construct meanings, sending messages to themselves and others about how they wished to be seen, and also building and challenging group identities. Identities and hierarchies were not objective facts, even though people might perceive them as such, but existed only because actors accepted them and tried to reproduce them in practice. Above all, meanings were disputed. Hodder argued for a contextual or postprocessual archaeology which explored what objects and contexts of activity meant to prehistoric people, and the need

for interpreting specific, not general meanings. Unlike most other approaches in archaeology, the contextual approach, close to thick description, seeks to ask questions such as 'Why was this particular shape or decoration of pot used rather than any other?', 'Why were the tombs this shape?', 'What specifically did the tombs mean?' It is only by asking such questions that we can understand the way in which material culture was socially active and was involved in long-term change. (Hodder 1992: 22–3)

This would be a better archaeology than the functionalist and reductivist new archaeology. But, Hodder also insisted, postprocessual archaeology was not just aesthetically preferable to other forms. It was the *only* form which made sense, because "in archaeology *all* inference is via material culture. If material culture, all of it, has a symbolic dimension such that the relationship between people and things is affected, then *all* of archaeology, economic and social, is implicated" (Hodder 1986: 3).

But, he recognized, actually doing postprocessual archaeology was no simple thing:

> In the construction of the cultural world, all dimensions (the height and colour of pottery for example) already have meaning associations. An individual in the past is situated within this historical frame, and interprets the cultural order from within its perspective. The archaeologist seeks also to get 'inside' the historical context, but the jump is often a considerable one. (Hodder 1987b: 7)

Postprocessualists developed various ways to make the leap. The main one was to contrast different contexts of activity. Like cultural historians, they recognized that while evidence might always come to us already implicated in representational strategies, these strategies were not all the same. If a particular site had impressive ritual buildings but uniform housing and simple, poor, burials, we might conclude that in this culture self-promotion was problematic. There may have been rich people, who might have won prestige through funding communal rituals, but directly claiming high status by building palaces for themselves, or tombs to rival the houses of the gods, was not appropriate. Postprocessualists quickly established ideology as a major concern.

Their methods were initially dominated by structuralism: because there were no informants to give clues about meaning, prehistorians had to treat what they dug up as signifiers standing in essentially arbitrary relationships to signified ideas. This was productive, but tended toward formalism. Christopher Tilley (1990: 65–6) observes that "Different aspects of the archaeological record may be regarded, from this perspective, as embodying a series of transformational homologies or inversions of the same structured relations of difference ... But the meaning[s] of the structures recovered have been interpreted through grafting various Marxist, hermeneutic and poststructuralist perspectives ... to structuralist forms of analysis." Meaning, the object of the enterprise, had to be imposed in blatantly intrusive ways, initially through ethnoarchaeological analogies, but increasingly by drawing on poststructuralist (and particularly literary) theory.

Like cultural historians, postprocessual archaeologists moved from being fact grubbers to being mind readers. Some describe themselves as "historians of the long-term" (Hodder 1987a). In his original critiques of functionalism, Hodder (1986: 77–102; 1992 [1982]: 92–121) suggested that Robin Collingwood's (1946) view of history as empathetic re-imagination might be a more useful model for archaeologists than Binford's natural-science approach. But Hodder seems to have been little more involved with what historians actually do than Binford; as examples of historical practice he cited Weber and Sahlins. Among his students, Shanks and Tilley (1989: 7) urged that "to forge an acceptable practi[c]e of archaeology . . . we need to take history *seriously*," but their discussion of "archaeology – history" remained at the severely abstract level of Nietzsche, Adorno, and Ricoeur (1987a: 16–22). Similarly, their critique of evolutionary thinking owes much to Giddens and Sahlins, but little to historiography (1987b: 137–85). Most of the comments on archaeology as history which came out of a postprocessual conference at Cambridge in 1991 were even more rarified (Hodder *et al.* 1995: 141–78).

Despite postprocessualists' rhetoric, the 1980s historical turn was less serious in archaeology than in other social sciences, largely, I think, because it went on within frameworks inherited from 1960s arguments about culture history vs. culture process, and ultimately from late nineteenth-century divisions of academic labor. To the extent that sociologists and anthropologists talk about history, postprocessualists take over their language. They have been excited by what they have read in Bourdieu, Giddens, and Sahlins, but they have taken history at second-hand from them, feeling little need to engage directly with historians.

Words and Things

Taking cultural history seriously means thinking on all three temporal levels described by Braudel and Giddens. And this requires a shift away from grand theory, toward more prosaic concerns – creating the densest possible texture of data and the tightest chronology. Text-aided archaeologists are particularly well placed to begin these shifts.

There are many ways to do this. I work mainly through what Andrén calls a method of correlation, looking for similarities between the structure of the material record and the members of a past society's verbal accounts of themselves. Andrén suggests that correlation often assumes that there is an association between the references of artifacts and texts. Correlations are thus based in large measure on perceptions of what is probable, which is ultimately defined by different research traditions. What can be seen in one perspective as an innovative correlation may seem uninteresting or impossible from a different point of view. (Andrén 1998: 166)

Andrén is right to say that such arguments are probabilistic and can only be true on the terms of a specific interpretive community. But that is the nature of all historical arguments (e.g., Appleby *et al.* 1994; McCullagh 1998). I follow up Andrén's emphasis on competing research traditions in Part II. But I also put special emphasis on the interpretive communities of the ancient Greeks themselves. Greek writers represented material culture as something to use creatively, in the same way as words, to construct images of themselves and the world around them. They knew that ways of dressing or building houses were different from styles of speech, but they implicated material culture in the same rhetorical games as words. Material culture was ambiguous, and they felt that it required linguistic interpretation. We make most sense of Greek material culture by using the closest analogies, the Greeks' own discussions of it.

It is easy to pile up examples. In our earliest sources, Homer put down much of Odysseus' success to his ability to apply *noesis*, "intelligence," more effectively than anyone else to the material *semata*, or "signs," he came across in his adventures. Throughout the *Odyssey* he identified meanings which eluded others, and took advantage of this to further his own ends. The hero had to be adept at reading nonverbal cues, from architecture to smiles (Nagy 1990: 202–22; Lateiner 1995). And in later centuries, when we have more literary evidence, the complexity of reading material culture and its embeddedness in the same contests over meaning as the written sources are clear. I discuss archaic debates over the meanings of Near Eastern artifacts in chapter 5; and by the fifth century tragedians were, if anything, even more interested in the ambiguities of material symbols. Aeschylus took it for granted that the audience of his *Agamemnon*, staged in 458, would pick up the nuances of its famous carpet scene. By unrolling a purple carpet between her returning husband's chariot and the entrance to the palace, Clytemnestra trapped Agamemnon between either belittling his own authority by refusing to step on such a symbol of kingliness or hubristically soiling the wealth embodied in the filmy material. The play turned on his vacillation in the face of the material trappings of power (Crane 1993). Where our evidence is densest, in the fourth century, any good orator knew that a passing reference to hairstyle, choice of cloak, or tableware spoke volumes about his rivals' wicked intentions (Ober 1989).

Classical historians sometimes respond to the ancient obsession with material culture with mechanical direct interpretations (I. Morris 1992: 17–21). The method is simple: we read the texts, which tell us that object A signifies idea B, etc. Symbolism is a code. We find out what A means, and our job is easy. We look at a carved Roman sarcophagus and can say that the snake means death, the olive means life, the egg is a sign of rebirth, and so on.

These one-to-one associations are not necessarily wrong, but our sources make it clear that things were more complicated. Even when we have texts directly relating to the objects we have dug up, we can rarely assign "the meaning" to an artifact, or assume that it had any such meaning independent of its context of use. A gold cup in a grave may mean something very different from one given to a god, or displayed in a dining room. The best example is the so-called "Orphic" graves of the late fourth and third century. The people who cremated a man at Derveni in Macedonia around 350 used grave goods much like those in other rich burials, but burned with him a papyrus roll describing an afterlife radically different from the mainstream Hades (Themelis and Touratsoglou 1997; Most 1997). Gold cups had different religious meanings for different buriers (I. Morris 1992: 17–18, 104).

Some associations carry over from one context to another, and in that sense we can speak of an irreducible core of meanings given to gold cups by a particular group at a particular moment; but many important meanings were entirely context-dependent. To pour libations to the gods from gold cups as the Athenian fleet sailed for Sicily in 415 was a fine and patriotic thing (Thucydides 6.32), but to say that a man took pride in owning gold cups was to imply that he lacked the qualities of the true citizen (Demosthenes 22.75). To say that your enemy went round positively bragging about his cups was even worse – it evoked images of antisocial hubris (Demosthenes 21.133, 158). When Andocides (4.29) wanted to convince a jury that Alcibiades was beyond the pale of civilized society, he took advantage of these associations by alleging that Alcibiades tried to create the impression that gold vessels belonging to an Athenian embassy were his own, not only pretending that cups made him a better man, but even lying about owning them.

To bury a gold cup with a dead relative may have been even more hubristic. In the roughly 3,000 fifth- and fourth-century graves known from Athens, there is not a single example of this (I. Morris 1992:

108–27), although we know from exports to Thrace that Athenian craftsmen made superb precious tableware. The literary sources do not give us "the meaning" of gold cups, which we can then apply to our finds. But they do give a sense of the semantic range of artifacts, the possibilities available to the people who used them, and the limits of plausible interpretation.

Verbal and nonverbal languages are not the same. Geertz, one of the main advocates of what he calls the "life is a text" model in anthropology, notes (1983: 33) that its "proponents incline toward the examination of imaginative forms: jokes, proverbs, popular arts," but have been less successful – indeed, have hardly tried their hands – at examining institutions, worship, or war. The gaps between material culture and texts are even more pronounced. Discussing archaeologists' borrowings from linguistic structuralism, Ernest Gellner observed that "the whole point is this: . . . the entities used in [linguistic] symbolism and communication operate under a rather special economy, without scarcity. Or, better, the other way around: symbolic systems choose as their units, their vehicles of communication, elements whose cost approaches zero" (Gellner 1985: 150). That is patently not true of the material world, whose symbols are very much governed by rules of scarcity. An Athenian could not just decide to flaunt gold cups, as Andocides' story about Alcibiades, true or not, illustrates. First he had to get hold of some.

We need different intellectual tools to analyze pottery than poetry, but we should analyze both correlatively, within the same cultural framework. Pots and poems were used by the same people, who – in case we should be foolish enough to doubt it – make it clear in their writings that they employed both in efforts to construct and contest categories. The resolutions differed from one context to another, but there is no reason other than the defense of academic boundaries for us to lump together all material culture, regardless of context of use, as one discourse and to separate all verbal culture as another, so that we can look for "the mismatch between texts and archaeology [which] can articulate important contradictions between operative social contexts" (Small 1997: 218). I argue in Parts III and IV that we must examine verbal and nonverbal languages together, comprehensively, in contextual detail, to identify cleavages which often have little to do with the medium through which people expressed them.

Borrowing another Geertzian phrase, all these categories of evidence are the remains of models *for* reality as well as models *of* reality (Geertz 1973: 93). Neither texts nor artifacts are radically thinned descriptions against which thick descriptions based on the other can be tested. But looking for the intersections of arguments based on such different forms of evidence ties our interpretations to themes which would have made sense to the ancients, and thickens our descriptions.

Andrén closes his book (1998: 180) by asking "Is it possible for one and the same person to master artifact and text, and the scientific traditions surrounding them, in such a way that new, interesting, and meaningful contexts really can be constructed?" We expect prehistorians not only to know the full range of archaeological data, but also to understand excavation and survey methods, and shifting theoretical debates. Historical archaeologists need to do all of these things, but also need to know the primary textual evidence, the difficulties of locating and reading the texts, and the arguments raging among text-oriented historians. To do anything less would be the equivalent of a prehistorian deciding to work only with survey data and ignore excavated material, or perhaps to take no notice of the secondary literature.

David Austin, discussing the state of medieval archaeology, complains:

> Try discussing 7th-century Poland without mentioning the Slavs, or 13th-century rural England without reference to the manor, and our credentials as commentators on the past would be seriously questioned by historians. We allow ourselves, therefore, to be compelled to integrate, and this carries with it the obligation to understand primary written sources, how to extract social or economic meaning from them, and how to apply them to the locations and communities we are researching . . . After a career of reading the documents, the history and the historical geography of the medieval landscape of Britain, for example, I would earn no discredit from my colleagues if I were to say that I had little time, inclination or energy to take on the whole framework of social theory and anthropology, the main disciplines to which our prehistorian colleagues have turned . . . The fact is that we have been so trapped by the agenda set by historians and so weighed down with the paraphernalia of medieval history that we scarcely feel able to interpret and analyse in the modes of contemporary archaeology. When we do try, we are accused by historians of, at best, irrelevance or lack of scholarship, and at worst of uttering jargonistic claptrap. (Austin 1990: 12–13)

It is asking a lot for one person to control so many fields, but as Americanists realize, the whole promise of historical archaeology lies in combining approaches, potentially transforming both text-based historiography and archaeology. Our educational institutions may not encourage people to feel equally comfortable with Chaucer, abandoned fourteenth-century villages, and Bourdieu; but that is no reason not to try.

The Structure of This Book

I divide the rest of the book into three pairs of chapters and a conclusion. I have already mentioned the importance of the institutions within which we work and the audiences we imagine in shaping research. In Part II I consider these factors in the history of archaeologies of Greece. I ask why archaeologists ask the questions they do, why they collect particular kinds of evidence to answer them, and specifically why archaeologists of Greece rarely think of what they do as cultural history. Tensions run high between those who would align Greek archaeology with anthropological archaeologies of other parts of the world and those who think it is doing just fine, but in chapter 2 I argue that this opposition is unproductive. We can only understand the issues historically.

A hundred years ago, eminently sensible people made reasonable decisions about how to organize scholarship. They found solutions to aesthetic, institutional, and political dilemmas, and worked out ways to align Greek archaeology with science while maintaining connections to high-status philology and contributing to burning questions of the day about the origins of Europeanness. They won general agreement that Greek archaeology was fundamental to the humanities. But it is as if their very success prevented later generations from moving on. In the 1990s we face different questions, for which our long-standing academic confinements are no longer so appropriate, and which threaten the prestige and funding enjoyed by classical archaeologists. Historical analysis of our own subject is not narcissism; only in this way can we understand why we have asked some questions and not others. And only when we know this can we respond to our situation, which makes new questions more interesting than some of the old ones. Throughout the book I return to this issue of how we decide what are important questions to ask.

In chapter 3 I explain why I think Iron Age Greece is an important time and place; why I think certain things about it are more important than others; and why I think certain combinations of evidence are more promising than others. In the 1890s academics finally accepted Schliemann's discovery of Bronze Age civilization as a fact, and at the same time, Flinders Petrie cross-dated Mycenae with the Egyptian New Kingdom. This created an unforeseen problem: there was a four-century gap between the end of the Mycenaean world and the first Greek poetry. Until the 1930s this "Dark Age" was a low-status field, receiving little serious attention, but after 1945 it became a major focus of research, particularly in Britain. Some historians redefined the Dark Age as a Heroic Age, arguing that Homer reflected Iron Age rather than Bronze Age society. Archaeologists continued to see the Iron Age as a Dark Age, but now said that a uniquely Greek way of life was created in this Dark Age (and particularly the eighth century). I examine how these radically opposed views co-existed and how they fused in the 1980s. Post-war Dark Age scholars transformed this field from an intellectual backwater into the site of an epochal transformation, when "the Greeks" stepped onto the stage of history. These were the claims that drew me to Iron Age Greece in the early 1980s; they continue to make it worth thinking about and arguing over.

I use intellectual history to denaturalize the questions we ask. By taking our forebears seriously, setting them in context and thinking of them as real people, rather than putting them on pedestals or reviling their stupidity, we make their questions and methods make sense. We see what they tried to do; we see why we maybe should not try to do the same things any more; and, hopefully, we develop some humility about our own claims. Looking at things on a timescale several generations long makes it easier to grasp how serious and fair-minded appraisal of the evidence then available constrained ideas, but also how external forces – power, money, politics – shaped what parts of that evidence people took seriously, and what they thought it meant. But above all, a historiographical approach shows in ways that nothing else can that it is up to *us*, here and now, to set the agendas for archaeology. There is nothing in the data themselves to tell us what is important. If anything, scholarship works the other way round, with our decisions about what is important determining what we count as data. We decide, and the more we know about the forces which influence our decisions, the more scientific we can be.

Classical scholarship has many strengths, but one abiding weakness is the survival of the positivist idea that researchers fashion bricks for some communal building project. If we all make bricks properly, the theory runs, someone will eventually put them together into a giant edifice of knowledge, like the great classical encyclopedias. Classicists often talk as if engaging with other scholars' arguments, taking the time to check references, re-read sources, break down the case into its component parts, and offer alternative interpretations is a profound personal attack, an act of vandalism against the sacred structure, rather than the highest compliment one specialist can pay another. I cannot share this attitude. None of us enjoys seeing work over which we have labored long hours picked apart and called superficial, speculative, or misguided. But doing history is a conversation. The conversation may not reach definitive answers, but history as an academic discipline is done in the act of arguing. I offer Parts III and IV in this spirit. Each consists of two quarrelsome chapters, examples of history as what Lucien Febvre, the founding father of the *Annales*, called *combats et débats*: that is, arguing about ideas, evidence, and methods, and in doing so trying to shape what friends, colleagues, and students think is worth talking about.

In Part III I set out an area for debates which I think makes the archaeological/cultural history of the Iron Age worth doing. I build on the intellectual history in Part II: ancient Greece is important partly because our forebears made it so. For the past two-hundred years, westerners defined classical Athens as the fountainhead of European-ness, the beginning of a unique cultural tradition setting us apart from (and above) the rest of the world. Late twentieth-century academics look on this grand narrative with suspicion, and in some circles anything to do with ancient Greece is tainted by association with Eurocentric charter myths. Some feel we should forget Greece. I believe precisely the opposite. The appropriation of Greece within this ideology demands that we continue to debate categories which intellectuals of the last two centuries have made into some of the most potent symbols of western identity. A new theory about the Parthenon frieze or Socrates' skin color is front-page news, and it is the height of folly for academics to abandon this ideologically charged subject to the platitudes and deceptions of politicians and advertising agents. We need to take ancient Greece seriously and to bring to bear on it the same intellectual tools we apply to other parts of world history.

And when we do so, I suggest, we find a second reason to study this small, far-off land. The Greek evidence resists appropriation, stubbornly failing to fit our frameworks. This was an odd place. In particular, I argue, Greek ideas about equality, often seen as the origins of liberalism and democracy, utterly confound the categories of thought which archaeologists bring to complex societies. Troublesome societies like Greece show up the limitations of our frameworks better than abstract analysis.

The interest of these questions dawned on me in 1993, when some people seemed intent on making the 2,500th anniversary of Cleisthenes' political reforms into a line of power from Athens to modern representative democracy. In the flurry of activity that year, I found myself thinking more and more about what ideas of equality made the institutions of democracy possible. In chapter 4, I look at literary sources from fifth- and fourth-century Athens. Engaging with the words Athenian men used to describe their political system makes democracy an issue in cultural history. My central question is what made democracy *thinkable*: that is, how and where people drew imaginary lines within the community, saying that some were full members and some were not. What the Athenians called *demokratia* was the rule of men. Athenian men systematically downplayed wealth and class while raising ethnic, gender, and cosmological distinctions to unusual heights. In Athens, poor, local-born men inherited the earth. Athens was no paradise, but it remains important because it was *different* – it fits into no ready-made modern schemes.

In chapter 5 I ask how such a society came to be. I examine poetic constructions of the self across the seventh and sixth centuries, arguing that we see the creation and then the collapse into each other of anti-thetical "elitist" and "middling" ideologies of the good community. These competing visions created opposed identities. The former blurred gender distinctions, and linked aristocrats with gods, heroes of the past, and rulers of the east, to create a single distinction between nobles and commoners. The latter did the opposite. I explore the tensions and antagonisms between the two worldviews, suggesting that ideas of time and space were central to these.

Part III is not what most of us would call archaeology. Material culture plays only a small part, and I will doubtless be accused of returning the field to its "handmaiden to history" role. But the methods I follow are central to my vision of archaeology as cultural history. Text-aided archaeologists and archaeologically minded historians too often concentrate on one kind of evidence and rely on secondary syntheses for the other. I believe that the best opportunities lie with people who are equally at home with written and mute evidence, knowing the potential and the limits of both. In chapter 5 I argue that archaic poetry provides a framework for reading the material record, but I also emphasize its limitations. Panhellenizing processes generated our texts, creating poetry relevant to all central Greek cities but specific to none, dealing with themes of enduring interest, but which cannot be tied to specific events. The poems leave us with a sense of archaic central Greece as a unit, but blur diachronic and regional distinctions within it; and most serious of all, the texts only appear in the late eighth century, right in the middle of the changes we most need to examine.

In Part IV I try to connect texts and artifacts. I draw on Darnton's methods (pp. 10–11 above), tracing ideas of the ancient race of heroes and the wonders of the east back to around 1000 BC. I concentrate on the site of Lefkandi, but put it into a larger context, combining micro- and macro-archaeologies, empathetic and statistical approaches, and material and mythological evidence. I argue that a "Dark Age" began in central Greece in the late eleventh century with the formation of a new social and cultural order, which made a usable past out of the ruins of the lost Mycenaean age. I see continuities between ideas about Greekness, the heroes, and the east which took shape in the tenth century and those of archaic and classical times, but also see profound discontinuities in the eighth century, in which the Dark Age cultural traditions took on new meanings. Against recent revisionists, I insist on the importance of the eighth-century transformation, which permanently changed concepts of wealth, gender, ethnicity, and cosmology, and created the patterns which I identify in the archaic literary sources. It was a rupture of Foucauldian proportions. The new identity of the male citizen was created, and along with it the preconditions for extreme gender inequality, large-scale chattel slavery, male democracy, and an astonishing cultural explosion. A mixed bag indeed.

Part II

2

Archaeologies of Greece

In this chapter I ask why Greek archaeology has not been the kind of cultural history I described in chapter 1, and suggest why we might now rethink the field along these lines. Until recently, discussions of Greek archaeology have been ahistorical, opposing rigid models of traditional/empirical and new/theoretical scholarship.[1] I try to move beyond this opposition. But I seek neither easy remedies for perceived ills nor celebrations of past triumphs. Disciplinary history is not a miraculous form of auto-analysis which straightens out the hidden quirks of communities of scholars simply by airing them publicly. But it does force us to face the fact that our academic practices are historically constituted, and, like all else, are bound to change.

The Argument

In the late eighteenth century a bundle of new ideas about European-ness emerged. One of them was what I call *Hellenism*, the idealization of ancient Greece as the birthplace of a uniquely European spirit. To make sense of Hellenism I modify Trigger's (1984) division of archaeologies into three types, each representing a different way to appropriate the past. His first type, nationalist archaeology, fosters unity within a state by studying its ancient greatness; the second, colonialist archaeology, justifies the control of one region by another by showing (to the dominators' satisfaction) that the dominated were always inferior; and the third, imperialist archaeology, supports worldwide ambitions by downgrading local histories. What makes the archaeology of Greece different is that Hellenists created a *continentalist* past by insisting on Greece's unique, even superhuman, qualities. There were disputes over which nation had the strongest claims on

Greece, but northwest Europeans agreed that collectively they
monopolized this heritage. This made nationalist uses of ancient
Greece by contemporary Greeks problematic. Classical glories
bolstered Greek pride and unity, like any nationalist archaeology; but
classical antiquity had been defined in advance by west Europeans.
Greeks were cast in the role of living ancestors for European civilization, and archaeology only reinforced this.[2]

Art was always important to Hellenism, but archaeology played a
minor role through most of the nineteenth century. But Greek archaeology changed profoundly in the 1870s. Some classicists saw this as a
threat to Hellenism. By 1900 all archaeologies of Greece were
absorbed administratively and intellectually into the field of "classics,"
under the general control of philologists, and classical archaeologists
severed their connections with other archaeologies. The archaeology
of classical Greece was effectively neutralized. Other archaeologies,
including Aegean prehistory, diverged from classical archaeology in
methods and theories.

Since the 1970s doubts about Hellenism have encouraged debates
about the field's direction, but there have been few attempts to understand *why* different schools of thought have such trouble communi-
cating. I do not argue that "traditional" archaeologists of Greece are
stuck-in-the-mud reactionaries, evil geniuses scheming to preserve
white male supremacy, or victims of false consciousness. Instead I
assert archaeology's historical specificity and our need to face changes
in the groups which pay for, produce, and consume our research. The
kind of archaeology which has dominated Greece for a century succeeded on its own terms, but its audience is shrinking, as part of a
greater set of changes. Fields of inquiry which are perceived, rightly
or wrongly, as merely offering a foundation myth for western
supremacy have been marginalized within an academic culture which
has little time for such ideas.

I concentrate on how the archaeology of Greece was brought within
Hellenism, and what is happening now that framework is crumbling.
Deprived of Hellenism, classics may disintegrate into its components,
with Greek archaeology coming under the wing of anthropological
archaeology; or it may reorganize itself from within to continue to
provide distinctive models of the Greco-Roman past. I identify three
main responses within the discipline: first, ignoring the situation;
second, reasserting Hellenism; and third, moving on to ask what is
useful about a Greek archaeology without Hellenism.

I suggest that archaeologists of Greece must think about
what Hayden White (1973: 31) calls the "prefiguring" of the object
of study, "the poetic act which precedes the formal analysis of the

field, [in which] the historian both creates his object of analysis and predetermines the modality of the conceptual strategies he will use to explain it." I argue that the archaeology of Greece was formalized in and after the 1870s as an innocuous subdiscipline within classics; that later generations were supremely successful in pursuing this vision; and that this vision was itself a product of a particular set of historical circumstances which is now passing away. The cultural archaeology in this book is an attempt to *refigure* the discipline. "Refiguring," as I use the word, has two dimensions: first, examining the history of Greek archaeology to understand how changing circumstances have undermined nineteenth-century assumptions about what is a worthwhile object of study (Part II); and second, returning people to the center of an intellectual landscape which has been dehumanized (Parts III and IV). Simply seeing "anthropological" archaeologies (themselves enmeshed in similar problems) as the salvation of Greek archaeology or the source of corrosion of its standards obscures the need to think about what an archaeology of Greece is *for*.

Bourdieu explains that

> When research comes to study the very realm within which it operates, the results which it obtains can be immediately reinvested in scientific work as instruments of reflexive knowledge of the conditions and the social limits of this work, which is one of the principal weapons of epistemological vigilance. Indeed, perhaps we can only make our knowledge of the scientific field progress by using whatever knowledge we may have available in order to discover and overcome the obstacles to science which are entailed by the fact of holding a determined position in the field. And not, as is so often the case, to reduce the *reasons* of our adversaries to *causes*, to social interests. We have every reason to think that the researcher has less to gain, as regards the scientific quality of his work, from looking into the interests of others, than from looking into his own interests, from understanding what he is motivated to see and not to see. (Bourdieu 1988: 15–16)

The difficulty is how to explain patterns of thought and behavior without sinking into implausible conspiracy theories. Bourdieu observes that "What may appear as a sort of collective defense organized by the professorial body is nothing more than the aggregated result of thousands of independent but orchestrated strategies of reproduction, thousands of acts which contribute effectively to the preservation of that body because they are the product of [a] sort of social conservation instinct" (1988: 150).

Great Divides

I identify three major boundaries defining Hellenist archaeology. Borrowing Colin Renfrew's (1980) terminology, I call these "great divides." Renfrew suggests that one reason why classical archaeology is so different from other archaeologies is that it has a "great tradition" of detailed reporting, which its practitioners see as obviating the need for explicit theorizing. He traces this concern for detail to philology, but otherwise adopts a timeless perspective. There is a classical great tradition; its absence in other fields has created a great divide; this must be bridged.

Concern for detail matters in all archaeologies, but an *exclusive* concern with detail was one strategy for neutralizing the threat that archaeology posed to Hellenism. As Hellenism comes under pressure, the great tradition suffers with it.

I will return not just to this divide, but also to two others. Through them the archaeology of Greece was made safe for Hellenism by being *de-peopled*. Power, conflict, and social change – major concerns for real people – have not been legitimate topics. Individuals appear only as Great Men, whether Pheidias the inspired artist or Pericles the wise statesmen, whose conscious decisions directly transform the passive material record.

The second divide is within Greek archaeology, and Renfrew exemplifies it. Much of his paper's impact came from his double legitimacy as a leading anthropological archaeologist and also as a field archaeologist in the Aegean. Since the 1890s, academics have drawn a line through the Iron Age. I return to this in chapter 3; for now, we need only note that the time before the Dark Age is not properly "classical". Very different theories and methods are tolerated in it, and are even encouraged in a kind of *trasformismo*, which allows those whose ideas cannot fit into classical archaeology to enter the professional elite without friction so long as they remain in the time before 1200 (like Renfrew, Disney Professor of Archaeology at Cambridge, former Master of Jesus College, Cambridge, and now a life peer). Most Bronze Age archaeologists are culture historians, but since the 1960s a substantial minority has found more profit in contacts with prehistorians of other parts of the world than with classicists. Renfrew made outstanding use of systems theory to explain the rise of complex society in the Cyclades in the third millennium, and went on to integrate this into an overview of European prehistory (Renfrew 1972; 1973). His model called for evidence which was not collected in most Greek fieldwork. Since Schliemann the Bronze Age has been the soft underbelly of Hellenism, where unconventional ideas slip in.

But I am most concerned with the third divide, between archaeology and history. Most classical archaeologists come from backgrounds in philology, which involves reading ancient Greek historians. But Hellenist archaeology is fundamentally different from the notion of archaeology as cultural history that I propose. Hellenist archaeology is saturated in historical texts, but does not *produce* historical texts. Rather, archaeology becomes a source of illustrations for accounts based on other sources. This "bits-and-pieces" approach is a barrier to developing archaeology as cultural history.

The written word, even when excavated on inscriptions or coins, is separated from and made prior to other artifacts. White (1987: 1–57) argues that emplotting historical writing into narratives presupposes a desire to moralize events; by arranging their texts in austerely non-narrative forms, archaeologists make it impossible to tell stories of importance (see pp. 52–7 below).

Hellenism

The Roman Past

Frank Turner suggests that "until the late eighteenth century most educated [west] Europeans regarded their culture as Roman and Christian in origin, with merely peripheral roots in Greece ... In contrast to this visible, tangible and persuasive Roman influence, the Greeks simply had not directly touched the life of Western Europe" (1981: 1–2). Language was the main part of this heritage. Roman art had been collected in the Middle Ages, and Renaissance artists sought inspiration in Roman sculpture and architecture. In the early sixteenth century French kings collected Roman statues as part of their claim to be "the new Rome," but Greek remains attracted little attention. The ancient world permeated elite life, but it was a textual world, and a Latin one at that. This Latin prehistory is vital for understanding Greek archaeology.

In the western empire by AD 400 even an intellectual like Augustine knew little Greek (*Confessions* 1.13). Latin, however, remained the international ecclesiastical and diplomatic tongue. Vernacular political and literary writing displaced Latin in the fourteenth century, but Latin-teaching did not fade away. Quite the reverse: one of the main dimensions of the Italian renaissance was a new sense of the past. Petrarch and other humanists saw a radical discontinuity between Roman antiquity and the present. They argued that the present was generally inferior to antiquity, yet held out the possibility that by sustained and serious study of Roman remains, the moderns might appropriate antiquity's excellence and even improve on it. Legend has it that Brunelleschi figured out the secrets of architecture by clearing garbage away from standing ruins to see how Romans had joined blocks and built foundations, while Poggio Bracciolini and Niccolo Niccoli scoured the monasteries of Europe recovering Latin manuscripts and perfecting philological methods which, they insisted, could not only tell genuine Roman texts from forgeries, but could also grasp the essence of antique virtue, and help to perfect mankind.

In the fifteenth and sixteenth century educators redefined Latin as part of the moral education of a gentleman. Roman stories required acquaintance with Greek history, but this came from Latin sources. Political theory continued to depend on Roman history. After the Glorious Revolution of 1688, parallels were regularly drawn between England freed from the Stuarts and Republican Rome, freed from its kings in 509 BC, as examples of balanced polities. Dryden and others acclaimed Latin poetry, especially Virgil's polished *Aeneid*, as describing the ideal constitutional monarch. Latin models dominated English high culture to the extent that the early eighteenth century is often called the Augustan Age. The ideals of the Enlightenment – power, sophistication, reason – were echoed in contemporary perceptions of Rome.

Johann Joachim Winckelmann

The shift of interest from Rome to Greece – the rise of Hellenism – began in the mid-eighteenth century. For some historians, one man is decisive: Johann Joachim Winckelmann (1717–68). Winckelmann was librarian and president of antiquities at the Vatican. Before his arrival, papal administration of antiquities had been haphazard, but he took the situation in hand. Based on knowledge of finds passing through Rome, he wrote a two-volume *Geschichte der Kunst des Alterthums* (1968 [1764]). Winckelmann adapted for Greek sculpture a four-stage scheme proposed for poetry by J. J. Scaliger in 1608. His first stage, the time before the Athenian sculptor Pheidias (mid-fifth century BC), was "straight and hard"; the second, or Pheidian, was "grand and square." The third stage, in the fourth century BC, he named after Praxiteles, and called it "beautiful and flowing"; finally, in later centuries, art was imitative.

Winckelmann was massively influential. He went beyond earlier antiquaries by explaining not just individual objects from the past but providing a whole new aesthetic. Herder, Goethe, Fichte, and Schiller all looked at antiquity through his eyes. But internalist perspectives obscure more than they reveal in this case, and Schnapp (1996: 179–273) shows Winckelmann's place in a larger story. Starting from a crude externalist level, Winckelmann and his success were partly a product of German cultural resistance to France, the self-proclaimed "new Rome." By the 1760s intellectuals opposing the French use of Rome could draw on knowledge of the far east and the new world to construct ideological alternatives, but Greece was still the obvious alternative to Rome. Even in its subordinate position in early modern classical scholarship, Greece had richer associations than China, India, or the Americas.

By the late eighteenth century, interest in Greece was spreading. The French and American revolutions made all republicanism, even Roman, suspect to conservatives. English scholars sometimes drew political analogies with Athens in seventeenth-century debates about the division of powers, but they began doing so far more around 1770, at first to show the evil of democracy, and later to exemplify its "constitutional morality" (Turner 1981: 187–234; Roberts 1993; pp. 55–7 below). In France, the questions about liberty raised by the revolution were often debated through comparisons with Athens. Benjamin Constant did this self-consciously in his 1814 *Spirit of Conquest and Usurpation*; more often, it was embedded within larger projects. The promotion of Greece was also useful within the British elite. In the eighteenth century the universities reached the low point of their prestige. Emphasis on Greek grammar gave bourgeois teachers a weapon against the slothful aristocracy.

Winckelmann also belonged to the still wider intellectual revolt of the "counter-Enlightenment." He was a key figure in the rise of Romanticism,[3] the search of the free soul for truth and beauty in spontaneous, natural creation. Narrowly construed, this was a militant trend among young German, British, and French artists. More broadly perceived, it was a major intellectual transformation. Charles Nodier wrote that "this last resort of the human mind, tired of ordinary feelings, is what is called the romantic genre: strange poetry, quite appropriate for the moral condition of society, to the needs of surfeited generations who cry out for sensation at any cost" (quoted in Hugo 1957: 58).

Romantics had little use for empires like Rome, Egypt, and China. Small, intense communities, full of spontaneous emotion, originality, and childlike innocence were more interesting. The cultured Virgil was less exciting than the rustic Homer; Rome seemed decadent and corrupt next to the Greeks' simplicity and hardness; and Roman art was derivative compared to Winckelmann's interpretation of the liberty of Greek sculpture. Youth and vitality were all, and Winckelmann made ancient Greeks the "natural children" of Europe. This was, as Turner says, "an exceedingly useful and influential fiction" (1981: 42). Greece was the fountain from which European culture sprang, and Winckelmann showed his readers paths back to it.

The German idealization of Greece had important effects on classical archaeology. Although by the 1670s English and French travelers were visiting Greece, German intellectuals felt no such need. In spite of invitations, Winckelmann never went to Greece, and his friend Johann von Riedesel is the *only* German known to have been there before 1800. German scholars rejected the physical experience of the ideal.

They made ancient Greece a metahistorical concept, freeing the Hellenes from normal canons of analysis. Formulaic responses to an idealized Greece seemed called for. Alexander von Humboldt, Prussian education minister 1808–10 and a key figure in the rise of Hellenism, thought that Germans should see Greece "at a distance, in the past, and removed from its everyday reality – only thus should the Ancient World appear to us" (quoted in Constantine 1984: 2).

German Classics

Most eighteenth-century European scholars were aristocratic men of letters. They developed rigorous methods for describing antiquities (Schnapp 1996: 238–42), but only in Germany did professionalized university researchers and teachers appear so early. The University of Göttingen was established in 1734. Between 1763 to 1812, Heyne trained a corps of classical scholars there, including von Humboldt. The overarching research paradigm was the concept of the *Volksgeist*, or spirit of the people. Paradoxically, critical skills helped enshrine the Greeks as being beyond historical criticism. The Greeks' impurities were purged in the fires of source criticism, to leave a race beyond comparison.

The new field of *Altertumswissenschaft*, the "science of antiquity," was important in Prussian political ideology. Von Humboldt was appointed as education minister to repair national morale after Napoleon annihilated the Prussian armies at Jena in 1806. He made *Altertumswissenschaft* the basis of his new *Bildung*, an almost religious experience through education, to rescue the fallen national spirit. He wrote that

Our study of Greek history is therefore a matter quite different from our other historical studies. For us the Greeks step out of the circle of history. Even if their destinies belong to the general chain of events, yet in this respect they matter least to us. We fail entirely to recognise our relationship to them if we dare to apply the standards to them which we apply to the rest of world history. Knowledge of the Greeks is not merely pleasant, useful or necessary to us – no, in the Greeks alone we find the ideal of that which we should like to be and produce. If every part of history enriched us with its human wisdom and human experience, then from the Greeks we take something more than earthly – something godlike. (von Humboldt, quoted in Cowan 1963: 79)

Few other nations adopted the full German system, but German scholarship was recognized as the most rigorous, and *Altertumswissenschaft* was vindicated as a moral strategy by Prussia's rapid revival after 1813. Hellenist *Bildung* was part of a package of liberalizing reforms in 1807–12, but after a student revolt in 1817–19 reaction set in. *Bildung* was more and more restricted to a meritocratic elite educated at Gymnasien. Beginning in the 1820s new Realschulen increasingly focused on science and modern languages. The *Humanismus–Realismus* debate which followed was essentially between the controllers of different institutions over shares of the student market and access to rewards. Within classics, a parallel debate grew up between a liberal historical wing (the *Sachphilologen*) and a narrowly philological and "scientific" wing (*Sprachphilologen*), which had important consequences for archaeology. Classically educated graduates monopolized jobs in the state sector, education, and law, but by the 1880s graduate unemployment was climbing. One response was to increase science education in the universities; another was to favor the bourgeoisie by reducing secondary school attendance among the children from the lower classes. By 1900 the pro-science response won out.[4] Yet despite classics' declining prestige in Germany, it was at this time that the system was most eagerly emulated overseas.

Hellenism, Orientalism, Imperialism

The earliest surviving definition of *to Hellenikon*, "Greekness," comes from Herodotus: "we are one in blood and one in language; those shrines of the gods belong to us all in common, and there are our customs, bred of a common upbringing" (8.144). He framed it in opposition to "the east" in his account of the Persian war of 480–479 BC, and nineteenth-century scholars defined ancient Greece as the fount of Europeanness in a similar way.

In the eighteenth century Egypt was regularly paired with Rome as an ancestor of European civilization. When Napoleon invaded Egypt in 1798 he envisaged a two-pronged French regeneration of the country, through scholarship and empire. The revived Egypt would then help renew Europe. His defeat and the British occupation of Egypt in 1801 ended this, but the academic project remained intact. The first "modern" orientalist, Silvestre de Sacy, typifies French responses. He won his influence precisely by reducing the orient to something which could be analyzed without leaving Paris' libraries. Sacy's orientalism allowed Europeans to know the east better than those who actually lived there. This had particular appeal in Germany, where three factors – professionalized academics, the tradition of nontraveling scholars, and the absence of imperial involvement – produced a situation where few orientalists visited the east before the 1870s.

Beginning with Sacy himself in 1805, some orientalists achieved status as political advisers, but orientalism made itself subordinate to classics. Hellenists worked on Greece, whence Europe came. Orientalists worked on incompletely developed or degenerate cultures, which defined what Europe was not. Only a few orientalists resisted this model. There were of course differences among them: some tied archaeology to the Hebrew Bible, others to secular scientific principles. And those oriented toward the Bible split further, into groups hoping excavation would confirm its historical narrative, and those influenced by German Higher Criticism. Epigraphers and fieldworkers often saw the field in entirely different ways, and their fragmented professionalization, with scholars scattered among different university departments or attached to museums, amplified conflicts (Kuklick 1996: 99–122). But one guiding principle united most orientalist scholars: that the orient was important in the distant past, and even then mainly as a place from which the Greeks had taken ideas which they brought to fruition.

Other disciplines urged this role onto orientalists, and by the 1930s Hellenists were so confident that they wrote the east out of the history that mattered altogether. Once again German archaeologists went to extremes. Kossinna even claimed that writing was a Stone Age Germanic invention (Trigger 1989: 166). Said suggests that "Most often an individual entered [orientalism] as a way of reckoning with the Orient's claim on him; yet most often too his Orientalist training opened his eyes, so to speak, and what he was left with was a sort of debunking project" (1978: 150–1). Many orientalists were self-professed Hellenists, who showed their love for Greece by denigrating the east.

The Greek War of Independence

The Greek War of Independence (1821–30) brought Hellenism and orientalism together. Western philhellenes sought to regenerate Greece, which would then regenerate Europe. But there were crucial differences from Napoleon's program for Egypt. In the 1820s, directly controlling Greece was unthinkable. Politics and Romantic visions of Greece were mutually reinforcing. The agents of Greek renewal would be the Greeks themselves, with help from individual philhellenes, not imperial administrators.

The twists and turns of the war which broke out in 1821 complicated this. When Greek resistance crumbled in 1826, the Great Powers directly intervened, crushing the Turkish fleet at Navarino in October 1827. The Greeks were now to run their own country, but under a Bavarian king and regents chosen by westerners. Hellenism was thus in a very different position from orientalism after 1830. Greece, unlike Egypt, *was* renewed, but the attitudes of westerners toward modern Greeks were complex. The philhellenes drove a wedge between ancient and modern as surely as the orientalists. Fallmereyer (1830: 143–213) argued that Slavs had entirely replaced Hellenes, and it became common to suggest that the modern Greek population was one of "Byzantinized Slavs," not heirs of the Hellenic *Volksgeist*. The Greeks were caught in an extraordinary cultural bind. Michael Herzfeld suggests that

> the West supported the Greeks [in the war] on the implicit assumption that the Greeks would reciprocally accept the role of living ancestors of European civilization . . . Greece may be unique in the degree to which the country as a whole has been forced to play the contrasted roles of *Ur-Europa* and humiliated oriental vassal at one and the same time. (Herzfeld 1987: 19)

Herzfeld (1987: 50) points out that "Unlike their European patrons, the Greeks were not seeking a return to a Classical *past*; they were instead seeking inclusion in the European *present*." They were simultaneously Europe's oldest state and its youngest nation. Many educated Greeks argued that they had thrown off the influence of the Church and the Turks, but they generally accepted their negative image. The peculiar position of Greece, free yet dependent, meant that its relations to the west were even more complex than those of the Arab world. Some within the new political elite wanted to forge a western-style nation-state from the diverse groups within Greece. Many intellectuals were as keen as westerners to promote a Hellenist antiquity, giving Greece a special place in Europe (Kotsakis 1991: 65–70), but this also perpetuated Greek reliance on western approval of how they used their heritage.

The Invention of Archaeology

Hellenism had developed without much input from archaeology. Philology, the study of the words of the ancients, was the most important resource for rejuvenating modernity. Artifacts were unlike the evidence most classicists worked with, and related to different aspects of antiquity, offering insights into everyday life and change through time. Many classicists were uncomfortable with this. In the late nineteenth century some archaeologists questioned Hellenism, but they were swiftly neutralized. Archaeology was reconstituted as an unthreatening subsidiary skill, just as orientalism had been reduced to throwing the edges of Europeanness into sharp relief.

I see four main factors at work in this process.

Greek Art

Seventeenth-century visitors to Greece had been interested in ancient art, and this intensified in the eighteenth century. In 1751 the Society of Dilettanti in London sent James Stuart and Nicholas Revett to Athens to sketch its ruins, and in 1758 Le Roy published his *Ruines des plus beaux monuments de la Grèce*. Artists began to demand exposure to the physical remains of Greek art, hoping that by returning to the source, they could hold back corruption (especially industrialism and materialism) and salvage western society.

What counted as adequate exposure escalated. Greek pots unearthed by Sir William Hamilton, British ambassador to Naples, gave the first direct contact. In 1772 Hamilton sold his collection to the British Museum for a staggering 8,000 guineas. When Josiah Wedgwood threw the first six vases at his new factory in 1769, he decorated them with scenes from Hamilton's pots; and when Hamilton published his second collection in 1791, he made the books cheap so that young artists could use them as models.

But sculpture and architecture from Athens itself were much more highly esteemed. In 1784, the Comte de Choiseul-Gouffier, French ambassador to Constantinople, sent Fauvel to Athens as his agent, armed with a permit to draw and make casts of antiquities. He also secretly ordered Fauvel to "Take everything you can. Do not neglect any opportunity for looting all that is lootable in Athens and the environs. Spare neither the living nor the dead" (quoted in St. Clair 1983: 58).

Lord Elgin's embassy illustrates the escalation. When Elgin left for Constantinople in 1798, his architect Thomas Harrison persuaded him that books no longer excited European designers. But by making casts of actual objects in Athens, Harrison suggested, Elgin could change the course of English art. Elgin took up this idea enthusiastically. When the British drove France out of Egypt, Elgin won a permit to excavate and to take away whatever he found. Whether he could tear statues off buildings is less clear. He pulled down houses on the Acropolis and found statues beneath them, and dug a huge statue out of a garbage pit at Eleusis. He even planned to work at Mycenae and Olympia.

But for all their artistic influence, neither the "marbles" nor "Etruscan" vases contributed much to Hellenist discourse. Even the painters who visited Greece represented its ruins as extensions of a formalized, literary past. The idea that antiquities could challenge visions of the past was never raised. Rather, "Writers appealed to Greece as an allegedly universal human experience, but the moral and social values of genteel upper-class English society set the parameters of that prescriptive experience" (Turner 1981: 51).

Nationalism

Philology gave westerners tools to trace a line of power from ancient Greece; archaeology went one step further. A museum full of Greek art showed a country's civilized status.[5] The unseemly 1812 squabble over statues taken from Aegina shows the lengths people would go to, as French, Bavarian, and English agents chased the shipment round the Mediterranean. But like artists, governments used antiquities to illustrate Hellenism, not to explore it. Once a country had an acceptable stock of antiquities, interest declined. The Greeks' own responses to their past are more complex, however.

Altertumswissenschaft

Germans interested in antiquities were pulled by two contradictory forces. On the one hand were Winckelmann's methods; on the other, philological *Altertumswissenschaft*. By the 1870s there was some concern that applying rigorous, comprehensive, and detailed analysis to antiquities could stimulate new ways to see the past, which might not fit within Hellenism. Leading British classicists certainly feared this would happen. A large, detailed excavation which treated the minutiae of its finds as seriously as textual critics treated theirs would produce evidence for daily life and change through time which could not be handled adequately within the existing frameworks.

As so often, an outsider who did not share conventional wisdom brought on the crisis. Heinrich Schliemann began to dig at Troy in 1870. He was an outsider to *Altertumswissenschaft*. His wealth freed him from institutional controls, and although his early seasons were more destructive than instructive, he won international fame by showing that excavation could go beyond recovering sculpture.

German nationalism changed rapidly with the country's unification in 1871. Schliemann demonstrated German preeminence in yet another field. Most German classicists scorned him (see pp. 85–6 below), but his triumph created a new sense that archaeology could be a source of national pride. The small French artistic school at Athens had been a focus for patriotism since 1846 (Radet 1901: 150), and in the age of empire the Great Powers all scrambled to assert their status in Greece through academic imperialism. Greece thus differed again from the Near East by remaining a neutral state with room for all to establish physical presence on her sacred soil through scholarly institutes. The German Archaeological Institute set up a branch office in Athens in 1874, the year Schliemann started digging Mycenae.

Schliemann showed the potential for rigorous archaeology in Greece, but it was Ernst Curtius (1814–96) who synthesized excavation and *Altertumswissenschaft*. Curtius began trying to raise money to dig at Olympia in 1852. In a memorandum to the Prussian Foreign and Education Ministries in August 1853 he argued that Germans had a duty to their national culture to excavate Olympia: the French were committed elsewhere, and the Greeks lacked the inclination and resources. There was some interest in finding statues of athletic victors, but despite having Alexander von Humboldt and the Kaiser as supporters, Curtius' plans broke down when German officials balked at Greek laws banning antiquities exports. It took Schliemann's finds, and the possibility that he might move from Troy to Olympia in 1873, taking the glory of the expedition away from the state, to dissolve the obstacles. In 1874 Prince Friedrich intervened personally with King George of Greece, and in 1875 Curtius began to dig.

Curtius insisted that finding sculpture was not his goal. He wanted to clear the entire precinct, to understand its plan. Alexander Conze had dug with similar aims on Samothrace in 1873 and 1875, but Curtius worked on a vastly larger scale, employing more than 500 laborers in 1880. Although recording and collection were minimal by modern standards, Curtius generated artifacts and information in unprecedented quantities. He found artwork and buildings named by ancient authors, but the more mundane finds created problems. Marchand (1996: 91) suggests that one of the long-term results of Olympia was that it "brought to light material inaccessible – and, the implication was, unappealing – to the man of general neohumanist *Bildung*." Scientific archaeology did not fit into traditional Hellenism; "archaeology undermined the highly romantic, idealized image of ancient Hellas which provided ruling class ideology, and on which dons and public school masters could wax lyrical" (Bowen 1989: 177). Far more than Troy or Mycenae, Olympia needed a new technical language and a new kind of text. Both drew more on the archaeology in other parts of the world than on Hellenist procedures.

World Archaeology

Modern archaeology probably began in Denmark around 1800 with Christian Thomsen's chronological research. The writings of the next generation of Danish archaeologists, particularly J. J. A. Worsaae (1821–85), have been interpreted as treating local prehistory as a source of national pride in the face of fears of French and German cultural domination. But Barthold Niebuhr, Denmark's most important classicist of this period, forms a complete contrast. Niebuhr turned his back on Denmark: he wanted to study at Göttingen (his father refused and sent him to Kiel, then a Danish city). As soon as he could, he abandoned the Danish civil service to join the Prussian government.

Niebuhr's internationalism (or at least pan-Germanism) epitomizes the differences between Hellenism and prehistory. A properly scientific archaeology of Greece needed to draw on the Scandinavian approach to artifacts, tying seriation to stratigraphy, but its goals still had to come more from men like Niebuhr, not Worsaae. If classical archaeologists took the prehistorians' ideas about good questions and appropriate audiences too seriously, they risked confusing their field's claim to speak to all western Europeans about their origins.

The idea that *all* archaeology was an independent science with its own goals and methods and observation language was potentially as subversive for Hellenism as it was attractive to some archaeologists. Greek material culture need not be tied to Hellenism; anthropologists or historians could study it, and even nonclassicists. It was in classical archaeologists' interests to make their subject distinct, emphasizing scientific skills like knowing how to control stratigraphy, classify pottery sequences, and date artifacts; but they could not afford to cut themselves off from classics, which had vastly higher prestige than archaeology. Archaeologists who were devoted Hellenists, as most of those active in Greece were (professional architects like Wilhelm Dörpfeld as much as philologists), used their methods and skills to carve out a niche within classics. If classical archaeologists ignored new developments, their archaeology would not live up to the highest standards of science. But left unchecked, these forces could make Greek archaeology largely independent of classics.

The Battle for Greek Archaeology

Writing Archaeology

Much was at stake, but by 1900 Greek archaeology had been neutralized. The problems were resolved by banishing people from archaeological discourse, sometimes reintroducing them at the end of the story as Romantic beings who by spontaneous decisions altered a passive material culture. The standard archaeological text became the artifact-centered monograph, describing the architecture, sculpture, small finds, or pottery from a specific site. The archaeologist's goal was to fit this model as comprehensively as possible. The ideal strategy was to spend several seasons excavating a major sanctuary or city, publishing it as a series of books. Olympia provided the model, with five volumes of *Ergebnisse* (1896–7). The level of detail in these works is astonishing.

The problem with Hellenist archaeology is not its commendable level of detail, but the idea that mastery of artifacts is *all* that there is. Anything not visible from the archaeologist's vantage point, itself chosen on the basis of assumptions which are rarely made explicit, is *a priori* not worth discussing. The choice of vantage point *prefigures* the historical field: it is a poetic act, determining what can be talked about. In the late nineteenth century, archaeologists of Greece decided that the ideal creative persona compiled and classified excavated data in a multi-volume site report.

Narrative had been the major literary form for antiquarians. Even authors who published private collections concentrated more on stories about artistic development or mythology than on publication in the modern sense. In the 1880s, nonnarrative texts took over. Adolf Furtwängler's (1885) catalog of the vases in Berlin was a landmark. Eschewing old-fashioned narratives, he classified 4,221 pots by fabric, period, and shape, and attributed them to specific styles. Between 1880 and 1914 long-term projects to publish complete corpora of sculpture, sarcophagi, coins, and vases began.

Marchand (1996: 104–15) argues that in the 1870s German classical art historians turned away from Winckelmann's interests toward a semi-scientific model. Analytical texts had great appeal. White (1987: 26) suggests that "To many of those who would transform historical studies into a science . . . [a] discipline that produces narrative accounts of its subject matter as an end in itself seems theoretically unsound; one that investigates its data in the interest of telling a story about them appears methodologically deficient." Nonnarrative texts aligned archaeologists with *Sprachphilologen*. They could feel more scientific than *Sachphilologen* for whom re-presentation in narrative was the highest form of explanation. Grafton (1991: 215) shows that from the perspective of *Sachphilologen*, philologists "did not read (*lesen*) ancient literature [or the material record], they read it to pieces (*zerlesen*) in their frenzied search for raw materials from which to make new lexica and handbooks – but never a new vision of the past." The new archaeologists of the 1880s prefigured categories of artifacts as the objects of analysis, and ordering them stylistically/chronologically as the main form of explanation. Scholars could dispute others' orderings, subdivide or blur categories, or fight over chronology. But only antiquarians or eccentrics would go beyond this.

The scientific site report and catalog made narrative inappropriate. Archaeology could not tell a story challenging narratives based on ancient texts (themselves often narratives in the first place) and could not, therefore, challenge literary scholars. By producing "analyses" rather than narratives, Greek archaeologists won scientific status but surrendered the disciplinary high ground – the right to shape the story of the relationship between Greeks and the west – in return for a small but secure niche within Hellenism.

Some archaeologists resisted these pressures, but once they abandoned the security of their place within classics they lost influence. Three British figures illustrate this. The earliest is Charles Newton, a keeper of antiquities at the British Museum. Newton was a pioneer in fieldwork, excavating classical sites in Turkey in the 1850s. He was not particularly interested in using Greek art to combat modernity. He rejected the "childhood of Europe" approach, and tried to use a range of evidence to explore everyday life and religion. He was more in tune with contemporary anthropology than most classicists. He was as Eurocentric as any Hellenist, but his evolutionary interests had the potential to begin an archaeological critique of Hellenism. Through the 1860s he used the many vases he had given the British Museum to show students new ways to explore Athenian society (Turner 1981: 117).

Among the few who followed his lead was Jane Harrison, one of the first women undergraduates at Cambridge. She later recalled:

> We Hellenists were, in truth, at that time [in the 1860s] a "people who sat in darkness," but we were soon to see a great light, two great lights – archaeology, anthropology. Classics were turning in their long sleep. Old men began to see visions, young men to dream dreams. I had just left Cambridge when Schliemann began to dig at Troy. (Harrison 1965 [1921]: 342–3).

The possibility of an anthropological Greek archaeology was felt all over Europe. German classicists defeated it completely, but in Britain a few anthropological archaeologists achieved professional success. Harrison's first book was a conventional treatment of sculpture, but soon she was using evolutionary anthropology, French sociology, and artifacts to argue that the Olympian gods developed from older spirits. She saw an evolution from matrilineal to patrilineal descent and derived all Greek religion from ritual (Harrison 1903; 1912). But archaeologists showed little interest in her work; her followers in the "Cambridge School" were mainly philologists. After the First World War her books became bywords for the dangers of reading too much outside classics, and her evolutionary approach completely disappeared.

The most successful anthropological archaeologist was William Ridgeway. He combined archaeology, anthropology, and German comparative philology with interests which seemed highly eccentric to 1880s classicists. Ridgeway thought he had been denied a fellowship at Caius College, Cambridge, in 1881 by "partisan feeling," and the editors of the new *Journal of Hellenic Studies* blocked his influential paper "The Authors of Mycenaean Culture." The editors ultimately resigned, but they created a long-term precedent for obstructing unusual contributions. Ridgeway felt that he received the same treatment from the journal in 1887 and 1895 (Ridgeway 1908: 11, 16). His work was fiercely resisted in the 1880s. He returned to Cambridge from Cork in 1892 not as a classicist but as part-time Disney Professor in the Faculty of Archaeology and Anthropology. In spite of 34 years in the chair, his presidency of the Royal Anthropological Institute, and a knighthood, he had no more impact on classical archaeology than Newton or Harrison.

Greek Historiography

But the failure of Newton, Harrison, and Ridgeway did not make Hellenist archaeology the only possibility. Once secure within classics, archaeology could become the handmaiden of history; archaeologists and text-based historians could work toward common goals. But this did not happen.

Athens was important in early nineteenth-century liberalism. Unlike connoisseurs who used Hellenism to revitalize western art, liberal historians used Greece to revitalize politics through a kind of comparative analysis, in which modernity was found wanting. If a historical archaeology emphasizing change had emerged anywhere, it would have been in 1850s London, when Newton was shaking up the British Museum. In the same years, liberal historians were mounting politically explicit attacks on conservative treatments like William Mitford's ten-volume *History of Greece* (1784–1810). To George Grote, a banker and leading Whig, Mitford's *History* was a major prop for antidemocratic ideology. Greek historians remember Grote the fact-grubber, but forget Grote the politically engaged critic of knowledge. He argued that

> There is no historical subject whatever which more imperiously demands, or more amply repays, both [liberal] philosophy and research; and when we recollect the extraordinary interest which the classical turn of English education bestows upon almost all Grecian transactions, and the certainty that a Grecian history will be more universally read than almost any other history, we regard it as highly important that the most current work in this country on the subject should be fairly and correctly appreciated. (Grote 1826: 280)

The problem was partly methodological; Grote observed that "we are made painfully sensible of the difference between the real knowledge of the ancient world possessed or inquired for by a German public, and the appearance of knowledge which suffices here" (1826: 281). Grote was rightly proud of his mastery of Continental skills, but what he wanted was (liberal) understanding of Greece *by the public*. He made his political agenda clear, suggesting that Mitford's high reputation

> is a striking proof how much more apparent than real is the attention paid to Greek literature in this country; and how much that attention, where it is sincere and real, is confined to the technicalities of the

language, or the intricacies of its metres, instead of being employed to unfold the mechanism of society, and to bring to view the numerous illustrations which Grecian phenomena afford, of the principles of human nature. It is not surprising, indeed, that the general views of Mr. Mitford should be eminently agreeable to the reigning interests in England; nor that instructors devoted to those interests should carefully discourage all those mental qualities which might enable their pupils to look into evidence for themselves . . . few works would more effectually conduce to this than a good history of Greece. (Grote 1826: 331)

Grote was too busy as a left-winger in Grey's Whig government to write such a history. But after the disastrous 1841 election, he began a fully political *History of Greece* (12 vols., 1846–56).

British readers in the 1850s took it for granted that Greek history provided lessons on modern politics. Only the content of the lessons was disputed. The prospects were good for a historical archaeology which could contribute to these arguments. But by the 1880s ancient historians turned away from Grote's generation's faith that politics – either British or Athenian – could regenerate society. Two factors were at work. First, professional academics replaced men of letters like Grote (Heyck 1982). They claimed to be more scientific, but not to be social critics. Second, the Third Reform Bill of 1884 and Gladstone's 1886 Irish Home Rule Bill scared many educated people off liberal policies. Greek historians did not respond to mass politics by returning to Mitfordian views – Grote had made this impossible; instead, as Turner concludes, "Students of and participants in the democratic politics of England in the last third of the century repeatedly denied that modern democracy resembled the democracy of Athens" (1981: 251). By 1900 a Grotean historian arguing that Athens held political lessons for modernity would have seemed hopelessly out of date. This remained true until the 1970s.

In France, different developments led to similar results. Already in 1764 Rousseau had argued that his contemporaries could not renew themselves through Hellenism, because modern states were too different from ancient poleis. After the revolution major thinkers like Condorcet, Chateaubriand, Volney, and Constant continued to look to Athens to understand Paris, but drew different conclusions from Mitford or Grote. Constant argued that in ancient states warfare, direct political participation, and action were linked. In modern states, commerce, politics mediated through representation, and reflection went together. Modern man loved civil liberty, not political liberty. Unlike Grote, French historians emphasized slavery, representing Athenian citizens as an aristocracy ruling a subjected population. By

1815 most French historians, particularly those associated with fledgling scholarly institutions, advocated what Pierre Vidal-Naquet called a "bourgeois Athens," important for its philosophy and art, but not its politics. Between 1850 and 1900 this model went virtually unchallenged (Vidal-Naquet 1995: 117).

In Prussia, scholars in the 1820s were in retreat from the early liberal associations of Greek studies, reacting against student uprisings and fears that philhellenes returning from Greece might create a domino effect (see p. 47 above). German histories of Greece moved toward either Rankean political analysis or high culture.[6]

A Greek archaeology aligned with Grote would have been a very different field, more like Newton's vision. But even in the 1850s it was difficult for archaeological innovators to think about this. Institutions hardened and scholars' liberalism softened in the 1880s, the very years that classical archaeology was becoming established. A great divide between philological historians and archaeologists came to seem natural.

A Case Study: Americans and Greeks

Recent studies of archaeology and nationalism (Kohl and Fawcett 1995; Díaz-Andreu and Champion 1996; Atkinson *et al.* 1996) show how much institutions and ideas vary between countries, even though a higher level of generalization clearly reveals a single trend. Rather than offer a broad but superficial survey of Hellenist archaeology, I will examine a single national tradition in more detail. The obvious candidate is American archaeology. By 1939 American archaeologists were the most significant foreign presence in Greece, and so they have remained (see Dyson 1998).

Charles Eliot Norton

Charles Eliot Norton has a good claim to be the founding father of American classical archaeology. In him all four factors discussed on pp. 48–52 above came together. Norton described the humanities as

> the strongest forces in the never-ending contest against the degrading influences of the spirit of materialism . . . The need is great, I say, for those who hold the humanities in this esteem, and above all for those who recognise in classical studies, largely interpreted and rightly understood, the quintessence of the humanities, to unite in the assertion and maintenance of these studies. (Norton 1900: 8)

Norton became Harvard's first Lecturer in the History of the Fine Arts as Connected with Literature in 1874. The German Institute at Athens opened that year, and Norton's decision in 1879 to create an Archaeological Institute of America (AIA) was precipitated by hearing that Richard Jebb was trying to set up a British School at Athens. Norton felt that Americans could match European scholarship. Dort suggests that "two objectives, to secure for America its due share in the fieldwork in the lands of antiquity and to bring great works of Classical art to this country, were clearly the primary motives in Professor Norton's mind" (Dort 1954: 195). Norton himself said in 1880 that "what we might obtain from the old world is what will tend to increase the standard of our civilization and culture . . . [if] we are even to have a collection of European Classical Antiquities in this country we must make it now" (quoted in Hinsley 1985: 55).

He was also in touch with world archaeology, and tried to reconcile this with Hellenism. His first circular in 1879 advertised the AIA as a society "embracing the sites of ancient civilization in the New World as well as the Old." The second series of the *American Journal of Archaeology* (*AJA*) was announced in 1885 as "devoted to the study of the whole field of Archaeology, – Oriental, Classical, early Christian, Mediaeval and American" (quotations from Donohue 1985: 3, 5).

But right from the start there were struggles between world archaeology and Hellenism. Norton was pulled in several directions. He never questioned Hellenist control over Greek archaeology, and wrote to Carlyle in 1880 that "My interest in this new Archaeological Institute of ours springs from the confidence that it may do something to promote Greek studies among us" (cited in Sheftel 1979: 5). But his archaeology was Romantic and preprofessional. He admired Curtius, but worried about the would-be scientific archaeology. Addressing the AIA in 1899 he observed that "a pitfall has opened up before the feet of the archaeologist . . . there is risk in the temptation, which attends the study of every science, to exalt the discovery of trifling particulars into an end in itself" (Norton 1900: 11).

By then, the AIA's polymathy had collapsed. The *AJA*'s editor was "desirous that American Archaeology in particular should once more become an important feature of the work of this Institute, and that it should find more frequent representation in the pages of this JOURNAL" (Wright 1897: 3–4), but after 1890 the AIA did little outside the Mediterranean. A few essays on nonclassical archaeology continued to appear in the *AJA* into the 1930s, but AIA members were fully aware of the narrowing of the Institute's vision (Dyson 1998: 160–7). Alice Donohue suggests that

> Although interest in the New World was mandated in the founding documents of both the AIA and the *AJA*, American subjects, despite the best attempts of its students, did not receive the same emphasis as classical topics. By the early years of the twentieth century the divergence between Old and New World studies became serious enough to necessitate extensive discussion and some practical readjustments. In hindsight, it is clear that centralization in a field expanding so rapidly in so many directions could never have been sustained for long; *it was natural* that organizations and publications should grow in response to the needs of the various areas of concentration. (Donohue 1985: 8; emphasis added).

There was nothing natural about this split. Larger and more diverse groups like the American Historical Association and the American Anthropological Association did not break up. American archaeology broke into classical and nonclassical wings because those working on Greece fully accepted Hellenism, had few interests outside the classical tradition, and held higher status within and outside the academy. Many hoped to improve society through classics. Hinsley (1985: 56) suggests that "To men of Norton's background and education the burden of public enlightenment was tangible and serious, a noblesse oblige that served at the same time, they believed, as the surest route to peaceful, gradual social improvement in community and nation." Americanist archaeology was unimportant in this agenda.

The American School of Classical Studies at Athens, which opened in 1881, contested European dominance and helped organize professional archaeologists under the aegis of classics, "afford[ing] to young American scholars similar advantages to those offered to their pupils by the French and German schools already existing there" (Norton 1900: 5). The School was digging by 1886. After mixed results outside the Greek state at Assos and Cyrene, the School had an unqualified success with Charles Waldstein's massive excavation at the Argive temple of Hera in 1892–5, following the Olympia "big dig" model (Dyson 1998: 68–85). It yielded art treasures and generated the wealth of smaller finds on which archaeologists had started to depend to define themselves as a distinct group, leading to the inevitable monographs. But it also helped make the most prestigious fieldwork so expensive that only the foreign schools of the Great Powers could carry it out (see Dyson 1989: 215–16).

The Athenian Agora

Every foreign dig in a sense increased Greek prestige, but simultaneously underwrote western control over Greece's heritage. In 1885,
Norton learned that the Metropolitan Museum was expanding
and would have room for new finds. He raised money and looked
for a good site. Delphi seemed most promising. However, the French
had dug there in 1861, and had first claim. Further, the village of
Kastri overlay the site, and would have to be moved, at great
cost. Some Americans felt it would be unethical to seize Delphi
from the French, but others thought it would be a triumph. In 1889,
W. G. Hale wrote to Norton, saying (according to the AIA secretary's
summary):

> Tricoupi [i.e., Trikoupis] stated unequivocally that we could have the
> concession if we came with the money. He said the French "were not
> patient persistent excavators."
> "The advantage to the country would be greater if another nation
> [than Greece] should undertake the task. Greece needed to be more
> widely known. The work of the Germans at Olympia has benefited the
> country more than if the same excavations had been accomplished by
> Greeks."
> "The Greek Archaeological Society would prefer to have the
> Americans undertake the work." (Quoted in Lord 1947: 59)

The heritage of Olympia was unquestioned: the French and the Greeks
were undesirable because they did not reach these standards, and it
seemed that only the Americans had the money. The French ended up
making trade concessions to secure their rights, and feeling that the
Greeks had led the Americans on, to raise the site's price (Amandry
1992).

Concentrating on periods of historical glory is typical of Trigger's
"nationalist archaeology," but again there is a difference: every excavation and expropriation of land added as much to Athens' image as
the frozen origin of western civilization as it did to a sense of the Greek
nation. Greeks had faced an archaeological dilemma since liberation.
The majority felt strong links with the Byzantine and Orthodox past;
classical antiquity mattered most to those with western connections
and education. Often wealthy, they formed archaeological organiza-
tions all over the country after 1829. New street plans for Athens in
1831 and 1834 treated the city as a museum of European origins as
well as a nation's capital, shifting the whole settlement north to expose
the ancient Agora. However, this open space soon filled up with

houses. Successive governments limited building, but in 1924 officials decided that if a large excavation was ever to take place, it must begin soon.

The context is important. In 1922 Greece had suffered a shattering defeat at Turkish hands, and in 1923 surrendered extensive territories. Over a million refugees fled. The population of Athens nearly doubled between 1920 and 1928. October 1923 saw a military coup, and in April 1924 a plebiscite abolished the monarchy. A display of Greek prestige might help Venizelos mollify the growing reactionary elements in Greek politics. However, the Archaeological Society was practically bankrupt. In the whole period 1924–44 it conducted just two small digs in Athens (Petrakos 1987). The state had no money to buy out the 7,000–10,000 residents of the Agora, and parliament rejected a bill of expropriation. Greek authorities hinted that the Americans – the only archaeologists who might raise such sums – might carry out the project. Armed with an anonymous gift of $250,000 from John D. Rockefeller in 1927, the American School's chairman Edwin Capps won the concession and expropriation went ahead, despite strong opposition from displaced locals.

The Agora raised Hellenist archaeology to new heights. In 1931–9 alone, Rockefeller contributed $1,000,000; 365 buildings were demolished and 250,000 tons of earth removed from an area of 16 acres. In 1891, the American School had conceded that its students dug less well than the French and Germans (Lord 1947: 81); by 1936, Leslie Shear Sr. had trained so many students that he could work in eight different parts of the site. Vast quantities of data were recorded in highly effective ways (Shear, Sr. 1938: 314–18). In 1928 the AIA recognized the School as the main American institution in Greek archaeology, with sole responsibility for the Agora (Lord 1947: 205). In the same year the Greek government ruled that any foreign field-worker first had to win approval from his or her school in Athens (Zaimis and Petridis 1928: article 2). In December the School completed its monopoly by forbidding Americans to collaborate with Greek archaeologists without its permission. In 1929 Capps announced that the School would have its own journal, which appeared in 1932 as *Hesperia*.

Dynamic leaders like Capps and Shear transformed American archaeology in Greece. The Agora was the culmination of the big-dig approach; even other foreign schools could not compete. It generated a wealth of material that has kept researchers busy ever since, cataloging and publishing in the canonical manner, masking the need for explicitly theorized approaches to the historical significance of the evidence. When there is so much to do just controlling the material, other concerns must be secondary. The program is self-reinforcing. If any group within the profession had been systematically excluded from the data, it might have challenged the dominant practices; but in practice exclusion from unpublished artifacts meant exclusion from the field, and the artifactual discourse remained intact. The 1930s, a decade of uncertainty and relativism in the human sciences, was the golden age of Hellenist archaeology; as Dyson (1998: 158–216) puts it, it saw "the triumph of the establishment."

Beyond Hellenism

Seventy years after the Agora project began, Hellenist archaeology has lost its innocence. In this section I examine the factors at work since 1939, from the individual to the epistemic. I emphasize massive economic, social, and intellectual changes. The scholarly terrain laid out in the late eighteenth century, which gave Greek archaeology its institutional goals one hundred years later, has shifted beneath our feet.

When fieldwork resumed after the German occupation, it differed little from prewar research. Postwar digs were generally smaller than those of the 1930s, but the strategy remained the same. However, this was not a foregone conclusion. By mid-1944 Communist-dominated EAM/ELAS guerillas controlled most of Greece. At Yalta Stalin recognized British interests, but the country rapidly slid into civil war. This ended in October 1949 with the complete defeat of the Communists (see Iatrides and Wrigley 1995).

A Communist victory would have aligned the Greeks' archaeology with Soviet practices, requiring a reorientation toward ethnicity, the material bases of society, and class conflict. We can only guess how western archaeologists would have reacted, but there may have been problems with obtaining permits and funding fieldwork in a Communist country. Hellenist ideals could have survived, but archaeology would have developed differently if cut off from excavation. The civil war and the Marshall Plan averted this.

John Beazley

During the 1940s, with fieldwork so difficult, the study of museum collections grew in importance. Lecturing at London University on "The Future of Archaeology," John Beazley observed that

> It is sometimes thought that the museums have been worked through, and that for fresh light on ancient art and archaeological problems the

world is dependent on new excavations. Our [ideal] student will not be of this opinion, but will realise that from the enormous stores of objects already above ground, secrets incalculable in number and importance can be won by keen and patient scrutiny. (Beazley 1989 [1943]: 100)

Beazley had begun systematic studies of Greek vases as early as 1910, but they came to fruition in the new postwar atmosphere in staggeringly comprehensive catalogs attributing tens of thousands of Athenian vases to artists, schools, manners, circles, etc. (Beazley 1956; 1963). Dietrich von Bothmer suggests that "His example served as an inspiration and challenge to his friends, colleagues, pupils, and followers – museum curators, university professors, excavators, students, collectors, and lovers of antiquity alike." Beazley transformed "What had been in the nineteenth century the prey of diverse and divergent scholarly stabs at a complex and confusing mass of minor monuments ... into a proper discipline, well ordered and sorted out, in which no aspect had been neglected" (von Bothmer 1987: 201). Some art historians represent Beazley as a pure empiricist, operating in a theoretical vacuum (e.g., Oakley 1998), but as James Whitley (1997a; cf. Neer 1997) points out, this depends on the strange assumption that Beazley's virtual silence about theory and method means that he *had* no theory and method, rather than being a theoretical stance in its own right.

As often happens in the humanities, Beazley's "unqualified success, essentially unchallenged authority, and general reluctance to explain in print how he looked at vases" (Kurtz 1983: 69) created their own problems. Von Bothmer (1987: 201) has said that "I do not believe that Beazley himself would ever have considered his word to be the last, for he never stopped acquiring new knowledge or refining and perfecting his method," but Martin Robertson (1991: 9) argues that "The main work [of attribution] *has* been done ... other approaches are and should be in the forefront of study now." The question "where do we go after Beazley?" is often raised.

One response has been to spread research downward and outward, toward lesser-known artists, or regions and periods formerly considered peripheral. Another is to return to narrative, but without questioning the depeopled landscape. Pseudo-biographical monographs of individual artists and studies of the evolution of specific motifs multiplied in the wake of Beazley. The major exceptions are scholars influenced by structuralism and feminism (e.g., Bérard 1989; Goldhill and Osborne 1994), but their cultural histories remain eccentric.

Beazley did not explicate his "keen and patient scrutiny" beyond saying that it "consists of drawing a conclusion from observation of a

great many details" (Beazley 1918: v). Kurtz (1983: 69) suggests that
he drew on methods pioneered by Morelli in studies of Italian Renaissance painting. Robertson (1985: 26) endorses this, concluding that
"Beazley in his early articles is clearly working under the direct
influence of Morelli and Berenson in their studies of Italian vase painting; and he treats Attic red-figure too unquestioningly, I feel, as an
entirely comparable field." If so, Beazley used the Renaissance analogy
as an alternative to a sociology of Attic vase painting. Robertson
suggests that

> by distinguishing the development of Attic vase-painting (black-figure,
> red-figure and white-ground) in terms of individual artists – master and
> pupil, colleagues and rivals, who learned from and influenced one
> another – he saved us from a schematic structure like that by which we
> distinguish the phases of Minoan or Helladic pottery; and instead we
> are able to watch the way in which the art was shaped by real men over
> three hundred years, much as we can watch the way the painters of
> Florence or Siena or Venice shaped the programme of their schools over
> later centuries. (Robertson 1985: 19–20)

But this is not really the case. Beazley showed no interest in how real
people shaped Athenian art. His categories are no less schematic than
taxa like Late Helladic IIIC1c; they just have friendlier names. When
Beazley did talk about social context he relied on literary sources, with
archaeology used in the classic Hellenist manner, for illustrations (see
Beazley 1989 [1943]: 99). Beazley advanced archaeology by creating
an incomparably tight ceramic chronology for sixth- through fourth-
century Athens, but alienated human agency still further. He provided
the appearance of a humanistic discipline but absolved archaeologists
from thinking about what vases were for.

Economy and Society in Greece, 1949–99

Dyson (1989) suggests that economics changed classical archaeology
more than anything else. In the 1930s and 1940s big digs were
cheap for foreigners: favorable exchange rates and Greek financial
underdevelopment made western money go a long way. In the 1950s
Karamanlis' more orthodox fiscal policies changed this. Transporting
experts and students to Greece each summer and hiring gangs of
workmen got harder. As before the war, archaeologists with private
incomes worked year-round in Athens, but there were fewer excavations big enough to generate material to employ teams of scholars in
its description. Costs rose still more with the energy crisis of 1973.

Some excavators adopted intensive recovery techniques sustaining the flow of artifacts, but this generated materials requiring nonclassical expertise. Other turned to survey. It is inexpensive, but, like the seeds and bones from intensive excavations, the artifacts it finds require new skills. The first systematic intensive surveys in Greece were carried out by Bronze Age archaeologists, and the first post-Bronze Age specialist to organize such a project was Michael Jameson, as much a text-based historian as an archaeologist.

Struggles against colonialism made the 1960s and 1970s difficult for Eurocentric archaeologies in Africa, Asia, and the Americas. In Greece, the most serious challenges came after the 1981 election of the socialist PASOK party on a platform which, for the first time since 1947, questioned American hegemony. Attitudes toward the west hardened. Since 1928 Greek law had limited each foreign school to three excavation permits each year (Zaimis and Petridis 1928: article 2; 1932: article 37), but loopholes were now closed and the law was enforced more rigorously (Merkouri 1982: articles 2–3; Kardulias 1994). In 1988 the law was extended to surveys.

Anthony Snodgrass

Anthony Snodgrass led the first serious revolt against Hellenist archaeology. He came into British classical archaeology in the 1950s by a conventional route, with an Oxford dissertation on archaeological evidence for Iron Age armor and weapons. Snodgrass made a thorough collection of the evidence (1964). British classicists were colonizing the Dark Age in the 1950s, applying Beazleyan methods to its pottery, producing analytical studies (see chapter 3). However, it remained chronologically marginal, its problems and methods overlapping with those of Bronze Age archaeology. Further, the questions Snodgrass addressed had been formed largely by text-based historians.

Andrén (1998: 23, 121–6) notes that pioneers in historical archaeology generally concentrate on "protohistory," where archaeology can fill the gaps between fragmentary texts. Responding to this opportunity, Snodgrass put the finds on a sound quantitative footing. He demolished impressionistic accounts of the change from bronze to iron and went beyond "filling the gaps" to challenge models of social change in archaic Greece (Snodgrass 1965). The fact that he worked on iron weapons also distanced his work from classical archaeology. The objects had little aesthetic appeal, and perhaps for this reason had never been subjected to systematic analysis. Snodgrass had most in common not with art historians but with Iron Age archaeologists of other areas, and he addressed their questions.

Snodgrass argues that

> ancient history and Classical archaeology have ... come much closer together. Once historians extend their interests from political and military events to social and economic processes, it is obvious that archaeological evidence can offer them far more; once Classical archaeologists turn from the outstanding works of art to the totality of material products, then history (thus widely interpreted) will provide them with a more serviceable framework ... As a result of this rapprochement, it will be difficult for a future researcher to embark on an historical subject in the field of Archaic Greece without becoming involved in archaeological questions, or vice versa. (Snodgrass 1980a: 13)

Like many Bronze Age archaeologists, he saw demography as a prime mover (Snodgrass 1977). From this concern he became, after Michael Jameson, the first major post-Bronze Age scholar to champion intensive survey.

Shanks (1996: 132–43) speaks of a "Snodgrass school" of social archaeology. If this is valid, its first feature is eclecticism. Quantification, wide-ranging comparisons, and varied interdisciplinary borrowings are all grist to the mill so long as they lead to new ideas about ancient society. Its second characteristic is overlap with ancient history. Snodgrass has pursued social archaeology into the fifth century BC, and some of his students have gone on to Roman times (Alcock 1993). By sweeping away barriers between archaeological and historical practice, Snodgrass put the idea of Greek archaeology as cultural history on the agenda.

Epistemic Change

We could build up an explanation for current challenges to Hellenist archaeology from these details. The difficulty of generating traditional kinds of evidence stimulated new ways to use material already available, or to create new kinds of evidence from cheaper projects. One response, pioneered by Snodgrass where classical archaeology met ancient history and prehistoric archaeology, was to concentrate on social meanings and contexts of deposition. This encouraged interest in how archaeologists in other parts of the world tackled similar problems, and provoked a crisis of confidence. As an internalist analysis, this has much to recommend it. But it is only part of the story.

The debates within Greek archaeology coincided with a fragmentation of the anthropological archaeologies in which the critics seek salvation. Both phenomena form parts of a wider change, as *all* human sciences have been transformed. The expressions postmodernism and postmodernity began to be heard in the mid-1970s, first among architects and then across the humanities. If anything, these words are even harder to define than Romanticism or Hellenism. Novick suggests that for historians postmodernity "is symbolic of a circumstance of chaos, confusion, and crisis, in which everyone has a strong suspicion that conventional norms are no longer viable, but no one has a clear sense of what is in the making" (1988: 524).

Definitions abound. Christopher Jencks, who popularized the word postmodernism in architecture, sees the key as "double coding," an ironic awareness of the impossibility of freedom from the constraints of what has already been said and done. Architects draw eclectically on earlier styles in a pluralist spirit: "the architect must design for different 'taste cultures'... and for differing views of the good life" (Jencks 1991: 8). The most popular argument is that postmodern architecture, literature, art, and scholarship abandon the modernists' imposition of a single international style in favor of participation with users of cultural products, in a piecemeal approach allowing choice and individuality. The pose is ambivalent, at once criticizing links between space, speech, or action and relationships of domination, and yet mocking the naiveté of attempts to escape complicity in them.

Some on the Left see this decentering of the subject into a pastiche of overlapping discourses as a retreat from political engagement (Eagleton 1996). Fredric Jameson (1989) argues that this caused the waning of affect, as the anxiety of self-conscious solitude evaporated; the disappearance of depth models, such as the dialectical distinction between the essential and the apparent, the Freudian between latent and manifest, the existential between authentic and inauthentic, and the semiotic between signifier and signified; and the loss of a genuine sense of the past as different. He calls postmodern culture shallow and schizophrenic. Jürgen Habermas goes further: defending "the project of modernity," a philosophical current running from Kant and aimed at grounding reason in a universal logic, he represents postmodernism as the culmination of twentieth-century despair in objective rationality, and thus as neoconservative (Habermas 1984). Directly responding to Habermas, Jean-François Lyotard agrees that postmodernists reject "making an explicit appeal to some grand narrative, such as the dialectics of the Spirit, the hermeneutics of meaning, the emancipation of the rational or working subject, or the creation of wealth," but argues that "Postmodern knowledge is not simply a tool of the authorities; it refines our sensitivity to differences and reinforces our ability to tolerate the incommensurable." Knowledge becomes "many different language games – a heterogeneity of elements. They only give rise to institutions in patches – a local determinism" (Lyotard 1984: xxiii, xxv, xxiv).

Others disagree with some or all these points. David Harvey (1989) questions the modern/postmodern divide that others see as so fundamental, pointing out that indeterminacy of meaning and constant flux were central to modernist thought. In *The Communist Manifesto*, a core text, Marx and Engels summed up the 1840s by saying that

> The bourgeoisie cannot exist without constantly revolutionizing the instruments of production, and thereby the relations of production, and with them the whole relations of society . . . Constant revolutionizing of production, uninterrupted disturbance of all social conditions, everlasting uncertainty and agitation distinguish the bourgeois epoch from all earlier ones. All fixed, fast-frozen relations, with their train of ancient and venerable prejudices and opinions, are swept away, all new-formed ones become antiquated before they can ossify. All that is solid melts into air. (Marx and Engels 1977 [1848]: 224)

For Harvey, postmodernity is an avant-garde trend which emphasizes this current in modernity over those which seek to master the chaos of capitalist relations by imposing fixity and order. He suggests that "both modernity and postmodernity derive their aesthetic from some kind of struggle with the *fact* of fragmentation, ephemerality, and chaotic flux" (Harvey 1989: 117). Modernity sought stability through institutions, and understanding through tearing aside the appearances which masked the hidden core underlying surface disturbances. Postmodernity revels in instability, loosening institutional controls and playing with the act of masking and the details of the masks themselves. As noted in chapter 1, all the human sciences have moved in the last thirty years from structure to culture, from depth to surface. Harvey argues that this shift among intellectual elites was driven by economic changes – the collapse of centralized, large-scale capitalist production in the face of smaller, more flexible units. Postmodernism tries to make sense of this but also fuels it by legitimating its consequences:

> Postmodernism has come of age in the midst of this climate of voodoo economics, of political image construction and deployment, . . . of new social class formation . . . the attempt to deconstruct traditional institu-

tions of working-class power (the trade unions and the political parties of the left), [and] the masking of the social effects of the economic politics of privilege . . . A rhetoric that justifies homelessness, unemployment, increasing impoverishment, disempowerment, and the like by appeal to supposedly traditional values of self-reliance and entrepreneurialism will just as freely laud the shift from ethics to aesthetics as its dominant value system . . . 'Once the poor become aestheticized, poverty itself moves out of our field of social vision', except as a passive depiction of otherness, alienation and contingency within the human conditions. When "poverty and homelessness are served up for aesthetic pleasure", then ethics is indeed submerged by aesthetics, inviting, thereby, the bitter harvest of charismatic politics and ideological extremism. (Harvey 1989: 336–7)

I emphasize the variety of theories about what has happened and why it happened because lack of consensus is one of the few features of postmodernity on which all agree. In a more cynical vein, Alex Callinicos suggests that

The discourse of postmodernism is therefore best seen as the product of a socially mobile intelligentsia in a climate dominated by the retreat of the Western labour movement and the "overconsumptionist" dynamic of the Reagan–Thatcher era. From this perspective, the term "postmodern" would seem to be a floating signifier by means of which this intelligentsia has sought to articulate its political disillusionment and its aspiration to a consumption-oriented lifestyle. (Callinicos 1990: 115)

The baffled observer could be forgiven for seeing in all this nothing more than a fog of waffle and academic posturing, but there are some shared themes – the decentering of the subject and rejection of single viewpoints; the piecemeal use of the past without regard for context; and the refusal of totalizing metanarratives which provide coherent meaning in history. Postmodernists often reject traditional ways of identifying truth and objectivity, making literary criticism rather than science the model for inquiries into the human condition. The center collapses. Some scholars hold to Eurocentric models like Hellenism; others seek new certainty in quantification; others still adopt forms of relativism. The dividing lines are not always political. Many Marxists resist postmodernism's tendency to fragment scientific knowledge into incompatible discourses, and postmodern philosophers like Jean Baudrillard have become darlings of the Right. Some established disciplines are disintegrating into subspecialties which cannot speak to each other.

These attitudes are antithetically opposed to the aims of classical scholarship since the late eighteenth century. Tracing the west's descent from Greece is anathema to the concerns which are coming to dominate academia. W. Robert Connor has sketched the effects of this on classics. He suggests that the dominant view before 1960 was that

> since our universities advanced the public good by educating citizens, and (it was to be hoped) leaders, these future power-holders should study power and its implications within the intensely political cultures of the Greeks and the Romans. In doing so, they would gain perspective on their own society, discover the values that should govern the use of power and at the same time be introduced to the literary tradition that shaped their culture. Thus the universities would contribute to a better world. This was a powerful rationale until driven topsy-turvy in the struggles of the late 1960s. Suddenly the noble rhetoric came home to roost. Student radicals and once-trusted colleagues told us if we wanted a better world, then the universities had better become vehicles for social and political change, here and now. Everything except immediate political reform became suspect. We all know the arguments and battles of that era and the reaction that set in in the 1970s. The results are evident today: a concentration on private concerns and sometimes even private worlds. Fantasy literature cohabits happily with guides to success and affluence. (Connor 1989: 29)

The net result was that classicists

> have lost something, for one of [the] effects is that it is much more difficult for the classical humanities to claim a central role in liberal education. And if the claim is made, it is much more difficult to deliver the goods . . . What do we have to put in the place of the old educational rationale that selected, presented and interpreted a canon of classical writers because of their critical concern with power and the holders of power? We have lost that rationale and not yet found a substitute. (Connor 1989: 34)

Nineteenth-century classical philology had held the academic high ground; by adjusting to a fragmented postmodern intelligentsia it concedes this position. If classicists persevere with established goals and methods, they may sink into the kind of obscurity that enveloped Egyptology after 1880; if they embrace the new, they have to surrender their claims to a superiority that needs no demonstration, and prove their value. It is a double bind.

Alternative Archaeologies

So it is not just that classical archaeologists have not kept up with the gurus in Ann Arbor or Cambridge. Other archaeologies are just as implicated in the intellectual movements of the last thirty years.

New archaeologies emerged at the same time in Britain and America, and though there were differences, both offered testable truths in a world where old verities were disintegrating. New archaeologists wrote their own history in internalist and celebratory modes. David Clarke suggested that archaeology was moving through a three-stage process from consciousness to self-consciousness to critical self-consciousness, when "attempts are made to control the direction and destiny of the system [i.e., archaeology] by a closer understanding of its internal structure and the potential of the external environment" (1973: 7). He saw archaeology as powered by introspection, its "loss of innocence." Binford presented the rise of the new archaeology as a personal odyssey away from innocence. He saw his adoption of Hempelian logic winning over younger and open-minded archaeologists by its self-evident superiority over older methods, as he moved from losing his job at the University of Chicago to a standing ovation at the 1966 meeting of the American Anthropological Association (Binford 1972: 6–13). He represented new archaeology as a break with the discipline's past, declaring history – the history of his discipline as well as the discipline of history – redundant.

These pseudo-histories are as crudely dualist as anything in Greek archaeology. Patterson and Trigger offer instead critiques concentrating on economics and institutions. Patterson (1995: 42–6) describes a traditional "eastern establishment" coming under attack in the 1960s from a more professionalized "core culture" based in the midwest and south, championing the new archaeology (Binford (1972: 11, 340) explicitly casts his hostility toward Robert Braidwood in these terms). Patterson sees similar forces in Britain around 1980, explaining postprocessualism as "a commentary on and critique of the highly centralized, hierarchical organization of the British archaeological community; of the high levels of marginal employment experienced by recently trained archaeologists; and of the neoliberal transformation of British society during the Thatcher years" (1995: 138).

Trigger sees American new archaeology as part of the transition from colonialist to imperialist mentalities. He links its success to the

1960s economic boom, and a confident middle class writing materialist naturalizations of its position as the inevitable outcome of evolution. The new archaeology fitted American pragmatism by justifying
its findings as socially useful while castigating other archaeologies
as irrelevant; and, Trigger argues, its generalizing thrust fitted US economic and military interventionism by implying that local traditions
were unimportant. All could be subsumed within a single American
discourse. Trigger (1989: 315) links its emphasis on demography,
ecology, and catastrophe theory in the 1970s to failures in American
foreign policy, especially in Vietnam, and growing middle-class
uncertainty.

For Trigger economic upheavals in the 1970s made the new
archaeology's second phase relevant for insecure middle classes in
other western nations. But while American new archaeology progressed from colonialism (denigrating native American culture) to
imperialism (justifying American interventionism), British new
archaeology retreated from colonialism toward nationalism, or at
least Eurocentrism. The second radiocarbon revolution of the 1960s
undermined diffusionist prehistory, and Renfrew's work (1972; 1973)
on multiple invention and systemic change might be seen as part of a
similar rethinking of orientalism, creating a distinctive European
trajectory as early as the neolithic.

Few archaeologists rushed to find a place within postmodernism
until the mid-1990s, but their work is now well represented in series
like Blackwell's *Social Archaeology* and Routledge's *Material Cultures*.
Many postprocessualists simply ignore the new archaeology, but the
1990s have also seen a healthier development. Some archaeologists
have sought middle ground, accepting postprocessual emphases on
agency, symbolism, and ideology, while retaining new archaeology's
interests in ecology, hypothesis testing, and generalization (e.g.,
Preucel 1991; Yoffee and Sherratt 1993).

Conclusions

I am not arguing that archaeologists of Greece should become postmodernists. But I am saying that over the past forty years the Hellenist idealization of Greece as the unique origin of the west has fallen
apart. Since Greek archaeology worked largely to defend that idealization, its value is open to question. Many critics within Greek
archaeology want to reorient work toward a wider archaeological
audience. The problem is that there is no united community to appeal
to. Anthropological archaeologists are if anything even more divided

than classicists. The new archaeologists' faith in themselves as disinterested scientific observers now seems naive, but no persuasive case has yet been made for alternative sources of legitimacy.

I see three possible responses for archaeologists of Greece. The first is to deny the problem. Judging from the papers in leading journals and at the annual meetings of the Archaeological Institute of America, this is the most popular position. If enough scholars do this, then classics may stick to its well-trodden paths, following the example of Egyptology 150 years ago, which purchased the right to continue its narrow work by surrendering to classics as unimportant the right to define Egypt.

The second response reasserts Greece's transhistorical relevance. James Redfield (1991) notes a "natural opposition between philology and democracy," calling philology a form of traditional authority at odds with modern society. Classicists might cast themselves as defenders "of a certain standard" (as Redfield puts it) in resistance to general decline, as intellectuals have often done. Casting Hellenist learning as a critique of society's ills constitutes a radical political agenda, and Victor Hanson and John Heath have stepped forward in this role. They argue that classicists are driving themselves out of business, as "Irrelevancy, incoherence, and professional self-promotion have become blood brothers in a perverse kind of suicide pact" (Hanson and Heath 1998: 151). In response, they offer America at the millennium's end "Greek wisdom" (1998: 36–58), a legacy of "Constitutional law, private property, the distinction between religion and politics, [and] the chauvinism of a middling class" (1998: 40). They conclude that "Every aspect of the ancient Greek world reveals the ideas and principles that have defined the shape – and determined the course – of Western culture" (1998: 58). They suggest that

the death of the Greeks and Romans means an erasure of an entire way of looking at the world, a way diametrically opposite to the new gods that now drive America: therapeutics, moral relativism, blind allegiance to progress, and the glorification of material culture. The loss of Classical learning and the Classical spirit as an antidote to the toxin of popular culture has been grievous to America, and it can be sensed in the rise of almost everything antithetical to Greek ideas and values: the erosion of the written and spoken word; the rise of commitments, both oral and written, that are not binding; the search for material and sensual gratification in place of spiritual growth and sacrifice; the growing conformity of urban life at the expense of the individual and the ethos of individualism; ahistoricism and a complete surrender to the present; the demise of the middle class. (Hanson and Heath 1998: 159)

Hanson and Heath suggest that if professors of Greek did their job properly, and reached those who run America's corporations, "Much could have been learned in the 1980s from the Greeks, and much of the misery of our winner-take-all craze avoided" (1998: 155). "Greek wisdom" is accessible via detailed study of a small fixed group of works which enshrine – for those educated to read them – eternal moral values (1998: 214). In a cynically professional sense, Hanson and Heath offer more hope to classicists than head-in-the-sand approaches, since they would make the Greeks as basic to higher education as von Humboldt did. But they offer little to even the most conservative archaeologist. They are concerned only with a small group of authors. Material culture matters only "if you can see that archaeology is but a tool, not the bridge [to Greek wisdom] itself" (1998: 184).

The third response is to recognize that the structure of Greek archaeology in the last hundred years is the outcome of particular historical circumstances, which have now passed away. For a century the simple fact that the objects archaeologists studied came from Greece justified the discipline's existence and lavish funding. That is no longer the case, but there are no easy alternative sources of legitimacy at hand.

"Problematizing" is the most overused word in the humanist's vocabulary, but it is the best one for describing the task facing Greek archaeologists. Ignoring the narrowness of the nineteenth-century definition of the subject, rejoicing in it, or condemning it are all equally pointless. At the close of the twentieth century, we need to ask what benefits studying ancient Greek material culture brings anyone. To say this is not to reject disinterested scholarship in favor of political agendas; our century-old obsession with chronology and attribution is itself ideological, and moreover, belongs to an ideology which is hard to maintain at the millennium's end.

The most fruitful response, I believe, is not to try to turn the clock back to a golden age when classicists were decent people, but to rethink the decisions of the 1870s. An archaeology of Greece will be more useful if it turns away from the goals philologists set up a hundred years ago, and bridges the great divides I identified on pp. 40–1 above. The first was between classical and anthropological archaeologies. This is where Snodgrass concentrates his discussion. My disagreement is not with the notion that archaeologists of Greece must understand the theories, methods, data, and conclusions of anthropological archaeologists of other areas, but rather with the assumption that this will cure all our ills.

The second divide was between classical and prehistoric archaeologists. Many Aegean prehistorians already have strong links with anthropological archaeologists in other regions, with obvious benefits for their research. Attempts to cross the Dark Age and bring prehistorians' methods into classical Greece have already produced results, most notably through intensive surface survey.

Both these changes are important. But I think that bridging the third divide, separating archaeologists from historians, holds the greatest promise. Making archaeology cultural history means refiguring our thought in two ways. First is the sense intended by White (1973) in discussing the *prefiguring* of the historian's intellectual landscape: we have to shift our perspective. Too often classical archaeologists make describing the material record as it exists in the present the ultimate goal. Doing cultural history means treating the evidence as the means rather than the end, concentrating on the uses of material culture in antiquity, even if this means that we spend more time talking about objects which have *not* survived than those which have. The second sense follows directly from this. In abandoning conventional perspectives, we fragment our field of vision into the countless points of view of actors *in the past* – that is, we refigure classical archaeology in the sense of treating material culture as something used by real people in pursuit of their everyday goals.

James Wiseman (1980) suggests that many problems would disappear if American classical archaeologists studied, as they often do in Europe, in Archaeology departments rather than in Classics departments. The implication of my argument is that this is only partly true. Archaeologists of Greece need as much contact with ancient historians and literary critics as with anthropologists and other archaeologists. In the late nineteenth century, it was important for classicists to insulate Greek archaeology from disruptive outside influences. Now precisely the reverse holds. But breaking down barriers has costs. Most obviously, if we expect archaeologists of Greece to be comfortable with concepts developed in studies of ancient Mesoamerica, the French Revolution, or reception theory we cannot expect them to be as familiar with the philosophy, literature, and languages of the ancients as classicists expect them to be.

Archaeologists of Greece must overcome formidable obstacles if they are to transcend their appointed role as an inferior kind of classicist. Not the least of these is the field's institutional structure. Most Greek archaeologists (particularly in North America) are employed in university departments of Classics, not in departments of Anthropology, Archaeology, or History. To be useful, they must contribute to a Classics curriculum, which usually means teaching languages and mythology rather than world archaeology, its methods, or its theory. As in late nineteenth-century Germany, expectations about the labor market exercise powerful constraints on how academics reproduce their field. Breaking with these constraints – that is, choosing to have internalist, intellectual concerns override externalist, institutional ones – calls for more courage than tenured professors normally need to show, although, of course, it is the students with degrees in a new classical archaeology who will run the risk of unemployment. But the constraints and risks are of our own making, the outcome of countless local decisions, played out in every appointment or promotion case – what is the proper field of study for a Classics department? Should there be independent Archaeology departments? How can we best study the ancient Mediterranean within our institutions? It is up to us to reproduce or overturn our century-old models, as we see fit.

In trying to refigure Greek archaeology as cultural history I want draw attention to the particular forces which at various points influenced the field's development, and to tease out the implications of past practice for future work. Archaeologists of Greece often seem unaware that *any* historical forces are involved in what they do. My aim in this chapter is to stimulate self-consciousness in thinking about what Greek archaeology is for. The next step, I believe, is to show that archaeologists of Greece are doing something that is *worth* doing: that we are earning our place in the sun, rather than inheriting it.

3

Inventing a Dark Age

Introduction

The Iron Age was long a border land in Hellenist archaeology, but Snodgrass (1998a: 132) can now say that "Within a single generation, [this] conspicuously neglected episode of protohistory has been changed into an intensively studied field." Before 1870 there was no concept of an Iron Age; Greece before the seventh-century lyric poets was imagined as an Early or Heroic Age, represented by Homer. By 1870 most members of the first generation of professional academics agreed that we could know very little about this. Unexpected new data shattered this consensus – first, Schliemann's discovery of the Greek Bronze Age, and then Flinders Petrie's synchronism of the fall of the Mycenaean palaces with Egypt's Nineteenth Dynasty, around 1200 BC. This left five centuries between Mycenae and the lyric poets. Classicists reversed the 1860s consensus and revived the idea of a historical Heroic Age, now set before 1200. Bronze Age archaeology was important and interesting, because Homer and the finds illustrated each other, and Homer stood at the beginning of western literature. But Homer told us little about the succeeding period, and its archaeology cast little light on the bard. This was a Dark Age, or the Greek Middle Ages, which made it uninteresting. Philology drove archaeology. Science required that fieldworkers record Dark Age materials if they came across them, but hardly anyone devoted much of his career to this period (for women it was slightly different). The Heroic Age was interesting, important, and worthy of serious scholars' attention. The Dark Age was not.

The distinction between a pre-1200 Heroic Age and post-1200 Dark Age broke down after 1945. Milman Parry's theories of an oral Homer, the decipherment of the Mycenaean Linear B script, and the accumulation of post-Mycenaean finds undermined Homer's standing as a guide to Bronze Age life. Moses Finley argued first that Homer told us most about the tenth and ninth centuries, and second that this period held the key to the long-term economic and social development of ancient society.

At the same time, British archaeologists were also rethinking the period. Driven more by an empiricist urge to fill a gap than by wanting to link material and literary culture, this school retained the Dark Age model, but argued that it *was* worth study. The prewar distinction between a Bronze/Heroic Age and an Iron/Dark Age was transformed into a postwar distinction between a philological Heroic Age and an archaeological Dark Age. Both groups now agreed that the Iron Age was important, but wrote very different accounts of it. Yet there was no confrontation between the two models. Instead, a series of great archaeological syntheses quietly swept the field in the 1970s, although in the process the archaeologists' art-historical agenda fragmented.

When I began graduate work in 1981, a new consensus had emerged, led by Anthony Snodgrass' *Archaic Greece* (1980a) and Oswyn Murray's *Early Greece* (1980). It made the eighth century a decisive moment for Greek civilization. Around 1200, the Mycenaean palaces burned down, and Bronze Age civilization rapidly declined. By 1100 Greece entered a Dark Age of isolation, simple social structures, and demographic collapse. This ended around 750 in a population boom, the resumption of long-distance travel, an economic transformation, and the rise of the Greek city-state. The eighth-century revolution changed ancient history.

The 1980s were the high point for social archaeologies of Iron Age Greece. In the 1990s some scholars question whether events around 1200 and 700 really do bracket the Iron Age as a distinct period. Instead, they emphasize continuities from Bronze Age through archaic times, or argue that until 480 Greece belonged to an east Mediterranean *koine*. It is too early to tell what kind of post-synthesis Iron Age will emerge, but the major debates now concern these challenges.

In this chapter, I ask why we have prefigured the Iron Age like this. I argue that scholars have faced new ideas and data fairly and with scrupulous attention to detail. But they have usually incorporated these into preexisting disciplinary structures (the historical/archaeological distinction, and the subordination of both to philology) and professional agendas (the relevance of research to a relatively inflexible canon of Greek authors), rather than using them to challenge these programs. These structures and agendas have done most to shape our ideas of what the Iron Age was really about. They have resisted the challenges of new data, and have mitigated the influence of ideas from other parts of the academy. As in chapter 2, I am not trying to debunk earlier researchers by showing that professional structures shaped their thought: that is what professional structures are for. But unless we understand why scholars cared about certain things fifty years ago and not about others, we cannot grasp what they were doing; nor what in their work is still valuable today; nor why certain debates are important in the 1990s while others remain on the sidelines.

Before the Dark Age

Thucydides (1.1–12), writing around 400 BC, provides our earliest narrative account of Greece before 700. He relied on similar evidence to what we use 24 centuries later: legends, Homer, archaeology, and ethnographic analogy. He saw a steady growth in Greek power up to the Trojan war, followed by disturbances and population movements. Progress then resumed, continuing to his own day. He dated the major disturbance, the Dorian invasion, eighty years after the fall of Troy, adding that "Greece enjoyed scarcely any peace for a long time" (1.12), but moved straight on to describe the Ionian migration and the eighth-century colonies in Sicily, saying simply that "All these were founded after the Trojan war."

Snodgrass (1971: 7) points out that in contrast to modern models, "Thucydides' story is one of a consistent, if extremely slow, progress; there is no 'crest' in the heroic age followed by a 'trough' in the dark age, partly because one of his aims is to modify the poets' assessment of the achievement of the heroic age." The first modern attempts to read Homer as history ignored this contrast and created an "early" period by forcing the epics into Thucydides' framework. Abandoning earlier allegorical readings, some eighteenth-century readers saw Homer in a proto-Romantic vein – "Blackwell and Gravine, Wood and Merian labored to knock Homer off his Ionic pedestal, to strip him of his austere classic robes, and to deck him out with the rough staff and furry cloak appropriate to a storyteller at a tribal campfire" (Grafton et al. 1985: 10). Grittiness and reality were all-important for Romantic Homerists, particularly in Britain, where readers tended to envisage a homogeneous period from the peopling of Greece until the first Olympiad in 776 BC.

The two best-known eighteenth-century British histories illustrate this. Temple Stanyan, in his *Grecian History* (1739), divided the chapters covering Greece down to 510 BC geographically rather than chronologically, each treating one city-state in the Heroic Age. He followed Bishop Usher's dating system, counting roughly 1000 years before the fall of Troy. Following Eratosthenes, he placed this in 1184/3 BC (Stanyan 1739: preface, p. 12; main text, p. 55). For Stanyan, the war "properly put an end to the *infancy* of Greece" (p. 39), but apart from noting – like Thucydides – that "Whatever *Troy* suffered, the *Grecians* had no great reason to boast of their conquest" (1739: 55), he identified no real changes between pre- and postwar Greece. Again like Thucydides, the detail of his story declined after the return of the Heraclidae; after 43 pages on Argos from its foundation to the fall of the kings, which he put around 1000 BC, for the next 250 years he simply commented that "In this state the *Argives* flourished for many ages" (1739: 61–2).

Stanyan's account changed after 1000 because his sources contained few postwar stories. He insisted that "The first from whom we receive any tolerable light into the *Grecian* affairs, is *Heredotus* [*sic*]" (1739: preface, p. 5), but relied on Homer and later mythographers in his first five chapters. He professed equal scorn for those who questioned Homer's reliability and those who "greedily catch at the least remains of antiquity," but was determined to save Homer from the critics. He held that Homer had good information about the Trojan war period. He did not discuss Homer's date relative to the war, but did argue that "neither was Homer the first and only author, (as some will have it) who gave an account of this expedition. There are several recorded before him, from whom undoubtedly he copied" (main text, pp. 40–1).

William Mitford (p. 55 above) was more critical of authorities, and disagreed with both Usher's and Isaac Newton's high chronologies for the foundation of Sicyon, the oldest polis. Stanyan had noted the problems, but still followed Usher (Stanyan 1739: 15). Mitford, however, asserted that "scarcely a wandering hunter had ever set foot in Peloponnesus so early as the period assigned by chronologers even to the founding of Argos" (Mitford 1784: 25–6). Despite his idiosyncratic politics, Mitford's outline of early times differed little from Stanyan's. He identified a single phase from the coming of man to archaic times. Echoing Stanyan, he called the capture of Troy "a dear-bought, a mournful triumph" (1784: 80), but described no consequences beyond dynastic problems. In the marginal notes, he cited Thucydides 1.1–12 as his source.

For Stanyan and Mitford, Homer gave direct access to the age before the city-states. Mitford, following Herodotus (2.53), placed Homer around 850, but disingenuously asserted that no ancient writer dated the fall of Troy itself. Ignoring not only Eratosthenes' precise date of 1184/3 but also Thucydides' placing of Homer "much later" than the Trojan war (1.3), Mitford (1784: 228–35) argued that Homer lived before the return of the Heraclidai, so less than eighty years after the war. Homer thus became almost a primary source, believable even on details. Mitford's only criticism of the legends is revealing: he conceded that Agamemnon never sacrificed Iphigenia, but only because Homer did not mention it (1784: 77). He defended Homer at length against "some grave writers of late" who dared assert that the Trojan war was only a story (1784: 81–4).

But even while Mitford's volumes were still appearing, a radical philological approach was gaining ground in Germany. This is best known through Friedrich August Wolf's *Prolegomena ad Homerum* (1985 [1795]). Wolf argued that Homer had stitched the *Iliad* together from older folk lays. Mitford (1784: 85) suggested that Homer was best as a guide to "the manners and principles of his age." Wolf did not comment directly on historical interpretation, but his theory was used in the nineteenth century to support arguments that the *Iliad* was useful *only* as a source for the general ethos of Homer's own time, long after the Trojan war.

Wolf's success defined the terms of the "Homeric Question" for the next 150 years. As Frank Turner sums it up,

> The Question was . . . in fact a series of questions about the composition of the *Iliad* and the *Odyssey*. Those included: Did the two epics have a single author? Under what conditions were the epics composed? Was there an original core to the *Iliad* or to the *Odyssey* upon which a later longer poem had been composed? What was the relationship of the *Iliad* to the *Odyssey*? . . . it was the emergence of philology as a core discipline in German universities that made the questions surrounding Homer problematic for a significant group of scholars. The Homeric Question became a vehicle whereby philologists worked to assert their cultural superiority in European and more particularly German intellectual life. Homeric criticism constituted an arena in which academic philological virtuosos could display their skills in transforming two of the monumental works of Western literature into objects of academic analysis. (Turner 1997: 123)

On one side were the Wolfian analysts (or separatists, or disintegrationists). They usually argued either that Homer was the author of a short Ur-*Iliad*, around which other poems coalesced to form the inconsistent masterpiece we call the *Iliad*; or that Homer stitched together earlier short folk lays to form a huge poem. On the other side were the unitarians, who argued that Homer was a lone, inspired bard who composed the *Iliad* as a single great poem, in more or less the form we have it. There were few pure analysts or unitarians, but the rhetoric on both sides gives the impression of two radically opposed schools of early Greek poetics and history.

Two factors encouraged polarization. The first was nationalism: Unitarianism was generally seen as British, Analysis as German. This fed a second stereotype, that German philology was merely one dimension of a more serious Teutonic aberration, the higher criticism of the Bible. These overtones perhaps did much to push non-British or German scholars away from the debate. Diderot had translated Stanyan into French as early as 1743, but Greek history remained less popular in France than Roman. When early nineteenth-century French writers touched on this period, they took a line like the British. Clavier, for instance, treated Homer as a primary source in a narrative history from Inachus to archaic times (Clavier 1809: preface, pp. 11–12), and engaged in chronological debates with Newton (preface, pp. 25–40). Fauvel, upon excavating Late Geometric graves at Athens in 1812, simply followed Herodotus (1.105; 2.44; 6.47) and Thucydides (1.8) in assuming that such strange pots were made by oriental colonists (cited in Poulsen 1905: 10). But by mid-century, French writers just ignored the entire Anglo-German debate. The most remarkable text is Numa Denis Fustel de Coulanges' *La cité antique* (1864). Fustel was a leading light in the reactionary Catholic circle around empress Eugénie. Ferociously anti-German, he rejected all methods pioneered by philologists across the Rhine and wrote a polemical tract barely mentioning contemporary scholarship. He argued that all Indo-European societies were founded on ancestor cults focused on tombs outside the house, which caused Greek and Roman society to be based on agnatic descent. Classical history was the story of struggles between kinship and politics. These periodically came to a head in revolution, which, Fustel argued, was always bad.

Early Greece was also useful in political debates within nation-states. Mitford drew warnings from history about the dangers of republicanism. He argued from Homer that "absolute MONARCHY ... was unknown among the Greeks as a legal constitution. The title of KING therefore implied with them, as with us, not a Right of Absolute Power, but a Legal Superiority of Dignity and Authority in One person above all others of the state, and for their benefit" (1784: 250). He claimed that "Monarchy with us perfectly accords with the Grecian idea of Kingly government" (1784: 255). By reading Homer as a record of early times, Mitford concluded that British-style monarchies had flourished in the Heroic Age, only to be replaced in archaic times by republics. He implied that if England was to avoid the mob rule of the Grecian republics, it had better make sure that its monarchs did not go the same way as Homer's.

Mitford's picture of Greece aroused liberal ire (see pp. 55–6 above). Connop Thirlwall was the first to reply in detail, with an eight-volume *History of Greece*. Turner (1981: 211) calls Thirlwall "the first British historian to bring the vast accomplishments of German classical scholarship into the service of Greek history," but as Mahaffy noted (1890: 13), Thirlwall bent the rules of source criticism to suit himself, and used legends extensively. Discussing the origins of the Greeks, for instance, Thirlwall struck a stern pose on evidence, suggesting that "if no such person as Hellen had ever existed, his name would sooner or later have been invented" (Thirlwall 1835: 80); but he then accepted almost the whole genealogy. On reaching the Trojan war, while arguing that "the poet . . . did not suffer himself to be fettered by his knowledge of the facts" (1835: 157), Thirlwall nevertheless concluded that "According to the rules of sound criticism, very cogent arguments ought to be required to induce us to reject as mere fiction a tradition so ancient, so universally received, so definite, and so interwoven with the whole mass of the national recollections, as that of the Trojan war" (1835: 151). Unlike Mitford, Thirlwall constantly emphasized the problems of using Homer, but his position that Homer was a source for the Trojan war as well as for the manners of his own age was closer to Mitford than to Wolf. Again like Mitford, Thirlwall made the Heroic Age a homogeneous pre-lyric period: "What [Homer] represents most truly is the state of Grecian society near to his own day; but if we make due allowance for the effects of imperceptible changes, and for poetical colouring, we are in no danger of falling into any material error, in extending his descriptions to the whole period which we term the Heroic" (1835: 159).

In the preface to his *History of Greece*, Grote explained that he began writing to refute Mitford, but Thirlwall had already done this. Grote then insisted, presumably to avoid offending his old school friend, that he only went ahead with his books because they were already far advanced when Thirlwall's appeared (Grote 1846a: iii–iv). Despite the praise he heaped on Thirlwall, Grote disagreed with him completely over the Heroic Age.

Grote favored a compromise between analysts and unitarians, seeing books 1, 8, and 11–22 of the *Iliad* as a core *Achilleis* (1846b: 118–209), but argued that no history could be based on mythology (Grote 1843). Grote acknowledged that legends could include factual information, but saw no way to distinguish between genuine stories and plausible fictions. He concluded that the Trojan war was

essentially a legend and nothing more. If we are asked whether it be not a legend embodying portions of historical material, and raised upon a

basis of truth... whether there was not really some such historical
Trojan war as this, our answer must be, that as the possibility of it
cannot be denied, so neither can the reality of it be affirmed....
Whoever therefore ventures to dissect Homer, Arktinus and Leschês,
and to pick out certain portions as matters of fact, while he sets aside
the rest as fiction, must do so in full reliance on his own powers of
historical divination, without any means either of proving or verifying
his conclusions. (Grote 1846a: 321)

Grote was more consistent than his predecessors, insisting that Homer
was useful for historians *only* as a source for contemporary manners.
He held that "the very same circumstances, which divest [the epics']
composers of all credibility as historians, render them so much the
more valuable as unconscious expositors of their own contemporary
society" (1846b: 57). Grote spent 72 pages reconstructing the customs
of Homer's own day, which he placed around 800. For Grote, history
began in 776, with the first Olympiad. Before this, we could say
nothing. All the chronological studies of earlier events, going back to
Newton and Usher, were worthless (1846b: 34–57).

   Grote's vision was controversial. Some saw his agnosticism as the
mark of a pedestrian mind. John Stuart Mill, for instance, wrote to
Carlyle in 1833 that Grote "is a man of good, but not first-rate intellect, hard and mechanical, not at all quick; with less subtlety than any
able and instructed man I ever knew" (quoted in Momigliano 1952:
11). So far as John Stuart Blackie was concerned (1866: 247), Grote
"declares war against all literary, all poetic instinct, and all the common
sense of common men in the matter of Homeric poetry," and for
Andrew Lang (1910: 234), Grote was "an excellent banker, but no great
poetic critic." Yet to William Geddes (1878: iv), Grote's reading of
Homer was the only one that was "scientifically tenable." By the 1860s
this latter view had won over most British and German readers.
Grote was a better philologist than his rivals, and even in the more
conservative atmosphere after 1870, there was no way to return to
pre-Grotean views. There was growing consensus that we could know
little about Greece before the eighth century, and that even then,
knowledge was restricted to customs, not politics.

Inventing the Dark Age, 1870–1939

Schliemann's Heroic Age

Heinrich Schliemann had abandoned his education in 1836, at the age
of fourteen, only returning to Homer in 1866 after a colorful career in

several businesses, including the California Gold Rush. By then, his belief in a real Troy made him an old-fashioned crank. But his finds, beginning at Troy in 1870, changed everything.

Schliemann called for a totally new vision of early Greece. He argued that there really had been a Heroic Age, associated with the Mycenaean palaces, for which Homer was a reliable source. At some point the palaces burned down and the Heroic Age ended. This had to be before the seventh century, but could not be dated more precisely. Schliemann's thesis flew in the face of scholarly orthodoxy.

Institutional developments gave the ensuing controversy a sharp edge. Academia was being professionalized, with salaried scholars replacing clergymen and socially committed men of letters. Philologists asserted the rigor of their scholarship, and classical archaeologists assimilated themselves to these standards. Schliemann's lack of training, destructive methods, and frequent changes of mind exposed him to charges that he was no scientist. In America, Stillman opposed him, but Schliemann won public opinion to his side. In Britain, the first professional classicists lined up against Schliemann, who again sought popular support. His position was peculiar; the German excavator's discoveries supported the older British unitarian model of a truthful Homer. Schliemann marketed his views skillfully, asking Gladstone to write a preface for his book *Mycenae*. Gladstone hesitated, feeling that Schliemann should approach Charles Newton. But Schliemann insisted, and Gladstone relented.

Schliemann carried the day. By 1914 most Hellenists argued or assumed that Homer described a real Heroic Age. The decisive argument was of course his spectacular finds, precisely where Homer said they should be. Classicists wanted to be scientific, and to the best of their abilities faced the new evidence. The 1860s consensus that the Heroic Age was a legend and that Homer only told us about eighth-century culture collapsed. Bronze Age archaeology transformed historical models, but was absorbed into philological agendas. In 1914, the Homeric Question still dominated scholarship. For twentieth-century unitarians, Homer was a Bronze Age poet, whose works survived intact to archaic times. For analysts, he was a ninth- or eighth-century editor of Bronze Age lays. Classicists rejected the historical implications of Grote's position while preserving his philological methods, much as prehistorians did with Childe's archaeology (p. 19). Scholars changed their views in the light of new finds, but consistently allowed institutional forces to shape the importance of that evidence.

The debates were particularly sharp in Britain, where Homer's ideological weight increased through the nineteenth century. The one

issue over which Gladstone (1857: 1–56) and Jebb (1907: 565–7) agreed
was that the poems should be central to elite education. They disagreed
over whether amateurs like Schliemann and Gladstone or profession-
als like Jebb should control interpretation. Jebb denounced Schliemann fiercely. He insisted (1887: 38) that "the Homeric Greek exhibits
all the essential characteristics and aptitudes which distinguish his
descendant of the classical age," and could not possibly belong to a
distant prehistoric world. Classicists debated the issue in the *Journal
of Hellenic Studies*, the major mouthpiece of the emerging classical
profession in Britain (see p. 54 above). Jebb insisted that Hissarlik was
not Troy, and that Mycenae and Tiryns were Byzantine fortresses.
Others sided with public opinion (and, as it turned out, the facts)
against Jebb's authority.[1] By the late 1880s the tide had turned in
Schliemann's favor. Even in Germany, an entrenched analyst like Carl
Schuchhardt admitted that "for certain parts of his descriptions,
Homer can have had no other models before him but those of
Mycenaean art and civilisation" (1891: 313).

Homer was firmly linked to the palaces. The only form of dissent
was circumlocution. In his widely read *Hellenic History*, George
Botsford only cited Homer once in 23 pages on the Bronze Age,
and in an ambiguously worded passage suggested that Homer "may
have composed both the *Iliad* and *Odyssey*, not by incorporating
earlier lays or by merely adding to an existing epic, but by totally new
creations, yet from tradition contained in extant songs . . . The life
he pictures is not homogeneous but a mingling of the traditional
and the ideal with contemporary facts" (1924: 43). But even this
tactful evasion was a minority position. Mahaffy claimed that "even
the most trenchant of sceptics does not now deny that there must be
some truth in legendary history" (1890: 18); Isham (1898: 3) simply
stated that Schliemann had discovered "the Mycenaean period, the
life of which no one seriously doubts that the Homeric poems
reflect."

J. B. Bury's changing views illustrate the growing strength of
Schliemann's position. In the first edition of his *History of Greece* Bury
took an analyst position. The original *Iliad* described the wrath of
Achilles and death of Hector, and was expanded in the ninth century
into something like our poem, while the *Odyssey* only took shape in
the eighth century. Each poem had two historical layers. He agreed
with Schliemann that "The old Achaean poet, doubtless, reflected
faithfully the form and feature of his time" (1900: 67), but also made
the redaction important. Homer reflected the rise of the city-state,
which he dated in a marginal comment on p. 72 to the tenth or ninth
century. In the margin of p. 74 he suggested that the Thersites episode

was "composed in the 9th century," as a royal reaction against new ideas of citizenship. Bury's original picture was multilayered, more optimistic than Grote, but lacking Schliemann's certainties. But in the second edition Bury's doubts largely evaporated. He simply stated that "Our earliest written record, the *Iliad* of Homer, refers to the peoples and civilisation of Greece in the thirteenth century ... the picture which Homer presents is a consistent picture, closely corresponding, in its main features and in remarkable details, to the evidence which has recently been recovered from the earth" (1913: 5, 50). In his entry on "Homer" for the *Cambridge Ancient History*, Bury was still more confident:

> Since the poems were not, on any theory, composed till about three centuries after the Trojan War, the natural place for considering them and questions associated with the name of Homer might seem to be not here but at a later stage of our history. There is, however, a good reason for anticipating chronology. The Homeric poems tell us almost nothing directly about the history of their own age. It is the civilization of the Mycenaean age they reflect. (Bury 1924: 498)

The new orthodoxy had its own problems. In 1871 Palaiologos had found rich graves outside the Dipylon Gate at Athens, which clearly defined a post-Mycenaean *Dipylonzeit*. In the 1880s most archaeologists put the end of the palaces as late as the tenth century, making for a short *Dipylonzeit*. Schuchhardt (1891: 316) was typical in placing the transition around 1000. If the palaces lasted so long, it was easy to claim that a ninth- or eighth-century editor knew Mycenaean poetry. But in 1890 Petrie published Mycenaean pottery from Nineteenth-Dynasty Egypt, fixing the fall of Mycenae around 1200.

As with Schliemann's finds twenty years before, Homerists faced the evidence, even though it complicated their theories. Lang (1906: 315–19) made explicit what many probably assumed, that the epics were composed before 1200 and then preserved in Linear B on papyrus until the alphabet was invented, when they were copied into the new script. Others tried different lines. Bury argued that medieval Germanic epics showed that oral poets could preserve historical facts; and further, that "the immeasurable superiority of the Greeks in the art of poetry ... implies an intelligent, lucid, and discriminating method in grasping and handling the material" (1924: 512–13). Leaf (1915: 296) claimed that Bronze Age poetry was the pride and joy of post-Mycenaean Ionian kings, so "Under such conditions it need cause no surprise if the tradition of the Achaian age was religiously preserved intact ... The tradition was the hall-mark of the aristocratic poet, and it was all the more tenaciously maintained because he had to compete with other poets who were not aristocratic."

One way or another, by 1914 most Homerists agreed that the poems reached more or less their modern forms around 700, but described the Mycenaean world which had ended around 1200. Petrie was as important as Schliemann for creating the Iron Age as a category: scholars now confronted not a brief transition from palace to city-state, but a major epoch about which they knew little.

The First Dark Age

Between 1870 and 1914 concepts of early Greece changed beyond recognition. Debates growing out of the Homeric Question now seemed old-fashioned. Historians reconstructed the years before 700 as two periods – a Mycenaean age, which Homer described and which cast light on the poems; and a post-Mycenaean world which Homer did not describe, and did not fill out the poems' background. It was clear that knowledge of this half-millennium was woefully inadequate, and only archaeologists could fill the gap. Yet few were interested in doing so.

On the face of it there were three good reasons for scholars to be interested in the Iron Age. First, many felt that the coming of the Dorians perfected the Greeks' racial mix (J. Hall 1997: 4–13). Scientific racism was a major force in these years, and when skeletons were available, skulls could be measured to prove that the Dorians were Aryans. When there were no bones, debates heated up over whether certain painting styles were Dorian.

The second factor was the feeling that the origins of Greek art lay in the Iron Age. Excavations produced more and more Iron Age pottery, and art historians catalogued this, identifying regional styles and fixing their chronologies. But only one monograph on Iron Age art came out before 1939 (Schweitzer 1917). Peter Kahane completed a study of Attic Geometric pottery in the 1930s, but never published it.[2] Archaeologists apparently felt that their energies were better spent on other periods. Beazley covered 1200–750 for the *Cambridge Ancient History* in one sentence: "Between the flourishing of the Creto-Mycenaean civilization, and the geometric period proper, there lies a long period which has been named, not very happily, the proto-geometric: a period of cultural decay, doubtless of invasions and incessant conflict" (Beazley and Robertson 1926: 580). Less art survived than from archaic Greece, but Beazley was also clear that cultural decline robbed these materials of interest.

The third reason for interest was the consensus that Greek religion took shape between 1200 and 700. This inspired some fieldwork. The British School pressed directly to the earliest layers of the temple of Artemis Orthia at Sparta from 1906, publishing them promptly. In George Macmillan's opinion (1911: xx, xxii), this, not Knossos, was the School's most important project. At Olympia, Curtius found much redeposited Iron Age material between 1875 and 1881, which Furtwängler (1879; see pp. 51–3 above) quickly published. On other sites, though, early phases of worship were less appealing. Schliemann's discoveries had less impact on scholarship in France than in other countries, where they were accommodated to Fustel's evolutionary scheme without disturbing it. Victor Duruy, for example, simply avoided the issue, arguing that since the Greeks had believed their legends, historians should do the same (1887: 45; cf. Mahaffy 1890: 30). Most French historians glossed over early Greece (e.g., Francotte 1922: 3–8; R. Cohen 1939: 35–56). French archaeologists were equally unexcited. Excavations began on Delos in 1873, but there were no significant soundings to Geometric levels until 1904, and the first major publication came only in 1934. Picard summarized the early deposits in a lecture in 1947, but not until 1958 did Gallet de Santerre publish a monograph on the pre-archaic sanctuary (Plassart 1973). Likewise, the leaders of the "grande fouille" at Delphi in 1892–1901 did not explore early levels, which waited till the 1920s (Bommelaer et al. 1992).

Archaeologists were not very interested. Dark Age finds usually came out of digs aimed at other periods, as at Olympia, the Kerameikos in Athens (where excavations of fourth-century tombs began in 1863, but Dark Age graves only received systematic attention in 1927), Knossos, and the Athenian Agora. Classical archaeology was text-driven, trying to illuminate philology, not challenge it.

Post-Mycenaean Greece was significant mainly as an annoying gap. For Martin Nilsson (1933: 1), Homer "stands in the morning twilight of Greek history and looks back to a preceding age, which according to him was an age of much more brilliant glory and valiant men than the age in which he himself lived. The question is whether Homer can help us to bridge over the gulf of the dark ages which separate the historical and the Mycenaean age of Greece." The Iron Age was "the poorest and darkest epoch in all Greek history except for the Stone Age" (1933: 246). The concept of a Dark Age rapidly took hold (e.g., G. Murray 1907: 29; Bury 1913: 57). Gilbert Murray (1907: 55) saw it as "a chaos in which an old civilization is shattered into fragments, its laws set at naught, and that intricate web of normal expectation which forms the very essence of human society torn so often and so utterly by continued disappointment that at last there ceases to be any normal expectation at all."

For the stories classicists wanted to tell in the 1870s–1930s, the Iron Age was not an attractive period, and few archaeologists in Greece took research goals from European prehistory. In Snodgrass's words (1971: vii), the Dark Age appeared as "an unsatisfactory interlude, interrupting any pattern of continuous development, yet not providing the positive evidence needed to demonstrate a fundamental change in direction."

Nothing illustrates the marginality of the Iron Age better than the partial feminization of its study. Women directors were more prominent on Dark Age sites than on those of other periods. Two of the earliest large Dark Age digs were carried out on Crete by Harriet Boyd Hawes (1901) and Edith Hall (1914), even though both were by choice Minoanists (Allsebrook 1992; Bolger 1994). The division of labor was far from complete, and some men did excavate Iron Age sites in Crete, while Boyd Hawes (1908) dug Minoan sites. But even her major Bronze Age project, at the village of Gournia, was peripheral at a time when the leading archaeologists dug up palaces and archives. It remained until recently the only large-scale excavation of a Minoan village.

The most exciting pre-archaic archaeology was excavating a palace linked with a Homeric hero, as Schliemann did at Troy and Mycenae. Other archaeologists tried to repeat this. The most elusive was Odysseus' palace on Ithaca. Schliemann briefly searched for it, and Wilhelm Dörpfeld spent thirteen years on Lefkas in the belief that it was the Mycenaean Ithaca. In 1931, Lord Rennell of Rodd instituted a British project on Ithaca, with William Heurtley as director. Heurtley also failed to locate a palace, but did find important Iron Age deposits. Heurtley published some of these, but devolved considerable responsibility onto Hilda Lorimer and Sylvia Benton.[3]

Darkness and Heroes, 1945–1980

The New Heroic Age

If 1875–1900 saw the Mycenaean world defined as an exciting Heroic Age and the Iron Age as an uninteresting Dark Age, after 1945 historians redefined both models. Two developments were particularly important. The first was gradual. Before the war, fieldwork in Serbia led Milman Parry (1971 [1928–37]) to conclude that Homer was an oral poet, and Parry's former assistant Albert Lord (1960) spread understanding of orality, undermining arguments like Bury's or Leaf's about the transmission of poetry across the Dark Age.

The older models still had champions. When Moses Finley declared Grotean agnosticism about the Trojan war in a radio broadcast in October 1963, several senior scholars joined in defending the war's historicity (Finley et al. 1964). One of them, Geoffrey Kirk, argued for a compromise in the new edition of the *Cambridge Ancient History*, preserving a unitarian monumental composer whose poetry was passed down by memory, but putting him in the Dark Age, and seeing few Mycenaean survivals (Kirk 1975 [1964]). Kirk was less radical than many Parryans, but his essay contrasts sharply with Bury's in the first edition of the *CAH*.

The second development was abrupt. In 1952, Michael Ventris deciphered Linear B, confirming that the Mycenaean palaces rested on an economic base completely different from that of Homeric society. Moses Finley (1981 [1959]: 199–232) argued that the Mycenaean palaces had more in common with the Near East than with Homer.

Finley came to ancient history from a social science background, and was more interested in debates among social and economic historians than in illuminating the canon of Greek authors. In his first book he adapted Karl Polanyi's model of reciprocity to argue that classical Athens was a complex economy in which money and markets were important, but which could not be called capitalist (Finley 1952). He then tried to explain how this socioeconomic formation had come into being. Borrowing another Polanyian model, Finley suggested that in contrast to classical civic reciprocity, Mycenaean palaces were redistributive economic systems, and the key to understanding Athens lay in explaining the shift from redistribution to reciprocity. This made the Dark Age important.

Borrowing also from Marcel Mauss, Finley argued in *The World of Odysseus* (1954) that the Homeric economy rested on gift exchange, which created and expressed hierarchy among the heroes. Drawing on Parry and making analogies with *The Song of Roland*, Finley also argued that Homer reflected neither Mycenaean times nor his own, but an intermediate point, around 900 (Finley 1954: 48).

In Finley's vision, Homeric-style gift economies replaced Mycenaean redistributive economies around 1200. At some point between 800 and 500, these systems of graded statuses went through a second transformation, into a world where free and equal citizens practiced reciprocal exchange. Finley offered a "highly schematic model of the history of ancient society. It moved from a society in which status ran along a continuum towards one in which statuses were bunched at the two ends, the slave and the free" (Finley 1981 [1964]: 132).

In 1959, Finley published the first in a series of papers giving his explanation for the transformation: slavery. Archaic social revolutions like that leading to Solon's reforms at Athens in 594 swept away the Homeric spectrum of statuses, replacing it with a situation in which men (women were conspicuously absent from Finley's story) were polarized into two groups of free and slave (Finley 1981 [1959–65]: 97–195).

By the mid-1960s Homer had been separated from the Bronze Age. When Finley reissued *The World of Odysseus* after 25 years, his main changes were to delete sections attacking the Mycenaean model, because "Today it is no longer seriously maintained . . . that the *Iliad* and *Odyssey* reflect Mycenaean society" (Finley 1979: 10). So complete was the shift that John Bennet begins his recent survey "Homer and the Bronze Age" by asking "why even devote space in a work summarizing late-twentieth-century Homeric scholarship to what might seem to be a non-question?" (1997: 514). Yet Finley stimulated little further research until the late 1970s. In part, this may be because few ancient historians shared his political commitments. Like Grote after 1870, his reasoning might persuade them, but his sense of the significance of history need not. Further, Finley himself largely abandoned the period. He perhaps felt that he had settled the main problems, and after 1958 never again published on Homeric society, moving instead onto the later phases of his "schematic model."

Finley redefined the Aegean Bronze Age as the fringe of a broader Near Eastern palatial system, and the Iron Age as a hierarchical and complex world of heroes, from which classical citizen society emerged. For the first time, post-Mycenaean Greece was important within a larger historical narrative.

The New Dark Age

Archaeologists embraced the Iron Age even more enthusiastically. As with Parry's influence on Homeric philology, there were prewar roots. Dorothea Gray (1954: 240) suggested that interest dated from the 1930s, with the British excavations on Ithaca and at Karphi; and Vincent Desborough began his studies of Protogeometric pottery as a student at the British School at Athens in 1937–9. But major monographs only appeared in the 1950s, and postwar archaeology differed sharply from prewar versions in focusing heavily on art history. Religion lost ground, and though migrations were invoked to explain art styles, focusing on invasions became an east European specialty.

The accumulation of unanalyzed finds was important. Nikolaos Verdelis (1958) systematized Protogeometric pottery from Thessaly, Gallet de Santerre (1958) put the early remains on Delos in order, and Paul Courbin (1966) classified Geometric pottery from French work at Argos. But the principal Dark Age archaeologists were British. Hilda Lorimer's *Homer and the Monuments* (1950) was the most systematic study of Homeric archaeology since the 1880s, and the first to treat the Iron Age as seriously as the Bronze Age. But Desborough's *Protogeometric Pottery* (1952) was the landmark, revolutionizing Dark Age studies by making it possible to compare regions systematically; and from 1957 through 1960 J. Nicolas Coldstream, like Desborough as a student at the British School at Athens, extended similar treatment to the end of the Dark Age in a dissertation published as *Greek Geometric Pottery* (1968).

It is not obvious why so many British archaeologists colonized the Iron Age, nor why their interest tended toward panhellenic systematizations rather than publishing finds from British excavations like Knossos or the 1948–51 work at Smyrna. If fieldwork were the main factor, Tübingen, the home of Karl Kübler, excavator of the Kerameikos, should have been the postwar Dark Age center.

The British archaeologists do not explain the new interest. Desborough (1952: xv) said only that he wanted to study the interrelations of Protogeometric styles; he drew in other evidence, such as the graves which the pots came from, "to support this general picture." Similarly, Coldstream described his work as "Being concerned exclusively with style and chronology" (1968: 3). The books create the impression that studying this large body of poorly known material was such an obvious thing to do that it needed no explanation: as Coldstream put it (1968: 1), "for the art historian, the study of Geometric pottery is an end in itself." Perhaps we see here the expansion of the Beazleyan model, firmly established in Britain by the 1950s, and looking for new outlets.

The historians' arguments about the Iron Age are conspicuous by their absence from these books. Desborough described his 1964 book *The Last Mycenaeans and Their Successors* as a historical inquiry into the period down to about 1000, but never mentioned the new approaches to Homer; his bibliography does not even include Finley's *World of Odysseus*, a decade old when Desborough's book came out. Desborough explained that "I intend to use the archaeological evidence as the basic material, at the same time assuming as true the existence of major movements of population as given by the [literary] tradition" (1964: xvii).

This split was a new development. Until the Second World War Homerists and Bronze Age archaeologists were expected to have a basic grasp of each other's fields. In *Homer and the Monuments*, for example, Lorimer (1950: viii) explained that Parry's demonstration of the antiquity of some formulae called for a book like hers, collecting all the archaeological evidence from the coming of the Greeks to Homer's own day. Lorimer had different goals from Desborough; she closed her book not with a summary of the material evidence but with a long account of what archaeology told us about the Homeric Question (1950: 462–528). Myres and Gray's *Homer and His Critics* (1958) and Wace and Stubbings' *Companion to Homer* (1962) shared similar aims, but like *Homer and the Monuments*, both owed much to the prewar period. Myres' book began as lectures at Bangor in 1931, was revised for more lectures at Harvard in 1937–8, delayed by the war, and completed by Gray after Myres' 1954 death; while Wace had planned the *Companion* before the war, and (like some of the contributors) died before Stubbings could complete the book. Some chapters in the *Companion* clung to the old model placing Homeric society in the Mycenaean palaces, while Myres, Gray, and Lorimer all preferred a composite picture, stressing the mix of Mycenaean and Iron Age material culture in the poems. All three books brought together texts and archaeology, assuming that philological interest in Homer must precede interest in archaeology.

By the 1960s, these books looked old-fashioned. The new social historians of the Heroic Age and the new art historians of the Dark Age apparently saw little to gain from each other's work. Massive systematizations like *Protogeometric Pottery* and *Greek Geometric Pottery* may have done more to divide scholars than to unite them. Each book included a section of "historical conclusions," but neither was what social historians recognized as an historical synthesis.

The First Social Archaeologies

Chester Starr made the first serious effort to treat archaeology as social history, in *The Origins of Greek Civilization* (1961). Starr worked mainly in Roman and modern history, but had combined textual and visual evidence in novel ways. In 1953 he decided to apply similar techniques to the beginning of classical civilization. He accepted some of Finley's views on Homeric society (Starr 1961: 123–38), but was not primarily influenced by *The World of Odysseus*. Instead, he based much of his argument on the newly published pottery from the

Kerameikos, and on study of museum collections in 1959–60.[4] He explained that

> The historian ... will use this pottery with due circumscription. He may – indeed must – go beyond the limited range of most modern studies of the material, for specialists restrict themselves to descriptive or morphological classification with the aim of setting the chronology of evolution and the interrelationships between the different fabrics. This is a highly useful and necessary foundation which reduces the masses of scattered finds to orderly terms; but it is not all the story. On the other hand, the careful student will not be able to follow in their details the overly subtle, at times virtually mystical interpretations of early Greek pottery which have occasionally been advanced. (Starr 1961: 101)

Origins had its own share of idealism and racial theorizing, but Starr's social questions were very different from Desborough's connoisseurship. Starr (1974) perceptively argued that Desborough's approach was not just unhistorical, but antihistorical. Starr wanted to go beyond pottery to a totalizing model. He identified two major discontinuities. The first meant that "the pattern of civilization which we call Greek emerged in basic outline in the eleventh century BC"; the second, that "The age of revolution, 750–650, was the most dramatic development in all Greek history ... Swiftly, with simple but sharp strokes, the Greeks erected a coherent, interlocked system politically, economically, and culturally, which endured throughout the rest of their independent life" (Starr 1961: 99, 190). Desborough had anticipated Starr's first argument, seeing in late eleventh-century Athens "certain innovations which were to affect almost the whole Aegean, and [which] can be considered the starting-point from which developed later Greek civilization" (Desborough 1952: 298); and the idea of an eighth-century renaissance had been around since the Dark Age was defined. But instead of dividing post-Mycenaean Greece into aesthetic periods, as Desborough did, or equating it with a static "Homeric society," as Finley was forced to do by limiting himself to written sources, Starr constructed a dynamic model, emphasizing change through time and regional contrasts.

The Archaeological Syntheses

In the 1970s, the three major British Dark Age archaeologists produced syntheses of the scattered reports and forbidding specialists' monographs (Snodgrass 1971; Desborough 1972; Coldstream 1977). These were massively influential, shaping the field for the next twenty years. Desborough and Coldstream worked largely within postwar art-historical traditions; only Snodgrass (1971: viii), already interested in wider social questions, singled out Starr as an influence. Desborough and Snodgrass (Coldstream's survey only begins around 900) made the twelfth century an abrupt break. The Mycenaean heritage disappeared in the Aegean region by 1100, lingering only in attenuated forms in backward areas. They agreed that in the eleventh century Aegean society diverged from the rest of the Mediterranean. Snodgrass (1971: 237–49) linked this to a collapse in long-distance trade after 1025: the Aegean lost contact with the outside world, and adopted an iron-based economy. Regionalism became more pronounced, and an "advanced" area took shape in the Aegean (Snodgrass 1971: 374–6). They also agreed that the Dark Age ended in a major eighth-century revival.

Snodgrass (1971: 378–80; 1987: 188–210) grounded this in economics. He quantified Dark Age burials and argued that there was a population explosion in the eighth century, at Athens reaching 4 percent per annum, as fast as human populations have ever grown. He saw population growth and agricultural intensification driving increasing social complexity and ending the Dark Age of small, mobile, egalitarian, and perhaps pastoral groups. Competition for good land triggered political centralization. The new city-states resorted to frequent and intense warfare, overseas colonization, and cultural developments such as temple-building, larger sacrifices, and veneration of long-dead ancestors who might secure claims to land (Snodgrass 1977; 1980a: 15–84).

Snodgrass's archaeological vision of a Dark Age stood in sharp contrast to Finley's text-based post-Mycenaean Heroic Age. As Snodgrass sums this up (1993: 35), "There is a long-standing division of opinion between those who believe that Greek society of the Early Iron Age was in general rather egalitarian, and those who on the contrary hold that it was markedly stratified. Broadly speaking, archaeologists have tended to make up the former group and historians . . . the latter." For Finley (1970: 93), it made little sense to speak of a Dark Age: "In the sense . . . that *we* grope in the dark, and in that sense only, is it legitimate to employ the convention of calling the long period in Greek history from 1200 to 800 a 'dark age.' " Starr's vision, on the other hand, recalled Gilbert Murray's: "During the Dark Ages . . . men struggled to survive and to hold together the tissue of society" (1977: 47). The prewar temporal distinction between a Mycenaean Heroic Age and a post-Mycenaean Dark Age was replaced by a methodological distinction between two different post-Mycenaean periods: a text-based Heroic Age and an artifact-based Dark Age.

Perhaps there should have been an academic debate to rival that of the 1880s, but nothing like that happened. Snodgrass (1974) used comparative anthropology to renew Lorimer's argument that Homer mixed elements from many periods, while Finley (1979: 155) accused Snodgrass of a "confusion between objects and institutions." Gladstone and Jebb would have thought this tame, but it was a classic paradigm shift: with no sustained debate in print, the archaeological model quietly swept the field. The clearest evidence is institutional. In the 1970s early Greek archaeologists swept the top British university positions. Coldstream and Snodgrass took the chairs in classical archaeology at London and Cambridge respectively, and Desborough returned to Oxford. Outside Britain, the publications of the four major conferences on Greece between 1200 and 700 suggest that by 1980 linguists and philologists, as well as archaeologists, took Snodgrass's archaeological model for granted (*Annuario della Scuola Archeologica di Atene* vols. 59–61 (1981–3); Hägg 1983a; Deger-Jalkotzy 1983; Musti *et al.* 1991). The first chapter of Oswyn Murray's *Early Greece* presented the archaeological model of the Dark Age as a matter of fact (O. Murray 1980: 13–20).

Paradoxically, the syntheses' success helped reorient Homerists toward Finley's and Polanyi's questions (most recently, Donlan 1997; Tandy 1997). Abandoning Finley's claim that Homer reflected a functioning society around 900, they found a compromise: there was a true Dark Age between 1100 and 800, but the eighth century was like the Heroic Age, connected to the archaeological model via Snodgrass's population explosion and state formation. Gregory Nagy found an explanation for the contrast between archaeological evidence for regional variation and the homogeneity of Homeric society, arguing that "this poetic tradition synthesizes the diverse local tradition of each major city-state into a unified Panhellenic model that suits most city-states but corresponds exactly to none" (1979: 7).

This success requires explanation. I suggest that the crucial factor was that archaeology produced thicker and more dynamic descriptions than philology. Until the end of the 1960s archaeologists created what seemed to outsiders a narrow form of art history, generally hidden in dense technical monographs. But the 1970s syntheses, especially Snodgrass's, changed this. They incorporated regional variation and changes from century to century, while older visions derived from Homer provided a single, static model. In providing a *bigger* picture and linking it to compelling questions about social evolution, the archaeologists could claim to have produced a *better* account.

The heart of the new Dark Age archaeology was comprehensiveness. Historians often complained that there was not enough evidence to say anything about the Dark Age, but by combing the journals and collecting every reference to graves uncovered in urban expansion, archaeologists amassed large data sets; and by publishing site lists, they allowed others to replicate their research. In an unusually explicit statement, Snodgrass explained that

> The method of this work is empirical . . . it is to examine the whole period in chronological sequence scrutinizing the evidence as it comes, assembling the facts and endeavouring to face them. This sounds banal enough, but in this instance it involves abandoning the normal priorities of the historian, the literary scholar or the Classical archaeo-logist . . . This method also entails an almost obsessional insistence on chronology. Much of the material that is available is trivial in itself and ambiguous as to the conclusions that can be drawn from it; yet this same material has some security as a basis for broader understanding of the period, in a sense in which no inference or analogy from better-known periods or regions can be secure. (Snodgrass 1971: vii)

Snodgrass extended the traditional rigor of classical archaeology to all artifacts, and concentrated as much on contexts of deposition as on the objects themselves. This inductivist, empiricist approach is the greatest methodological legacy of the 1960s and 1970s: whether inspired by Marxist, feminist, or poststructuralist questions, a Dark Age archaeologist must amass *all* the evidence, showing what belongs to broad patterns and what is unique.

Beyond Synthesis: Since 1980

The Snodgrass School

In the late 1970s, Finley and Snodgrass both held chairs at Cambridge, which emerged as a center for early Greek scholarship. Shanks (1996: 132–43) even speaks of "the Snodgrass school of Iron Age studies." The flood of studies of the Iron Age from Snodgrass's students is probably the most sustained scholarly attack on this period in its history. The first group of these books developed Snod-grass' social archaeology, but examined smaller areas in greater detail, using more quantitative tools, and looking to readerships in other archaeologies (I. Morris 1987; Morgan 1990; Whitley 1991a). They shared many of Snodgrass's questions, but sometimes reached different answers.

My own book *Burial and Ancient Society*, based on research done between 1981 and 1986, bears the marks of this context. I followed

Snodgrass's emphasis on demography, but also Finley's on citizenship and slavery. Processual archaeologists searched for hierarchical rank in burials, and postprocessualists for ideology. I had come of age in the strongly class-divided industrial world of the English Midlands in the 1970s (Paul Willis's classic *Learning to Labour* (1977) could almost have been written about my own comprehensive school). Wealth-based inequality seemed obviously the issue most worth study. Moving from Birmingham University to Cambridge in 1982 only intensified this feeling.

I argued that eighth-century Athenian graves did not reflect a shift from an egalitarian to a stratified society. Instead, as often seems to be the case in the archaeological record in other parts of Iron Age Europe and the Near East, between about 1025 and 750 funerals drew a line within the community. Most excavated burials belong to just one section of the adult population, while other adults and most children were disposed of in ways which have low archaeological visibility. Drawing on Homer, I argued that this distinction was based on rank: the excavated graves belong to an upper class, what the Greeks called *agathoi*, or "good people," while the lower orders (*kakoi* or "bad people") were disposed of in ways we rarely find. I suggested that the excluded *kakoi* were dependants of the wealthier *agathoi*, who controlled most of the land. In the eighth century, this ritual distinction collapsed. I accepted the concept of a Dark Age framed by twelfth- and eighth-century ruptures, but reinterpreted them. The eighth century did not see the return of hierarchy to Greece; rather, it was the origin of the social order of free citizens and chattel slaves which dominated Finley's work, and, if anything, a time of *weakening* aristocratic power. I combined postprocessual assumptions with the empirical methods of Dark Age archaeology, connecting them to the arguments of Finley's social history.

The first "Snodgrass school" studies were very much social histories of culture, treating burial, worship, and style as ways to get at underlying realities. As Shanks observes (1996: 137), "Material culture functions to express social structure; the *style* of this functioning is inexplicable." A second wave of books in the later 1990s turned away from these issues, raised questions about the construction of ethnic and gender identities, borrowing from cultural and art histories as much as from social archaeology (J. Hall 1997; Shanks 1999). They have links with the earlier books, but rely less on quantification and total material assemblages, and move away from Snodgrass's sociological questions. In this, they share much with developments among other groups of scholars.

Religion and Art

Few French scholars have concentrated on the Iron Age, but François de Polignac (who studied with Finley and Snodgrass as well as with Jean-Pierre Vernant) combined structuralism with social archaeology in *La naissance de la cité grecque* (1984), examining how formative poleis used sanctuaries to define their boundaries. He supported Snodgrass's view of religion as central to state formation. But the rewritten version *Cults, Territory, and the Origins of the Greek City-State* (1995a) presented a more complex picture, using new evidence for Dark Age cults to argue for more gradual changes. The eighth century remained important for him, but less so than for the Snodgrass school; and he concluded that we are at a "point that the traditional term 'Dark Ages' is not used any more" (de Polignac 1995b: 7).

Other French scholars also wrote about the Iron Age in the 1980s, and like de Polignac's recent work, they downplayed the breaks around 1200 and 700, seeing more gradual developments. Schliemann's work had received similar treatment in France, with the ruptures it implied being minimized to preserve Fustel's evolutionary model (p. 89 above). This long-term historiographical tradition may be Fustel's strongest legacy.

One strategy is to project classical institutions back to Mycenaean times. Henri van Effenterre argues for continuities by refusing to characterize Bronze Age society in terms of the palaces. He suggests that these were foreign impositions on an egalitarian *Volksgeist* going back to the "coming of the Greeks" in the third millennium (1985: 68). Van Effenterre sees beyond the palatial sphere "a communal life – can one already say 'political'? – in which certain traits seem to hint at or prefigure the system which would be that of the [classical] *cité*" (1985: 96). Pierre Carlier even identified Bronze Age "communities practicing an embryonic form of democracy" (1984: 130). He subsequently modified this, suggesting that while "it would be an exaggeration to speak of village democracy ... Nonetheless, the Mycenaean *damoi* constitute a primary form of collective organization and perhaps lie at the origin of the demes of a city like Athens" (1991: 87).

This idea bears directly on my core arguments in Parts III and IV. Carlier's main claim is that in Linear B *kekemena* meant land held in common, and that its occurrence with the word *damo*, the ancestor of classical *demos*, shows that communal village structures were important (1984: 68 n. 369). But the philology is not so straightforward (Carpenter 1983), and Carlier's reasoning is circular. Finley saw the methodological problem forty years ago: "To hit upon 'village', or 'collectivity' [as translations for *damo*], even as a convention, is to introduce a very precise and far-reaching interpretation through the back door . . . not one of these meanings is contextually determined or controlled; they have all been deduced philologically" (Finley 1981 [1957/8]: 209). If we use classical literature to deduce the meanings of *damo* and *kekemena*, then claim that we have discovered semantic continuities from the Bronze Age to classical times, and that these reflect institutional continuities, we have not done very much.

Van Effenterre projects classical concepts of citizenship back to the Bronze Age by equating Linear B *ereutero* with the classical Athenian word *eleutheros* or "free man." He argues that *ereutero* means "he who owes nothing to anyone. He already existed. Freedom remained the primary quality of the citizen" (1985: 155). But the semantics of these words undermine this association. *Ereutero* "connotes the space within which autonomy in relation to the palace is possible: autonomy for produce and perhaps also for men" (Garlan 1988: 29). This is a far cry from the Athenian citizen as an *eleutheros* (chapter 4). We can trace the history of the classical word *eleutheria*, normally translated as "freedom," in detail. *Eleutheria* was an aristocratic rallying-cry against tyranny in the late sixth century, then a democratic catchword in the fifth, only to be turned against democracy by philosophers in the fourth (Raaflaub 1985). Given such changes in just two centuries, we should not assume fixed meanings across the previous eight, and on that basis hypothesize sociological continuities.

Carlier's link between Mycenaean *damo* and classical *demos* also ignores well-documented linguistic shifts. In archaic Greece, *demos* was a flexible concept, shifting meanings through time and according to context, sometimes denoting the whole community, sometimes all the community except its leaders (Donlan 1970). Given clear evidence for tactical manipulation of the word between 700 and 500, it would be naive to assume earlier stability across almost a millennium.

A second strategy is to abandon social historians' and archaeologists' interest in politics and the state altogether in favor of traditional French concerns with religion and art (pp. 56–7 above). De Polignac criticizes social archaeologists for dwelling on the polis (*la cité*), "interpreted as a type of society and political organization understood by reference to the model of the classical city-state and its institutions." He asks "whether it is necessary . . . to forget the polis to think about society [*oublier la cité pour penser la société*]?" (1995b: 7, 9). Some art historians feel the same way. Sarah Morris concludes that:

> It may be time for a reform of our current adulation of "the state" in early Greece, a specter which has acquired a monolithic, nearly

totalitarian set of powers over contemporary scholarship. In my view, community-by-consensus evolved slowly, gradually, and continuously since the Late Bronze Age . . . without the "explosion" or "renaissance" attached to the 8th century. (S. P. Morris 1992a: xvii)

Calling the Iron Age an "overworked" field, she begs "please, no more Early Iron Age dissertations!" (1995: 184–5). Redefining the boundaries of the Dark or Heroic Ages changes the stories we might tell and the value of studying the period.

The Problem of the East

Hellenism sundered Greeks and orientals. No one could deny Near Eastern influences on seventh-century art and literature, especially Hesiod's *Theogony*, but like any paradigm, Hellenism could push anomalies to one side. If the Dark Age was the infancy of Greece, the eighth and seventh centuries were its impressionable adolescence, when it uncritically followed the lead of others, before it reached maturity in the sixth century, keeping what was best from its youth and shedding the rest. As always, though, a few people were obsessed with the awkward cases. When Martin West wrote a commentary on the *Theogony*, he could not avoid the orientalizing question, concluding that "Greece is part of Asia; Greek literature is a Near Eastern literature" (1966: 30–1). In a familiar pattern, West's philological mastery won respect, while his historical conclusions were treated as eccentric. But this changed in the 1980s. Walter Burkert's *Die orientalisierende Epoche* (1992 [1984]), a careful philological study of Greek and Akkadian literature, showed the pervasiveness of contacts in the eighth and seventh centuries, while Martin Bernal's *Black Athena* I (1987) demonstrated how classicists had for two centuries ignored this issue.

Burkert's work was a catalyst for classicists uncomfortable with Hellenism. In her important study *Daidalos and the Origins of Greek Art* (1992b), Sarah Morris goes further than Burkert or West, arguing that from the Bronze Age through the archaic, the Aegean was part of an east Mediterranean cultural *koine*. Aegean-Levantine connections did not collapse after 1100; rather, preclassical Greece was always an "oriental culture" (1992b: 101–49). Only the Persian wars of 480–479 caused a reaction against the east, and a "deliberate disarticulation in the classical period" (1992b: xx) of the multicultural archaic society. She asserts that this oriental culture, especially its religion, was continuous from the Bronze Age through the Iron Age, justifying the use of the term "early Greek" to embrace the second and first millennia. The epigraphic definition of historical periods creates an artificial "Dark Age," which must then be "reconciled" with the "inconsistencies" of more faithful records of that continuity, poetry and archaeology . . . the origins of Greek urban culture begin before 1200 BC, with a demise, not a highpoint, in the fifth century. (S. P. Morris 1992b: 115, 124)

This long "early Greek" period has more in common with pre-Schliemann (even pre-Grote) scholarship than with the postwar Dark and Heroic Ages. In conference panels, public debates, and special issues of journals, classicists mapped out new areas for debate in the early 1990s. The big questions now concern which areas of the Near East played the greatest part (Egypt? Anatolia? the Levant?), when the major transmission of ideas took place (in the Late Bronze Age, in the seventh century, or continuously?), and whether we are dealing with Greek borrowing or a common culture. These questions often took shape in angry reaction against Hellenism. They energized the field, but the philologists and classical art historians who formulated the new agenda took little inspiration from work on the same issues in cultural history and anthropology. "Orientalized" approaches potentially constitute a paradigm shift, and a cultural history along the lines I sketched in chapter 1 must confront the issues they raise; but I argue in Parts III and IV that these questions, though productive in the 1980s, are now too limited.

For instance, Burkert criticizes "the tendency of modern cultural theories to approach culture as a system evolving through its own processes of internal economic and social dynamics, which reduces all outward influences to negligible factors," going on to argue that

> It may still be true that the mere fact of [Greek] borrowing [from the Near East] should only provide a starting point for closer interpretation, that the form of selection and adaptation, of reworking and refitting to a new system is revealing and interesting in each case. But the "creative transformation" by the Greeks, however important, should not obscure the sheer fact of borrowing; this would amount to yet another strategy of immunization designed to cloud what is foreign and disquieting. (Burkert 1992: 7)

Burkert attacks one of Hellenism's truisms, the radical distinction between Greeks and orientals. But he does so by reinforcing another, the depeopling of antiquity, reducing it to monolithic cultural blocks

of "Greece" and the "Near East." This has little in common with
the cultural history I described in chapter 1. Similarly, West's only
analysis of cultural dynamics in a 650-page survey of west Asian
influences on Greek poetry is that "Culture, like all forms of gas, tends
to spread out from where it is densest into adjacent areas where it is
less dense" (1997: 1).

These studies are empirically rich but conceptually impoverished.
Concentrating on "the sheer fact of borrowing" rules out what
Chartier (1988: 102) sees as the basis of proper cultural history, "a
definition of history primarily sensitive to inequalities in the
appropriation of common materials or practices." The actors in these
stories are dehistoricized cultural systems; what Hellenist scholars had
split into two such systems is reunited as one.

Burkert points out that his emphasis "is not to preclude more subtle
interpretations of Greek achievements as a consequence" (1992: 8), and
more recent studies take greater account of agency and contested
meanings. Margaret Miller argues in *Athens and Persia in the Fifth
Century BC* that "No complex society will respond monolithically to
the same stimulus. The richer the texture, the more varied the
response, because alien objects have potentially different meanings and
different uses for different social strata" (1997: 247). But instead of
examining how different groups of Athenians used Persian objects to
construct identities and debate the forms of the good life, Miller reifies
"social texture," suggesting that Persian material culture appealed to
an undifferentiated elite because in the fifth century "the social texture
was increasingly rich and increasingly in need of external status-
differentiation" (1997: 251). Miller's book is an important advance,
but Whitley (1994a: 60–2) had already shown the need for a more
sociologically nuanced approach to orientalism in archaic material
culture. I want to go further still in this direction, by drawing, like
Whitley, on developments in fields outside classics. Criticizing what
they call "the stereotypical 'among the so-and-so' mold" of ethnography, Akhil Gupta and James Ferguson suggest that

> whatever associations of place and culture may exist must be taken as
> problems for anthropological research rather than the given ground that
> one takes as a point of departure; cultural territorializations (like ethnic
> and national ones) must be understood as complex and contingent
> results of ongoing historical and political processes. It is these processes,
> rather than pregiven cultural-territorial entities, that require anthropo-
> logical study. (Gupta and Ferguson 1997: 4)

The "billiard-ball model" of the world as a bag of discrete, bounded
cultures does not work in the late twentieth century. It may work

better for other periods, but that is something to demonstrate, not assume; and in the east Mediterranean Iron Age, which saw drastic changes in the amount and forms of long-distance travel, it is particularly necessary to begin analysis with active, thinking agents – as Gupta and Ferguson put it, "In place of the question, How is the local linked to the global or the regional? then, we prefer to start with another question that enables a quite different perspective on the topic: How are understandings of locality, community, and region formed and lived?" (1997: 6).

As we shall see in Part III, Greek literature makes it clear that "the east" was a thoroughly contested category. Some Greeks embraced an imagined east; others denounced their own imagined east savagely. Sarah Morris's interpretation of "early Greece" represents one of the points of view in the Greeks' long debate; the old Hellenist model is quite close to another. But cultural history requires us to come to terms with the whole range of ideas.

Conclusion

The ways other people prefigure a field often look odd until we set them in context and get a feel for why what may strike us as peculiar questions seemed like good ideas at the time. The major point of disciplinary history is to make us realize that our own categories may be no more sensible than anyone else's. Research programs are arenas for debate. We carry out these debates through the available evidence, within frameworks inherited from the past, facilitated by the institutions where we work, and molded by the expectations about audiences which these institutions encourage. We need to know as much about the positions from which we view the past and the external forces which affect us as we do about the evidence itself. Maybe we really can transcend the points in time, space, and the social order at which we find ourselves, and attain a panoptic perspective; but the only hope of doing so is to discuss these factors openly.

Disciplinary history is partly an exercise in relativism, but to understand all is not necessarily to forgive all. My research project will doubtless seem as odd in fifty years as Lorimer's and Desborough's seem to me now. I hope that my work will stand the test of time, but since readers are just as much prisoners of time and space as writers, I see no point in worrying about this. I write about what in the past seems important to me, here and now, hoping to persuade others to share my views. In Part III I explain why I think an archaeologically informed cultural history of Iron Age Greece is worth doing, and in

Part IV I disagree with the gradualists who would blur the differences between Iron Age and Bronze Age Greece as well as between Greek and other Mediterranean societies. They have failed to grasp how social archaeology changed the field forever, and have profited even less from the 1980s revolution in cultural history. They remain grounded in the dogmas of pre-1970s classical archaeology with its bits-and-pieces methods and systematic occlusion of agency, power, and conflict.

Part III

4

Equality for Men

Introduction

In Part III I explain the way I prefigure Iron Age archaeology. I draw on several of the lines of thought I described in Part II, but emphasize the Anglo-Saxon tradition going back to Mitford, finding in Greece a good way to think about politics, equality, and justice. This, I believe, is no bad thing. The 1990s have been called the decade of democracy. From Beijing to Berlin, challenges made in the name of the power of the people have shaken totalitarian regimes; and the same academics who so spectacularly failed to predict this are now coming forward to tell us what it all means. Their most remarkable discovery is that history is now over. According to Lutz Niethammer (1993) we have entered *posthistoire*, much like what Francis Fukuyama (1992) calls "the end of history." The great historical dialectic is played out, and capitalism and representative democracy have proven decisively superior to all other arrangements. There will be lots more events, but history is reduced to its narrowest sense of one-damned-thing-after-another. Institutions and ideas have reached their final form.

If history has a *telos*, it should also have an *arche*, which the vagaries of the calendar promptly supplied, in the 2,500th anniversary of Cleisthenes' reforms at Athens. The democratic revolutions of 1989–92 could be interpreted as the end of a two-and-a-half-millennium cycle. Barry Strauss has identified the central issue this model raises:

> Democracy, which exists today, began at Athens. In other words, democracy has a genealogy ... [A]ny such genealogy is also an ideology ... The notion that democracy began among the citizenry of Athens – and not in Sumer, nor in ancient Israel, nor in Rome, nor at Calvary, nor among slaves, nor in Anglo-Saxon England, nor in the Puritan Congregation, nor among the Iroquois, nor in the acephalous

communities of non-urban societies, nor in the tradition of Classical republicanism, nor in early capitalism, to take just some of the alternate genealogies that have been offered – implies an ideological choice. (Strauss 1997: 141)

What is involved in this ideological choice? Is classical Athenian *demokratia* really connected to modern pluralistic democracy? To answer these questions, I suggest, we first have to ask what made ancient democracy *thinkable*. This requires two more questions – what Athenians thought equality was; and why they extended it to all local-born adult men, regardless of wealth, family, education, or any other criterion, but to no one else. To my mind, these questions give Iron Age archaeology its point, just as related questions gave Heroic Age history a point for Finley. But we can only answer them by weaving words and things into a single cultural history.

Setting up the issue this way exposes me to charges of teleology. De Polignac (1994: 18), for instance, insists that we need "to remove the study of society and cult in the Geometric and Archaic periods from the conceptual framework imposed through hindsight by the model of the Classical city." I disagree. It is precisely the classical city which makes the Iron Age important. I fall back on a point made by Chartier (1993: 7): "History stripped of all temptation to teleology would risk becoming an endless inventory of disconnected facts abandoned to their teeming incoherence for want of a hypothesis to propose a possible order among them." As social historians point out, critiques of metanarratives regularly turn out to be merely arguments for alternative metanarratives, as when Catherine Morgan (1994: 108) argues that "the fact that the polis *sensu stricto* occupied a relatively short period in the political life of even the most renowned Classical states should make clear the importance of considering the longer-term evolution." Her story focuses on the large, loose states of western Greece; it might end in Hellenistic or Roman times, rather than classical. She consequently finds different things important in the Iron Age. The problem is not *whether* we emplot Iron Age data within some narrative. I know of no serious deconstructionist interpretation of the Iron Age which does otherwise. Rather, the question is *what* is the most significant story to tell about this period – if, indeed, any story is significant.

Equality and Democracy

I begin at the end of my story, in fourth-century Athens, where the sources are fullest. Mogens Hansen proposes that "it was the political institutions that shaped the 'democratic man' and the 'democratic life', not vice versa" (1991: 320). Hansen's account is *procedural*, emphasizing rules; I argue that a longer historical perspective shows that institutions did not determine identities, and that we must balance his approach with a *normative* account, examining attitudes and values (cf. Sartori 1973: 3–15). A democratic constitution, I suggest, was one possible outcome of the emergence of egalitarian culture within broad male citizen communities. This culture is what is special about Greece, and what most needs to be explained.

I structure my analysis around what Robert Dahl calls the "Strong Principle of Equality." He suggests that

> It is obvious . . . that the emergence and persistence of a democratic government among a group of people depends in some way on their *beliefs* . . . among a group whose members believe that they are all about equally well qualified to participate in the decisions of the group, the chances are relatively high that they will govern themselves through some sort of democratic process. (Dahl 1989: 30–1)

This Strong Principle of Equality rests on two further propositions:

> *All members are sufficiently well qualified, taken all around, to participate in making the collective decisions binding on the association that significantly affect their good or interests. In any case, none are so definitely better qualified than the others that they should be entrusted with making the collective and binding decisions.* (Dahl 1989: 98)

The first of these propositions is what Dahl (1989: 55, 85–6, 167) calls the Principle of Equal Consideration of Interests. This affords each citizen equal respect and a right to be heard, but reserves the possibility that some citizens may know what is in everyone's best interests, and may be qualified to make the decisions for all. I suggest that something like the Principle of Equal Consideration appeared in the eighth century, and something like the Strong Principle of Equality in the late sixth. I focus in Part IV on the first of these transformations, and plan to explore the second in detail elsewhere.

The Strong Principle of Equality is not a synonym for democracy. But when enough people hold views of this kind, it becomes possible – even logical – to respond to the fall of an oligarchy with new conceptions of majority rule, instead of simply finding a different group of guardians. This is what happened at Athens in 508/7.

A Strong Principle of Equality within a bounded citizen group crystalized over much of Greece between *c.* 525 and 490. As Dahl implies, once this has happened the establishment of democracy is not so surprising. What *is* surprising is that such a mentality gained the upper hand in the first place.

The Athenian Strong Principle of Equality rested on what I call the middling culture of civic manhood. The most important cultural category was the *metrios* or *mesos*, the "middling man." Such a man was supposed to be moderate, restrained, respectable, and pious. Men who went beyond this role took risks. If their actions were construed as expanding their honor at the expense of others, they faced disapproval or even legal penalties. Athenians were still more wary about personal links beyond the polis. Claiming special status because of outstanding ancestors was unusual; friendship with non-Athenians, particularly eastern potentates, was dangerous; and few Athenians claimed privileged links with the gods. On the rare occasions that Athenians tolerated such claims, they so hedged them around that specialness in one sphere could not be converted into dominance in others. There were citizens who did not share this view of the world, and they constantly challenged middling values.

This chapter is an exercise in model-building. A model, or ideal type, is *not* just a summary of the surviving evidence; rather,

> An ideal type is achieved by the one-sided *accentuation* of one or more points of view and by the synthesis of many diffuse, discrete, more or less present and occasionally absent *individual* phenomena, which are arranged according to those one-sidedly emphasized viewpoints into a unified mental construct. In its conceptual purity, this mental construct can never be found empirically in reality. It is a *utopia*. (Weber 1949: 90)

A model is a tool for doing a particular job. It simplifies and selects from the complexities of real life to show how the most important factors work. Other historians, asking other questions, will want to build other models.

There are three main ways to argue about models. First, while a model does not have to account for all data, it must fit the facts. If too few pieces of evidence support it, or too many contradict it, it is not useful. It is relatively easy to test goodness-of-fit with quantifiable models, so long as we can agree on the parameters and their relevance, but qualitative ones require lengthy exposition. Second, while empirically sound, a model may identify the wrong variables, and another scholar may show that looking at different factors produces a more powerful model. Third, scholars may conclude that the question which the model addresses is just not important, in which case they may focus on other features of the evidence. In practice, of course, the three responses overlap.

Greek historians often seem confused about models. Some, recognizing that no model can accommodate all data, decide they may as well do without one. Setting sail without charts on a sea of details, they try to incorporate every ancient statement into their narratives, even if it means sacrificing conceptual rigor and explanatory power – what Finley (1985: 61) called the "Tell all you know about X" school of historiography. Others act as if models are nothing more than simplified descriptions of reality. Thus Gabriel Herman (1993; 1994; 1998) and David Cohen (1991; 1995) have each constructed valuable models of Athenians behavior, the former representing Athenians as unusually cooperative people, eschewing the violent pursuit of honor, the latter seeing typically "Mediterranean" aggression lurking behind the texts. But rather than setting such models against each other and asking which is right, we might more profitably focus on what each tells us, and the situations in which each is useful.

We find a broad range of attitudes and behaviors in the Athenian sources. I am not claiming that middling values always and in all situations ruled Athenians' lives; only that *to meson* was (1) a powerful native model and (2) provided the values which made democracy thinkable. To understand Greek democracy, we must first understand this worldview, on which the Athenian Strong Principle of Equality rested. But to do that, we must recognize the partiality of *to meson*, and I devote considerable space in Part III to opposition to middling values and arguments about the boundaries of the good society. But part of the point of modeling the middle is to throw into sharper relief the evidence which does not conform to this view of the world: to quote Weber again (1968: 21), "The more sharply and more precisely the ideal type has been constructed, thus the more abstract and unrealistic in this sense it is, the better it is able to perform its functions in formulating terminology, classifications, and hypotheses." My goal in this chapter is to construct a model of *to meson* as precisely as possible, allowing me to formulate the classifications and hypotheses which I pursue in the next three chapters.

After describing the middling ideology and the visions of equality it entailed, I turn to competing visions of the good society, and how the dominant middle suppressed them. I conclude by turning to those outside the middle, particularly women, slaves, and aliens.

Classical Middling Culture

The Literary Evidence

Following common practice, I divide the literary sources into two groups. The first, which I discuss in this section, consists of about a hundred public speeches delivered in lawcourts, political assemblies, and state war funerals between 430 and 320 BC, and roughly forty dramas performed in state festivals, mainly in the late fifth century. I discuss the second group of sources on p. 130 below. To varying degrees, texts in the first group express a middling culture, praising the citizens' restraint and collective wisdom.

These middling texts were written by educated men, but despite their elite context of production, they (or something very like them) were delivered orally before mass audiences. Anyone could attend the theater and orations over the war dead; any male citizen over twenty could attend the political assembly; and any over thirty could serve on juries. Birth to citizen parents determined citizenship. No other factor of wealth, occupation, education, or kinship mattered.[1]

State dramatic festivals drew audiences of up to 15,000, while over 6,000 citizens (from a total adult male citizen population of perhaps 30,000 in the fourth century) attended the assembly's roughly forty meetings each year. Juries numbered from 201 to 2,501 citizens, depending on the charges. 1500 or more citizens would sit in courts on each of the roughly 200 trial days each year. All these bodies were busy. Hansen (1991: 156) calculates that between 403 and 322 the Assembly passed some 30,000 decrees. To encourage the poor to participate, the state began paying jurors a small stipend around 460, and extended this to the assembly in 403. By about 350, citizens also received a stipend to attend the theater on festival days. In these contexts, Athens' leading men engaged in public discussions before mass audiences, submitting to their judgment, according to popular norms and values. Josiah Ober argues that the speeches they delivered were social dramas, in which elite speakers and mass audiences entered into productive shared fictions:

> Theater-going citizens "learned" to suspend disbelief . . . This "training" helped jurors to accept elite litigants' fictional representations of their own circumstances and their relationship to the Athenian masses. The complicity of speaker and audience to create and accept dramatic fictions regarding social status was an important factor in the maintenance of Athenian social equilibrium. (Ober 1989: 153–4)

Middling Men

Speakers assumed that Athens was a community of *metrioi*, or "middling men." The *metrios* was said to be content with "a little" money (Aeschines 3.218), yet Demosthenes (29.24) and Isaeus (7.40) could use *metrios* to describe some of the richest men in Athens. By *hoi mesoi,* "those in the middle," Athenians did not mean a "middle class" in an economic or occupational sense. The *metrioi* were defined primarily through their attitudes, which determined how they would use their wealth. Any *metrios* who had sufficient means had no cause to pursue still more wealth (Dinarchus 3.18). The *metrios* possessed *aischune,* self-respect (Aeschines 3.11), which brought his appetites under control. He exercised restraint in sexual matters (e.g., Aeschines 1.42; Demosthenes 54.17) and drinking (Demosthenes 54.15) as well as in spending, quietly minding his own affairs (Hyperides 4.21), doing good for family and community alike (Dinarchus 2.8).

Speakers assumed that *all* citizens, except those whom they defined as enemies, belonged to the middle. They formed, in their own eyes, a community of restrained, sensible *metrioi* who shared *homonoia,* "same-mindedness." Demosthenes (25.89) suggested that *aischune* was the key to *homonoia,* while Andocides (2.1) held that because the polis was a common possession of all citizens, all saw things in similar ways. *Homonoia* generated *philia,* the glue which held the community of true *metrioi* together. *Philia* is usually translated as "friendship," but it carried a much stronger sense of interdependence. *Philoi* are those people on whom we not only can, but must, rely. Aristotle commented that popular opinion equated *homonoia* with the *philia* felt between citizens (*Ethics* 1167a26–9), and that democracies had most *philia,* since their citizens were most equal (1161b9–10).

Speakers represented the community of *metrioi* as being under constant threat from marginal groups lacking its virtues. A man judged to stand at any extreme – that is, not in the middle – was one who lacked control. In Jack Winkler's words (1990: 45–6), he was "socially deviant in his entire being, [a man] whose deviance was principally observable in behavior that flagrantly violated or contravened the dominant social definition of masculinity . . . the *kinaidos,* mentioned only with laughter or indignation, is the unreal, but dreaded, antitype behind every man's back." The language of class was a major idiom for thinking about these extremes. When a speaker called a rival rich, especially a young rival, he implied that his enemy was prone to hubris, defined by Nick Fisher (1992: 1) as "the serious assault on the honour of another, which is likely to cause shame, and lead to anger and attempts at revenge." Aristotle (*Rhetoric* 1378b28–9) explains that "they think that in this they show their superiority," and Fisher (1992: 493) concludes that hubris was "constantly seen as a major crime, endangering the cohesion of the community as well as the essential self-esteem and identity of the individual."

Poverty, on the other hand, forced a man to do undignified things, exposing him to exploitation. David Halperin (1990: 99) suggests that in popular thought the poor, "deprived of their autonomy, assertiveness, and freedom of action – of their masculine dignity, in short – were in danger of being assimilated not only to slaves but to prostitutes, and so ultimately to women: they were at risk of being effeminized by poverty." When Athenians called themselves *metrioi* they imagined one another as self-sufficient farmers on their own land, heads of households, married with children, pious, responsible, and self-controlled (cf. Hanson 1995: 87–8). The phalanx of hoplites was a key metaphor for the solidarity of the citizens. No more than half the citizens qualified as hoplites, but for Athenians, that was not the point. The funeral orations spoken over the war dead represent them all as hoplites (Loraux 1986: 34, 37, 98, 151), even though losses among the poorer oarsmen were often heavier. What mattered was that every citizen was a *metrios* and a *philos*, and all shared *homonoia*.

By general agreement – a willing suspension of disbelief – Athenian men thought of each other as *metrioi* and *philoi*. "Rich" and "poor" functioned as categories of exclusion. The philosophy of the *metrios* was a useful democratic fiction, a structuring principle guiding behavior. A full share in the community, and its politics, flowed from the fact of being born a free male: as Halperin bluntly puts it (1990: 103), "the symbolic language of democracy proclaimed on behalf of each citizen, 'I, too, have a phallus.' "

Athenian citizen society was egalitarian, but in a very particular sense. Equality in one sphere of life inevitably means inequalities in others. Modern liberal societies privilege equality of opportunity, the belief that everyone has an equal right to compete for life's rewards, but sanction inequalities of outcome. Critics would help the underprivileged by restricting the equal freedoms of the successful, through policies such as affirmative action, or banning private education and healthcare. Champions of the various models of equality accuse one another of treating people unfairly. Similarly, in fourth-century Athens supporters of "geometric" equality could claim that democratic "arithmetic" equality was unfair: by giving all men equal voting power, it treated them unequally in terms of competence and virtue (F. D. Harvey 1965).

Depending on political choices, different "spaces" for equality appear obvious or natural. Amartya Sen (1992: 15) points out that "critiques of egalitarianism tend to take the form of being – instead – egalitarian in some *other* space." Conflicts cluster around attempts to impose such choices on others. In most situations, one group imposes its view that a particular quality – wealth, birth, strength, education, beauty, or whatever – is *the* dominant good. Claiming to monopolize it, they try to convert their monopoly over one good into monopolies over others. Thus in a plutocracy, equal rights to make money and dispose of it freely allow the rich to create inequalities in other spheres, such as politics, subsistence, or health. There will be pockets of nonconvertibility – it may not be possible to buy divine grace or beauty – but the holders of the dominant good will struggle to breach these citadels of resistance.

Michael Walzer observes that "since dominance is always incomplete and monopoly imperfect, the rule of every ruling class is unstable. It is continually challenged by other groups in the name of alternative patterns of conversion." Thus, against the plutocrats, a nobility might hold that certain goods – say, land, high office, dignity, and royal favor – cannot be bought. If they are successful in advancing their claims, plutocracy might gradually give way to aristocracy, with genealogical distance becoming the standard for judging equality, and wealth following in its train – "all good things come to those who have the one best thing" (Walzer 1983: 11).

In Athens, the one best thing was male citizen birth. Other goods, even money, could only be converted into citizenship under extraordinary circumstances. The exclusion of women and the near impossibility of naturalization were not unfortunate quirks in an otherwise admirable system. The strong principle of equality was essentialist – in Bourdieu's neat formulation (1984: 24), "Regarding existence as an emanation of essence, [essentialists] set no intrinsic value on [their] deeds and misdeeds . . . They prize them only insofar as they clearly manifest, in the nuances of their manner, that their one inspiration is the perpetuating and celebrating of the essence by virtue of which they are accomplished." Athenian funeral orations took this for granted (e.g., Thucydides 2.42; Plato, *Menexenus* 234C). Every Athenian man was a *metrios*, deserving equal respect and an equal share in the polis, unless he forfeited it. What mattered was that Athens was a group of *metrioi*. Every *metrios* had a share in the community, and no one else had any share at all.

At least, that was the idea. In practice, Athenians recognized that noncitizens had all kinds of claims. The law of hubris protected aliens and even slaves (Demosthenes 21.47), even though this seems inconsistent with the assumptions running through much Athenian writing (so much so that modern scholars regularly attempt to explain the Demosthenes passage away). Similarly, in the fourth century Athens set up special maritime courts to help aliens in town on business, and allowed some slaves to accumulate their own resources.

The middling ideology's dominance was imperfect and contested, and it had to reach compromises with other visions of equality. I return to these below; but given such beliefs, the logical way to reach decisions was to assemble as many citizens as possible, and find out what they agreed to – in the common Greek expression, to bring matters *es meson*, into the middle of the community. A community which saw itself in this light met the conditions of Dahl's Strong Principle of Equality (p. 111 above). But the fullest theoretical statements of this come not from champions of democracy, but from its most acute critics. In one dialog, Plato has Protagoras argue that virtue can be taught. Socrates rejects this claim. Protagoras then recounts a myth justifying democracy through a theory of ontological equality (*Protagoras* 320c–28d). Protagoras claims that when Zeus created the world, he allowed Epimetheus to distribute powers to each animal. But by the time Epimetheus came to humans, he had run out of gifts. Zeus sent Hermes to give mankind respect for others, a sense of justice, and political wisdom. Zeus ordered him to give a share in each of these gifts to everyone. Plato has Protagoras conclude:

> Thus it is, Socrates, and from this cause, that in a debate involving skill in building, or in any other craft, the Athenians, like other men, believe that few are capable of giving advice, and if someone outside those few volunteers to advise them, then as you say, they do not tolerate it – rightly so, in my submission. But when the subject of their counsel involves political wisdom, which must always follow the path of justice and moderation, they listen to every man's opinion, for they think that everyone must share in this kind of virtue; otherwise the state could not exist. That, Socrates, is the reason for this. (Plato, *Protagoras* 322d–23a)

Plato has Socrates argue that Protagoras' theory is incoherent. Classicists disagree over whether Plato portrayed Protagoras fairly. But for Plato's critique to have seemed worthwhile, even to his philosophical friends, we have to assume that ideas something like these were current. The norms of democracy were taught through involvement in public speech (pp. 137–8 below); only its critics wanted explicit, written theorizing. As Eugene Genovese says of another slaveholding society (1969: 216), "They wished their ideology to be careless, pragmatic, inarticulate, disorganized, lazy; only political fanatics, philosophers, and lunatics can live any other way."

The most formal account of the middle comes in Aristotle's *Politics* (1295a25–96a22). This text may have been notes for lectures Aristotle gave at the Lyceum, his philosophical school at Athens, and was certainly written for small groups of educated discussants, not mass audiences. Aristotle suggests that virtue (*arete*) is the mean (*mesotes*) in all things, the exact midpoint between excess and deficiency (*Ethics* 1106a14–1107a27). Consequently, the middle course of life is the best

(*Politics* 1295a38). He argues that every state is divided into three parts, the rich, the poor, and *hoi mesoi*. The rich are prone to hubris and the poor to evil-doing, so neither have true *philia*. Middling men should therefore control politics.

But it is not clear who Aristotle's *mesoi* are. His *mesos* hold "middling and sufficient" property (1295b40), but Aristotle does not define this. Ober (1991: 119–20) sees Aristotle's *mesoi* as the lower ranks of the leisure class, perhaps 5 percent of the citizen body. Ste. Croix (1981: 71–6) thought Aristotle meant a wider group, while Finley (1983: 10–11) even argued that the *mesoi* did not fit into Aristotle's categories at all. Aristotle did not see *hoi mesoi* as the backbone of democracy. Rather, he argued that states controlled by the property-less had reckless democracies (1296a3). A state dominated by the middle would be a *politeia*, or "constitutional state," not a democracy (1293–4). Scholars have tried in vain to make sense of these passages, but their ambiguity may be an important part of Aristotle's thought. The *Politics* was not an objective account of social relations. Aristotle tendentiously redefined popular concepts (Nightingale 1996). For him, *demokratia* was not the rule of the many but the rule of the poor, regardless of numbers (1289b2–5). By definition *hoi mesoi* could not dominate a democracy, though he conceded that democracies lasted longer than oligarchies because they honored *hoi mesoi* more (1296a13–16). Aristotle reshaped popular ideas of the middle way for his own ends.

Making the Middle Work

Democratic Politics and the Middle

The middle was one way to structure experience. It was a class- and gender-based ideology, working in the interests of less well-off men but leaving room for others to use it for their own ends. The main problem was that whenever Athenians did bring matters *es meson*, speakers always had conflicting opinions. To some Athenians, the obvious conclusion was that the middling ideology – and democracy – were nonsense. But Athenians accommodated conflict within the middling ideology by claiming that their rivals were not really *metrioi* at all. Anyone who disagreed with the community was not a *philos* but an *echthros*, an enemy. Only men who were foreign, slave-born, or bribed by foreigners could possibly mislead the people so grievously. Speakers regularly argued that their opponents fell into one or more of these categories, rhetorically casting one another out of the community. Prosecutors emphasized their longstanding feuds with rivals, making enmity a semiformal relationship, not to present themselves as fractious individuals, but to portray their enemies as men no reasonable citizen would befriend. By hounding rivals through the courts (sometimes for generations), speakers preserved Athens' perfection by exposing those who lacked middling values (Ober 1989: 149–50, 167, 180–1). They could even reinterpret the city's conflict-filled politics as a constant state of *homonoia* (Loraux 1991).

Being a middling Athenian was complicated. As a community, Athens had a reputation for boundless energy and self-aggrandizement. Thucydides had a Corinthian speaker say:

> An Athenian is always an innovator, quick to form a resolution and quick at carrying it out . . . And so they go on working away in hardship and danger all the days of their lives, seldom enjoying their possessions because they are always adding to them. Their view of a holiday is to do what needs doing; they prefer hardship and activity to peace and quiet. In a word, they are by nature incapable of either living a quiet life themselves or of allowing anyone else to do so. (Thucydides 1.70)

Thucydides' Corinthians were making a rhetorical point, trying to stir the Spartans into action, but this also seems to have been Thucydides' own opinion (8.96). He had Pericles assert in his funeral oration over the war dead that all citizens needed to be involved in the affairs of the polis (2.40), but private speakers nevertheless went out of their way not to give the impression that they thought they were better than others. This fiction was not always easy to maintain. Speakers would present their arguments as common sense, prefacing them with expressions like "you all know," or even claimed to be bad orators, quiet citizens drawn unwillingly into the limelight. Thus Aeschines (1.31) maintained that as long as a man was good, his words would be useful, simple and awkward as they might be.

The Athenian conceit was that collectively they were the most dynamic men in Greece, but that individually they were virtually interchangeable. All men looked after their own concerns, but would do whatever was needed for the group. In the words of Thucydides' Corinthian, "As for their bodies, they regard them as expendable for the city's sake, as though they were not their own; and each man cultivates his own wisdom, again with a view to doing something notable for the city" (1.70).

This created certain tensions. Democracy needed men who would step forward to advise the assembly. But their actions set them apart from most citizens, who rarely spoke before these huge gatherings.

This automatically made claims to "middleness" suspect. Fourth-century Athenians recognized a group (probably never more than 100 strong) whom they called *rhetores*, or "politicians." The *rhetor* addressing the assembly needed to persuade his fellows that he was qualified to give advice everyone should follow, and might need to present himself as special. Demosthenes (18.320) reminded a jury how he had "revealed himself" in the great crisis of 338: "I made better speeches than any other man, and everything was carried out by means of my decrees, my laws, my diplomacy." Therefore, he said, because of this earlier demonstration of specialness, the jury should now vote with him. Yet a few minutes earlier, he had insisted that the *rhetor* simply expressed the wishes of the people (18.280). In another speech, Demosthenes (9.54) excused himself for going against the wishes of the people by suggesting that some demon had possessed them. But on closer inspection, even at 18.320 Demosthenes qualified his claims to specialness: he came to the fore in 338 in an open competition in patriotism, winning because he was most patriotic, while his splendid, horsebreeding rivals gained the upper hand by compromising with foreigners. Even his unique qualities merely distilled the patriotism every citizen held. *Rhetores* took care to limit the implications of their claims.

In a famous passage, Thucydides (6.16) had Alcibiades say in a heated debate in 415 that the Athenians should listen to him because he won honor for them the previous year by taking three prizes in the chariot race at Olympia; but Thucydides prefaced the speech (6.15) by explicitly saying that Alcibiades' horsebreeding and other extravagances made most citizens suspect and fear him. Through rhetorical devices such as Demosthenes', "the illusion was maintained of the simple man relating the unvarnished truth to the representatives of the demos, who would apply their collective intelligence in arriving at a just verdict" (Ober 1989: 176). Even the most ambitious *rhetor* wanted to appear as a *metrios*, and in Thucydides' eyes Alcibiades' error lay in failing to do so.

Inherited Excellence

One of the commonest critiques of liberal concepts of equality of opportunity is that successful people pass on various forms of capital to their children, who begin life's race ahead of the children of the less successful. Athenians tried to limit some of the scope for this. Appeals to the deeds of ancestors were problematic. Walter Donlan argues that in the face of popular resistance "ancestry could not stand alone as the determinant of class superiority." Some men did risk resentment by acting as if their families made them special, but generally they did this by suggesting that their own behavior was exceptional, and then claiming, in Donlan's words, that "Intellectual and moral proclivities are traced back to character, which, in the final analysis, is determined genetically" (1980: 139). The significance of *eugeneia*, "good birth," was constantly debated. A character in a fragmentary tragedy expresses the middling model well:

> It is an excessive statement if we praise *eugeneia* in mortals. For long ago, when first we came to be, and earth, our mother, brought mortals forth, the land impressed a like appearance on us all. We have no peculiar trait (*idion*); good birth (*to eugenes*) and low birth (*to dysgenes*) are a single stock, but time, through custom, has made [good birth] a thing of pride. (Euripides, *Alexander* fragment 52.1–8)

The story that all Athenians were autochthonous, born from the soil itself, was an important civic myth. It left no room for some men to claim better birth than others, reducing such appeals to matters of custom (*nomos*) asserted against nature (*phusis*).

Yet some men were determined to dispute this. Alcibiades is again a good example. Thucydides (5.43) says that in 421 the Athenians did hold him in high regard because of his family, but attached less importance to this than he himself did, preferring to follow Nicias' advice. Some historians see *gennetai*, men (like Alcibiades) who belonged to descent groups called *gene*, as a well-defined aristocracy of birth. They suggest that *gene* dominated archaic poleis, but after 500 gradually lost influence. A century ago Weber (1976 [1896]: 149–51) showed this was wrong, and Felix Bourriot (1976) and Denis Roussel (1976) have repeated the demonstration. *Gene* hardly feature in archaic literature; they gain, not lose, significance after 500. They were not survivals of an archaic aristocracy, but classical fictive kinship institutions. Further, Roussel (1976: 71–4) showed that while some texts use *gennetai* use as a synonym for "noble," others do not. Stephen Lambert (1993: 31–57, 107–12; cf. Bourriot 1976: 1347–66) argues that the *gene* were merely subdivisions of the phratries or brotherhoods to which, he suggests, all citizens belonged; and even their status as descent groups can be questioned.

Some fourth-century *gennetai* invented histories representing themselves as an ancient aristocratic order (Bourriot 1976: 694–710), but this made little impression on the dominant discourse. Demosthenes (18.10) summed this up by claiming to be better born than Aeschines, but immediately adding that "you know me and my family to be – not to put this offensively – as good as any other *metrioi*."

Athenians generally avoided claiming more than this in public speech, and the few passages where men do stress *eugeneia* illustrate the strength of the middling ideology. Around 397, one Teisias charged that Alcibiades had stolen a team of race horses from him. Alcibiades was now dead, but his son of the same name had just reached adulthood, so Teisias sued him. Isocrates wrote a speech *On the Team of Horses* in the younger Alcibiades' defense. This was a tricky issue, given how orators bandied around the epithet *hippotrophos*, "horsebreeding," to imply that rivals lacked middling attitudes. Lycurgus (1.140), for instance, insisted that no man who bred horses and raced chariots deserved gratitude from the people, and for Demosthenes (61.23), horsebreeding meant elitism. Neither Teisias nor Alcibiades can have expected popular sympathy in a feud over race horses. Perhaps because of this Isocrates (16.25–8) adopted a bold strategy. Rather than insisting he was a *metrios*, he had Alcibiades emphasize his lineage's nobility. His father came from the *genos* of the Eupatridai (literally, "well-born ones"), and his mother from the Alcmaeonids, who had intermarried with the Pisistratid tyrants, and whose founder Alcmaeon was the first Athenian to win an Olympic chariot race. But Isocrates then brought this genealogy back within the middling universe. The family's real honor, he suggested, stemmed from the Alcmaeonids' refusal to share in the tyranny, and subsequent exile. Still better, Cleisthenes, the founder of democracy, was an Alcmaeonid. From them, the younger Alcibiades inherited *philia* for the demos. This extraordinary sleight-of-hand wraps *eugeneia* in democracy: Alcibiades claims special standing because his ancestors make him specially democratic.

In an oration probably delivered the next year, an unknown speaker also drew attention to birth in a remarkable way (Lysias 18.10–12). In 404/3, a narrow oligarchy known as the Thirty controlled Athens. They subsequently became a standard image for nonmiddling, tyrannical government (Wolpert 1995). Democratic exiles began a civil war. The speaker was then a boy, and claims that when the Spartan king Pausanias came to Athens, the democrats placed him and his brother on the king's knee. The democrats told Pausanias that the Thirty would kill children like these, because of their birth and wealth. Pausanias was moved, and backed the democrats, bringing the war to a rapid end. Given such a history, the speaker suggests, the democracy should not strip him of his property.

Examples could be multiplied. Men could exploit special ancestry, but always translated *eugeneia* into appeals to middling values. The past was not a source of personal honor; rather, the demos appropriated the very language of aristocracy. Lysias (30.14), Aeschines (1.124), and Dinarchus (3.18) all asserted that the demos were collectively the real *kaloikagathoi* ("beautiful and good," or "gentlemen"), and Lysias (19.14) also treated *eugeneia* as something defined by the people as a whole.

The Claims of Family

A city of interchangeable middling men required its members to identify primarily with the citizen community. However, there was general agreement that the *philia* within an *oikos*, usually translated "family" or "household," was even more intense than that uniting the polis. Many citizens probably experienced tensions between the two kinds of *philia* at some point. The same Pericles who renounced family and friends to demonstrate his loyalty to the people, even giving Athens his estates in 431 to avoid embarrassment from his guest-friendship with the Spartan king (Thucydides 2.13), was said to have begged the assembly to enfranchize his last surviving but illegitimate son, making an exception to the citizenship law he himself had proposed (Plutarch, *Pericles* 7, 36).[2]

Theorists dramatized extreme results. Tragedians explored how communal *homonoia* could fragment as citizens furthered their own *oikoi* at the cost of everyone else's, while Plato (*Republic* 457c–61e) wanted to abolish the family altogether. In everyday practice, Athenians marked out spaces for familial *philia* which did not threaten civic *philia*. The normal stance was that the only life worth living was public (*ta koina* or *ta demosia*), while private life (*ta idia*) was weak and womanish (e.g., Thucydides 2.40; Demosthenes 19.203–4; 24.192–4; Aristotle, *Ethics* 1163b5–15; *Rhetoric* 1361a). In public men should be autonomous citizens, ignoring private concerns. To make this work, speakers manipulated the public/private boundary. Isocrates (16.22) and Lycurgus (1.149) maximized the private sphere for tactical advantage by claiming that only the act of holding state office was public, while everything else belonged to "the other life," of no concern to anyone else. They chopped up civic space into thousands of secret enclaves. Other times, writers asserted that everything outside the physical walls of the home was public, to be judged by the whole polis (e.g., Lysias 16.11–12; Xenophon, *Memorabilia* 4.4.1–2, 4.6.14). Aeschines (1.122; 2.182) claimed that his whole life was public, lived out before the gaze of other citizens. Andocides (1.149) went even further. Accused of betraying his father, he pleaded that the citizens as a whole were his father, brothers, and children. David Cohen (1991: 74) suggests we imagine Athenian ideas of privacy as being like onion skin: any layer potentially counted as private in relation to other layers.

The middling man should head a household, and should defend its status, but the household itself was submerged beneath the public space. The good citizen could not claim special honors from his family, but had to defend its standing. The physical space of the house assumed tremendous importance in this (see pp. 149–50 below). Crossing its threshold without an invitation was a serious offense, almost like penetrating the body (e.g., Demosthenes 21.79; 47.52–6). Those allowed into the courtyard might still be kept from an inner, more private, area (e.g., Lysias 3.23; Demosthenes 37.45–6). Entering the core of another man's house was hubristic (Lysias 1.4, 25, 36; Demosthenes 18.132), diminishing his manhood, and requiring strong responses. Athenian law apparently allowed citizens to kill adulterers or thieves found in their homes, although, as Herman (1993) shows, when Euphiletus did just this (Lysias 1) he risked seeming to put his family's honor above the peace of the polis as a whole.

Man and God

Athenian civic discourse, then, made it difficult to claim grandeur through links with the past, although some managed it. The Gephyraian *genos* paid no taxes (Demosthenes 20.29, 127), albeit for good democratic reasons: they descended from Harmodius and Aristogeiton, whose assassination of Hipparchus in 514 was popularly believed to have triggered the fall of the tyranny. The Eteoboutadai monopolized priesthoods of Athena Polias and Heracles Erechtheus, while Kerykes and Eumolpidai always provided priests for the Eleusinian Mysteries, and the Eumolpidai had private religious laws (Aeschines 2.147; Lysias 6.10). Other *gene* also had their own cults.

Relationships with the gods were fundamental to Greek self-definition. Most famously, when Herodotus (8.144; p. 45 above) defined Greekness, religion loomed large. Mainstream religion placed mankind *es meson*; in Vernant's telling phrase (1980: 130–67), sacrifice suspended the Greeks between the beasts and the gods. Aristotle (*Politics* 1319b25) consequently urged democratic reformers to abolish private cults.

Athenians did admit that some citizens stood closer to the gods than others. Conceding that these few could reach outside the community to the divine realm drastically qualified middling beliefs, yet we hear little of men converting this into other kinds of power, beyond late stories that the Eteoboutadai could display family portraits in the

Erechtheion shrine on the acropolis (Plutarch, *Moralia* 843E; Pausanias 1.26.5). Athenians tolerated these exceptions, but fenced them in with popular religious power. Even the Kerykes and Eumolpidai were regulated, and shared control of the Mysteries with two magistrates chosen annually by lot from all citizens aged over thirty (Lewis 1981: no. 6 = Fornara 1983: no. 75). Nearly all priesthoods ran along these lines (Garland 1984). Isocrates (2.6) even said that "they believe that the office of . . . priest is one that any man can fill." Anyone was free to sacrifice without the mediation of religious specialists, and Herodotus (1.132) was astonished that Persians needed to call on a magus for every offering. Insofar as Athens recognized religious specialists, their authority was informal. The assembly even queried the Delphic oracle in 480 (Herodotus 7.140–3), and when the people judged that oracle interpreters had misled them in 413, they attacked them (Thucydides 8.1).

Another way to forge special links with the gods was by heavy spending on worship. Citizens could represent this as winning divine favor for the whole community, but it also gave rich sponsors of sacrifices opportunities to claim special standing. Wealthy men could represent their religious activities as middling acts of piety and obedience to the law (e.g., Isaeus 1.39; 2.36; Isocrates 13.43), but Aristotle (*Ethics* 1123b19–21) saw both sides of the equation. Spending on votives, sacrifices, and everything concerning the gods always brought honor, he said, because these were for the common good (1123a4–5). But, he went on, a poor man could never win honor in this way, because if he spent a lot on sacrifices it would be inappropriate and ridiculous (1122b27–33; see also p. 276 below). Xenophon had Socrates agree; he saw Critoboulos' lavish sacrifices as being good for everyone, but particularly for Critoboulos, justifying his prominent position. However, Socrates added, Critoboulos thereby trapped himself. If he stopped the sacrifices, both the gods and his fellow-citizens would be angry (*Estate Manager* 2.5–6). Neoptolemos illustrates the ambiguity. He won honors from his community of Paiania for restoring a shrine and from the polis for other religious acts (Woodhead 1967: no. 116; Plutarch, *Moralia* 843F), but Demosthenes represented him as a sinister figure whose excessive wealth threatened the citizens (21.215).

One response was to make fun of men who thought their sacrifices made them special (e.g., Theophrastus, *Characters* 21.7; Menander, *Dyscolus* 447–53). I discuss this technique further on pp. 134–8 below. Another was to reduce rich men's sacrifices to relative insignificance: Athens as polis put on festivals and sacrifices dwarfing what even the richest man could do. Few rich classical votives have been excavated, but temple inventories record spectacular offerings, almost all from poleis not individuals (D. Harris 1995). The archaeological evidence for animal sacrifice consists chiefly of sheep/goats or smaller animals (M. H. Jameson 1988: 90–3), and the five extant sacrificial calendars from rural demes provide for similar small feasts (Whitehead 1986: 176–99). Cattle sacrifices were largely restricted to state-funded festivals. On one occasion in 410/9, in the depths of the financial crisis after the Sicilian expedition, Athens spent 5,114 drachmas on cattle to sacrifice at the Great Panathenaea (when assembly pay was introduced in 403, each man earned half a drachma per day); and in 334/3 a group of officials sold off the hides of about 1,500 sacrificed cattle (Lewis 1981: no. 375.7). The animals were paid for largely from liturgies imposed on rich men, some of whom, as we know from court speeches, claimed that this showed their devotion to Athens and therefore justified special treatment. But the anonymous late fifth-century political pamphleteer known as the Old Oligarch (2.9) saw only class exploitation, with the state forcing the rich to pay for the poor to eat beef.

Athenians took popular control of sacrifice very seriously. One of the fiercest disputes in Athenian religious history came in 399, when Nicomachus, who had been busy for years revising the law code, was prosecuted for neglecting some traditional rites while introducing new ones (Lysias 30; Andocides 1.81–9). Nicomachus seems to have imposed extra liturgies on the rich by expanding state sacrifices, while unnamed opponents wanted to cut back. Connor (1991: 52–4) relates this trial to broader struggles over popular control of religion, which also surfaced in Socrates' impiety trial in the same year.

Socrates apparently virtually renounced sacrifice. This earned him mockery in 423 in Aristophanes' *Clouds*, but in the delicate situation of 399, he seemed such a threat that the demos executed him. They were prepared to use legal force against anyone who reconstructed cosmological space. According to Plutarch (*Themistocles* 22; see n. 2 on p. 314), a key event in Themistocles' fall from favor in the 470s and subsequent flight to avoid prosecution was his decision to build a temple to Artemis Aristoboule (i.e., Artemis of Wise Counsel, alluding to his own counsel at the battle of Salamis) next to his house, with a statue of himself in front of it.[3] Themistocles tried to convert military prestige into religious honors, but misjudged things. Athenians saw no need to take away the inherited privileges of the Eteoboutadai or Eumolpidai, but Themistocles' self-promotion was too dangerous.

Middling Men and the Wider World

Some men tried to elevate themselves by forging links outside their poleis. In the *Wasps* (lines 1176–1207), performed in 422, Aristophanes

mocked Bdelycleon's pretentious attempts to make his father Philocleon into an aristocrat. Bdelycleon assumed that telling stories about
experiences at Olympia or on embassies was an important part in this
would-be elite style. Philocleon disrupted the process, though, by
coming up with domestic stories (*kat' oikian*) about a cat and mouse,
while his foreign travel was limited to serving in the fleet. His only
contact with an Olympic athlete was sitting on a jury that convicted
him. For Aristophanes' humor to make sense, his audience had to recognize Bdelycleon's observation that "that's the clever set's conversation" (1196). Athenians needed to send men on embassies (Miller 1997:
109–33), and wanted the glory of Olympic victories, so opportunities
for such self-promotion were rife; but the demos also wanted to
control the interpretation of these activities.

One way for a man to define himself as part of a larger world was
through marriage outside Athens, but this was consistently represented as something tyrants did, and which no middling citizen would
want to do. Vernant (1980: 60) argues that the use of marriage to forge
political alliances with members of other poleis declined sharply after
507. Marriage was still a good basis for political alliances, but these
were now largely within Athens (Davies 1971: table 1), and exclusively
so after the law of 451/450 requiring double endogamy for citizenship.

The most important form of spatial extension was *xenia*, ritualized
guest-friendship with men in other poleis. Athenians did not ban
xenia, perhaps because of its religious dimension, but they limited its
implications. Athenians portrayed *xenia* as a feature of would-be aristocrats, in conflict with middling citizenship. Herman (1987: 8) suggests that "at times the horizontal ties of solidarity which linked
together the elites of separate communities were stronger than the vertical ties which bound them to the inferiors within their own communities." Fellow-citizens might see the man with many guest-friends
as a potential traitor, ready to trade in the middling polis for a broader
world of his peers: "Throughout Greek history, it was the community
that arrayed itself against the one-time hero, against *xenoi* [guest-
friends] plotting its plundering, subjection and exploitation . . . In the
Greek world of the cities, then, unlike the modern world, the notions
'treason' and 'patriotism' had overtones of class conflict" (Herman
1987: 157, 160). Alcibiades is again the classic example, but the theme
also runs through Demosthenes' confrontation with Aeschines in 330.
Demosthenes claimed that on embassies to Macedonia Aeschines
schemed with his *xenos* king Philip, while he himself was a loyal
citizen, avoiding such ties.

The most problematic overseas ties were with the east. As Miller
(1997) shows, a steady trickle of Athenians had direct contact with

Persia, and there were plenty of Persian artifacts in Greece. Part of Bdelycleon's plan to make Philocleon an elitist, for instance, was to squeeze him into a Persian cloak (Aristophanes, *Wasps* 1132–56). Some public architecture drew on Persian designs, perhaps to claim that Athens had replaced Persia as an imperial power. But in public speech Persia was the archetype of decadence, passivity, hubris, and servility – everything the community of middling citizens was not (E. Hall 1989). For Herodotus and Aeschylus (in his tragedy *The Persians*, performed in 472), Persian softness accounted for their defeat at Greek hands in 480. Herodotus imagined the world as a rough rectangle, with Greece at the center. To the east lay the Persians, to the north the Scythians, to the south the Egyptians, and to the west, barbarians of lesser interest. In climate and geography, these extremes mirrored each other; so too in customs and temperament (Hartog 1988). Herodotus was notorious for admiring elements in Egyptian, Persian, and Scythian culture, but his explanation for the Greek victory came down to what Paul Cartledge (1993: 60–2) calls "Herodotus' law": only Greece, in the middle, perfectly balanced geography and climate, producing free, strong, and brave men. To drive home the point that the Persian wars were ultimately about different kinds of manhood, Herodotus ended his account with the tale of how around 550 Artembares had proposed that the Persians abandon the mountains and move to the plains. Cyrus refused, replying that "From soft countries come soft men" (9.122). Greece produced hard men.

Conclusion: Athenian Spacetime

In her study of the Pacific island of Gawa, Nancy Munn argues that competition for fame (*butu*) is central to male self-definition. When a Gawan gets control of an imporant kula shell, he in effect extends himself through space, by being present in the minds of men on other islands when they talk about that shell, and through time, when men still to come will remember his possession of the shell. In a densely worded passage, she explains that

> the action system involves the means of generating a continuum in which the ongoing present (spatiotemporal field) is experienced as continually surpassing itself, engaging the future; and the past is continually being engaged within the present which surpasses it. I refer to this process – in which expectation and past reference (and coordinately, different spatial references) are regularly being formed within the present – as one of spatiotemporal synthesis . . . sociocultural action systems (or the activities through which they become operative) do not simply go

on *in* or *through* time and space, but they form (structure) and constitute (create) the spacetime manifold in which they "go on." Actors must
"make" this manifold, thus concretely producing their own spacetime.
(Munn 1983: 280)

A man who does well as a shell-giver and -receiver literally expands
his own spacetime, "as if the name takes on its own internal motion
traveling through the minds and speech of others" (Munn 1986: 105),
while the spacetime of an unsuccessful man shrinks: he becomes like
a man asleep, or even dead.

The concept of "spacetime" is widely used by anthroplogists, but
not ancient historians. Yet it is a powerful tool for making sense of
Athenian middling culture. Munn notes links between Gawan *butu*
and Homeric *kleos* (Munn 1986: 292 n. 14). Like the Gawan, the
Homeric hero sought to extend himself through time and space. But
by the fifth century, the good *metrios* did precisely the opposite. His
middling ideology was presentist and localist. Its good man was happy
to be like all other Athenian citizens. The community as a whole
wanted endless fame, and according to the funeral orations the hoplite
who fell for Athens won a share of this collective fame. But anyone
who tried to define *himself* by reaching outside the Athenian male
community courted disaster. Aristocratic and heroic genealogies were
problematic; so too special relationships with the gods. Marriage
outside the polis would cost a man's sons their citizenship, and pointedly making guest-friends outside Athens invited charges of treason.
Connections with the east were most dangerous. Understanding this
spacetime is the key to explaining Athenian male egalitarianism and
democracy.

Contesting the Middle

Munn (1983: 280) notes that in Melanesia "Different action systems in
the same society can construct different spacetime formations."
Minority groups in Athens developed very different ideal spacetimes.
I commented on p. 114 that our sources break down into two groups.
I now turn to the second category, texts which were probably meant
to circulate in written form. Their audience was small. 5–10 percent of
Athenian citizens were literate, and even among them "literacy" must
be understood in a restricted sense. Some of these sources mimic performance contexts midway between mass gatherings and private readings, such as conversations at drinking parties where the "clever set"
engaged in philosophical and political discussions.

Many of these texts oppose middling culture, and were probably self-consciously subversive, aimed at like-minded readers. Some sources link writing, and particularly lawcodes, with equality (e.g., Euripides, *Suppliant Women* 433; Aristotle, *Politics* 1286a9–17, 1278b5–8), but others are suspicious of writing, as a technique associated with the east, secrecy, and tyrants. Deborah Steiner (1993: 227–41) explains this tension as part of democracy's struggle to tame this technology: most Athenians felt that writing lent itself to manipulation by intellectual elites, and had to be wrested from them and neutralized by being performed publicly in speech. For example, Athenians wanted written laws, but not professional jurists who might control them. Even after the reforms of 403 it was panels of ordinary citizens who made law, and laws rarely guided decisions in detail. Instead, it was up to the protagonists to tell jurors what laws were relevant, while the citizens listened and decided on the basis of middling common-sense what was just (Demosthenes 39.40) – that is, who conformed to *homonoia* and *philia* and who did not. Aristotle (*Constitution of Athens* 9.1) saw this freedom to interpret law as a bastion of democracy. Written lawcodes underwrote equality because ordinary citizens interpreted them through public speech.

Most fourth-century texts were produced by men who considered themselves an intellectual elite. Ober (1998) suggests that one of Plato's, Aristotle's, and Thucydides' major goals was to create an intellectual space from which to challenge the hegemonic claims of middling ideology. In differing ways, they argued that real truth lay deeper than the appearances which passed for truth in democracy. Plato offered the most sophisticated critique of popular discourse. He contrasted the opinions, *doxa*, of the many with the true knowledge, or *episteme*, which only philosophers could attain. He suggested that ordinary understanding stood in the same relationship to truth as did the shadows cast on a cave wall to the creatures who cast the shadows. It is as if ordinary men are chained up, only able to see the shadows on the wall, while philosophers break the chains and turn to the light. At first they are dazzled by what they see, but soon they understand that all they had known before was mere illusion (*Republic* 514e–521c). Consequently, making communal decisions according to what the masses believed was madness. The good man should heed only the wise few (e.g., *Crito* 43e–48a), and government will only be perfect when philosophers become kings (*Republic* 471c–473e). The problem was that no one who saw the light could survive in democratic politics, because he would have to oppose the will of the masses, who would eventually execute him (*Apology* 31e–32a). Andrea Nightingale (1995: 10) suggests that " 'philosophy' as Plato conceived it comprised not just an analytic inquiry into certain types of subjects but a unique set of ethical and metaphysical commitments that demanded a whole new way of living." Plato responded by withdrawing from public life into an oppositional community, formalized in his philosophical school at the Academy, a short walk outside the city walls.

Some critics were less alienated. Old Comedy involved a kind of institutionalized critique (see p. 134 below), and Ober (1996: 143) supposes that "in each village and neighborhood of the polis there were men and women who could be counted on to interrogate, humorously or angrily, various aspects of the current order of things." A common claim was that only men rich enough for a life of leisure could cultivate true wisdom, dignity, and restraint. In a sense, this argument simply restricted the claims of the middling ideology to a narrower group. The Old Oligarch, for instance, held that

> among the best people [*to beltiston*] there is the least unrestraint and injustice, the most precise concern for things of value; but in the demos there is the most ignorance, disorder, and vice. For poverty has a strong tendency to lead them into shameful ways, along with the lack of education and the ignorance that lack of money causes for some people. (Old Oligarch 1.5)

His sentiments could be those of a middling orator, except that he restricted goodness to a few "best men," defined against the demos. The mass of ordinary citizens were *poneroi*, "people of no account" (1.1), who recognized that virtue was inborn in the worthy (*hoi chrestoi*) but also that true virtue was inimical to their class interests (2.19).

Kurt Raaflaub (1989: 60–8) has usefully constructed an imaginary debate between a democrat and a critic, basing every statement on views expressed in the sources. He shows that democracy's opponents did not reject equality. Rather, they claimed that democracy was *not* equal. Its arithmetic equality treated all men as equal by birth. This, they argued, ignored more important spheres of life, unfairly treating as equals men whose virtue or cultivation made them unequal.

The middling ideology dominated classical Athens, but ordinary citizens rarely tried to extend its principles into all spheres, creating equality of condition or outcome by insisting that no one could be richer, better educated, or more politically active than anyone else (Thucydides 2.37–40). Athenians did not insist on wealth, land, or influence strictly following equal dignity. This was not because they only valued equality of political opportunity, as Hansen concludes

(1991: 83–5), but because opposition from the rich made it difficult. Further, they did not need equality of resources to guarantee the basal dimension of equality of attitude and respect between citizens. Some archaic states did cancel debts, redistribute land, control inheritance, or even massacre the rich, but after 500 this only happened when states were destabilized through war (Link 1991; Gehrke 1985).

Jonathan Parry and Maurice Bloch's model of "transactional orders" may help us make sense of this. They observe that in many (perhaps all) societies, most people identify a long-term transactional order comprising correct relationships between mortals and gods, men and women, old and young, rich and poor, etc. The middling ideology was the dominant long-term transactional order in classical Athens. If the cosmic order is to work properly, people must reproduce these norms without thought of personal advantage. Nearly everyone likes to think they do this, but at the same time they do have personal interests and a living to make. We all have one foot in the world of short-term gain. Parry and Bloch suggest that:

> all these systems make – indeed *have* to make – some ideological space within which individual acquisition is a legitimate and even laudable goal; but . . . such activities are consigned to a separate sphere which is ideologically articulated with, and subordinate to, a sphere of activity concerned with the cycle of long-term reproduction. (Parry and Bloch 1989: 26)

People seek a balance. They convert gains in the short-term order into the reproduction of the long-term, interpreting personal advantage as a good thing, to everyone's benefit. In different situations and among different groups, this balance is constructed in different ways. Parry and Bloch continue:

> While the long-term cycle is always positively associated with the central precepts of morality, the short-term order tends to be morally undetermined since it concerns individual purposes which are largely irrelevant to the long-term order. If, however, that which is obtained in the short-term individualistic cycle is converted to serve the reproduction of the long-term cycle, then it becomes morally positive – like the cash "drunk" in Fiji or the wealth given as *dana* in Hindu India. But equally there is always the opposite possibility – and this evokes the strongest censure – the possibility that individual involvement in the short-term cycle will become an end in itself which is no longer subordinated to the reproduction of the larger cycle; or, more horrifyingly still, that grasping individuals will divert the resources of the long-term cycle for their own short-term transactions. (Parry and Bloch 1989: 26–7)

Like the members of any community, middling Athenians tolerated alternative visions of equality, rooted in other spacetimes, so long as they did not threaten basal civic equality, the morally superior long-term transactional order. Men who lurked in philosophical schools saying things other citizens could not understand were not automatically immoral. But they might be. If their activities appeared to be converting the long-term good of the polis into their own short-term good, as when former followers of Socrates overthrew democracy and constituted themselves as the Thirty in 404, philosophy began to look very suspicious indeed. Socrates had opposed the Thirty, but in 399 the democracy executed him anyway. Aeschines (1.173) said this was because they were angry over his connections with the oligarchy; while Plato (*Statesman* 299c) implied that it was because Athenians thought he was trying to be cleverer than the laws. Similarly, most of the time symposiasts could go about their merry business, but when it suited them, the *metrioi* could attack, and those symposiasts suspected of undermining democracy by profaning the mysteries in 415 were mercilessly hounded down.

Civic Culture: Institutionalized Gossip

There are late stories that Athenians routinely persecuted intellectuals, but these are probably apocryphal. Ordinary Athenians defended the long-term transactional order against other patterns of conversion not through a reign of terror, but through the day-to-day hegemony of a civic culture which marginalized critics: a kind of institutionalized gossip. Fear of ridicule can be essential to the formation of identity (Herzfeld 1985: 79–84), working, in David Gilmore's words (1987a: 50), as an "invisible fist" punishing those who deviate too far from expectations.

Athenians would have agreed. Aeschines (1.128–9; 2.145) called Rumor a goddess, equating her with the will of the masses, and a later commentator on his speeches claimed that the Athenians set up an altar to Rumor. Aristotle (*Rhetoric* 1400a23–9, 1416a36–8) observed that the only way to fight gossip was with more gossip. Athenian gossip mocked both those who fell short of communal standards and those with pretensions to rise above them. In his study of Fuenmayor, an Andalusian agrotown of 8,000 people, Gilmore (1987a: 60–4) constructed a three-level typology of gossip, beginning with nosy neighbors talking in the street, moving to nodes of talk like hairdressers' shops and bars, then to occasional town-wide gatherings such as harvests or carnivals. Athens was no face-to-face community, and its gossips dealt with scale in similar ways (Hunter 1994: 97–100; S. Lewis 1996: 9–23). But they also added a fourth level, effectively insti-tutionalizing gossip as a major focus of civic culture. Unlike the townsfolk of Fuenmayor, Athenian citizens were not subjects in a larger territorial state; they *were* the state. The Andalusian carnival is subversive and oppositional, and was even banned under Franco (Gilmore 1987a: 96–125), but Athenian "festivals of gossip" were not only state-supported, but even used state violence to back up communal judgments.

The most remarkable example is late fifth-century Old Comedy, performed in major festivals which drew crowds of thousands. In this context, comic poets stepped into the persona of wise guide of the city, charged with ritually expelling deviants responsible for the commu-nity's ills. Like abusive bards at modern carnivals, the poets attacked real individuals, fictional characters, and stock groups, but always within generic constraints. Ralph Rosen (1988a: 78) suggests of the most famous of these feuds that "the details of the quarrel between Aristophanes and Cleon can easily be seen as an elaborate fiction, capable of traveling from play to play, gaining new additions and twists, and furnishing the poet with new inspiration." Aristophanes gives us the voice of the comic "I," criticizing departures from the norms of an ideal community. The *Wasps* provides good examples. In an economic arrangement only possible in drama, the wealthy and cosmopolitan Bdelycleon (meaning "Cleon-hater") locks his impov-erished, jury-obsessed father Philocleon ("Cleon-lover") in the house. When the chorus of vindictive old jurymen comes to free Philocleon, Bdelycleon complains to them that Athens has gone mad:

> Example. You don't want sardines for supper; what you want
> is a nice, fat, juicy sea-bass. So down to the MART you go,
> and BUY a nice, fat, juicy sea-bass. And the man next door,
> – who, incidentally, just happens to sell sardines – starts up:
> "Sea-bass, huh? That's real rich food – expensive, too.
> TOO expensive for a real Athenian democrat. Hey, Mac –
> why the bass? You want to bring DICTATORSHIP [*tyrannis*] back?"
> (Aristophanes, *Wasps* 493–5).

Fish was expensive, and Greek thought linked it to self-indulgence and lack of control over the appetites (Davidson 1997: 3–35, 288–90), so the neighbor might be cutting Bdelycleon down to size in an accept-able way. But Aristophanes immediately undermined this, by por-traying the man next door not as civic-minded but out for his own profit. He mocked both the pretensions of those who would live off fish and the pettiness of those who would resist them at a time when there were real villains, like Cleon, gobbling up public goods on a much bigger scale.

Aristophanes claimed that his attacks stung Cleon so badly that Cleon took him to court, but we should beware of taking statements by the comic "I" as referring to anything outside a world of comic discourse. Gossip works by denying the victim's self-image, and feeds on anger. If a victim ignores ridicule, he or she asserts that the attacker is beneath notice. The greatest success for pranksters in modern Mediterranean abuse is to drive a victim to respond, admitting that it hurts; if the victim refuses, the prankster may pretend that he or she responded. Rosen (1988a: 64) argues that "Aristophanes' allusions to an indictment by Cleon [w]as one element of a fiction of hostility between them propagated by the poet. Such a fiction would be eminently self-serving and self-congratulatory, since the more trouble the poet claims to have received from Cleon, the more this would reflect [his] power and effectiveness."

But the differences between ancient and modern festivals are again more instructive than the similarities. In Andalusia, the upper classes (*los ricos*, *los grandes*, or *los capitalistos*) simply ignore the antics of *los pobres*, leaving town or staying home during carnivals (Brandes 1980: 24–5). The poor of Fuenmayor know that this does not mean that the rich fear them: the elite pursue *separación*, what Gilmore (1987a: 102) glosses as "a wider encompassing tradition of elite exclusivity . . . the elite disparage and disdain the culture of the people." Poor villagers feel they inhabit a different world from the rich, and even their own festivals underline this. Brandes (1980: 30) suggests that poor men in Monteros view themselves as childlike in comparison to the dignified rich.

The contrast with democratic Athens could hardly be sharper. Cleon presumably did not enjoy public abuse, but was perhaps complicit in it. Being ignored by Aristophanes might be worse than any ridicule. The would-be elite took comedy very seriously. The Old Oligarch experienced it as a class weapon:

> they [the poor] don't permit the general populace to be made the butt of comedies and to be ill-spoken of, in order that they may hear no evil about themselves. But they encourage comedies about individuals, if someone wants to lampoon one, knowing well that the object of comedy is rarely the populace or the majority, but a rich or highly born or powerful person – whereas few of the poor and vulgar are made fun of in comedies, and not even those unless it is for being busybodies and trying to get more than the common people have, so it's no grief to them when such types are the butt of comedy. (Old Oligarch 2.18)

The most famous example is Aristophanes' attack on Socrates in the *Clouds*, which Plato saw as a factor in Socrates' execution in 399. Aristophanes portrayed a "stage Socrates, carried around on the stage machinery, claiming that he walks on air and babbling a great deal more nonsense" (Plato, *Apology* 19c). This was a stock figure, but that was probably why it worked so well to crystalize gossip against philosophers' antisocial habits. The words Plato put into Socrates' mouth at his trial could almost come from a modern Mediterranean ethnography:

> These, then, are my accusers. They are many in number. Their accusa-
> tions have been in existence for a long time now. In addition, they made
> them to you at a time of life when you would have been especially likely
> to believe them, since some of you were children, and others, young
> men; and they were accusing in a case that had literally gone by default,
> since no one was speaking for the defense. The most absurd feature of
> the case is this: it is not even possible to know or to tell you their names,
> unless there chances to be a comic poet among them. Some were moved
> by envy to slander; others themselves believed what they were saying.
> Both groups kept trying to persuade you. All of them are very difficult
> to deal with, for one cannot even bring them before the court as wit-
> nesses and refute any of them; one literally has to shadowbox with them
> in one's defense and try to refute them, though there is no one to answer
> one's questions. (Plato, *Apology* 18d–e)

It was in the lawcourts that the Athenians gave teeth to their gossip. Ober's theatrical metaphor for Athenian politics (p. 114 above) cap-tures the continuity between institutions. Lawcourts and assemblies functioned even more pointedly than the theater as gossip writ large (Hunter 1994: 101–11). Prosecutors scrutinized defendants' whole lives, making even the smallest acts (real or not) speak volumes. A way of walking and choice of cloak (Demosthenes 19.314; 36.45), carrying a cane (Demosthenes 27.52), choices of hairstyles (Lysias 16.18–19; Aeschines 1.64; 3.118), fondness for dainty foods (Aeschines 1.65), keeping overdressed courtesans (Demosthenes 48.52–5), and many other foibles signified a rival's contempt for the equal dignity of citi-zens. And in these contexts elite speakers courted disaster – defeat might cost them not only face but also property, citizenship, or their lives. Gilmore (1987a: 33) describes public opinion in a modern village as being "ever watchful, unforgiving, exacting. It is everyone and it is no one . . . people always say that it is *el pueblo* (the people) or the town which gossips or pillories or ostracizes or admires." This applies equally to Athens, except that Athenians backed up opinions with state power. Its starkest expression was a kind of annual unpopularity contest, *ostrakismos*, in which the citizens could send a threatening man into exile for ten years.

Through sitting in institutions of public speech, Athenians learned how to contain those who stepped forward to advise the people: how to be democratic citizens, and how to press that persona onto others. Plato had Meletus, one of Socrates' accusers, say that young Athenians learned virtue by listening to speeches in the lawcourts, council, and assembly (*Apology* 24e–25b); and had Protagoras tell Socrates that all citizens taught political virtue – " 'you're spoiled, Socrates,' he said, 'in that everyone teaches virtue to the best of his ability, so you think that no one does – just like if you asked who teaches the Greek language you wouldn't find anyone' " (*Protagoras* 327e).

The Problem of Wealth

The greatest issue for civic culture was wealth. By general agreement, inequalities in wealth were like inequalities in intellect, eloquence, or any other sphere: they did not matter until they challenged equality of respect between all men. Most writers agreed that so long as a rich man showed he shared the values of *metrioi*, then his wealth was his own business (e.g., Xenophon, *Memorabilia* 2.4.6; 3.4.12; Lysias 16.9–12; Isocrates 15.276–85; Demosthenes 20.24; 21.210; 23.246; 58.65; Aristotle, *Politics* 1256a1–1259b22). The best way to demonstrate a middling mentality was by sharing wealth with the people. As part of their *philia*, all citizens should feel *charis*, a sense of appreciation, toward one another. The rich man should express this through gifts to the polis. The citizens would judge whether a gift was given in the appropriate spirit of *charis* (Ober 1989: 226–30, 245–7). If it was, the people would return the donor's *charis* by supporting him; but a man who lacked *charis* was no *metrios* (e.g., Lysias 30.6; Demosthenes 18.131).

Athenians developed a wide vocabulary for "the rich" (*hoi plousioi, hoi euporoi*, etc.). They normally applied these words to a leisure class of just 1,200–2,000 citizens who did not have to work for a living (Davies 1981: 6–14, 28–35). Much of the time, these words had neutral connotations. A man's wealth only became a public matter if his use of it seemed hubristic. When speakers wanted to put opponents into this category they might describe "the rich" as posing a collective threat to democracy. Thus Demosthenes (21.140), attacking Meidias, told jurors "this is why you band together, so that when you find yourselves individually worse off than others, whether in wealth or *philoi* or anything else, you may together prove stronger than any one of your enemies and so check his hubris." Isocrates took a different line, looking for sympathy for the rich by complaining that Athenians saw them as worse than criminals (15.160). His argument presupposed that ordinary citizens felt that this attitude was unfair, and that the simple fact of wealth should not divide the community. When Demosthenes (21.211) suggested that Meidias would not suffer too terribly if he had to live on the same resources as ordinary Athenians, it was not because wealth was inherently wrong, but because Meidias was hubristic.

The Athenian rhetoric of wealth is radically different from what ethnographers report in the modern Mediterranean. In most contemporary situations male honor is class-bound. The poor feel they are at the mercy of the rich: they depend on them for jobs, often for housing, for aid in hard times, and dare not stand up to their patrons (Davis 1977: 81–101, 107–25). Villagers generally blame this humiliating dependency on the concentration of land in a few hands. Many villagers are rural proletarians. Most Andalusian men are landless laborers, harvesting other men's olives for their livelihood. They teeter on the brink of disaster while surrounded by vast estates. One worker said that "Our land is superabundant and rich . . . The only problem is that it is divided among only a handful of people (*cuatro personas*). The rest of us have nothing" (quoted in Brandes 1980: 31). Class hatred, which can erupt into violence, is a fact of life. Jacob Black-Michaud (1975: 160–78) calls this situation – the combination of relative and absolute land hunger – "total scarcity," arguing that it both intensifies class conflict and pits poor households against one another, encouraging a zero-sum, agonistic view of honor.

Some classicists, impressed by the commonness of this situation in the modern Mediterranean, argue that large-scale patronage and rural dependency are adaptive responses to Mediterranean ecology. If ancient texts say little about this, then they mislead us, reflecting an ideology which denied the facts of life, concealing elite domination behind a mask of egalitarianism (e.g., Gallant 1991: 143–69, drawing on Mediterranean models like Davis 1977 and Gellner and Waterbury 1977). David Small (1997: 220) suggests that "Although it may seem unusual to the historian to argue for patronage in ancient Athens (see Millett 1989), to an anthropological archaeologist there are some extremely strong cross-cultural arguments for its existence. Of prime importance is the environmental frame, one that has been witnessed in several cultures to require a dependence of small farmers on large landowners for subsistence insurance." This allows the model to override data, rather than following Weber in using an ideal type to highlight the peculiarities of the particular case, which can then modify the original abstraction (I. Morris 1997a).

Even as a description of contemporary relations, "Mediterraneanism" – a situation where a few men dominate landholding, the poor are dependants, and all men compete against each other for honor, which is focused on controlling female chastity – is suspect. Herzfeld (1980) shows that this model cannot describe the range of relationships in modern Greece. He suggests instead a spectrum, ranging from marginal, poor villages like Glendi on Crete, where the most valued ethic is an aggressive *egoismos*, to well-off villages like Pefko on Rhodes, where most men define *filotimo* (honor) as a cooperative value.[4] Projecting "Mediterraneanism" back to classical Greece, ignoring the Athenians' own statements, exacerbates the problems. Braudel (1972) and Le Roy Ladurie (1974) suggested that concentrated landholding like that in the modern countryside only goes back to the late sixteenth century AD. In the fifteenth century, small proprietors enjoyed a golden age of relatively even land distribution and considerable independence. Anthropologists like Davis (1977: 5–6, 12–15, 255) and Gilmore (1982: 178–9, 187), who assert that "Mediterraneanism" goes back to antiquity, ignore this evidence.

The limited classical Athenian data suggest that land was distributed relatively equally among citizens. In this regard, Athens had more in common with fifteenth-century Languedoc than twentieth-century Andalusia. We know roughly the area of cultivable land in fourth-century Attica and the approximate population, and can calculate the income that the leisure class needed each year to maintain their lifestyles. Robin Osborne (1991: 128–36; 1992) and Lin Foxhall (1992) independently suggest that if the richest 2,000 families earned their wealth solely from land, and if all crops were roughly equally profitable, then the top 7.5–9 percent of the citizens must have owned about 30–35 percent of the land. There are hints that 15–30 percent of the citizens owned no land or not enough to guarantee subsistence, leaving the remaining 60–75 percent of the citizens holding roughly 50 percent of the land. This is certainly unequal. Everyone in Athens knew that some citizens were richer than others. But in emphasizing inequality, Foxhall (1992: 159) and Osborne (1992: 25) overlook the more important point, that in comparative terms – the only way to judge such matters – this landholding pattern is *extremely* egalitarian.

Economic historians often quantify land distribution through Gini's coefficient of inequality, scoring distributions from 0, or total equality, where everyone holds exactly the same amount of land (as in the legend of Lycurgus' distribution at Sparta), to 1, where all the land belongs one person (Aristotle's vision of seventh-century Attica, where "all the land was in the hands of a few" (*Constitution of Athens* 2.2), would score close to 1). The Gini coefficient (*G*) is a crude index, but its merit is robustness. It works even in cases like Athens, where our data are few or far between. If we had more information we could produce a more nuanced Lorenz curve, but even with just three or four data points, we can calculate *G*, with a margin of error of no more than ±10 percent.

Calculating Gini coefficients for Athens requires many assumptions, and Osborne and Foxhall stress that their figures may underestimate elite landholding, since the rich needed the cash equivalent of *at least* this amount of land. But they also assume that the rich generated their wealth *solely* from the land, which was not the case. Edward Cohen (1992: 191–207) shows that many rich Athenians engaged heavily in what they called the "invisible economy," a world of cash transactions and loans, in which large sums circulated, and in which slaves, aliens, and women were active. Athenians kept quiet about involvement with banks and quick profits, which could easily be interpreted as seeking personal short-term gain over long-term benefits to the polis. They much preferred to represent themselves as honest middling farmers growing crops in the time-honored way. Osborne and Foxhall take this image at face value, but as Cohen shows, there were substantial profits in the invisible economy. I see no obvious way to weight the two uncertainties, and so proceed with Foxhall's and Osborne's figures as best estimates.

The Gini coefficient for fourth-century Athenian landholding is .39 by Foxhall's calculations, and .38 by Osborne's. Both figures are lower than any of the seven scores calculated for different parts of the Roman empire by Richard Duncan-Jones (1990: 129–42; *G* = .39 to .86). Roger Bagnall (1992) calculates scores for four nomes in late Roman Egypt; all are higher than the Athenian scores (*G* = .52 to .71).[5] The 1292 census from Orvieto in Italy (Waley 1968: 28) scores .62. Davis (1977: 88) calculates scores for seven rural Mediterranean communities in the 1950s–1970s; only two scored lower than Athens (*G* = .22 to .87). We could extend the list, but the point is already made: landholding was unusually egalitarian in fourth-century Athens.

Our data are poor, but calculating Athenian *G* scores and comparing them with other Mediterranean societies is surely better than assuming that the rich dominated landholding and that the poor depended on their largesse, despite the Athenians' own sense that this was untrue. And other indices point the same way. When data are too poor even for a Gini coefficient, historians often treat the proportion of the total arable land in the single largest estate as a rough guide. In Duncan-Jones's Roman cases, this ranged from 7.6 to 21.6 percent. The

largest known fourth-century Athenian estate, Phainippos' in
[Demosthenes] 42, covered just 0.1 percent of Attica's arable land (Ste.
Croix 1966). Alison Burford (1993: 67–71) suggests that this was as
big a farm as Athenians would tolerate, and Aristotle says that Solon
and other lawgivers limited the amount of land anyone could buy
(*Politics* 1266b17–19). Estates confiscated from Adeimantos and
Oionias in 415 were much larger, but these were on Thasos and
Euboea, subject states within the Athenian empire, not in Attica. The
Athenians in effect exported economic inequality.

Finley (1983: 41) suggested that Athens was characterized by a
broad mass of roughly equal landholding citizens. Many may have
struggled on the edge of viability, as Gallant (1991) argues, but they
were better off than those modern Mediterranean countrymen who
depend on patrons because their properties are below the minimum
needed for subsistence. Foxhall (1997: 132) notes that "A modern
Methana household would be somewhere near the bottom of the
thetes, on the basis of the figures which have come down to us," i.e.,
at the very bottom of the property classes set up at Athens in 594.
Athenians were relatively well-off.

The sources describe three main ways to work the land. A man
could (a) till it himself, with family and/or extra labor; (b) hire a super-
visor to oversee laborers; or (c) rent it out. The first was probably
normal for most citizens. Typical plots were just four or five hectares,
close to the minimum viable. Michael Jameson (1977/8; 1992) suggests
that Athenians responded to pressure on the land by buying a slave or
two to work alongside them, intensifying production. He sees the rich
as using larger gangs of slaves, with supervisors. Ellen Wood (1988:
42–80) argues that the rich preferred to rent out their land. Rather than
buying slaves, they would lease to poorer citizens, thus generating
income and also providing the poor with larger plots, without anyone
needing to turn to slave labor. Osborne (1988: 127) shows that a great
deal of land was rented each year, but all known renters were rich,
rather than Wood's tenant class. Much depends on how we interpret
the language used to describe labor. Jameson's argument, that words
like *ergates* and *ergazomenos*, literally meaning "worker," refer to
slaves, is the more convincing. But regardless of this philological
debate, Burford makes an important point (1993: 178): all our evidence
is for short leases, and "tenancy obviously did not create the long-
lasting relationships of landowner and tenantry typical of some land
tenure in England." Whether citizens worked alongside slaves on their
own land or as tenants on someone else's, there is no evidence for a
significant rural proletariat.

Paul Millett (1989) further suggests that state pay acted as a topping-up mechanism to see poor citizens through bad times without having to ask the rich for handouts. Once the poor had control of the state in fifth-century democracy, they effected a downward distribution of wealth through its institutions. According to Aristotle:

> Pericles was the first man to provide payment for jury service, as a political measure to counter the generosity of Cimon. Cimon was as rich as a tyrant: he performed the public liturgies lavishly; and he maintained many of his fellow demesmen, for any man of Laciadae who wished could go to him each day and obtain his basic needs, and all his land was unfenced, so that anyone who wished could enjoy the fruit. Pericles' property was insufficient for this kind of service. He was therefore advised by Damonides of Oe (who seems to have been the originator of most of Pericles' measures, and for that reason he was subsequently ostracized) that since he was less well supplied with private property he should give the people their own property; and so he devised payment for the jurors. (Aristotle, *Constitution of Athens* 27.3–4)

The story may be a rationalization, but it illustrates Athenians' perceptions of their circumstances. Poor citizens used democracy to vote themselves pay which did away with dependency on men like Cimon, who had made a fortune from booty in Athens' wars against Persia.

Small (1997: 220) holds that "the argument that state disbursements to the demos for service in the assembly or courts, or in the navy, offset their indebtedness cannot be supported, because we lack any statistical information (how much was paid out, how wide was the disbursement, what effect did it have on the commons' financial power, etc.)." This exaggerates the difficulties. Aristotle's quantification (*Constitution of Athens* 24.3; and even more so Aristophanes, *Wasps* 707–11) is problematic, but evidence for the size of the fleet allowed Rosivach (1985) and Gabrielsen (1994: 105–25) to generate a rough idea of the impact of pay. Contrary to the assertions of upper-class ancient authors, few Athenians supported themselves completely off state pay, but there was enough money in circulation to create a buffer against personal patronage.

In conclusion: there were patron–client dyads in classical Athens, as there are in the modern Mediterranean countryside. Finley (1983: 46) was surely right that Cimon was not the only Athenian who used his wealth to create a following. But the local context is important. "Patronage" is not a monolithic construct which a society either has or does not have. In Athens, popular power – political and financial

– circumscribed the opportunities open to the rich so severely as to transform patronage into something new. In the 460s, Pericles led a move away from Cimonian patronage by acting as a steward of the state's resources. Rather than imposing a distant analogy onto evidence it will not fit, we should take inspiration from Herzfeld's discussion (1984: 446) of another putative pan-Mediterranean model: "it is the framework, rather than the ethnographic [here, historical] studies it supposedly organizes, that should be rethought and perhaps even jettisoned in favor of something more productive."

Any reconstruction necessarily simplifies what must have been complex patterns of landholding, but the ideal of the *metrios* as an independent farmer does seem to conform reasonably well to lived experience. Some poor Athenians doubtless drifted into towns; others survived by combining intensive labor, including that of family members and slaves, on their own sub-size plots with renting land, seasonal wage-labor, and state pay. Life was hard for many, but freed from direct handouts from the rich, most citizens could imagine themselves, and others, as independent *metrioi*.

Given the weakness of our evidence, we cannot disentangle causal relationships between egalitarian landholding and middling beliefs. Agrarian equality need not generate political equality: in western Germany in the seventeenth century, for example, peasants held some 90 percent of the land, but it was princes, not the peasants themselves, who gained political power at the expense of the nobles (Brenner 1985: 56). In the fifth century BC, though, it seemed natural to men who had enough land to be largely economically independent of rich neighbors that they should be equal to them in honor, and should make decisions democratically. Simultaneously, it seemed natural to men who saw the state as a community of middling citizens that there should be a fairly even distribution of land, guaranteeing all citizens' independence, and that the state should act to extend this through pay and other forms of redistribution. Economics, politics, and ideology turned together in a tight circle. If the even distribution of land broke down, with some citizens becoming very rich and a large group depending on them, the middling ideology would falter, and democracy become untenable. As Hanson puts it, "Only a settled countryside of numerous small farmers could provide the prerequisite mass for constitutional government and egalitarian solidarity" (1995: 27). But the converse also held: if the middling ideology weakened, and oligarchy replaced democracy, it would be easier for the rich to concentrate land. All this came to pass in the third century and after, but in the fifth and fourth, the middling citizens could make the world and their view of it conform tolerably well.

The Excluded

The middling ideology constructed male citizen society as pure, homogeneous, and consensual. I have discussed citizens' perceptions of their relationships with the gods, the dead, and non-Greeks; I now turn to their relationships with people who were co-residents in the geographical community, but not members of the political community.

Women

The middling ideology relegated women to the margins. Even among the critics of democracy, only Plato (p. 124) and to a lesser extent Xenophon (p. 148) questioned this. Women had no political rights, and legal rights only through a male *kyrios* or "master" (usually her father, husband, brother, or son). Their economic rights were limited. Inheritance was patrilineal; if a man's only direct heir was female, she functioned as a residual heir, to be married off to the nearest male kinsman. The law only allowed women to make contracts for amounts valued below one *medimnos* of barley, enough to feed a family for a week. Resourceful women found ways around this (E. Harris 1992), but the assumption is clear: a woman was only connected to the community through her *kyrios*, because she was not a full being in the sense that a man was. Aristotle (*Politics* 1260a13) argued that while women did possess rational faculties, their minds lacked full authority (*akyron*). Consequently, nature equipped men to rule women (1259b2).

However, even in Aristotle's systematization, there were problems. Women were not citizens, since citizens were those who ruled and were ruled in turn (*Politics* 1275a23–24), but despite their exclusion, they made up half the population (1260b20). Their reproductive role further complicated matters – many cities (including Athens after 451/450) required double endogamy for citizen birth, which meant that Aristotle had to define "citizen mothers" who were also born from citizens on both sides of the family (1275b23). Cynthia Patterson (1986) and Edward Cohen (forthcoming) suggest that historians exaggerate women's exclusion by concentrating on politics and law. In doing so, however, classicists follow the models of Athenian men. Some women probably developed counterhegemonic discourses, but we cannot recover them. Johnstone (1998) shows that although many Athenian disputes involved women and slaves, the law required men to emplot their stories as conflicts between citizens; and Zeitlin (1996: 1–15, 341–416) demonstrates that even in tragedy, which gave women significant roles, male actors dressed as female characters were literally "playing the other," acting out male anxieties about gender relations, not giving voice to women.

Tragedy questioned gender roles by allowing women to intrude into politics, but also affirmed them through the disastrous results of such transgression. Women were set apart from men by the nature of their bodies, their concealment, their plotting, and their weaknesses. In comedy, Aristophanes imagined an Athens where women dictated foreign policy (*Lysistrata*) or took control of politics (*Assembly-women*), and even saw positive results; but his humor depended on the absurdity of the women's actions as inversions of all that made sense. In Praxagora's Athens feminine vices of promiscuity, gluttony, alcoholism, and deceit ran riot, in what Helene Foley (1982: 6) calls an "infantilized and privatized life of eternal festival." The order of women was the antithesis of *to meson*. In every way, the women in these plays produced by and for men reveal themselves as lacking middling attributes.

Ischomachus and His Wife

The most systematic discussion is Xenophon's *Estate Manager*, an early fourth-century philosophical text. Like Aristotle's account of *hoi mesoi* in the *Politics*, it pulls together the assumptions we find in other texts, and goes beyond them to construct an alternative. Xenophon begins by claiming to present a dialog between Socrates and Crito-boulos over managing an *oikos*, defined as all things which contribute to the individual's good. But most of the text has Socrates retell a conversation with Ischomachus, who had been pointed out to him as a man who was truly *kaloskagathos* (see p. 124 above). Embedded in this is yet another conversation, between Ischomachus and his unnamed wife.

Foucault (1985: 143–65) and Johnstone (1994) argue that Xenophon wrote the work not as a guide to farming but as a "manual of aristocratic style," describing "stylized labor" which set true gentlemen apart from those who worked for a living. Socrates was famously poor, and Xenophon has him insist that though he owns less than Critoboulos, Socrates is in fact richer, because he has all he wants, and Critoboulos does not (2.2–3). Socrates even persuades Critoboulos that a poor man can be good (11.3–6). Xenophon draws on middling ideas, but like the Old Oligarch (p. 132), deflects them in elitist ways. Ischomachus was clearly wealthy, and his good life depended on leisure.

Ischomachus says he married his wife when she was fifteen (7.5; Critoboulos says similar things at 3.13). He is proud that she knew nothing except spinning and ordering maids around (7.6). Socrates earlier told Critoboulos that a husband should train his wife in virtue (3.11), and Ischomachus did just this. He began her education "as soon as she was sufficiently tamed and domesticated so as to be able to carry on a conversation" (7.10). Xenophon used a common image of woman as an animal needing taming: Euripides' Medea (*Medea* 623) spoke of Jason's "newly tamed" wife, and Sophocles' Creon (*Antigone* 477–8, 579) of "bridling" Ismene and Antigone. Ischomachus' instructions deserve full quotation:

> Because both the indoor and the outdoor tasks require work and concern, I think the god, from the very beginning, designed the nature of woman for the indoor work and concerns and the nature of man for the outdoor work. For he prepared man's body and mind to be more capable of enduring cold and heat and traveling and military campaigns, and so he assigned the outdoor work to him. Because the woman was physically less capable of endurance, I think the god has evidently assigned the indoor work to her. And because the god was aware that he had both implanted in the woman and assigned to her the nurture of newborn children, he had measured out to her a greater share of affection for newborn babies than he gave to the man. And because the god had also assigned to the woman the duty of guarding what had been brought into the house, realizing that a tendency to be afraid is not at all disadvantageous for guarding things, he measured out a greater proportion of fear to the woman than to the man. And knowing that the person responsible for the outdoor work would have to serve as defender against any wrong doer, he measured out to him a greater share of courage. (Xenophon, *Estate Manager* 7.22–5)

Xenophon set up a series of polarities between the male and female spheres:

Male	Female
Agriculture	The house
Outside	Inside
Production	Consumption
Hardness	Softness
Aggression	Nurture
Endurance	Weakness

The gods gave each sex its qualities. Being indoors is good for a woman, but bad for a man; the reverse is true of being outside (7.30), which makes a body hard (5.4; 7.2). But Xenophon diverged from mainstream values in suggesting that a man could educate his wife so that these innate qualities became virtues rather than vices. The gods gave virtues (*aretai*) to each sex, and these were interdependent (7.27–8), so that a good marriage was a partnership (7.13). The properly trained wife blurred the boundary between male and female; at the end of Ischomachus' account, Socrates exclaimed "By Hera! By your account, your wife has a truly manly mind!" (10.1). Xenophon insisted that virtues could be taught, and that the truly good man could fashion a woman like himself. He made it clear that this was a novel attitude by having Critoboulos concede that he probably spoke less to his wife than to anyone else (3.12).

In believing that philosophical training challenged gender distinctions, Xenophon and Plato presumably followed their teacher Socrates. But even in Ischomachus' house, gender was hierarchical. A trained wife brought order to a house, converting her role as consumer into that of organizer (3.2–4), but the husband remained the one active producer, outdoors in public. Ischomachus lectured his wife on organizing the storerooms like those of a ship (8.11–23). The key was to train her appetites, so that she could control the weaknesses of her sex (7.6; 12.11–15), just as slave housekeepers must be taught self-discipline (9.11–12), and men must master their own desires (1.17–23). The trained wife wanted to work to increase the estate. Borrowing another popular animal image (p. 171 below), Ischomachus compared his wife to a queen bee, organizing labor in the household (7.17, 32, 33, 38).

But there was more to wifely work (*ergon*) than supervising servants. Ischomachus (10.2–13) said he once found his wife wearing cosmetics and high heels. He persuaded her that such deceits only made her *appear* more attractive, without affecting her being. To be truly beautiful she should dress modestly and get exercise walking around supervising slaves, or mixing dough and folding clothes. "I said that after she had exercised in that way she would enjoy her food more, be healthier, and truly improve her complexion. For compared with a slave, the appearance of a wife who is unadorned and suitably dressed becomes a sexual stimulant, especially when she is willing to please as well, whereas a slave is compelled to submit" (10.11–12). Greek authors regularly spoke of sexual activity between man and wife as "work" producing legitimate offspring, in contrast with *paidia* or "play," nonprocreative sex which did not (Carson 1990). Man's work was to produce food by plowing the land, and woman's to produce children through the *ergon* of legitimate sex, her body sowed through the sexual labor of her husband (DuBois 1988).

Woman's Space

Ischomachus' wife stayed indoors. When something had to be done outside, slaves should take care of it (7.35). Passages like this encourage historians to imagine the "oriental seclusion" of Athenian women, but this is clearly a mistake. We hear of women in many outdoor activities. Women had neighbors as friends, and vase paintings show groups of women. But the fiction of female isolation was central to male identity, and daily breaches created problems. Women's trips to wells and fountain houses were particularly frequent, and writers and painters represented these as places of frequent rapes and seductions. Aristotle (*Politics* 1300a7; 1323a5–7) complains that in democracies it is impossible to stop women from working, implying that prevention is desirable. Judging from Demosthenes (57.30–1), one response was to pretend that only foreign or slave women worked outside the home. Demosthenes' case required him to deny this, so he fell back on an alternative strategy: a free woman *could* do these jobs, but would not *want* to. It was the economic crisis after 403 which forced Euxitheos' mother and other free women to be wetnurses (57.35). Speakers used the topos of female seclusion to show what good men they were, diminishing other speakers' claims to middling manhood by suggesting that they could not control their women. This was, as Foucault said (1985: 22), "an ethics for men."

Household space was important. Athenian houses normally had several rooms around a courtyard, entered from the street through a narrow door (Nevett 1995; see figure 4.1). This threshold formed a major transition (see p. 125 above), and Lysias (3.6, 23) and Demosthenes (47.45–52) imply that there was also an inner area, the *gynaikon* or *gynaikonitis*, which was the special concern of women (cf. Lysias 1.9; Xenophon, *Estate Manager* 9.2–5). Nevett (1994) argues that Greek houses were sexually asymmetrical, with public areas used primarily by men, while the rest of the house was an appropriate area for women, but barred to outsiders. The theory was that women stayed in the least accessible parts of the house, "enclosed, hidden, guarded, dark" (D. Cohen 1991: 72). In an extreme case, a speaker claimed that his sister's and nieces' lives were so well-ordered that they were ashamed even to be seen by kinsmen (Lysias 3.6).

Gender was fundamental to the middling ideology. By virtue of their manhood, all citizens were equal; and real men kept their women out of sight. The house should join the city only through a narrow doorway; similarly, a woman should join civic society only through her *kyrios*. Experience might contradict this theory, but it still worked to marginalize and to fragment women. Whatever counterconsciousness women

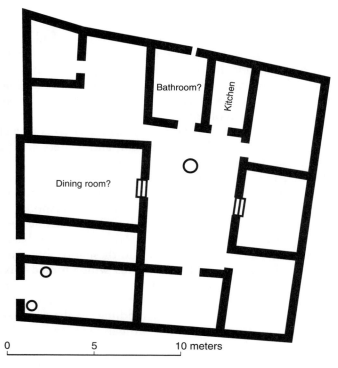

Figure 4.1 The floorplan of a typical Athenian house: Agora House C (based on *Hesperia* 20 (1951) 204, fig. 11)

developed was buried by Athenian male authors and in Athenian material culture (I. Morris 1998a: 211–20). The dominant culture denied women a place *es meson*, in the community of equal citizens.

Slaves and Metics

The exclusion of slaves was even more extreme. Athenian slaves were chattels, normally brought into Attica in small groups and sold. In Orlando Patterson's influential definition (1982: 13), "slavery is the permanent, violent domination of natally alienated and generally dishonored persons." Athens is the paradigmatic case. New slaves were inducted into the house with rites like those for new brides, and given new names, extinguishing their former identity. The law restricted violence against slaves (p. 117 above), but slaves could not bring suits against their masters. According to Aeschines (1.17), "It was not for the slaves that the lawgiver was concerned, but he wished to accustom you to keep a long way from hubris toward free men, so he banned hubris even against slaves."

Demosthenes (22.15) asserted that the difference between free men and slaves was that slaves answered for everything with their bodies. Comedies are full of casual humor about violence against slaves, and Aristophanes (*Wasps* 1298–9) jokes that Athenians call a slave "boy" (*pais*) regardless of his age, because he gets beaten (*paiein*). Slaves' testimony was only acceptable in trials if they had been tortured, again a subject for Aristophanic humor. In the *Frogs* (618–24), Xanthias offers a slave-boy up for torture, saying: "Tie him on the ladder, hang him up, beat him with a whip of bristles, take his skin off, twist him on the rack, pour acid up his nose, pile bricks on him. Give him the works." Aiakos accepts, responding "Why, fair enough. And if I hit your slave too hard and cripple him – the damages will be paid to you." However rarely litigants actually practiced judicial torture, audiences apparently found these scenes most amusing.

The ideology of slavery was stark. The slave was an *andrapodon*, a "man-footed creature," not fully human. Aristotle (*Politics* 1253b33–1254a1) argued that the only alternative to slavery was automation. Since that was impossible, then slavery was natural, and the gods had made certain people to be others' slaves. He suggested that

> that man is a slave by nature who is capable of belonging to another, and that is why he does belong, and he shares in reason so far as to apprehend it but not to possess it . . . Nature therefore wishes to make the bodies of free men and slaves different, the latter strong for necessary tasks, the former straight and unsuited for such occupations, but useful for a civic life. (Aristotle, *Politics* 1254b21–31)

He conceded that nonservile Greeks were accidentally enslaved in wars, and that some thinkers saw slavery as contrary to nature. Peter Garnsey (1996: 107–27) shows that Aristotle's theory in the *Politics* differs from his assumptions in the *Ethics*, and concludes that the full natural-slavery model, what Garnsey (1996: 107) calls "a battered shipwreck of a theory," was unique to the *Politics*. However, some of Aristotle's ideas recur in other texts. For Homer, it was a commonplace that the *doulion hemar*, "the day of slavery," took away half a man's worth. Herodotus (4.1–4) told a story that the Scythian men once conquered Media, and stayed there 28 years. The Scythian women, left alone, had sex with their slaves, producing sons. When the Scythian men returned, the slaves' sons fought them off, until the Scythians put down their weapons and attacked with whips. When the slaves' sons saw these, their essential nature came out, and they fled. The message is clear: the slave is less than a full man, lacking the qualities of the *metrios*.

There cannot have been fewer than 30,000 slaves in fifth-century Athens, and probably no more than 100,000. Slaves made up 10–30 percent of the population. But within these limits, there is no point playing what Finley (1980: 79–80) dismissed as the "numbers game." Slavery was widespread, and while there is no quantifiable evidence for employment, we hear of slaves in just about every role.

Some slaves were manumitted, though we have no idea how common this was. In many slave-owning societies, particularly in Africa, slavery works as a process, in which the slave may begin as a commodity but gradually enters the host community, acquiring kinship ties (Kopytoff 1982). But in Athens, this process was arrested early on. A freed male slave had little chance of becoming a citizen. Instead, freedmen who stayed in Athens became resident aliens (metics). Only a meeting of the assembly could confer citizenship on a metic. Naturalization of metics remained extremely rare until the second century (M. J. Osborne 1981–3), and Davies (1977/8: 111) observes that Athenians defended descent as the only criterion for citizenship with an intensity verging on paranoia.

Not all metics were ex-slaves; some were citizens of other poleis, who came to Athens for their own reasons. Many were poor, but some (including a select group of ex-slaves) were not. Cephalus, the Syracusan father of Lysias the orator and the host in Plato's *Republic*, was among the richest men in Athens, but neither his wealth nor his son's services to Athens led to citizenship. Metics had to pay a residence tax and place themselves under a citizen patron's protection. The story of Pasion, one of the few ex-slaves to become a citizen, is illuminating. We first hear of him around 400, as a skilled slave running a bank owned by citizens. Slaves and women were prominent in banking, perhaps because its role in the "invisible economy" exposed practitioners to suspicion of unhealthy involvement in the short-term order. But there were large profits to be made. Pasion prospered. By 393 he had bought his freedom and the bank. He made huge gifts to Athens during a military crisis, and was naturalized in the 370s. His son Apollodorus' language describing these gifts (Demosthenes 45.85) is revealing: he suggests that Pasion's generosity showed that by some miracle he really did share in the *charis* essential to Athenianness.

For Marxists, Athens is a prime example of the Slave Mode of Production, in which "The class opposition on which the social and political institutions rested was no longer that of nobility and common people, but of slaves and free men" (Engels 1972 [1884]: 180–1). But while we can call slaves a class in terms of their relations to the means of production, they never coalesced as a class. The best example is Thucydides' story (7.27) that in 413, when the Athenian fleet was destroyed and the Spartans occupied Decelea, more than 20,000 slaves took advantage of the situation – not by revolting, but by individual flight, only to be sold back into slavery. Cartledge (1985) explains the contrast between these events and the slave revolts of the Roman Republic or the West Indies through the fragmentation of Athenian slaves. Most slaves worked in tiny domestic groups which made organization difficult. Groups were larger in the mines, but these were heavily policed, and in the absence of mass enslavements of the Roman type, linguistic and cultural barriers further fragmented them (I. Morris 1998a: 197–211). Modern Marxists have to defend Engels' proposition that slavery was the fundamental contradiction in Athens by redefining such key terms as contradiction (Vernant 1980: 1–18) and class (Ste. Croix 1981: 63–9).

The worlds of the metics were similarly fragmented. When describing themselves in inscriptions or being honored by Athens, metics identified with their home poleis rather than as Athenian metics (Whitehead 1977: 27–34, 164–7). Many might have preferred Athenian citizenship to their own, but they accepted the principle of exclusion, and never acted as a group.

Conclusion: The Classical Middle

Most Athenian citizens imagined themselves as middling men. Using Munn's terminology, we might say that they drew their spacetime in closely around themselves, while claiming to produce for the polis a vast and eternal world of fame. They liked to believe that their community was homogeneous and consensual. And, the theory ran, since all citizens thought in much the same ways, it made sense for Athens to be a democracy. There were citizens who disagreed, believing that it was ludicrous to ignore dispararities in cleverness (or bravery, or wealth, or education) and treat all men born in the same town as equals. But most of the time middling citizens marginalized such men, who were more to be mocked than feared, particularly when the democracy controlled an empire. If a citizen did display attitudes undermining the middling principles, as Meletus thought Socrates did, and Demosthenes thought Meidias and Aeschines did, this bad seed had to be expelled. Speakers claimed that their rivals fell into this category, and dragged them through the law courts. Being too rich, too ambitious, too vocal, or any of a number of other aberrations attracted trouble, but one of the ideals of democracy was that it tolerated eccentricities which did not threaten it. So long as a man was at heart a *metrios*, then his peculiarities should be manageable.

There are important similarities between ancient and modern democratic ideologies, but there is no direct line from them to us. To understand Athens – that is, to say why Athenian social order rested on these particular beliefs about manhood, equality, ethnicity, and theology, rather than on other ideas which would have functioned equally well but would have produced a different world – we have to grasp the unique historical process through which Athenians made their middling male spacetime.

5

Antithetical Cultures

Introduction

Classical Athenian middling culture rested on a Strong Principle of Equality. The Athenian version of this strikes many today as misogynistic and chauvinistic, and no documented civilization had promoted chattel slavery on such a scale before. But the Athenians also insisted that within a small city-state, all local-born men were equals, regardless of any other criterion. That made the peculiarly Athenian type of democracy possible.

But what made classical middling culture possible? In this chapter, I follow Greek discussions of the good society back through archaic times. In doing so I broaden my argument from Athens to the whole Greek world. This is unavoidable. While nearly all classical literature comes from Athens, little archaic material does so. But it is also desirable: because as far back as written sources go, we see a version of the middling ideology, covering a large area. *To meson* was not an Athenian principle, but a Greek one. To understand Athenian democracy we need a panhellenic perspective.

I argue that from the eighth century on, the core features of the ideal middling man are already visible. But just as other visions of the good and other patterns of conversion constantly challenged classical Athenian middling culture, so too an alternative view opposed archaic middling beliefs. I call this the elitist ideology. This elitism, I suggest, was more virulent than classical critiques of democracy. The middling ideology drew a line around a community of equal male citizens, and denied the importance of other communities. Elitists, by contrast, identified an international aristocracy, including (to varying degrees) men, women, Greeks, easterners, gods, and heroes. True excellence only existed in this community: the champions of local community were mere peasants.

Discussing elite and popular culture in eighteenth-century England, E. P. Thompson suggested that "The plebeian culture cannot be analysed independently of [an] equilibrium; its definitions are, in some part, antitheses to the definition of the polite culture." Traditional historical approaches, Thompson argued, restrict us to the perspective of the aristocracy, who merely "saw beyond the park gates, beyond the railings of the London mansion, a blur of indiscipline." But, he argued, historians could reconstruct a "countertheatre of the poor" opposing elite constructions (Thompson 1991: 83, 41, 67–71). He saw the struggles of the poor against upper-class cultural hegemony as the major issue in eighteenth-century history:

> ruling-class control in the eighteenth century was located primarily in a cultural hegemony, and only secondarily in an expression of economic or physical (military) power. To say that it was "cultural" is not to say that it was immaterial, too fragile for analysis, insubstantial. To define control in terms of cultural hegemony is not to give up attempts at analysis, but to prepare for analysis at the points at which it should be made: into the images of power and authority, the popular mentalities of insubordination. (Thompson 1991: 43)

Like Munn's model of spacetime, the value of Thompson's concept of antithetical cultures lies in how it *fails* to fit the Greek case. Like Thompson, I put culture at center stage; but whereas his story is of popular resistance to a dominant aristocracy, in archaic central Greece it was would-be aristocrats who fought against the hegemonic culture of the ordinary citizens. I argue that ancient historians have read archaic poetry too literally, systematically mistaking one line of thought, what I call the elitist ideology, for an objective account of social relations, characterizing archaic poleis as "zero-sum" agonal societies dominated by feuding over honor. I suggest that the elitist position was a "dominant ideology" only in the sense that Abercrombie *et al.* (1980; 1990) use that expression: it reinforced solidarity *within* a would-be elite, persuading its members of the justness of their claims. But it had less influence on other groups. It was not a "false consciousness," duping people into accepting aristocratic authority. On the contrary, it was oppositional, working best outside the civic space, in the interstices of the city-state world, through interstate aristocratic ties and closed symposia; and a "middling" philosophy contested it on all points.

In this and the next two chapters, I make four arguments:

1   There were massive social changes across central Greece in the eighth century, producing a conception of the state as a community of "middling" male citizens.

2   Not everyone liked this. Those who did not argued that authority
    lay outside these middling communities, in an inter-polis aristoc-
    racy linked to the gods, the heroes, and the east.
3   Archaic social history is best understood as a conflict between
    these antithetical cultures.
4   At the end of the sixth century, the elitist ideology suffered major
    reverses. It became harder to claim wisdom denied to other citi-
    zens. Once this happened, citizen democracy became a plausible
    system of government.

The Literary Sources

28,000 lines of Homer and roughly twice that quantity of other poetry
survive from between 750 and 480 BC. Much of this is known only
from quotations in later authors or from Egyptian papyrus fragments.
The material is difficult to interpret. We know little about composition or performance, although many of the poems were in some sense
oral-derived. Later sources describe the poets' lives, but are largely
fictional. We cannot even take at face value what the poems themselves
say about their authors. Nagy (1990: 48 n. 40) suggests that much of
what comes down to us under specific poets' names was in fact formed
by broader processes: "the pan-Hellenic tradition of oral poetry
appropriates the poet, potentially transforming even historical figures
into generic ones who merely represent the traditional functions of
their poetry."
    Nagy argues that before the eighth century there was great regional
variety in oral poetry, but that by 700 some bards were traveling
widely. These poets observed discrepancies between local versions of
stories, and started producing poems relevant to all areas of Greece
but specific to none. They developed more fixed ideas about what their
subject matter, the vanished heroic age, had been like. They represented themselves not as recreating stories orally but as noncompos-
ing rhapsodes, reciting a fixed text. Local mythology was marginalized
in opposition to *alethea*, "unforgotten things," which authoritative
traveling bards claimed to know. As traditions coalesced, rhapsodes
retrojected Ur-poets into the distant past – first Homer, then Hesiod,
Archilochus, and a range of other personas, in bids for panhellenic
status. These poets were probably real people, but already in archaic
times they were submerged and reconstituted within the genre. Only
at the end of the sixth century, Nagy suggests, did individual poets
emerge as authors in anything like a modern sense (Nagy 1996).
    This is a controversial argument, but it accounts for some of
the peculiarities of the texts. The most striking is the poetry of

Anacreon. In addition to about 360 verses which go back to the sixth
century, philologists have known for centuries that more than 1,000
Anacreontic lines were written much later. A series of poets, active
into Byzantine times, stepped into a recognized poetic persona of
"Anacreon" to compose verse about love and wine (Rosenmeyer
1992). There are signs of similar processes in the 1,388 verses under
the name of Theognis. Lines 1103–4 seem to refer to early sixth-
century events, and line 894, criticizing the Cypselid tyrants of
Corinth, should date before 585. Most ancient traditions put Theognis slightly later, around 540; but line 775, worrying about a Persian
invasion, should belong in the fifth century. Further, 42 of Theognis'
verses are also attributed to other poets. Various explanations have
been put forward, but the most economical is to see the disputes
over authorship and over Theognis' city of origin (Megara in Boeotia
or Megara in Sicily?) as evidence for competing retrojections, and
the poems' chronological spread as reflecting a poetic persona of
"Theognis," into which anyone could step to compose in this genre
(Nagy 1985).

The mocking personas of fifth-century comic poets (pp. 135–6
above) descended directly from those of archaic iambic poets. The best
known, Archilochus, is often taken as the first individual poet,
reflecting on his own inner feelings. Yet his characters' names have
long aroused suspicion for the way they describe their bearers' functions in the poems. Miralles and Pòrtulas (1983: 22) argue that the
poems resemble the "trickster" genre known from all over the world,
in which a cunning Brer Rabbit figure with insatiable hungers outwits
opponents and unmasks their hypocrisy – he is "the outcast able to
cause someone else's casting out, the figure that has been excluded but
has the power to exclude." The most extreme casting out comes in a
paired set of traditions, first that Archilochus abused Lycambes so savagely that he hanged himself, and a second that Hipponax did the same
to Boupalos. It is possible that two poets drove their enemies to the
same form of suicide, but Rosen (1988b) more plausibly suggests that
these are two versions of a single literary topos. The fifth-century
comics Cratinus and Aristophanes represent themselves as heirs of
Archilochus and Hipponax, regularly alluding to their poems. Rosen
(1988a: 79) argues that "Cleon would have been for Aristophanes what
Lycambes was to Archilochus, and Bupalus to Hipponax." We know
that Cleon existed, but comedy mythologized him into a stock character (p. 136 above).

For my argument it makes little difference whether Lycambes and
Boupalos, or Archilochus and Hipponax, were real people or not. What
does matter is that they were all recreated in poetry as generic personas.

Several of Archilochus' characters appear in a third-century inscription (Kondoleon 1964), but rather than rooting them in external events, this only reinforces the picture of traditionalism. The text was set up by one Mnesiepes, a name meaning "he who remembers the words." We are dealing here with a long-term invention of tradition, as hellenistic Greeks appropriated old stories for their own ends.

These observations influence how we interpret the texts. We have to recognize continuities between certain groups of poets, and the constraining powers of genre. I see three implications. First, the main body of texts, from Homer's and Hesiod's hexameter epics, probably around 700, to the epinician odes, beginning around 520, can only be approached synchronically. Tracing an intellectual evolution within this corpus by stringing the poems together in supposed chronological order finds change by ignoring continuity, explaining all differences diachronically. Literary historians who do this act much like Mnesiepes, sharing in the invention of tradition.

Second, we cannot reconstruct specific events. Archilochus and Alcaeus may have been real people, singing about other real people, but when performing they stepped into persona. They sang through conventional tropes. When Alcaeus called Pittacus "fatty" and "base-born" (67.4; 75.12; 106.3; 129.21; 348.1; Kurke 1994) we should not assume that these insults were true, or even that the poet expected anyone to find them credible. A man singing Alcaeus took the part of the betrayed one, trying to recreate an ideal, homogeneous world by casting out the traditional enemy, just as Archilochus cast out of the community of decent folk his faithless lover Neoboule, a name implying "the fickle one," or as Hipponax cast out Boupalos the "bull-phallus" (Rosen (1988b: 32) more pointedly translates the name as "big-dick"), and as Demosthenes was to cast out Aeschines, with unlikely accusations of servile origin (Ober 1989: 268–79). The targets of abuse poetry may have been as real as Aeschines, but however these terms of abuse functioned, one thing is clear: if we take *anything* from these stories at face value, we stand to be seriously misled.

These are negative arguments, but the third is positive. Poetic tropes had immense cultural significance. We should think of these archaic traditions as co-existing discourses, always overlapping, but capable of being grouped into more-or-less coherent ideological hierarchies. In this chapter, I take up the arguments of Leslie Kurke (1992) that for analytical purposes we can simplify this shifting stock of attitudes into two broad traditions of thought, what I call the middling and elitist ideologies. The poets/traditions which I group as middling express many values which would later stand at the core of classical democracy; those I call elitist give voice to a radically opposed vision.

My distinction between middling and elitist voices is a simplifi-
cation, another ideal type (cf. p. 112). We cannot expect to subsume
all the attitudes expressed by a creative individual, let alone an entire
poetic tradition, under a single sociological rubric. For example, while
I treat Alcman as an elitist, in his fragment 17 he apparently adopted
a middling, iambic persona, calling himself the eater of everything
(*pamphagos*) who rejoices in common foods (*ta koina*) just like the
people (*ho damos*). Perhaps we see here disagreement over who
Alcman was supposed to be and what he stood for, an ambivalence
reflected in his "biographies." The tenth-century AD *Palatine Anthology* (7.18, 19, 709) calls him Lydian as well as Spartan, linking him
strongly to elitism, but the *Suda*, a roughly contemporary Byzantine
dictionary, made him a descendant of slaves, a quintessential iambic
outsider. There is no reason to suppose that either source knew more
about a historical Alcman than the other. Rather, the poets themselves,
along with categories like *to meson*, were contested.

Further, no creative artist always expresses the same outlook. I want
to move beyond the simple opposition of middling and elitist ideologies to a more flexible, but still one-dimensional, model of a spectrum
of values, with the middling and elitist ideologies as I construct them
representing its poles. Each poet might occupy not a point on this
spectrum but a span of its length, overlapping with areas occupied by
other poets. Some poets (particularly those like Phocylides, few of
whose verses survive) occupy a small space on the spectrum, present-
ing relatively consistent views; others, like Alcman, fill a broader
space. On the whole, the more we have of a poet's work, the more
space along the spectrum he or she takes up. The recent discovery of
new fragments of Simonides, for instance, expands the range of attitudes we can associate with him. One fragment speaks of gold, ivory,
and hubris, while another seems to tell a story of a journey to an island
to have sex with another man, leading to rejuvenation (21, 22 (West
1991/2)). What I separate as middling and elitist discourses might have
overlapped in practical consciousness. But there would have been
times, moments of conflict, when they separated into irreconcilable
ideologies; and there are indications in the texts that the poets did see
the world in terms of two competing models. I construct models to
clarify the most important themes in archaic social thought.

I could stay truer to the complexity of the evidence by abandoning
a one-dimensional spectrum for a multidimensional model, disaggre-
gating the attitudes toward class, gender, ethnicity, and religion which
I lump together to create my single middling-elitist spectrum. But as
in any exercise in making sense of reality, there is a trade-off. The
grander the model, and the more data it subsumes, the looser its fit
with reality, and the less well it accounts for every detail. The more

complicated and specific the model, and the more closely it describes the particular data, the less its explanatory power. The only way to appreciate the evidence in all its richness would be to reproduce the texts in full. Omission is the price of interpretation. We have to decide what kind of model we want on the basis of what questions we ask. For my purposes, a simple spectrum works best, accommodating much of the evidence but still providing a clear framework.

To some extent, the distinctions between middling and elitist poetry are generic. Scholars conventionally divide archaic poetry by meter into epic (hexameter), iambic (trimeter and trochaic tetrameter), elegiac (distich, or alternating hexameter and pentameter), and lyric (a variety of forms, sung to the accompaniment of the lyre or wood-wind). The boundaries were permeable, but lyric dominated the elitist tradition. In the middling tradition, lofty and serious thoughts about restraint and virtue were expressed in elegiac verse, and raucous humor in iambic, which, as Aristotle (*Poetics* 1449a) noted, imitated the rhythms of everyday speech. Hexameter was used in both traditions, with Homer in some ways standing at the head of the elitist ideology, and Hesiod of the middling; but in neither case is this clear-cut.

The Archaic Middle

The Concept of the Middle

Like fourth-century orators, archaic poets imagined *hoi mesoi* as self-sufficient farmers. Calling a man "rich" or "poor" excluded him from this group. And as in classical times, *to meson* was flexible. Xenophon and Aristotle adapted the language of the middle for their own ends; and in some archaic middling poets suspicions about the poor veer toward outright hostility. Theognis' attitudes are most complex (see Stein-Hölkeskamp 1997). He even urges listeners to "Drive the empty-headed vulgar herd with kicks, jab them with sharp goads and put a galling yoke on their neck; you will not find, among all the men the sun looks down on, a people that loves a master more than this one" (lines 847–50). His *mesoi*, like Aristotle's, form the middle of an aristocratic community, not a broad city-state. As we shall see, other poets, like Solon and Phocylides, conceived *to meson* more broadly; but some historians generalize Theognis' attitudes, assuming that archaic poleis excluded the poor.

They often link their readings of archaic poetry with the theory of a "hoplite reform," a putative change in weapons and tactics around 650 which gave new military power to an economic middle class, or *Mittelschicht* (e.g., Spahn 1977). The argument runs that when well-off farmers proved their military worth, aristocrats gradually granted them political rights. But the poor remained on the outside until 480, when Athenian rowers were decisive at Salamis. After this they too were brought into the demos, with Ephialtes' reforms in 462/1 recognizing this fact.

The evidence for these early fifth-century changes is poor (Ceccarelli 1993; debates in Morris and Raaflaub 1997), and that for the seventh century even worse (van Wees 1996; 1997; Raaflaub 1997). Nothing can be certain, but the *Mittelschicht* model perhaps reads archaic poetry too literally. When classical Athenians evoked *to meson*, it was an ideological category to which all citizens, regardless of wealth, could claim to belong. But we have no direct evidence for who counted as "middling" in any archaic polis.

When archaic poets used the word *demos*, they always meant either the entire male community, or, most often, all men except the rich; never all men except the poor (Donlan 1970). Philology gives no grounds for assuming a gradual economic widening of the category of *demos* from the seventh century through the fifth. Further, whenever archaic poets contextualize *to meson*, they link it with peasant attitudes. Commenting on Archilochus' fragment 19, a strident attack on elitist values (p. 185), Aristotle (*Rhetoric* 1418b) noted that Archilochus put these words into the mouth of Charon, a carpenter. Aristotle inferred that this was to avoid saying anything *agroikia*, "peasant-like," in his own voice. Hermann Fränkel (1975: 138) noted that at least since Homer (*Iliad* 3.60–1) "the carpenter was a stock example of the industrious man," locating these middling remarks firmly within the world of ordinary citizens. Sappho shared this assumption. She lamented that one of her circle, Andromeda, was obsessed with an *agroiotis*, "a peasant girl, dressed in a rustic smock, not even knowing how to pull her rags above her ankles" (57). In his comments on fragment 110, the grammarian Demetrius said that Sappho was mocking a rustic (*agroikon*) bride and bridegroom. What elitists did not like, along with anyone who did not like elitists, was assimilated to the peasantry. The middling ideology as expressed in archaic poetry was an upper-class literary refraction of what educated poets took to be the voice of the man or woman in the street.

The archaic middle may have had much in common with classical Athenian ideas: when middling poets sang about *to meson* they perhaps imagined a community to which *all* citizens, not just a small group of nobles, belonged. But there is little to gain from pushing the argument too hard. We just do not know how many citizens in archaic poleis realistically expected to be seen as *mesoi*. There is no good evidence that the *demos* gradually widened from the seventh century through the fifth, but the counterevidence I have adduced from Archilochus and Sappho is little better. The archaic middle may have included most local men, if only because in a world where the industrial base and "invisible economy" were so much smaller than in classical Athens nearly all Greeks were farmers (though we know little about how the land was distributed). But in the end, this issue may not be the most important one. However these poets imagined the middle, what we know about composition and performance suggests that virtually all surviving poems were "elite" in the sense that they were produced by and for elites of birth, wealth, and education. Unlike classical Athenian orations, which were delivered before mass audiences, most surviving archaic poetry was performed at small aristocratic drinking parties. The rivalry between the extant traditions was primarily a conflict within the highest social circles over what constituted legitimate culture. We have no direct evidence for what ordinary citizens thought about all this.

The elitist ideology belonged to a group which wanted to fashion itself as a ruling class by claiming to monopolize a high culture beyond the reach of the masses, while those wealthy men who sang about middling values in their symposia asserted their power by deliberately transgressing, conferring high status on values and objects excluded from the privileged aesthetics (cf. Bourdieu 1984: 40, 47–50, 88, 92–3). But the popular aesthetic was not simply a failure to grasp elitist tastes; it was a conscious refusal of them, among ordinary people as well as the elite. I suggest below that those aristocrats who adopted the middling position deliberately assimilated themselves to the values of ordinary citizens. They did not surrender their claims to constitute a ruling class: when a wealthy symposiast praised *to meson* it was a very different matter from when a poor farmer pronounced the same words. However, they claimed leadership as special members of the polis, not as a distinct aristocratic community of the kind which the elitist tradition created. Middling aristocrats did not struggle across the seventh and sixth centuries to create democracy. But the unintended consequence of their beliefs was that when the elitist ideology collapsed after 525, the general acceptance of middling values made democracy a real possibility; and whenever an oligarchy fell apart, as happened at Athens in 507, democratic institutions were a possible response.

Hesiod's Ascra

Hesiod's *Theogony* and *Works and Days* are among our earliest sources, probably dating around 700. They belong to broad east

Mediterranean theogonic and wisdom traditions, with strong parallels in the Near East (West 1997: 276–333, and pp. 167–8 below).

Hesiod describes himself as a Boeotian peasant, to whom the Muses gave the gift of poetry as he tended sheep (*Theogony* 22–35; *Works and Days* 633–40). He represents himself as the middling man incarnate – a righteous soul wronged by his own brother Perses, who, assisted by local lords, cheated him of his inheritance. The *Works and Days* warns Perses and the lords: Zeus is always watching, and will restore the cosmic balance.

There are important differences between Hesiod's good society and that of classical Athenian public speech, but many of the core elements of the middling ideology are already present in Hesiod (cf. Hanson 1995: 91–126). Like the classical *metrios*, Hesiod's good man is married with children (*Works and Days* 376–80, 695–705), ideally having land, two bulls (436–7), a slave woman (405–6), a hired laborer (602–3), and dependants of some kind, who receive rations (470, 502, 559–60, 573, 597, 607–8). Good men know that the gods fill the barns of those who order their works *metria*, "with due measure" (*Works and Days* 306). The gods reward hard work (303–14, 381–2); the only alternative is begging (397–400). The gods created two kinds of strife. One is evil and disruptive, but the other drives men to work hard (11–24). So long as men are pious, their labor contributes to the long-term good, perpetuating Zeus's cosmic order. But if they are impious, their gains are purely short-term, and corrode proper order.

Throughout, Hesiod's ideal community is male. Female forces had been disruptive throughout the history of the cosmos, and Zeus created women as a late addition, as part of the painful process of separating mortals from immortals (*Works and Days* 58–92; *Theogony* 570–612). Hesiod is angry, because while women cause evil and feed off men's labor, they are also necessary, and even desirable. Zeus made Pandora, the first woman, as a "beautiful evil" (*Theogony* 585), "like to a deathless goddess in face, like to a beautiful, lovely virgin in form" (*Works and Days* 62–3). Loraux (1993: 81–3) argues that for Hesiod there is nothing to Pandora but finery and surface beauty: woman is merely a trick. To perpetuate the world, men must live with women, who are drones (*Theogony* 594–601), using the lure of sex to win the fruits of man's labor (*Works and Days* 373–5), and draining his energy through their lusts (586). They linger idly indoors while men struggle outdoors in the winter (519–25).

A woman's greatest source of power is that gossip about her could dishonor her husband: "look all around you well, so that your marriage will not be a joke for your neighbors" (*Works and Days* 701). Women's sexuality is a threat, and needs surveillance. As in Athens, gossip was a major force for control (715, 719–21), even though Hesiod, like Aristophanes, criticizes others for gossiping too much. He advises Perses to avoid hotspots like the market and smithy (29, 493–4).

Hesiod never uses words such as *astoi* or *politai* for "citizens." His community consists of neighbors (*geitones*). This may mean that no concept of citizenship had yet emerged; but on the other hand, *geitones* had a long history as a poetic trope (e.g., Semonides 7.110; Alcaeus 123; Anacreon 354; Pindar, *Nemean* 7.87–9), continuing into fourth-century oratory (D. Cohen 1991: 85–90). Hesiod advises Perses that neighbors matter more than kin (*Works and Days* 343–5), and though the *philia* between brothers ought to be stronger than that between comrades (*hetairoi*), it is not always so (707–8). His neighbors live in a certain tension. A man must respect his equals but also be sensitive to slights, balancing rivalry with even dealings, helping friends and harming enemies (e.g., 23–4, 342–5, 709–13). He advises that "It's good to take a moderate measure from your neighbor, and good to pay him back in due measure [*metro*], or even more, if you can, so that if you're needy later, you'll find him sure" (349–51). A man should be welcoming but tough – "Let the price promised to a friend be fixed. And even with your brother, smile – and get a witness. For trust and mistrust alike will destroy a man" (370–2).

The good man's attitude toward "the poor" is quite like that of the classical *metrios*. They should not be mocked, but neither should they be trusted, for their empty bellies degrade them and make them lie (717–18; *Theogony* 26–8). Relationships with the rich were more complex. In the *Works and Days* (38–9, 202–12, 263–4), Hesiod calls the nobles (*basilees*) "gift-devouring judges" who rely on violence, not right: "The fools know neither how much greater the half is than the whole, nor what advantage there is in mallow and asphodel" (40–1) – that is, a fair share is better than unjustly seizing everything, and peasant foods are better than luxury. But in the *Theogony* (79–93), he praises the *basilees* to whom the Muses give honey-sweet tongues for settling quarrels. The whole people treat them like gods when they walk through their assemblies.

There is no contradiction here. The *Theogony* sets out the ideal of lordly power preserving the long-term transactional sphere, and the *Works and Days* shows it undermined by the world's unjustness. When the nobles show proper respect, the city flourishes; when they do not, Shame flees to Olympus and Zeus punishes the whole community. Hubris, another central fourth-century concern, then destroys the city (*Works and Days* 174–201, 213–18, 225–64, with Fisher 1992: 185–200, 213–16).

In both poems the *basilees* have a divine right to settle disputes, manifested in their eloquence and respect for gods and men. Here Hesiod's worldview is strikingly different from that of the fourth century. Hesiod's account of the *basilees'* virtues parallels Homer's in *Odyssey* 8.166–77, and both probably drew on a hexameter advice-poetry tradition (R. P. Martin 1984). Zeitlin (1986) shows that in classical tragedy, Thebes functioned as a poetic topos, symbolizing the place where things always go wrong. Ascra was just as much a topos: this was the place where Zeus's will, personified by the good *basilees* of the *Theogony*, is undermined by hubris. Marcel Detienne (1996: 55–67, 81–8, emphasizing *Theogony* 27–8) suggests that in Hesiod *aletheia* represents not abstract "truth" but the "magico-religious speech" of kings, poets, and seers, who have access to an invisible realm, and draw wisdom, justice, and prophecy from it. In the *Works and Days*, Hesiod judges the *aletheia* of the *basilees* by their behavior, and finds it wanting.

Like the *basilees*, Hesiod appeals to outside sources of authority, casting himself as a recent immigrant (*Works and Days* 633–40), an "exterior insider" (R. P. Martin 1992: 14) whose position at the edge of the community gives him privileged insights. Nagy (1990: 67) suggests that in Ascra "the function of the *basileus* 'king' as the authority who tells what is and what is not *themis* 'divine law' by way of his *dike* 'judgment' is taken over by the poem itself." The archaic elegiac poets form a bridge between Hesiod's attitudes toward the *basilees* and classical attitudes toward law as a product of civic deliberation. Elegiac poets frequently link themselves to semi-legendary lawgivers who went to Crete or Delphi to legitimate their codes, which they then wrote down and brought back within the community (Szegedy-Maszak 1978). Like Hesiod, these poets accept that law comes from divine sources outside the community, but unlike him, they want to ground it in the polis in concrete form, putting it increasingly under civic control. A third stage began around 500, as citizens took full authority for law. Martin Ostwald (1969: 55) argues that the sixth-century word for law, *thesmos*, implied "something imposed by an external agency, conceived as standing apart and on a higher plane than the ordinary"; while the fifth-century word, *nomos*, implied something "motivated less by the authority of the agent who imposed it than by the fact that it is regarded and accepted as valid by those who live under it."

For all its differences from the classical middling ideology, the *Works and Days* is the oldest example of a peculiarily central Greek conception of the good society as a community of middling farmers. That may be why it remained so popular in antiquity: along with the

Theogony, it provided a charter for the long-term religious/moral transactional order. In calling this vision "peculiarly central Greek" I do not mean to minimize its links with what Seybold and von Ungern-Sternberg (1993: 233–6) call "the east Mediterranean *koine* of the eighth century." But as so often with cross-cultural comparisons, the differences are as illuminating as the similarities.

There are strong parallels with Egyptian wisdom literature. The roughly contemporary *Instructions of Amenemopet* (Pritchard 1955: 407–10) agrees with Hesiod on many points, most strikingly that unrighteous profits are fleeting (9.16–10.13), but shares little of his male egalitarianism. Even in the superficially similar Middle Kingdom *Protests of the Eloquent Peasant* (Lichtheim 1973–80.I: 169–84), the good steward Rensi treats the peasant Khun-Anup in ways which would have been considered hubristic in Ascra. The tale begins with Khun-Anup's donkey eating a wisp of Nemtynakht's barley. Nemty-nakht then beat Khun-Anup and stole his donkey. Khun-Anup appealed to Rensi, who was interested because he thought Khun-Anup's beautiful rhetoric would entertain pharaoh. To prolong the speeches, Rensi listened in silence, forcing Khun-Anup to make nine petitions. After the third, the steward "had two guards go to him [Khun-Anup] with whips, and they thrashed all his limbs." In the end, Rensi granted the petition, but there is no suggestion that he treated Khun-Anup badly; indeed, Rensi is the fair-minded hero of the piece. The *Instructions of Onqsheshonquy* (Lichtheim 1973–80.III: 159–84) has stronger parallels with the *Works and Days*, but dates at least 500 years after Hesiod, and Peter Walcot (1962) argues that an Egyptian poet imitated the *Works and Days*. But even overlooking such issues, *Onqsheshonquy*, like other Egyptian texts, is far more hierarchical than the *Works and Days* (e.g., 7.12–15; 8.11; 17.17, 25; 18.7–8, 12).

The Hebrew prophets, particularly Amos, also have much in common with Hesiod (Walcot 1966; Seybold and von Ungern-Sternberg 1993). They describe themselves as outsiders to the traditional elite, mostly claiming to date to the eighth and seventh centuries. Amos (1:1), like Hesiod, calls himself a shepherd visited by God and inspired with a vision. The prophets criticize the concentration of wealth (Hosea 12:9; Isaiah 2:7). They accuse the rich of buying up the land (Isaiah 5:8; Micah 2:2) and being fraudulent landlords, cheating the poor (Hosea 12:8; Amos 8:5; Micah 2:1–2). As in the *Works and Days*, the rich judge the poor, and give decisions in return for bribes (Isaiah 1:23; Micah 3:11; 7:3). They spend their profits on luxurious buildings (Hosea 8:14; Amos 3:15; 5:11), clothes (Isaiah 3:16–24), and lifestyles (Isaiah 5:11–12; Amos 6:4). They hound the poor mercilessly. Israelite law theoretically canceled debts every seven years (Deuteronomy 15:1, 4), but the rich cruelly persecuted those in debt to them (Amos 2:6–8; 8:6). The prophets describe social and economic conditions much like Hesiod's Ascra, speaking for the poor (Isaiah 3:14–15; 10:2; 11:4; Amos 4:1; 5:12), insisting that God loves the meek, and that the rich are impious (Deuteronomy 10:18; Proverbs 22:22–3).

We might hypothesize a broad east Mediterranean egalitarianism in archaic times, or at least similarities between conditions in Israel and Greece. But there are two reasons to emphasize the differences between these regions as strongly as the similarities. The first is a source problem. Just as some classicists argue that "Ascra" is a literary topos and all the people in it traditional poetic personas rather than real individuals (e.g., Nagy 1990: 36–82; Rosen 1997), so too many Biblical critics (e.g., P. R. Davies 1992; 1996) suggest that much of the Hebrew Bible was written after the return from the Babylonian Exile in 539 BC, as a mythical charter for certain strands within Judaism. This was a period of intense conflicts between the descendants of those who were deported in 586 and those who had stayed in Israel, and both groups aggressively reinterpreted the past to justify their positions (e.g., Berquist 1995; Barstad 1996; Mullen 1997).

There is no agreement on whether social egalitarianism was a feature of Israelite society from the end of the Bronze Age, or was largely a fifth- and fourth-century fiction. But wherever we come down in this debate, it is even more important to note that while Hesiod, Amos, and Isaiah all pressure the elite to return to a way of life in keeping with Zeus's or God's expectations, there the similarities end. Whereas Hesiod's instructions call for the *basilees* to share power with the *geitones*, the prophets want the kings of Judah and Israel to reform the priesthood. King Hezekiah (717–687 BC) started this, but according to II Kings 22:8–23, king Josiah (640–609) found a hidden book (perhaps Deuteronomy) in 621, and forged a "second covenant" with God, setting the Israelites apart from their neighbors through purity laws. Egalitarianism and the good society are fundamentally different in the books of the prophets from what we see in Hesiod and the archaic Greek poets, being oriented toward religious prescriptions and the equal worth of souls, and much less toward secular control of law and diminution of social hierarchy.

Similar processes of population growth, concentration of wealth, and elite competition may have affected much of the Mediterranean in the eighth century. But their results varied, and by 700 a distinctive egalitarian middling ideology and sense of manhood was emerging in the Aegean.

The Elegiac Middle

The core of Hesiod's ideal persona recurs throughout archaic elegy, despite major changes in the sense of audience. Hesiod sang for all listeners, but he also knew songs limited to "those who understand" (*phroneousi*). He called these *ainos* (*Works and Days* 202), which meant "praise," and was aimed at a small group of "the wise." *Ainos* was also the root of *ainigma*, denoting coded speech. Theognis called his verses "*ainigmata* hidden by me for good men" (681). But despite being produced by and for aristocrats, "elegiac poetics in general amount to a formal expression of the ideology of the polis, in that the notion of social order is envisaged as the equitable distribution of communal property among equals" (Nagy 1990: 270). In this poetry some aristocrats came to terms with the polis of middling citizens while acquiring a useful weapon in intra-elite struggles. Poets and audiences could still see themselves as wise men possessing special wisdom and piety, which other citizens allowed them to convert into political leadership. What ordinary citizens said mattered: as in Ascra and classical Athens, gossip was a force for social control.[1] But this was no democratic ethos. Middling poets presented their symposia as the consummation of restraint and good sense,[2] in contrast to the elitists' desire for a distinct luxury culture, but "the wise" nevertheless claimed to know what was good for ordinary citizens better than the citizens did themselves.

To be in the middle was best. Solon called himself a shield over rich and poor; a wolf at bay among hounds; a lawmaker for good and bad alike; and a boundary stone at the midpoint between them (4c; 36.26–7, 18–20; 37.9–10; cf. 5; 24.1–4). Phocylides said simply "*mesos* in the polis I would be" (12; cf. 11), and for Theognis "the middle is best in everything."[3] Restraint and moderation were basic, expressed first as *aidos*, later as *sophrosune* (Cairns 1993: 160–75; North 1966: 12–18). The *metrios* needed moderate landed wealth, summed up by Phocylides in terms reminiscent of Hesiod: "If you want wealth, have a fertile farm: for they say that a farm is the horn of Amaltheia" (7). Theognis wished only "to be rich without evil cares, unharmed, with no misfortune" (1153–4). As in Hesiod and in the fourth century, the middle was defined against the poor as well as the rich. Men were constrained by poverty (Solon 13.41; Theognis 173–82, 383–98, 649–52, 1062), and poverty's victim "cannot say or do anything, and his tongue is tied" (Theognis 177–8). According to Theognis (267–70, 621–2, 699–718, 927–30; cf. Alcaeus 360), all men despised the poor, whose hungry bellies were to blame for their lack of dignity and self-control (Archilochus 124b; Hipponax 128, with West 1974: 148). For Solon, sufficiency ("luxury in belly, sides, and feet") was equal to the silver, gold, land, and horses of the rich (21.1–4).

If moderate wealth was the precondition for the middling life from the seventh century through the fourth, the ogre of greed was consistently its enemy. Some men pursued wealth by any means, setting no limits (Solon 13.71–6 = Theognis 227–32). Solon (13.7–11) and Theognis (145–8, 465–6, 753–6) agreed with Hesiod that unrighteous gains brought only ruin. Wealth and hubris were inseparable (Theognis 603–4, 731–52, 833–6, 1103–4). Solon described a decline into disaster very like Hesiod: "excess breeds hubris when great wealth follows men who do not have a complete mind" (6.3–4). Hubris then destroys the polis: "the citizens themselves, obsessed by greed, are prepared to ruin this great city" (4.5–6). In 594 Solon checked the slide by giving Athens *eunomia*, a "well-ordered world" which "makes all things wise and perfect among men" (4.39).

Archaic lawgivers paid attention to regulating women, and seventh-century iambus intensified Hesiod's misogyny. In *Works and Days* 60–1, Hephaistos created Pandora by mixing earth and water. In fragment 7 Semonides separated the two elements, having each represent one type of woman, then added a further eight animal types – the sow, vixen, bitch, ass, cat, mare, ape, and bee. Of these, only the bee was a positive image (cf. p. 148). Semonides played with traditional structures: animal fables were stock devices in iambic. Loraux (1993: 91) notes that the number of races was significant too: "Nine women for the suffering of men and the tenth for his joy, just as the Greeks endured nine years facing Troy, and Odysseus lasted nine years far from Ithaca, before procuring victory or return: these are symbolic numbers." Explicitly rooting his words in this mythological frame, Semonides ended the poem by referring to those who died at Troy for Helen's sake (7.117–18).

Semonides followed Hesiod in asserting that Zeus first made man without woman (7.1–2), and that woman was the greatest ill of all (7.96–7, 115–16). The evils of the races of women also elaborated the Hesiodic code. The woman of earth and the ass did nothing but eat, which was indeed true of women in general (7.25, 46–7, 101–2). The ass and cat offended by their lusts (7.48–9, 53–4), while the mare offended equally by her pickiness, only taking a mate under compulsion (7.62). The sow (7.2–6) revolted Semonides by sitting around in unwashed clothes in a house defiled by excrement, and the mare again upset him by doing the opposite, washing two or three times each day (7.63–4). But his most frequent complaint was about gossip. The vixen, bitch, and cat noticed everything, spreading evil reports and causing trouble (7.7–15, 55). Whether a man tried persuasion, threats, or smashing her teeth out with a stone, the bitch would not shut up (7.16–18). Semonides' highest praise for the bee was that she got no pleasure from gossiping about sex (7.90–1). But gossip was nonetheless crucial: nothing was better than being praised for having a good wife, as the woman of the sea could sometimes trick a stranger into believing of her (7.29–31), or worse than being laughed at for having one as ugly as the ape (7.74; cf. 6; 7.108–11).

Phocylides (3) boiled this tirade down to eight lines, which suggests that the tradition's outlines were well enough known that he could create the desired effect merely by alluding to it:

> And Phocylides said this: of four kinds are
> The tribes of women. There's the bitch, the bee,
> The savage-looking sow, and the long-maned mare.
> The daughter of the mare is swift, a runaround, and fair of form;
> The savage-looking sow's, neither good nor bad;
> The bitch's, bad-tempered and uncouth; but the bee's
> Is a good housewife and knows her work.
> It's her, dear friend, you should pray to get in desirable marriage.
> (Phocylides 3)

The ideal archaic middling man, like his Hesiodic predecessor and the good citizen of fourth-century orations, was under constant threat from excluded margins – women, the poor, and the rich, all sharing lack of control. To explore the dangers they posed to the *mesos*, I now turn to the elitist tradition.

The Elitist Tradition and the Conflict of Values

Homer's Heroes

In a sense, the elitist tradition begins with Homer. Our texts probably go back to late eighth-century oral-dictated poems (Janko 1998), albeit refracted through subsequent recensions and generations of Alexandrian scholarship. The *Iliad* and *Odyssey* describe the adventures of an ancient race of heroes. The former focuses on Achilles and a few critical days during the Trojan War; the latter, on Odysseus' return home after the fall of Troy. The stories are set in the distant past, but, returning to Grote's position (pp. 83–4 above), most historians now assume that the social background reflects eighth-century conditions (e.g., Raaflaub 1998). The one certainty, though, is that this is an imaginary world, what oral poet(s) in one eighth-century tradition thought a heroic world *ought* to have been like. They drew primarily on

contemporary values, constrained by generic and traditional expectations. The poems are thus tremendously valuable guides to eighth-
century thought, but there is no way to strip away the poetic
construction of a vanished world to find a documentary source for any
particular time or place (cf. I. Morris 1997b). Nagy (1979: 7) rightly
insists that "this poetic tradition synthesizes the diverse local traditions of each major city-state into a unified Panhellenic model that
suits most city-states but corresponds exactly to none." The heroic age
was a time when handsome, brave, strong, rich, and aggressive nobles
protected their followers. The weak accepted that they depended on
the heroes for their survival, and followed them into destructive wars
rather than seeing them dishonored.

Arjun Appadurai (1981: 201) observes that despite the importance
of historical narratives in legitimating the present, the past is rarely "a
boundless canvas for contemporary embroidery." There are always
constraints on what stories about the past are credible. The Indian
priests and villagers Appadurai studies know of official histories produced by literate elites, and accept that their own accounts must be
consistent with these. But there was no such written tradition in Dark
Age Greece. Instead, poets learned about the past from goddesses, the
Muses.[4] The more the Muses inspired a singer, the better his words,
and the more accurate his tale could be assumed to be. Odysseus
praised Demodocus' account of the fall of Troy by saying:

> Demodocus, above all mortals beside I prize you.
> Surely the Muse, Zeus' daughter or else Apollo has taught you,
> for all too right following the tale you sing the Achaians'
> venture, all they did and had done to them, all the sufferings
> of these Achaians, as if you had been there yourself or heard it
> from one who was.
> (Homer, *Odyssey* 8.487–91)

Odysseus had been at Troy, and so could judge the song's accuracy;
yet ordinary Phaeacians, who had not, also reckoned Demodocus the
best of poets (8.472). Throughout the *Odyssey*, audiences judge poets'
quality and truthfulness (e.g., 1.351–2; 8.496–8), letting them know
very clearly when they fall short (1.336–42; 8.536–41). A poet's
account had to conform with audience expectations of what the heroic
age was like, which could be fantastic, but ultimately had to rest on
their own experience of how the world worked. The poet "turns the
ideals of the present into the reality of the imaginary heroic past" (van
Wees 1992: 253).

But within these limits, there was room for competing historical
visions. Nagy (1979: 65) argues that Demodocus' song (*Odyssey*

8.72–82) reveals knowledge of a different *Iliad*, focusing not on Achilles' anger against Agamemnon, but on a quarrel with Odysseus; and Lord (1960: 194) even suggested that there was an *Iliad* where the embassy to Achilles in book 9 succeeded. Herodotus (2.112–20) knew another story, that instead of sailing to Troy with Paris, Helen spent ten years in Egypt. He says he learned this from Egyptian priests, but Stesichorus (192) already knew it in the sixth century, and perhaps also Hesiod in the seventh (fragment 358).

Those who liked Homer's representation of the heroic age encouraged it to be written down and promoted it as the authoritative account, fixing this vision of the past in a time when values were changing quickly (pp. 261–6 below). Homer's magnificent language showed that he was the most divinely inspired, and therefore most truthful, of all bards. I have argued (I. Morris 1986) that Homer presents the heroic age as a time when noble warriors ruled society with an iron grip, and that this picture was exceedingly convenient for eighth-century aristocrats.

The heroes were "touchy" (van Wees 1992: 109). They saw insults everywhere, responding to perceived slights with threats or violence. In a seminal study, Arthur Adkins argued that Homer had no words to criticize violence; *kakon* or *aischron*, "bad" or "disgraceful," only applied to men who showed weakness. Adkins concluded that

> If we examine the culture revealed by these terms of value, we discover a society whose highest commendation is bestowed upon men who must successfully exhibit the qualities of a warrior, but must also be men of wealth and social position . . . This is an aristocratic scale of values: but . . . it is reasonable to conclude that such a scale of values was generally acceptable. (Adkins 1960: 34)

Adkins suggested that Homeric society was in a constant state of struggle. The weak needed protection from the strong. Without heroes to defend them, families would lose their possessions and honor, beggars would be sold as slaves, and communities would be destroyed by rivals. Homeric society "was still much more an agglomeration of individual 'Cyclopean' households than an integrated society" (Adkins 1960: 54).

Van Wees (1992: 28–58) shows that much of Homer's society is internally consistent, as well as overlapping with later Greek practices. Homer made his heroes plausible by taking aspects of contemporary life and pushing them to extremes. The heroes are bigger, braver, stronger, and angrier than any men could be: yet they remain recognizable, acting in ways which people might believe that such big,

brave, strong, and angry men would act. The values of heroic life
overlap with those of Ascra, but Homer usually offers different moral
judgments. Hesiod insists that Zeus enforces morality, and reviles
basilees who give biased judgments, but Homer assumes that while the
gods and nobles like to be fair, "obligations to kin and friends have
priority over demands of justice" (van Wees 1992: 146). Similarly, all
Greek authors see hubris as a crime, and Fisher (1992: 176) concludes
that the word's overtones in Homer are "entirely compatible with
those found in our study of *hybris* in classical Athens." But there is
again a difference: Homeric hubris is punished not by the community,
as in Athens, or by Zeus, as in Ascra, but by an individual hero's violence (*bie*) or cunning (*metis*). If a victim of hubris cannot fight back,
he is more dishonored than the perpetrator.

In a key passage, Agamemnon decides to test Achaean morale when
the war is going badly by calling an assembly and telling the troops
that he wants to abandon the siege. The overjoyed Achaeans break
ranks and run for the ships, but are blocked by Odysseus. He persuades the *basilees* with soft words, and the mass with blows and abuse
(*Iliad* 2.188–206). When the Achaeans resume their places, the lower-
class Thersites criticizes Agamemnon and the other *basilees*. Odysseus
rounds on him, shouting:

"Stop, nor stand up alone against princes.
Out of all those who came beneath Ilion with Atreides
I assert there is no worse man than you are. Therefore
you shall not lift up your mouth to argue with princes,
cast reproaches into their teeth, nor sustain the homegoing . . .
If once more I find you playing the fool, as you are now,
nevermore let the head of Odysseus sit on his shoulders,
let me nevermore be called Telemachos' father,
if I do not take you and strip away your personal clothing,
your mantle and your tunic that cover your nakedness,
and send you thus bare howling back to the fast ships,
whipping you out of the assembly place with the strokes of indignity."
 So he spoke and dashed the scepter against [Thersites'] back and
shoulders, and he doubled over, and a round tear dropped from him,
and a bloody welt stood up between his shoulders under
the golden scepter's stroke, and he sat down again, frightened,
in pain, and looking helplessly about wiped off his tear-drops.
Sorry though the men were they laughed over him happily,
and thus they would speak to each other, each looking at the man next to
him:
"Come now: Odysseus has done excellent things by the thousands,
bringing forward good counsels and ordering armed encounters;
but now this is far the best thing he has ever accomplished
among the Argives, to keep this thrower of words, this braggart

out of the assembly. Never again will his proud heart stir him
up, to wrangle with the princes in words of revilement."
So the multitude spoke.
(Homer, *Iliad* 2.247–78)

This beating and the army's response have more in common with
Egypt than with Ascra (p. 167 above). Thersites was the paradigmatic
kakos, "bad man"; as Adkins explained (1960: 42), "to be *kakos* is to
be the sort of person to whom *kaka* [bad things] may be done
with impunity." The Achaeans are sorry, presumably because they do
want to go home, but feel that Thersites is the one who committed
hubris, in speaking up. By beating him, Odysseus restores the proper
order.

Classicists debate what this episode tells us about eighth-century
society; some think Homer questions the *basileis* by having Thersites
speak at all (Rose 1988; Thalmann 1988), and hear a critical tone
throughout the poems (e.g., Rose 1992: 43–91; 1997). But Nagy (1979:
259–62) sees a more subtle commentary on praise, blame, and the
social order in this Achaean assembly. He notes that Homer describes
Thersites' rebuke of Agamemnon as *neikos* (2.224), "blame," and that
in the past Thersites had made *neikos* against Achilles and Odysseus
(2.221). *Neikos* was a key word for describing iambic "blame poetry,"
like Archilochus' or Hipponax's verse; poetry which, in mocking
heroic values, was the opposite of Homeric praise poetry (Nagy 1979:
223–5). Like Archilochus, Thersites tries to get laughter out of others'
claims of social superiority (2.215). But Nagy suggests that in this
episode "Epos gets the last laugh on the blame poet" (1979: 262).
Homer provides a metapoetic commentary, and perhaps his own view
of the kind of (middling) man who would appreciate iambus. In opposition to a race of heroes defined by beauty, Thersites was "the ugliest
man who came beneath Ilion. He was bandy-legged and went lame on
one foot, with shoulders stooped and drawn together over his chest,
and above this his skull went up to a point with the wool sparsely
grown upon it" (2.216–19).

We are dealing with what Rose (1992: 160) has called "matters of
discursive conflict." Rosen (1990; 1997) sees Hesiod's account of his
one sailing trip, to sing in the funeral games of the hero Amphidamas
at Chalcis (*Works and Days* 618–94), as the reverse of the Thersites
episode, asserting the superiority of didactic over heroic poetry. The
opposition is explicit in *The Contest of Homer and Hesiod*, which has
the poets meet and compete at Chalcis. The audience wants to give
Homer the prize, but the judge awards it to Hesiod, because he praises
peace not war. The text presents the contest as a story told by the
Delphic oracle to the emperor Hadrian around AD 130. In such an

open-ended poetic tradition, it makes little sense to ask whether the text is genuine or a forgery; but it does matter whether the story went back to archaic times. The basic plot appears in a third-century BC papyrus, but there is nothing earlier. This raises an important issue, of how far it is possible to trace ideas back beyond their first textual attestation into effectively prehistoric contexts. I return to it on p. 233 below. But for my argument here, what matters most is that an elitist archaic poetic tradition appropriated Homer's heroic vision as one pillar to support a set of values in direct contradiction to those of the middling tradition.

Hoplites and Heroes

The hero's authority depended on military prowess. At the height of the battle for Troy, Sarpedon asked

> "Glaukos, why is it you and I are honored before others
> with pride of place, the choice meats and the filled wine cups
> in Lykia, and all men look on us as if we were immortals,
> and we are appointed a great piece of land by the banks of Xanthos,
> good land, orchard and vineyard, and ploughland for the planting of
> wheat?
> Therefore it is our duty in the forefront of the Lykians
> to take our stand, and bear our part of the blazing of battle,
> so that a man of the close-armored Lykians may say of us:
> 'Indeed, these are no ignoble men who are lords of Lykia,
> these kings of ours, who feed upon the fat sheep appointed
> and drink the exquisite sweet wine, since indeed there is strength
> of valor in them, since they fight in the forefront of the Lykians.'"
> (Homer, *Iliad* 12.310–21)

The image of the "good battlefield" was itself a rhetorical battlefield between the elitist and middling traditions. Proponents of a hoplite reform argue largely that the shift from individual heroes in Homeric battles to serried ranks in some seventh-century poets means that there must have been a tactical change around 650. But this evidence is itself implicated in competing constructions of the ideal warrior, and through this, ideals of the citizen and the community. Whatever the tactical innovations of the seventh century, in reading these poems we confront a *martial imaginary*, using images of battle to evoke whole ways of life. It is naive to act as if we can simply read away the poets' intentions to reach an unmediated military truth.

Historians often use the disappearance of references to heroic-style warfare to date the hoplite reform. The problem is that we only find heroic scenes in elitist poets, and hoplite scenes in middling poets. For example, Tyrtaeus praises both the virtues of moderation and the excellence of fighting in a hoplite phalanx; Mimnermus, on the other hand, extols wine, love, and general high living, but his sole surviving martial poem (14) describes in epic tones a hero rushing forward to rout Lydian cavalry.

Compare Alcaeus:

> . . . and the great house is agleam with bronze, and all the roof is full-dressed for the war god with shining helmets; white horse-hair plumes wave down from them – adornments for the heads of men. Bright bronze greaves hang round and hide the pegs – a fence against the arrow's might.
>
> Corslets of fresh linen and hollow shields lie thrown upon the floor. Beside them are blades from Chalcis, beside them many a belt and tunic. These we may not forget, since first we stood to this our task. (Alcaeus 140)

In describing the arms and armor hanging on the wall, Alcaeus uses epic terminology (*kunia, lophos, knamides*), which, as Denys Page (1955: 222) pointed out, is very like the way Herodotus (1.34) later describes Lydian armor. As well as heroizing, Alcaeus perhaps evokes the east – a technique central to elitists' self-perceptions. Anne Burnett (1983: 123–6) suggests that the first part of this poem creates a mood of calm and order, appropriate for a peaceful, shared feast; but in the second part, Alcaeus changes the pace. We move to a jumbled heap of weapons on the floor, described in non-epic terms, particularly *spathe*, the word for sword in comedy and colloquial speech. The contrast between ordered heroic arms and disordered everyday ones perhaps alludes to Alcaeus' main theme, the sordid fragmentation of the ideal fellowship, and civil war on Lesbos. The hero's weapons stand for the perfect aristocratic community, now broken up.

Rather than being objective accounts of military techniques, these passages are synecdochical: the part stands for the whole. When poets refer to heroic warfare, they evoke a larger package of heroic values, loyalties, and dependencies. Elitist poetry took for granted the Homeric appropriation of the heroic age, and the heroic warrior became a potent symbol. Like the Homeric battle tradition, Mimnermus and Alcaeus pushed the unpleasant real-world need for masses of infantry into the background.

Middling poets took a different view. For them, as for classical Athenian speakers, the phalanx stood for citizen solidarity (e.g., Tyrtaeus 10, 12; Callinus 1; Theognis 1003–6). Archilochus mocked the heroic model by describing in epic language how he abandoned his "blameless armament" (*entos amometon*) to a Thracian tribesman – but Archilochus didn't care, and found the whole episode amusing (5). He preferred a short, bowlegged man with his feet firmly on the ground to a tall, elegant, heroic officer (114). Begging was the only alternative to hard work in Hesiod (*Works and Days* 397–400), and to standing your ground in Tyrtaeus (10.1–14). These are not transparent accounts of tactical changes: they are exchanges between two poetic traditions, another example of Rose's discursive conflicts.

Luxury, Love, and the East

The heroic warrior was a useful image for elitist poets, but much of the lyric world was a far cry from the slaughterhouse of Troy. It was a place of delicacy, elaborate manners, sweet perfumes, and wealth.[5] All these themes were present in the heroic age, and Sappho (44.5–10) explicitly associated wealth with the heroes; but seventh-century poets shaped them into a new kind of elitist culture. Page DuBois (1995: 45–6, 192) sums this up by saying that while the poems of "the Sapphic corpus . . . , saturated with Homeric references, embody an awareness of the epic context, its militarism, its atmosphere of masculine combat and struggle," nevertheless "Sappho . . . takes up the discourses of Homer, Hesiod, myth and ritual, and while alluding to them, constructs another reality of nocturnal freshness, beauty, and yearning."

Sappho's simple statement "I love luxury" (*habrosyne*: 58.25) was the direct opposite of Phocylides' "*mesos* in the polis I would be." Luxury did not just make life pleasant – it collapsed the distances between the aristocracy and the gods, the heroes, and the great rulers of Lydia. Sappho described the gods as dressed in gold, living in a golden house, pouring drinks from golden vessels, and coming to worshippers who made offerings in similar golden cups (1.7–8; 2; 33; 54; 96.27–8; 103.6, 13; 123; 127). Bruno Gentili (1988: 83–4) observes that Sappho merged divine and mortal luxury in personal epiphanies, claiming to have "*privileged* religious experiences bringing closer communion with the god." Luxury bridged the gulf between mortals and gods. Sappho and her friends imagined themselves in a realm more like the heroic age than the seventh century. The gods moved among them. Sappho identified with Aphrodite as strongly as Odysseus did with Athena, and in fragment 129, Alcaeus "stands in an almost priestly relation" to Zeus, Hera, and Dionysus (Burnett 1983: 161). Lavish display made the aristocracy something more than human.

True aristocrats were comfortable using the east, moving within their own interpretation of Lydian culture. Homer had anticipated some of this. Classicists often argue that Homer makes no distinction between Greeks and Trojans, but Hilary Mackie shows that the *Iliad* "imagines a complete ethnography of speaking for either side," with Achaean speech being more outward-directed and aggressive then Trojan. She concludes that the "Differences drawn up between Greeks and Trojans are numerous, variable, and subtle, and they are not obviously reducible to any one evaluative scheme;" but, she continues, "In some respects the *Iliad* 'feminizes' the Trojans" (Mackie 1996: 5, 9, 80). The Trojans were softer and more luxurious than the Achaeans.

Homer's Phoenicians are equally interesting. Some were honest (*Odyssey* 13.272–86), though more often they were petty crooks and hucksters (e.g., *Iliad* 23.741–4; *Odyssey* 14.288–9; 15.415–16, 448–9, 459–70; Winter 1995). But Phoenician objects were wonderful. Menelaos rated a Phoenician silver krater given him by the king of Sidon as the "most splendid and esteemed at the highest value" among his treasures (*Odyssey* 4.613–19 = 15.113–19). A similar Sidonian silver krater "for loveliness surpassed all others on earth by far" (*Iliad* 23.740–8), and an ivory horse's cheek piece stained purple by a Maionian or Carian was fit to be laid up for a king's treasure (*Iliad* 4.141–5). Menelaos had spent eight years in Cyprus, Phoenicia, Egypt, Ethiopia, and Libya gathering treasure, which, it seemed to Telemachus, made his palace rival Zeus's – though Menelaos himself, unlike later elitist poets, quickly denied this (*Odyssey* 4.71–85). His beautiful wife Helen, Homer's most sensuous and erotic character, was also linked to the east. Her silver and gold treasures came from Egyptian Thebes, and she was skilled with Egyptian drugs (*Odyssey* 4.120–32, 226–32).

Lyric poets took Homer's notions of eastern softness and splendid material culture much further. Oriental luxury and power, by the late seventh century usually Lydian rather than Phoenician or Egyptian, became central themes,[6] particularly in emphasizing another Homeric theme, the beauty of the elite. For Sappho, the greatest praise for a woman was to say that she stood out even among the Lydian women (96.7–8). Sappho compared Anactoria's attractions to a host of Lydian chariots (16.17–20), both dangerous and alluring.[7] Decorated Lydian headbands showed off beauty at its best, although Sappho thought crowns of flowers were even prettier on blondes (98a). Sappho repeatedly linked floral garlands, soft beds, perfumes fit for queens, and robes colored with expensive Phoenician purple dye (e.g., 92; 98a; 132), as in the tantalizingly incomplete fragment 94:

     . . . truly I wish I were dead.
     Leaving me with many tears,

     she said to me,
     "Ah, what sad things have been ours,
     Sappho, and truly I leave you against my will."
     And I said these things to her.
     "Go, and fare well, and remember me,
     for you know what care we took of you.

     And if you don't, I want
     to remind you . . .
     . . . and all the good times we had.

     You put on so many wreaths
     of violets, and roses with me,
     and [crocuses?], by my side

     and around your soft neck
     you laid so many
     woven garlands of buds,

     and . . . with full fragrant
     perfume, fit for a queen,
     you caressed yourself,

     and on soft spread-out
     beds . . . you would
     satisfy your longing for tender . . ."
     (Sappho 94)

As DuBois says (1995: 178), "The words in Greek twine around each other, adjective modifying noun in such a way as to imitate the braiding of flowers, words plaited and wound together, creating a poem that is itself a garland, a crown for the recipient, for the reader."

Beauty, like luxury and Lydian objects, united Sappho's circle with the gods: "He seems to me equal to the gods themselves, that man, who sits opposite you and listens nearby to your sweet voice and lovely laughter . . ." (31.1–5). Erotic desire, "bittersweet Eros" (130), was the most important emotion, heightening sensation, transporting the lover to new levels, breaking down the very limits of mortality. Eve Stehle (1990: 108) argues that "Through her use of the gaze to dissolve hierarchy, Sappho creates the same kind of open space for unscripted sexual relations that the mythic pattern of goddess with young man makes possible. By this means Sappho can represent an alternative for women to the cultural norms."

Sappho's imagery is a perfect example of what Jack Goody calls a "culture of flowers," a common ideology among Eurasian elites, reveling in conspicuous diversion of energies into beauty, manners, dress, and perfumes, using flowers as central images. In most cases, this culture is opposed by one scorning wasteful spending on frivolity, which on occasion – as in ancient Israel or Greece – becomes dominant (Goody 1993: 422). Marcel Detienne discusses the logic of this opposition in Greece. Aromatic spices, consistently associated with the orient, "make it possible, through the power of their perfume, to bring together beings normally separated from each other" (1977: 62) – that is, perfumes forged vertical links between mortals and gods, and horizontal ones between men and women.

The huge numbers of Protocorinthian perfume flasks in archaic cemeteries and sanctuaries suggest that perfume was widely available. Foxhall concludes that "the less-well-off consumed such products occasionally (frequently, one might guess, on special occasions, with entertainment being a factor), while for the rich such commodities might have been what was expected every day." The poor might anoint their dead with local perfumes, while the rich might have Samian oil and spices from Egypt. Foxhall suggests we see "consumption of products through which the individual links him- or herself to larger, global sets of values and ideologies . . . Elites can feel themselves distinct, while the poorer can feel that they can step one rung up the ladder, at least for a moment" (1998: 305–6). Detienne (1977) argues that perfumes belonged to the sphere of Adonis, evoking the east, sexual hyperactivity, frivolity, seduction, expense, and nonproductive activities. Their direct opposite was all that was rotten, bad-smelling, wet, and impotent, leading to death and decay. Civic culture found the correct productive middle ground, in which serious men grew grain, and married couples had procreative sex (cf. p. 148 above). Individual Greeks could consume orientalizing goods according to their means, their attitudes toward the middle, and their personal sense of just where the boundary between sensible pleasures and elitist decadence fell. It was perhaps prudish to refuse to have anything to do with perfumes, fancy clothes, and nonprocreative sex, but on the other hand overindulgence could look distinctly suspicious.

Semonides' abuse of women begins to make more sense. Sexuality was religious and political as well as a matter of personal preferences. Semonides attacked the mare, who "every day bathes twice, sometimes three times, and anoints herself with perfumes; she always wears her hair deeply combed, and wreathed with flowers. A wife like this is a fine thing for other men to look at, but she's an evil for any man who owns her unless he's a tyrant or sceptered king, a man whose heart delights in such ornaments" (7.63–70). Marilyn Arthur observes that Semonides made misogyny a class-based critique of elitist culture (Arthur 1973: 47–48). But he also attacked the foul sow, wallowing in her own filth and disgusting odors. Just as Athenian festivals like the

Thesmophoria located citizens' wives between these two extremes (Detienne 1977: 97–8), Semonides' poem fixed the ideal wife – the productive bee – at the midpoint of olfactory, hygienic, and sociological codes. Woman's labor was crucial to this ideology – it could not be left unused, as in the sow's disdain for housework or the mare's for legitimate sexual union, but must be controlled by men for productive ends.

To some extent, elitist interest in finery, intense emotions, and physical pleasure constituted an alternative gender ideology. Kurke (1999: ch. 5) argues that by 500, elitist *hetairoi*, the "companions" who attended symposia, invented a new type of woman, the *hetaira*, as their counterpart. Anacreon and other poets distinguished *hetairai* from common *pornai*, "prostitutes," by their sophistication, grace, and elegance. Viewed from within the sympotic world, the gender hierarchy was strong, in that women were present to service men's sexual desires; but seen from outside, the remarkable thing about *hetairai* was their relative equality with male *hetairoi*, blurring the conventional barriers around male gatherings.

The east, luxury, beauty, and privileged relations with the gods merged. Aristeas, for example, who supposedly traveled all over Asia seeing mythical beasts in the seventh century (Herodotus 4.13–16), was also an ecstatic devotee of Apollo. Elite religion adapted eastern rites in the eighth and seventh centuries, and the same themes dominate the new "orientalizing" pottery styles. Among the most common seventh-century shapes are the aryballos and alabastron, small perfume flasks. The most widely distributed pots come from Corinth, often decorated in the Protocorinthian style (figure 5.1). Floral motifs, echoing the perfumes within the pots, were especially popular, consistently linked with eroticism (Shanks 1999: ch. 3). Shanks shows that Greek artists took over Near Eastern vegetal motifs and deployed them in a larger system – "the following themes are associated with the floral: youth, perfume, beauty and the erotic, cult and divinity, power, wine, refinement and a world more than that of ordinary life, a contrast to labour and agriculture, bread and marriage."

The aristocratic symposium, the performance context for much archaic poetry, had its own orientalizing revolution after 700, adapting special rooms and furniture from the east (Kyrieleis 1969; Fehr 1971; Dentzer 1982; Boardman 1990), particularly Palestine (Burkert 1991). Reclining on couches of Near Eastern type and using vessels with Lydian prototypes, aristocrats sang about Lydian dress, women, and military might, judging Greek life against these standards. The new symbols justified their users' claims to superiority – they virtually mixed with the gods themselves, just like the heroes, on whom

Figure 5.1 A mysterious scene on a Protocorinthian aryballos of about 675 BC, attributed to the Ajax Painter (Boston Museum of Fine Arts 95.12, after Hurwit 1985: 156, fig. 65)

society had depended for its very existence; and they felt like the powerful kings of the east.

Elitist sympotic culture directly opposed the middling ideology. Oswyn Murray (1990a: 7) notes that "The *symposion* became in many respects a place apart from the normal rules of society, with its own strict code of honour in the *pistis* [trust] there created, and its own willingness to establish conventions fundamentally opposed to those within the *polis* as a whole." The primary assets were beauty, youth, eroticism, love of wine, arcane mythological knowledge, and athletic skills. The games perhaps owed as much to the east as did the symposium, and both merged with ritual friendship to form a coherent culture beyond polis morality. No rules barred ordinary citizens from entering the games, but the level of skill required effectively did so;

and in any case, the scale of rewards made victory an avenue of rapid promotion into elite circles. Serious competitors constituted in their own eyes an interstate elite. Ordinary citizens enjoyed watching elite conflicts and honored the victors, much as classical Athenian jurymen watched wealthy litigants (Ober 1989: 144). But for the participants, athletic victory renewed the household's glory (Kurke 1991: 15–62). Just like correct use of luxury, having a victor in the family identified a true aristocrat, someone who stood close to the gods and heroes.

The orientalizing movement was a class phenomenon. Desire for eastern rites, dress, perfumes, images, and utensils was political. Those who adopted them pretended that they belonged to a grander and better world than the ignorant peasants around them. Curtin (1984) and Appadurai (1986) document similar situations in other cultures, with groups which feel unfairly excluded from power tending to welcome new and disruptive ideas, while more established groups resist novelties. What makes archaic Greece unusual is that here it was not some rising mercantile group or the overeducated young who felt excluded but the would-be aristocrats, and it was self-styled noblemen who looked to the past, the east, and the divine for justification, expanding their spacetime in opposition to the restrictive expectations of the middling ideology.

The middling poets resisted all these beliefs. To them, the elitists' gods looked just as frivolous as their wild heroic warriors and erotic uncontrolled women. In Xenophanes' eyes, the gods of epic represented "all that is bad and blameworthy among men – stealing, adultery, and deceiving one another" (11; cf. 10, 12–16). Far from being companions of the elite, as Sappho would have them, the middling poets' gods kept the ends of life hidden from all men.[8]

The east inspired the harshest attacks of all. For Phocylides "an orderly polis on a rock is better than crazy Nineveh" (5), and Xenophanes told how the Colophonians

> learned useless luxuries [*habrosynai*] from the Lydians,
> while still they were free from hateful tyranny,
> and went into the marketplace wearing all-purple robes
> no less than a thousand strong,
> rejoicing proudly in their gold-bedecked hair
> and bedewing their scent with studied anointings.
> (Xenophanes 3)

Xenophanes pointedly links *habrosyne*, the east, tyranny, gold, and perfumes. Tyranny itself was often linked to the east, and the word *tyrannos* may have been borrowed from Lydian. In fragment 19,

Archilochus has Charon the carpenter say "I don't care for Gyges the Golden's things, and I've never envied him. I'm not jealous of the works of gods either, and I don't lust after a magnificent tyranny. These are beyond my gaze." What he rejects is a virtual checklist of elitism – desires for wealth on the scale of the king of Lydia, to rival the gods, and (at least in the eyes of critics) to be a tyrant, the ultimate expression of hubris.

But perhaps the most effective attack on elite pretensions comes from Hipponax, who abuses the delicacy, eroticism, and orientalism which Sappho and others see as sources of social power. The dung-covered hero of fragment 92 finds himself in a toilet with a woman who performs an obscure act on his anus while beating his genitals with a fig branch. The fragment ends with a cloud of beetles whirring out of the filth. The woman is *lydizousa*, "talking like a Lydian"; it seems that the whole episode is so downmarket that it does not even involve a real Lydian. This is classic iambic abuse, making it hard to take the *habrosyne* ideology seriously, and that was surely the point.[9]

Conclusions

There was no way to transcend the polis in the middling tradition. Not even athletic victory brought a man closer to the gods and heroes, and Tyrtaeus (12.1–12), Xenophanes (2), and Solon (at least according to Diodorus 9.2.5) all rejected the ideal of the athlete in favor of more useful social types. The differences between the two traditions in the end came down to a single point. The elitists legitimated their special role from sources outside the polis; the middling poets rejected such claims. The former blurred distinctions between male and female, present and past, mortal and divine, Greek and Lydian, to reinforce a single distinction between aristocrat and commoner; the latter did the opposite. Each was probably guilty of disgusting and polluting behavior in the eyes of the other.

For elitists, a good community would embrace aristocrats from all over Greece, and even from beyond Greece. But this was rarely more than an oppositional dream: the "Greek aristocracy" was an immanent elite, an imagined community evoked in the interstices of the polis world – at interstate games, in the arrival of a *xenos*, or behind the closed doors of the symposium. In practical terms, fragmentation was stronger, as individuals pursued their own honor at the expense of class interests (Stein-Hölkeskamp 1989). Political power remained vested in independent poleis, where the middling ideology was generally triumphant.

The Emergence of Greek Democracy

Returning to Dahl's model, we might say that while elitist models drawing authority from outside the community remained strong, there were good arguments that some men really were so much better qualified than ordinary citizens that they should make the collective and binding decisions. It made sense to run poleis as oligarchies. But late in the sixth century, this ceased to apply.

According to Herodotus, there were several experiments with popular rule in these years. About a generation before Cleisthenes, Demonax of Mantineia was invited to Cyrene during a dynastic crisis. The Cyreneans followed an old tradition of arbitration, acknowledging that external sources of authority could override local factionalism: but once he arrived, Demonax divided the citizens into new tribes, set aside some land and offices for the kings, and "gave all the other things which the kings had formerly held into the midst of the people" (*es meson to demo*: 4.161). It is hard to know exactly what Herodotus meant, or even if the story is true, but he used similar language in three more passages. In 522, he says, Maiandrios wanted to give up his tyranny over Samos. He set up a shrine to Zeus as God of Freedom, and offered *isonomia*, "equality before the law," to the people (3.142). In a famous but bizarre tale, Herodotus claimed that in the very next year, the Persian noble Otanes proposed that the whole Persian empire should be a democracy (3.80). All these plans fell through, but Herodotus also mentions in passing that in 499 certain rich men were thrown out of Naxos by the demos (5.30), and that at some time around 500 Kadmos, tyrant of Kos, inspired by justness (*dikaiosyne*), "gave his rule into the midst of the Koans" (*es meson Kooisi*: 7.164), and moved to Sicily. He probably felt comfortable there: in 491, the Syracusan demos expelled their notables and set up their own democracy (7.155). Herodotus knew that not everyone believed his story about Otanes, so he bolstered it by emphasizing that in 492 the Persians set up democracies all over Ionia (6.43).

All these stories have well-known problems, and none should be pressed too hard (Robinson 1997: 103–22). The same is true of an inscription from Chios, dating around 550 or even a little earlier, referring to some kind of *bole demosie*, a "people's council" (Meiggs and Lewis 1969: no. 8 (trs. Fornara 1983: no. 19); Robinson 1997: 90–101). Unlike Herodotus' stories, we cannot dismiss the inscription as an anachronism, but we do not know who sat on this council or what it did.

But all problems aside, the chronological clustering of this evidence is striking.[10] Herodotus was not particularly interested in the origins of democracy, but just two generations after the facts, he mentioned in asides seven or eight episodes of varying credibility involving shifts in political power toward a broad male citizen community between about 525 and 490. It seems unreasonable to deny that there was a trend toward the demos seizing broader authority in the late sixth century. At Athens, democracy was established in a violent rejection of external authority, as the citizens rejected Hippias' base in the inter-state tyrants' club and Isagoras' in Sparta in favor of Cleisthenes' total commitment to the demos (see Ober 1996: 32–52). Changes in poetry and the archaeological record suggest that this was part of a wide-spread development in the last decades of the sixth century, and that democracy became thinkable with the collapse of the elitist ideology. This transformation was just as complex as that of the eighth century which I discuss in Part IV. I have summarized the material evidence elsewhere (I. Morris 1998b: 31–6), but the period 550–450 calls for fuller analysis than I can give it here, and I plan to return to it in a sep-arate study.

Around 520, aristocrats started commissioning odes in honor of returning athletic victors, to be performed by choruses in the home city. This poetry shared the victor's glory with the community. It was an old idea. The heroes had worried about what "someone" (tis) from the masses might say (de Jong 1987), but the new epinician poets went further, incorporating all the citizens into a single song. The praise of other nobles was now not enough. There was a crisis of praising.

A group of professional poets emerged, taking pay for their per-formances. They argued that ordinary praise was shapeless and futile, whereas they could focus it. Praise could be misdirected, becoming mere gossip.[11] The poets stepped forward as a neutral group, mediat-ing between mass and elite, turning aside envy.[12] Pindar at one moment called himself the guest-friend of Sogenes of Aegina (Nemean 7.61–5), at another an ordinary citizen (Pythian 2.13), identifying with each group as the need arose. Kurke (1991: 86–90, 135–47) argues that through careful use of references to guest-friends, Pindar reassured athletic victors that they still belonged to an interstate elite, even as he incorporated them among the citizens (e.g., Olympian 7.89–90; 13.3; Pythian 3.69–71; Isthmian 1.50–1; 6.66–72).

Epinician poets embraced the image of the middling citizen (Pindar, Nemean 11.47–8; Isthmian 6.66–72; Paean 1.2–5; 4.32–53), sharing middling attitudes about the corrosive forces of hunger (Pindar, Isth-mian 1.49) and poverty (Pindar, fragment 109; Bacchylides, Ode 1.168–71). Pindar agreed that the "middle rank" (ta mesa) had the most enduring prosperity (Pythian 11.52–3), praising those who pursued the mean, living justly (Pindar, Pythian 2.86–8; 3.107–8; 5.14; 10.67–8;

Nemean 7.87–9). Hubris was the most serious crime.[13] For Bacchylides, whoever had his health and lived off his own estate rivaled "the first men" (*Ode* 1.165–8).

But the epinician poets did not simply continue the middling tradition. They recognized an elite distinguished by more than just wisdom and moderation. Pindar baldly asserted that "the piloting of poleis is passed from father to son, in the hands of the nobles" (*Pythian* 10.71–2). Pindar divided the world into gods, extraordinary men, and ordinary men. For him, as Glenn Most puts it (1985: 75), "the gods are superior in that they always possess felicity, the extraordinary men in that they have, at least on one occasion and if only briefly, attained felicity." But this was not the fearless elite of Sappho and Alcman. Athletic victory still provided links with gods and heroes,[14] but the effort which went into these triumphs was now "in the common interest."[15] The nobleman's success obliged all citizens to repay it with *charis*, another key classical concept; and the poet then converted *charis* into safe praise.

Like the men in Xenophanes' symposia, Pindar's extraordinary men were wise enough to be pious. But Pindar also believed that the gods repaid piety with favor, which translated into wealth, to be spent on the games (Pindar, *Olympian* 2.53–6; 5.23–4; *Pythian* 2.56; 5.1–2, 14; 6.47). Their wealth became "a conspicuous star, truest light for a man" (Pindar, *Olympian* 2.55–6), illuminating the whole city. The only alternative to public spending was hoarding wealth in the darkness, hiding the family's fame.[16] Pindar's universe had no room for the Sapphic manipulation of luxury.

Epinician poets repeatedly described noblemen with their golden cups like the gods on Olympus,[17] and linked aristocrats' riches with those of the heroes.[18] But the poets nevertheless sided with the middling tradition in seeing an unbridgable gulf separating mortals from the divine. "One is the race of men, one is the race of gods," explained Pindar, "and from one mother do we both draw our breath; but a wholly sundered power has divided us, so that the one is nothing, while for the other, brazen Heaven remains secure for ever" (*Nemean* 6.1–4). No achievement was possible without the gods' help,[19] and no man could hope to equal the gods.[20]

Aristocrats were cut off from the east just as brutally. The Persians had crushed Lydia in 546, and according to Herodotus (1.71) had learned luxury as a result. In the fifth century, Persia was imagined as the major source of oriental luxury, and Lydia almost disappeared from poetry. Aeschylus' fragment 29, from the *Edonoi*, depicted Dionysus in Lydian dress, and Pindar (*Nemean* 6.16–18) offered Ajax a Lydian headband decked with song, which he then associated with a mythical priest of Aphrodite, bringing together several elements of the older elitist ideology. A fragment of Ion's satyr-play *Omphale*, about the mythical Lydian queen who enslaved Heracles for a year and made him dress as a woman, says "It is better to know Lydian perfume and myrrh and Sardis' ornaments of the skin than the manner of life in Pelops' isle" (Radt *et al.* 1977: no. 24). The themes are old, but we do not know who is speaking, or in what context; and given the anarchic humor of satyr-plays, we cannot even guess at the intended implications.

Lydia was reduced to little more than a source of music (Pindar, *Olympian* 5.19; 14.17–18; *Nemean* 4.45; 8.15; fragment 125; Bacchylides, fragment 14). By the time of Aeschylus' *Persians* in 472 eastern luxury was increasingly negative: wealth, softness, and hubris explained Persia's defeats in 490–479. As Miller (1997) shows, some Athenians did use Persian culture as a way to signal their sophistication. But the sources overwhelmingly deploy Persian luxury as a symbol for hubris and decadence (E. Hall 1989; Cartledge 1993: 36–62).

Shorn of external legitimation, aristocrats fell back on themselves and their poleis. The only alternative was to retreat to mystery cults, but as Detienne (1996: 120) notes, "the magi and initiates lived on the [social] periphery of the city, aspiring only to an altogether internal transformation." Even when transformed, the priest's superiority over ordinary men was purely interior. For those who stayed in the mainstream, essentialist definitions of nobility no longer held good. For Simonides there could be no "all-blameless man . . . built four-square, without blame, in hand, foot, and mind" (542.24, 2–3). The best a man could hope for was to avoid doing anything disgraceful, and to mind civic justice (542.27–9, 34–5). Not without cause does Gentili (1988: 63–71) speak of "Simonides' deconsecration of aristocratic values," or Detienne (1996: 107–17) of Simonides' demotion of *aletheia*, externally grounded truths, in favor of *doxa*, appearances. Virtue was relative, defined from the point of view of the polis. Simonides summed this up in an elegiac fragment: "It is the polis that teaches the man" (15 (West 1991/2)).

Dahl suggests that democratic government only works when most members of a group believe they are roughly equally qualified to participate in decision-making. The middling ideology was such a belief within late archaic male citizenries. It had been important since the eighth century, but between 525 and 500 all viable alternatives collapsed. No doubt many nobles, whether in Thebes, Aegina, or Athens, continued to believe they were special beings, but they increasingly conceded the need to be judged as such not just by other nobles, but also by their fellow citizens. Many must have continued to believe that aristocratic government should guide the people, just as praise and blame should be channeled through professional poets. The collapse of faith in external sources of authority did not automatically produce democracy, but it made democracy a possibility. Aristocrats had to make their way within communities of roughly equal men.

Preliminary Conclusion

In Part III I have argued that from 700 through 300 BC, the middling ideology pervaded Greek thought. In archaic times it was constantly challenged by a rival, elitist way of thinking, but around 500 elitism collapsed, ushering in an age of consensus. The fifth-century imagined community was one of moderate, equal male citizens, turned away from the past and the east. *Hoi mesoi* were less a *Mittelschicht* than an ideological construct, part of a pair of antithetical cultures, allowing *all* citizens to locate themselves in the middle if they chose to do so. In Walzer's terms, the one good thing was male citizen birth. All other goods flowed to the men who had it. To call a man rich or poor, to deny his middling status, was to cast him out of the ideal polis. In the late fifth century new forms of criticism took shape among the rich and highly educated, but along very different lines from the elitism of the archaic period (Ober 1998).

We have the outline of a cultural history of Greek egalitarianism, but no more than that. The texts have three severe limitations. The first is geographical. In chapter 4 I discussed Athenian evidence, and while the poets in this chapter come from several cities, the process of text formation, particularly the promotion of poetry to panhellenic status, had a homogenizing effect. We have a single "Greek" discourse, even though archaeological data and the stories in Herodotus and Aristotle indicate strong regional variations. Turning to material culture in Part IV, I argue that from the eleventh century on we see four main regional groupings (Figure 6.1). Most of the poets I have discussed in this chapter come from the central area, and it is here that we find most of the best-known classical citizen poleis, and the early democracies.[21]

Whitley (1991b: 344) notes the tendency of historians to extrapolate from Homer to a single "early Greek" society, concluding that "the problem [is] of sifting out those aspects which may refer to one type of society, and those which refer to another." But the problems go deeper. It is all too easy to think of Homer as a mirror to an external reality, but a defective one, and to see our job as being to use archaeology to smooth his distorting surface to produce a clear reflection of social realities. I argue instead that the epic was not some kind of bad history, nor archaic poetry some kind of bad documentary source. From the eighth century through the sixth, we are dealing with homogenizing literary constructions of what different groups of people wanted the world to be like. Homer set his constructions in a once-upon-a-time land of heroes; elegiac, iambic, and lyric poets in a contemporary but equally imaginary world. We cannot smooth the surfaces; but we can combine these ritualized literary discourses with material remains of other ritualized discourses, digging beneath panhellenizing poetry to see how far Greek communities agreed on what the good society should be like.

This leads into the second problem, which is sociological. The texts trap us within one particular realm of discursive conflicts, mostly associated with aristocratic symposia (Kurke 1999). We can trace conflicts within this sympotic world, but we get little sense of how those excluded from it shared its ideas or developed alternatives. I argue in Part IV that beginning around 750, the debates we see in the literary record also seem to have informed the practices which created the archaeological record, while before that date, the excavated evidence seems to be structured on significantly different principles.

This leads into the third issue, which is chronological. Since the written sources do not go back beyond 750, and Homer and Hesiod already reveal the strength of the middling and elitist ideologies, there is no way to demonstrate from the texts whether these belief systems were new phenomena in the eighth century, forces which emerged more gradually during the Iron Age, or elements of a timeless Greek "spirit." Only archaeology can clarify this question. I argue in Part IV that we see major changes in material culture toward the end of the eleventh century and again in the eighth century, and that these reveal profound shifts in spacetime: the roots of the Greek Strong Principle of Equality.

Part IV

6

The Past, the East, and the Hero of Lefkandi

Introduction

We know far more about Iron Age Greece than we did when the great syntheses appeared a quarter of a century ago. I hope to treat the full range of evidence in detail elsewhere, but for now I limit myself to the area around the shores of the Aegean, which I call "central Greece" (figure 6.1). I have argued that we can identify four regional material cultures, which took shape in the eleventh century and lasted into the sixth and beyond (I. Morris 1997b; 1998b). These regions were not homogeneous. No two archaeological sites are ever exactly alike, and grouping them into geographical units is always an interpretive act. Other archaeologists, looking at different elements within the overall assemblage, might come up with different spatial arrangements. Nor are the boundaries between the regions which I identify always clear-cut. But for all the definitional problems, this organization of the data clarifies more than it obscures. Snodgrass (1971: 228–68) saw similar regional patterns in pottery decoration, metal use, and building. His "advanced" regions of Protogeometric Greece correspond roughly to my central Greek area (Snodgrass 1971: 374–6), around the shores of the Aegean Sea. I step outside this area at several points, but focus on it here because this is where most of the city-states discussed in Part III are to be found, and because since the eleventh century it developed in ways unlike any other part of the Mediterranean.

Postmycenaean Culture

There were gigantic upheavals all across the east Mediterranean around 1200 (Ward and Joukowsky 1992; Gitlin et al. 1998). In Greece the Mycenaean palaces were destroyed and abandoned. Linear B,

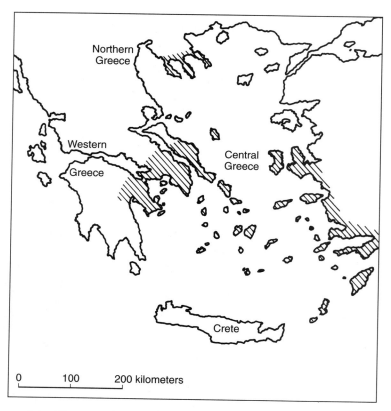

Figure 6.1   The central Greek material culture region

monumental stone architecture, and other "high" skills disappeared. Population fell by perhaps 75 percent between 1250 and 1100. Emigration from the core areas of Mycenaean civilization, famine, and disease must all have been involved. The palaces had controlled much of the agricultural economy, and their destruction perhaps spelled economic disaster.

At some sites, dislocations were fairly small: at Tiryns (figure 6.2), the Oberburg, where the palace had stood, was virtually abandoned around 1200, and a new town flourished below it on the Unterburg.[1] But other sites were evacuated, as people from the Argolid made new homes in the Cyclades, Chalcidice, western Greece, and as far afield as Cyprus and the Levant. There were attempts to preserve elements of Late Bronze Age culture in the twelfth century. House- and tomb-building, the worship of the gods, and much artwork

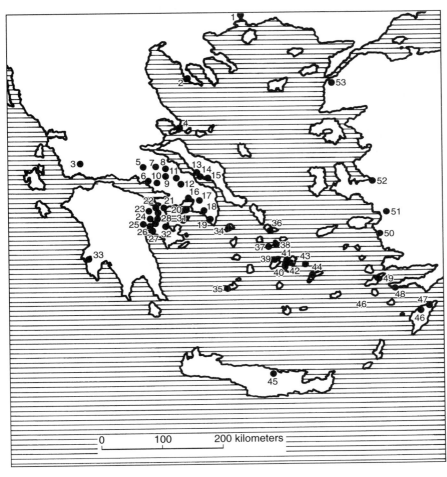

Figure 6.2 Sites mentioned in this chapter

1 Amphipolis	15 Eretria	29 Prosymna	43 Donoussa
2 Mende	16 Eleusis	30 Berbati	44 Minoa
3 Thermon	17 Athens	31 Athikia	45 Knossos
4 Theotokou	18 Lathouriza	32 Epidauros	46 Kameiros
5 Amphikleia	19 Anavyssos	33 Pylos	47 Ialysos
6 Andikyra	20 Salamis	34 Ayia Irini	48 Asarlik
7 Elateia	21 Isthmia	35 Phylakopi	49 Kos
8 Kalapodi	22 Corinth	36 Tinos	50 Miletus
9 Orchomenos	23 Klenia	37 Rheneia	51 Ephesus
10 Vranezi	24 Mycenae	38 Delos	52 Smyrna
11 Akraiphia	25 Argos	39 Koukounaries	53 Troy
12 Thebes	26 Tiryns	40 Iria	
13 Chalcis	27 Asine	41 Grotta	
14 Lefkandi	28 Heraion	42 Tsikalario	

continued along the same lines as in the thirteenth century. There was even something of a Mycenaean renaissance by 1150, perhaps a golden age for local aristocrats, now freed from palatial control (Rutter 1992). At Koukounaries on Paros, a Mycenaean-style mansion flourished in these years complete with a throne with ivory fittings (Schilardi 1984), and tombs at Perati include Near Eastern imports (Iakovidis 1969). At Mycenae, some fragments of wall paintings may date to the twelfth century, although there is still no evidence for writing after 1200.

By 1100 this was changing. New destructions and emigrations hit central Greece hard. Population declined sharply. Occupation continued at some of the larger mainland sites, but its character changed. At Tiryns, the Unterburg was burned and abandoned. Only one eleventh-century house has been found, and another just outside the walls, and a mere handful of tenth-century sherds. What we might call the "new frontier" in the islands, Achaea, and Cyprus foundered. Koukounaries and Lefkandi were burned, and squatters then eked out a shabby existence in the ruins. But by 1050 this too had ended. Phylakopi on Melos, Ayia Irini on Kea, and many other sites were destroyed. The richness of material culture declined after 1100. Regional variation increased, and long-distance contacts probably grew less common. In central Greece, the last traces of the Mycenaean way of life had effectively disappeared by 1000. In its place, we see the creation of what is normally called Submycenaean culture. Desborough saw this as covering all of central Greece, southern Thessaly, and Elis, characterized by "much the same sort of pottery, the same types of tomb, cist tombs or earth-cut graves, and similar types of ornament" (Desborough 1972: 75).[2]

The Dorian Invasion

Classical writers spoke of an invasion of Greece by the Dorians, which Thucydides (1.12) placed eighty years after the Trojan war, so in the late twelfth century. This might explain the transformation of central Greek material culture. It features prominently in discussions of the Iron Age, though the methodological problems are rarely spelled out.

There are two difficulties with the texts. First, Thucydides lived some 700 years later, and the most detailed accounts in fact come from Roman authors. There were many occasions when it would have been useful for various groups to fabricate stories, and Jonathan Hall (1997) shows that distinct myths of a return of Achaean Heraclidae and an invasion of Dorians were probably still being constructed and conflated well into archaic times.

Second, the sources contradict one another. We cannot judge from them whether we should think of one invasion or several, involving many people or few, over a short period or many decades. Archaeologists seeking to prove the legends true identify many intrusive objects in twelfth-century Greece, but all have good Aegean antecedents before 1200 (Vanschoonwinkel (1991) reviews the evidence). Yet since the sources are so vague about what was supposed to have happened, we cannot say whether this falsifies invasion theories or shows that infiltration began in the thirteenth century.

In the last twenty years archaeologists have identified a class of handmade, burnished pottery with few obvious links to Mycenaean styles, predictably christened "Barbarian Ware." Like other supposed fossils of invaders, Barbarian Ware occurs in pre-1200 deposits, and its relevance depends on how we imagine invasions to have proceeded. Small (1990) interprets the pottery as an economic response to the collapse of centralized ceramic production, which caused regression to simpler technology, but Rutter (1990) points to similarities in the styles of this pottery all the way from Corinthia to southern Italy, and suggests that migrations explain the data better. Despite detailed studies (e.g., Reber 1991), no one has yet identified an area where this pottery was the normal style before 1250 and which might be the invaders' homeland; but it is perfectly possible that "Barbarian Ware" was a hybrid style created in the process of movement itself. Hall (1997: 62) points out that the literary sources are as vague about the Dorians' supposed homeland as archaeologists are about Barbarian Ware's point of origin.

Linking wheelmade Submycenaean pottery to invaders is even harder. This simple and repetitive ware owed much to Late Helladic IIIC, even while abandoning many of its features (Snodgrass 1971: 28–40). At Corinth (although not at Mycenae and Tiryns) the two styles are stratified together, and at Asine Submycenaean develops organically out of Late Helladic IIIC.[3] Possibly Submycenaean and Barbarian Ware were both hybrids of local traditions and customs brought in from outside.

Some archaeologists associate the curvilinear, one-roomed houses which appear on Submycenaean sites with invaders. Such houses were common in the Aegean before 1600, but were largely (though not entirely) replaced by rectilinear houses in Mycenaean times (Mazarakis Ainian 1989). Michel Sakellariou claims that oval and apsidal houses with pitched roofs were easier to build and less permanent than Mycenaean multiroomed rectilinear houses with flat roofs, and that we should associate the new houses with nomadic invaders from the north (Sakellariou 1980: 118–26; 1981). The equation of house shape, subsistence, social complexity, and ethnicity is popular. Looking at eighth-century apsidal houses at Miletus, Gerhard Kleiner (1966: 21–2; 1970: 119) saw the homes and shrines of Carians who were displaced by Greeks living in rectilinear houses. At Smyrna, Ekrem Akurgal (1983: 31–2) linked curvilinear buildings with Aeolian-speaking Greeks, and rectilinear with Ionian speakers. At seventh-century Lathouriza, Hans Lauter (1985a: 69–70, 73, 77–8, 83) again assumed that nomadic immigrants built the apsidal houses.

None of these archaeologists provides any kind of middle-range theory. We might expect nomads to build temporary shelters rather than permanent houses, but we cannot read off economic behavior and ethnic origins from house plans so simply. Some modern nomads who live mainly in tents leave almost no material residues, while other tent-dwellers use stone bedding platforms and weights, leaving substantial remains. Roger Cribb (1991: 84–99) provides a typology of nomadic dwellings, from tents to permanent houses. In one example from Baluchistan, the only archaeologically visible difference between the stone bedding for a house and that for a tent would be that the former needed one postbase to support its roof, while the latter had three postholes for the tent poles. Eleventh-century central Greeks used the same wall construction techniques for their apsidal houses – mudbricks on stone socles – that Mycenaeans had favored for rectilinear ones. There is no reason to assume that apsidal houses *must* have been short-term shelters thrown up by mobile pastoralists, and there have been no attempts to identify the kinds of assemblages which Cribb (1991: 76) suggests might be typical of nomads. Eleventh-century central Greeks may have relied more heavily on meat and movement than the Mycenaeans, and there could have been population movements into the area. But so far there is no direct evidence for either.

Changes in burial have been treated in similar ways. Submycenaean graves were typically individual inhumations in stone-lined cists, either extended or contracted. Archaeologists often say that the shift from multiple to single burial after 1100 means that people abandoned the long-term planning implicit in chamber-tombs because they lacked confidence about the future. But the theories then diverge. Desborough (1964) argued that invaders from the northwest caused this uncertainty, while Snodgrass stressed similarities between the cist graves, handmade pottery, and apsidal houses of Submycenaean times and those of the Middle Bronze Age. He suggested that these material features had been suppressed in Mycenaean times by "exotic and essentially intrusive features"; beneath this veneer "there lay a substratum which we may now recognize as essentially Greek" (1971: 385). Dakoronia (1987: 145–52) combines these views, suggesting that

Middle Bronze Age culture survived through Mycenaean times in northwest Greece, and that invaders brought it back to central Greece in the eleventh century.

But Jonathan Hall argues that "The apparent impasse between the proponents and opponents of an archeologically visible Dorian invasion arises from the fact that both camps subscribe to the same fallacy – namely, that an ethnic group must necessarily be identifiable in the archaeological record" (1997: 128–9). Desborough and Dakoronia took it for granted that invaders clung to the customs of their homelands, and Snodgrass that cists, houses, and pottery were elements of a Greek ethnic identity. By 600 BC, apsidal houses and handmade burnished pottery were things of the past, and even cist burial was a restricted phenomenon; yet we would not say that archaic and classical Greeks were less Greek than those of the eleventh century. These approaches to the Dorian invasion rest on essentialist models of ethnicity, which break down when we confront the complexity of the evidence and the discursive, subjective construction of identity.

Whether cist-using invaders descended from the northwest or the locals decided to revive distantly remembered ways of life (or both, or neither), we are looking at *a series of decisions* which changed material culture. Through the twelfth century, many or even most of the people living in central Greece tried to reproduce something like the Mycenaean way, albeit without a palatial ruling class. By the late eleventh, few if any were doing this. We might attribute this to an indigenous population turning its back on the relatively recent Mycenaean past, perhaps recreating some idea of what they thought the pre-Mycenaean world was like. Or we might see newcomers displacing the locals and feeling no ties to the Aegean past, deliberately retaining their own ways and making no concessions to the customs of their new home. Either way, the result was that the Bronze Age symbolic order rapidly collapsed after 1075.

The End of the Old Order

Rather than continuing to argue over the invasion hypothesis, I want to focus on how this rejection of Mycenaean ways unfolded. The Submycenaean cemeteries in the mid-eleventh century create an impression of symbolic chaos, verging on anarchy, and of a wide range of attitudes toward the Mycenaean heritage. The eleventh century was a time of bewildering changes. Intensive surveys have identified virtually no definite Submycenaean sites in central Greece. This may

Table 6.1 Central Greece: Submycenaean graves

	Number of graves	Pottery		Metal	
		Mean	Gini	Mean	Gini
All areas	354	1.4	.51[1]	1.2	.83
Athens	193	1.1	.54	1.2	.88
Attica	105	0.6	—	0.2	.80–1.0
Lefkandi	24	1.9	.48	2.2	.65
Argos	15	1.0	.69	0.7	.77
Tiryns	5	1.4	.13	2.6	.52
Thebes	9	1.0	.67	0.9	.70

[1] Not counting Salamis graves.
Sources: see Snodgrass 1971: 203–7, plus: Athens, I. Morris 1987: 228–33; *AD* 33:2 (1978) 13; 34:2 (1979) 16–17; 38:2 (1983) 23–5; *AR* 1994/95: 4. Lefkandi, Popham *et al.* 1980. Argos, Hägg 1974. On Gini coefficients, see pp. 140–1 above.

be a result of the low visibility of eleventh-century potsherds, but excavations also suggest that site numbers fell off after 1100. Much of the countryside was probably abandoned, or left very thinly settled. Most people lived in small hamlets, occupied for anything from 50 to 300 years. Whitley (1991b) suggests they were organized around big men, and that the end of a chiefly dynasty might mean the end of a community. But there were also larger stable settlements, such as Argos and Athens, where the populations probably never fell below 1,000–2,000 people (I. Morris 1991: 29–34). Villages survived at the major Mycenaean sites in the Argive plain, but in Attica apart from the final burials at Perati no Submycenaean graves have been found outside Athens itself and the Salamis cemetery just ten miles away.

More than half of all known Submycenaean graves in central Greece come from Athens (table 6.1). We can explain some of this through the history of excavations. The discovery and publication of more than 100 graves at the Arsenal on Salamis was a stroke of luck; so too the thoroughness of the German excavators at the Kerameikos in publishing 115 graves around the Pompeion.[4] But even without these, we would still have 122 Submycenaean graves from Athens as against just 72 from the rest of central Greece. Intensive salvage archaeology at Athens in the wake of explosive urban growth in the 1960s and 1970s accounts for more of the pattern, but we should note that digs in Athens often find graves in groups of 8 to 15 (e.g., on Vassilisis Sophias, Kriezi, Drakou, and Erechtheiou Sts),[5] while outside Athens, graves usually occur singly or in pairs. There are some comparable groups – at Argos, 6 graves on Deiras hill and 7 in the Kourou plot; at Thebes, 9 at the Electran Gate; and at Lefkandi, 24 in the Skoubris field.[6] At Lefkandi Popham et al. estimate that they have excavated "no more than a quarter of the whole [Skoubris] cemetery" (1980: 103), so this burial ground might be comparable with the Kerameikos and Salamis. The Lefkandi Iron Age cemeteries spread over an enormous area, although most of the material seems to be somewhat later.[7] But Argos and Thebes have also seen intensive salvage work, and yet have nothing like the density or spread of Athenian graves. Athens looks like the largest site in eleventh-century central Greece. Legends said that after the Trojan war – presumably, in the twelfth and eleventh centuries – Athens became a center for refugees from disasters around Greece. There may be something to this: Athens grew as the central Greek countryside emptied.

Unlike twelfth- or tenth-century graves, most Submycenaean burials contain few grave goods – perhaps a pot, but often nothing at all (such graves are dated on stratigraphic grounds or by secure associations with similar graves which do contain objects). Yet – also unlike tenth-century graves – a few contain quite rich offerings. Thus at Athens, where the mean number of metal objects per burial was 1.2, Kerameikos gr. SM 108 held 20 bronze and iron rings, 31 bronze fibulas, 3 bronze pins, a bronze armband, fragments of glass, and 4 pots. Iron is restricted to rich graves in this period, such as Rendi St. gr. 8 in Athens, which held an iron ring along with 10 bronzes and a silver ring. At Lefkandi, where the mean was 2.2 metal objects, Skoubris gr. 38 held 2 gold earrings, 5 bronzes, 3 iron objects and 3 fragments of ivory; and in the slightly richer cemeteries of Tiryns, with a mean figure of 2.6 metal offerings per grave, the remarkable gr. 1957/28, a double burial of a man and a woman, is the last known burial for three centuries with bronze armor (a helmet and shield boss).[8]

There are several ways to interpret this. Most obviously, the disasters around 1100 may have impoverished central Greece, with what little wealth was left falling into the hands of village headmen, the heirs to the last Mycenaean local officials. Alternatively, we may be dealing with different attitudes toward grave goods, with a few buriers believing in lavish offerings, while others thought simpler rites more appropriate for seeing the dead off to the next world. Even given the imprecision of archaeological dating, it seems that the abandonment of Mycenaean traditions was anything but abrupt. While most people adopted the new cist-grave rite early in the eleventh century, some did not. On the Deiras hill at Argos, six chamber tombs continued in use well into the eleventh century, and tomb 20 was probably newly dug as late as 1050. On the western edge of central Greece, at Amphikleia and Elateia, chamber tombs probably stayed in use even into the ninth century.[9] But there are no clear correlations between the different elements of the funerary package. Some of the people who buried in cist graves on Salamis and in the Kerameikos deposited pots which look more "Mycenaean" than some of the vases in the chamber tombs at Perati, where multiple burial continued into the eleventh century.[10]

This was a time of rapid change and collapsing meanings. Burial practices had a fluidity we will not see again until the late eighth century. Most people switched to cist graves; some did not. Most also switched to the narrow and simple range of pots we call Submycenaean; some, again, did not. Grave goods were tremendously varied and unevenly distributed, in what Whitley (1991a: 96–7) calls "near-random and non-discriminatory patterns of deposition." The burials have an anything-goes quality, which for Whitley reflects a situation where few rules governed the creation of social identities. Gunther Krause (1975: 18–19) notes that this was the only period when even gender distinctions blurred at the Kerameikos.

At Asine, some rectilinear Mycenaean buildings continued in use alongside new apsidal houses until about 1000 BC (Wells 1983: 117), but at several sites where there is evidence of continuous occupation across the eleventh century, cist-grave cemeteries were cut into the ruins of Mycenaean houses (e.g., Argos, Asine, Mycenae, Naxos, Thebes, Tiryns). On the Athenian acropolis and at Iolkos in southern Thessaly, they were even carved into the crumbling debris of once-mighty palaces (Styrenius 1967: 22–3; Sipsie-Eschbach 1991).

One interpretation of this would be that Submycenaean settlement did in fact continue in the same locations as Mycenaean, and that as happened at twelfth-century sites like Lefkandi and Tiryns,[11] eleventh-century central Greeks dug graves between their houses or under the house floors; but because Submycenaean apsidal houses were so flimsy, the buildings themselves have been destroyed, leaving behind only the graves, dug safely beneath the surface. In the tenth century we have one definite case of intramural burial, in the Karmaniola area at Asine. Settlement continued here without interruption from the twelfth century through the eighth, and although there are no Submycenaean graves in the small excavated area, a series of eight Protogeometric burials has been found, beginning around 1000 BC (figure 6.3; Wells 1976; 1983).

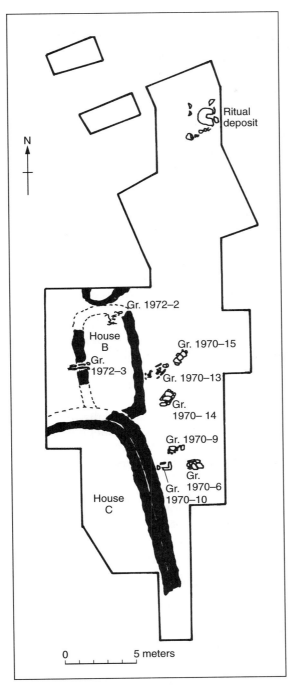

Figure 6.3 Houses and graves in the Karmaniola area at Asine (based on plans in Wells 1976; 1983)

However, this model does not work for other sites. Eleventh-century walls were found among the graves at Naxos, but these belonged to funerary structures, not houses (Lambrinoudakis 1988: 235). At Argos and Tiryns (Hägg 1974: 23–7, 79–82), little Submycenaean settlement material was found around the graves, and it is unlikely that there were originally houses above them; while at Mycenae Desborough explicitly concluded that "The likelihood of any of these tombs being intramural, in the sense of a burial in a house at a time when it was still lived in, seems rather small."[12]

By burying their dead in ruined houses but building their own huts elsewhere, Submycenaean Greeks created a new landscape. They seem almost to be declaring the Mycenaean world itself dead. They distanced themselves from the past instead of trying to reproduce it. People *chose* to dig graves into Mycenaean ruins or to avoid them, and to use new types of graves, pottery, and metalwork or to stick with the old ways, not as passive reponses to uncertainty, but because it seemed like the right thing to do in the circumstances. A much smaller number of people – again, through decision-making processes which we cannot observe – carried on using chamber tombs, or, like those who dug Asine gr. LH 12, a cist grave cut into the dromos of a twelfth-century chamber tomb (Frodin and Persson 1938: 158), assimilated their funerals to them. I can only see these decisions as being motivated by a desire to stay in touch with the Mycenaean past. But most of the choices being made by 1050 look like deliberate attempts to break with that past. Even if the basic skills needed to dig chamber tombs or build multiroom houses had somehow been forgotten, there were plenty of Mycenaean chamber tombs which could be re-used and houses which could at least be fixed up. Both things happened in the decades around 1100. But by 1050 most central Greeks distanced themselves from the past instead of trying to reproduce it.

Central Greece had become something of a ghost world. Practically every hilltop and harbor had had earlier occupants, and by 1050 the landscape was dotted with the ruins of a more glorious age. Just listing examples cannot evoke the atmosphere of these days. The experience of moving through a landscape so heavily shaped by a vanished race must be understood intuitively, but this is no easy task. Each age interprets ruins in its own ways, as Anton Bammer (1994) shows in his study of reactions to the remains of Ephesus over the past two centuries. For Georg Simmel (1968 [1911]: 261), "it is the fascination of the ruin that here the works of man appear to us entirely as a product of nature." In a speeded-up, frantic world, the creeping ivy and lichen on German castles anchored Simmel in a more authentic and reflective reality; while in early medieval France and Italy, the inhabitants of a shrunken world peopled the magnificent Roman villas now overtaken by forests and wild animals with devils and saints (Fumagalli 1994: 71–5), and Sarah Semple (1998: 121) speaks of "the demonization of the [prehistoric] barrow" in Anglo-Saxon England. But what of eleventh-century central Greece? Here the past was surely more tangible than the present; sturdy Mycenaean remains everywhere overshadowed the flimsy huts thrown up in their shadows. Boardman has suggested that

> The physical presence of the Bronze Age world must still have been strong, and in places like Mycenae and Cnossus overwhelming, in the centuries immediately following the collapse of the Mycenaean kingdoms ... its presence was a constant reminder to the Greeks of what life could be if the gods willed, and the challenge to emulate what had, perforce, to be attributed to the work of heroes, gods or giants, lay always before them. (Boardman 1982: 793)

Three or four generations of central Greeks had struggled to meet this challenge, but the next turned away from it. If any part of the Iron Age deserves to be called a Dark Age, then this is it. From some perspectives, such as that of the lower classes who built the Mycenaean palaces and labored to meet their quotas, or that of the local aristocrats held in check by the *wanakes* and their officers, the destructions around 1200 may have been a blessing. But by 1050 the costs of change – not just the loss of high civilization, but also disruption and massive mortality – outweighed the benefits to any group. Egyptian documents record crop failures at just this time (Kitchen 1986: 247). Ordinary people in central Greece may have been less vulnerable to shortages if they no longer had to support palatial elites, but without palatial buffering mechanisms, food crises could quickly become famine, disease, and depopulation.

The burials suggest that by 1025, Mycenaean values and ways of life no longer provided practical models. In their funerals people seem more concerned with showing what they were *not* than with what they were. Central Greeks had lost the sophistication of earlier times, and gave up the last efforts to reproduce the Mycenaean way; but seem not to have formulated any coherent alternative. This was perhaps as much a Postmycenaean as a Submycenaean culture (cf. p. 67). As Desborough remarked, "Altogether it is a strange mixture of an end and a beginning" (1972: 340). The old world had passed away; the new was not yet born.

The Bronze Shortage Hypothesis

In *Burial and Ancient Society* (I. Morris 1987) I argued that the chaos of the eleventh century ended with the creation of a new social structure, imposing order and stability on the Submycenaean flux. The best evidence comes from graves. Funerals divoded the world between an internally homogeneous elite, of perhaps one-quarter to one-third of the adult population, and excluded lower orders, whose remains have low archaeological visibility. The elite, I suggested, dominated landholding. This thesis has its critics (e.g., Sallares 1991: 122–9; Papadopoulos 1993; Humphreys 1993: 130–4), but the counterarguments have not persuaded me (I respond in I. Morris 1992: 78–80; 1993b; 1998c). All detailed reanalyses of the Kerameikos have supported the exclusion hypothesis (Whitley 1991a; 1994a; Houby-Nielsen 1992; 1995; D'Onofrio 1993), although they debate some of the historical implications I drew out of it; and Cavanagh (1996: 664) suggests that new finds from the Knossos North Cemetery support my extension of the argument to Crete.

We still know little about tenth-century settlements (Mazarakis Ainian 1997 collects the evidence), but as in the eleventh century, each region probably had one major site with a few hundreds or even thousands of souls, and a scatter of hamlets (p. 202 above). Of religion we know even less. Like burials and houses, worship had low visibility. Mazarakis Ainian (1997) suggests that much cult activity went on in the houses of chiefs, which, like burial, effectively drew a line within the community between those included in the most prominent rituals and those excluded from them. I return to this topic in chapter 7.

Here I want to extend these social histories of material culture. The late eleventh century, I suggest, saw not just the creation of a new, rigid social order asserting boundaries between haves and have-nots, but also a new way of seeing the world. This was as important for Greece's long-term development as the new social structures.

I suggested in chapter 1 that the best cultural history builds on social and economic analysis rather than abandoning it, and I want to start from one of the most important hypotheses yet developed about the Iron Age. Reviewing the evidence then available, Snodgrass noticed that just as iron grave goods started appearing regularly in central Greece (around 1000 BC on the chronology used here), bronze, gold, ivory, and other imported materials became rare. In Middle Protogeometric graves (*c.* 1000–950) iron even came into use for dress pins, rings, and fibulas, although these are much easier to make out of bronze. The pattern was so consistent that Snodgrass hypothesized a bronze shortage, caused by the final collapse of trade with the Near East. Central Greeks had probably learned the methods of ironworking from Cyprus by about 1050, and with their access to Anatolian tin drastically reduced, they turned to local iron ores for all their needs. This situation lasted until late in the tenth century, when bronze grave goods reappeared. By 900, Near Eastern finished goods were being buried with the dead (Snodgrass 1971: 228–68; 1980b).

There is abundant corroborating evidence outside Greece. No Greek objects found in the Levant or Cyprus can be dated confidently between about 1025 and 925, and Near Eastern politics provides a plausible context for the decline in contacts. The Egyptian *Story of Wenamun* (Lichtheim 1973–80. II: 224–30) describes Sidon and Byblos as powerful trading centers soon after 1100. As noted on p. 168 above, many scholars now suggest that the "historical" books of the Hebrew Bible were composed as late as the first century BC, and tell us little about actual events of the eleventh through eighth centuries (see van Seters 1983; P. R. Davies 1992). The archaeology of Iron Age II Israel also shows that the Biblical narratives need modification; yet the general picture is of a sharp increase in wealth and political centralization in the tenth century, which is at least consistent with the stories of the United Kingdom under Saul, David, and Solomon (Barkay 1992).

The Hebrew Bible says that by 1050 the Philistines had defeated the Israelites at Ebenezer (I Samuel 4: 1–10), and for three generations dominated the coast between Gaza and Mount Carmel, weakening the Phoenician cities through raids. Phoenician transport amphoras have been found in early eleventh-century tombs on Cyprus, but none date after 1050. Around 975 the Israelites broke Philistine power, and under Hiram I (969–936 BC) Tyre emerged as a center for long-distance trade, making commercial voyages in collaboration with Solomon of Israel to Ophir, perhaps down the Red Sea, and to Tarshish, perhaps in Spain (I Kings 9: 10, 10: 22; Briquel-Chatonnet 1992: 271–87). On their trips to the west Mediterranean, some of them visited the Aegean. Greek pottery once more shows up in the Levant around 900, traveling inland to the Sea of Galilee and the Amuq valley. Phoenicians were in the Aegean by 900, and craftsmen may have settled at Knossos and on Rhodes. A few villages on the Aegean islands and the west coast of modern Turkey had used central Greek pottery styles right across the Dark Age, but around 950–900 their numbers increase dramatically, perhaps indicating an expansion of settlement, or even the "Ionian migration" of later stories. Overall, it seems that central Greece and Crete were drawn into a wider economic system in the late tenth century.[13]

Snodgrass's powerful hypothesis provoked surprisingly little discussion. Iron Age archaeologists of other areas accepted and applied his model (Wertime and Muhly 1980; Sørenson and Thomas 1989a), but classicists, including those who call preclassical Greece an "oriental culture" (see pp. 102–3), have not responded. In returning to these data I defend Snodgrass's thesis that east Mediterranean trade declined after 1200 and all but dried up around 1050–1025, only to revive a century later. But I also complicate his interpretation, suggesting that recent finds show that central Greek behavior was not just a passive response to nondiscursive economic forces. Rather, people made sense of their changing world within existing systems of thought, but modified and even revolutionized those systems when they could not cope with the facts of life.

When Snodgrass formulated the bronze shortage hypothesis, virtually all the evidence came from graves. Table 6.2 shows the distribution of metals in the securely datable burials now known. Even making only crude distinctions between Submycenean, Protogeometric, and Early/Middle Geometric, there is a sharp movement away from bronze grave goods and toward iron after 1025, followed by an increase in the use of gold at the expense of iron after 900. But Snodgrass in fact argued that the few rich Protogeometric graves[14] all date either to the very beginning of Early Protogeometric, having more in common with Submycenaean traditions than with those of the tenth century, or else fall at the very end of Late Protogeometric, forming the beginning of the metal-rich ninth-century tradition. He argued that there was "a sequence of transition to iron, then intensive use of it, then of a partial reversion to bronze in the latest years of Protogeometric . . . Bronze prevails in the earliest and latest stages of Protogeometric . . . in between, the dependence on iron is general" (Snodgrass 1971: 237). If we group these final Protogeometric graves with the Early/Middle Geometric finds, then something like 85 percent of the metal grave goods in Snodgrass's bronze-shortage period (c. 1000–925 on the chronology I use here) would be iron. Our control over Dark Age chronology does not allow very fine distinctions, and we may want to focus just on the pattern in table 6.2, which is remarkable enough; but most experts do in fact date the graves in the way Snodgrass suggests. This would mean that all metals but iron virtually disappeared from central Greek burials between 1025 and 950.

When Snodgrass identified this pattern in the late 1960s, only Athens, Mycenae, Tiryns, and Theotokou in southern Thessaly had well published graves. All he could say of the rest of central Greece was that "conformity to Attic practices . . . is more loosely apparent

Table 6.2   Use of metal grave goods in central Greece, SM-MG

Period	Number of graves	Number of metal objects	Iron	Bronze	Gold	Silver
SM	376	354	6%	89%	4%	1%
PG	390	446	41%	48%	11%	0%
EG/MG	392	778	27%	45%	27%[1]	1%
Total	1,158	1,578	26%	55%	18%	1%

[1] Assuming just one gold ornament from Skyros in *BSA* 11 (1904/5) 78–80.
Sources: see table 6.1 above, plus: Athens: *AD* 34:2 (1979) 16; 38:2 (1983) 19; 40:2 (1985) 25–7; 43:2 (1988) 24. Attica: *AD* 40:1 (1985) 221–3; 42:2 (1987) 100; 46:2 (1991) 71; 47:2 (1992) 57. Argos: Courbin 1974; *AD* 26:2 (1971) 79; 27:2 (1972) 192, 197, 200, 205; 28:2 (1973) 95, 97–9, 115; 29:3 (1973/4) 219; 40:2 (1985) 86–8; 46:2 (1991) 91–2, 98–9; *BCH* 96 (1972) 162; *AE* 1977: 171–94. Argolid: Hägg 1974; Wells 1976; *BSA* 68 (1973) 87–101; *AD* 36:2 (1981) 105–7; 35:2 (1980) 124; 37:2 (1982) 85; Gercke *et al.* 1975: 27–8; *AAA* 7 (1974) 15–24. Boeotia: *AD* 27:3 (1972) 316; 29:3 (1973/4) 425, 439; 39:2 (1984) 126; *AE* 1976 chronika 12; Andreiomenou 1989; and see table 6.5 below. Corinthia: Salmon 1984; Dickey 1992. Euboea: See table 6.3 below. Cyclades: See p. 318 n. 41 below, plus Cambitoglou 1981: 99–102; *Praktika* 1978: 203. Dodecanese: See tables 6.6 and 6.7 below.

everywhere" (Snodgrass 1971: 237). There are more data now, but still only a handful of closely dated graves contradicts his pattern.[15]

The most important evidence is from Lefkandi. As table 6.3 and figure 6.4 show, the Middle and Late Protogeometric phases here saw more iron use and less bronze use. Catling and Catling (1980: 263–4) claim that the Lefkandian "bronze decline" was later than the one at Athens, but the most recent evidence for relative chronology (Catling and Lemos 1990: 94) synchronizes the patterns exactly.

The pattern has stood up to the test of new finds well, but seeing the changes as "an involuntary and to some degree temporary response to circumstances" (Snodgrass 1971: 239) may be to oversimplify them. When we look at metal use in detail, the similarity in patterns of deposition across central Greece fragments. Table 6.4 shows the use of iron, bronze, and gold for major artifact types at Athens, Lefkandi, and Argos, the three best-known Protogeometric sites. At Athens and Lefkandi, the shift from bronze to iron was also a shift in artifact types, from fibulas and rings to weapons and pins. Six out of every seven Protogeometric weapons and four out of five pins were iron, while

Table 6.3 Proportions of metal grave goods of different materials at Lefkandi

Period	Percentage of whole assemblage			Number of graves	Number of objects
	Iron	Bronze	Gold		
SM	6	86	8	23	49
EPG	23	74	3	12	39
MPG	39	33	27	13.5	33
MPG excluding heroon graves	56	28	17	11.5	9
LPG	34	27	39	32	155
SPG I	21	39	40	32.5	113
SPG II	14	25	61	25.5	131
SPG III	3	31	65	8.5	95
All graves	20	38	42	147	615
Raw numbers of objects	123	231	261		

Notes: Graves and grave goods dated as transitional (e.g., LPG/SPG I) are divided equally between the two phases. Gilt objects are counted separately under the material of the core object and under gold. Groups of small objects (beads, arrowheads) are treated as a single object.
Sources: Popham *et al.* 1980; 1993; Popham and Lemos 1996: table 1; *BSA* 77 (1982) 213–48; *OJA* 11 (1995) 103–7, 151–7.

many fibulas and rings continued to be made of bronze. At Athens, fibulas and rings made up 83 percent of the Submycenaean metal assemblage but only 27 percent of the Protogeometric, while weapons and pins increased from 18 to 70 percent. At Lefkandi, fibulas and rings declined from 80 percent of the Submycenaean assemblage to 49 percent of the Protogeometric, and weapons and pins increased from 20 to 38 percent.

We might derive two hypotheses from these data. Rather than reflecting a bronze shortage, changing tastes in dress might have caused increasing deposition of iron. Tenth-century men were dressed for burial with swords and spears, and women with pins, while fibulas and rings went out of fashion. Long, straight weapons and pins are easy to make out of iron; fiddly fibulas and rings are not. How can we tell whether changes in metal supply stimulated new fashions or

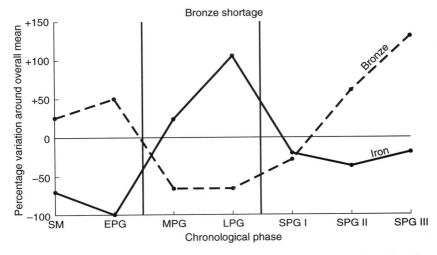

Figure 6.4   Bronze and iron use at Lefkandi, Submycenaean through Sub-Protogeometric

whether changes in dress create a false impression of changes in the metal supply? The external evidence for confusion in the Near East favors the former hypothesis, but much of the internal evidence is open to either reading. Where Snodgrass looked at the iron dress pins with bronze globes on their shafts and saw a sign that bronze remained desirable but was in short supply (1971: 232), Desborough inferred that "the addition of the bronze globe was the result of personal preference, not necessarily a sign of bronze shortage" (1972: 318).

But adding a third site, Argos, to the comparison tips the balance. Here the overall shift from bronze to iron is like that at Athens, but the proportion of the assemblage made up by weapons and pins actually fell from the Submycenaean figure of 63 percent to 39 percent in Protogeometric. Fibulas disappeared altogether (and were rare in burials anywhere on the Argive plain), but finger-rings more than made up for this, increasing from 18 percent of the finds to 61 percent. At Athens and Lefkandi, all of the small number of Protogeometric rings were bronze, but at Argos, 23 percent were iron. Further, while it is highly likely that iron weapons were recognized as superior to bronze ones (since iron continued to dominate this category after 900), Athenians and Argives did not think it was "natural" to make pins from iron. At all three sites, between 78 percent and 84 percent of Protogeometric pins were iron. The fact that iron was less favored for

Table 6.4 Uses of bronze, iron, and gold for major artifact types at Athens, Lefkandi, and Argos

	Total numbers of objects			Percentage of assemblage made up by artifact type
	Iron	Bronze	Gold	
a) Athens				
i) *SM*				
Weapons	1	2	0	1%
Pins	2	34	0	17
Fibulas	0	50	0	24
Rings	7	115	6	59
ii) *PG*				
Weapons	18	3	0	20
Pins	41	11	0	50
Fibulas	13	6	0	18
Bowls	0	2	0	2
Rings	0	5	4	9
iii) *EG/MG*				
Weapons	31	1	0	24
Pins	7	9	2	14
Fibulas	4	4	3	8
Bowls	0	29	0	22
Rings	5	1	17	18
Bands/diadems	0	0	18	14
b) Lefkandi				
i) *SM*				
Pins	2	7	0	20
Fibulas	0	20	0	44
Rings	0	12	4	36
ii) *PG*				
Weapons	29	0	0	18
Pins	27	5	0	20
Fibulas	9	43	0	33
Bowls	0	6	0	4
Rings	0	8	17	16
Bands	0	0	8	5
Attachments	0	0	7	4

Table 6.4 *Continued*

	Total numbers of objects			Percentage of assemblage made up by artifact type
	Iron	*Bronze*	*Gold*	
iii) *SPG*				
Weapons	19	0	0	7%
Pins	25	2	0	10
Fibulas	13	78	1	34
Bowls	0	12	0	4
Rings	0	1	74	28
Bands	0	0	13	5
Attachments	0	1	30	12
c) **Argos**				
i) *SM*				
Weapons	0	2	0	18
Pins	0	5	0	45
Fibulas	0	2	0	18
Rings	0	2	0	18
ii) *PG*				
Weapons	0	1	0	2
Pins	14	4	0	37
Rings	7	21	2	61
iii) *EG/MG*				
Weapons	16	1	0	10
Pins	30	41	0	41
Fibulas	0	7	0	4
Bowl	0	5	0	3
Rings	1	58	15	43

Notes: see table 6.3 above.
Sources: see tables 6.1–6.3 above.

pins in Submycenaean graves (6 percent at Athens, 22 percent at Lefkandi, 0 percent at Argos) is no surprise, since it was probably a valuable metal before 1050. But if the prominence of iron grave goods in Protogeometric times is simply a side-effect of the fact that it was easy to make pins from iron, it is hard to explain why the proportion of pins made of iron fell from 79 to 39 percent after 900 BC at Athens and from 76 to 42 percent at Argos (although at Lefkandi it increased, from 84 to 93 percent). The simplest explanation is that Athenians and Argives preferred bronze pins to iron ones, and when more bronze was available around 900 they switched over to it.

A change in dress at Athens and Lefkandi did not *cause* the change in the proportions of bronze and iron in the graves. Rather, both dress and deposition responded to an underlying decline in the availability of bronze and gold. I cannot see how else to interpret a find like the iron pin from a Protogeometric child grave at Tiryns, which had been carefully coated with bronze, to make it look like an all-bronze pin.[16]

But we should also draw a second conclusion. Buriers at Athens, Argos, and Lefkandi responded to the decline in long-distance trade in different ways. They mediated irresistible macroeconomic forces through ritual behavior, and analyzing grave goods is in the first instance an exercise in cultural history. It is much easier to make a long pin out of iron than to make a small fibula out of the same material. People at Argos and Tiryns gave up burying (and perhaps even wearing) fibulas in the tenth century. People at Athens closed the shrouds of their dead with fibulas less often after 1000 than before, but did not abandon them altogether. More than two-thirds of their Protogeometric fibulas were iron, despite the technical difficulties involved. The buriers of Lefkandi took a middle course, making one-sixth of their Protogeometric fibulas out of iron.

Evidence from other contexts also shows how central Greeks could at least control their responses to larger forces, and make sense of them on their own terms. A little settlement evidence is now available. Two bronze-and-iron door locks have been found in the huge apsidal building at Lefkandi Toumba, dating c. 1000–950 (Catling and Lemos 1990: 12, 27, 71–2), although given the peculiarities of the building, it is hard to know what to make of that (see pp. 218–38 below). Finds at Asine are more suggestive. Here only one Protogeometric burial in the small excavated area of houses, gr. 1970–15, contained metal, and fits the pattern of iron but no bronze (Wells 1976: 16–19). But the houses produced seven bronzes and traces of bronze- and iron-working (Wells 1983). These finds suggest that at least some bronze was available in tenth-century central Greece, which again means that buriers had an element of choice in the disappearance of bronze grave goods.

Chemical analysis of the bronzes from graves points the same way. Had central Greeks abandoned bronze grave goods as a mechanical response to declining tin supplies, we would expect that they would have tried to make the little tin they had go further, and that tenth-century bronzes would have a low tin content. But this is not the case. The tin content of the 102 analyzed bronzes from Lefkandi dating 1100–900 remained stable, at around 5 percent. Richard Jones (1980: 457) concludes that "there was a ready availability of the base metals to the metalsmiths at Lefkandi during the time span of the cemeteries." There are also some indications of where central Greeks might have found tin in the tenth century. A few east Mediterranean sherds have turned up in Middle Protogeometric contexts at Lefkandi, and local wares show stylistic links with eastern pottery styles (Catling and Lemos 1990: 56, 95); and important new excavations in Chalcidice have revealed Athenian and Euboean refuge sites flourishing through the eleventh and tenth centuries. Snodgrass (1994: 91) was among the first to point out that this means that central Greeks remained in touch with Macedonia, where central European tin was readily available.

There is more to these grave goods than the simplistic question of whether central Greece was an "oriental culture" in the tenth century. It clearly was not, but framing the discussion this way obscures the fact that grave goods were deposited by conscious actors, and that we can still observe some of the ways they manipulated economic facts. Tenth-century Athenians, Argives, and Euboeans had to come to terms with their own decline relative to the ruins filling their landscape; so too they had to face the decay of the ties that had bound them to a larger Mediterranean world.

Although they certainly had some bronze, in funerals between 1000 and 925 they emphasized iron objects, such as weapons and pins. What did this mean? Classical archaeologists often see such choices as "mere fashion," either too superficial or too psychologically embedded to be worth thinking about. But the roles of bronze and iron in the earliest Greek poetry suggest that this shift had two important symbolic overtones.

First, Homer consistently had the heroes at Troy fight with bronze weapons, restricting iron to similes drawing on his listeners' experiences. Hilda Lorimer pointed out the significance of this:

> The convention of bronze weapons in heroic poetry must have been maintained by generations of men who in battle never handled anything but swords and spears of iron . . . When within [two centuries] of the fall of Mycenae iron was fully established, there would at first be no impulse to make a change in the poems, since bards and audiences were alike aware that they were dealing with a past already of some remoteness and that iron weapons were a newfangled invention. (Lorimer 1950: 453)

In the eighth century the relationship between bronze and iron was *historical*: bronze was to iron as the race of heroes was to the contemporary world. Possibly this was a Homeric invention, but Lorimer's interpretation, that the notion that bronze was the metal of the past existed right through the Dark Age, is far more likely. This means either that when people turned away from bronze at the end of the eleventh century they were aware of drawing a line between themselves and that past, or (perhaps more likely) that with the hindsight of a generation or so, central Greeks realized that one more symbolic tie to antiquity had been cut. This may even have been welcome after generations of chaos. Just as they divided the community into a new elite and its dependants, the austere tenth-century rituals created order and coherence out of the symbolic anarchy described on p. 204 above.

Second, iron symbolically cut its users off from the east. It was a product of the local soil. I suggest that as contact with the east declined after 1050, and bronze and gold disappeared from funerals, iron came to stand as a symbol of the new, narrower horizons of the modern world. It was part of a presentist and inward-turned ideology.

Sørenson and Thomas (1989b: 17) distinguish between the Early Iron Ages of what they call " 'functional' societies, such as those in the Mediterranean and Western Europe, and 'ritual' societies, in Northern Europe and Scandinavia, in which wealth and attention are apparently channelled into ritual and religious activities rather than directly invested in infrastructure and in production." But the contrast may tell us more about the priorities of different groups of prehistorians than those of people in the past. There is little evidence for iron tools in Greece before the sixth century, and we should not think of the Dark Age as an "Iron Age" in the functional sense. But that does not diminish the importance of the shift from bronze to iron grave goods. At the end of the eleventh century iron took on a major role – arguably *the* major role – in burial symbolism. Iron defined the tenth-century elite order.

The Hero of Lefkandi and the Race of Iron

The Discovery at Toumba

Had I been writing twenty years ago, I could reasonably have claimed that this picture summed up the tenth-century graves. But in 1980 trial excavations on the Toumba hill at Lefkandi, adjacent to an important cemetery known since 1969, exposed traces of a large Protogeometric building (Popham *et al.* 1982; 1993; 1996; Catling and Lemos 1990).

During the *panagia* holiday that August, the landowner tried to bulldoze the site before the Archaeological Service expropriated the land, so he could build a summer house. He was defeated in this plan, but only after seriously damaging the middle of the building. Beginning in 1981, an Anglo-Greek excavation exposed a remarkable complex (figure 6.5). Two shafts had been cut into the bedrock. One contained two burials. The first was a man's ashes in a twelfth-century Cypriot bronze amphora, closed by a bronze bowl (figure 6.6). With the urn were a whetstone, and an iron sword, spearhead, and razor. The second burial (figure 6.7) was a female inhumation, adorned with an electrum ring, bronze and iron pins, and gold jewelry, including a gorget which is probably Old Babylonian, already a thousand years old at the time of burial (Popham 1994: 15). By the right shoulder was an iron knife with an ivory pommel. The second shaft held the remains of four horses, and a monumental krater stood over the graves. The whole group was enclosed by a massive apsidal building, some fifty meters long (figure 6.8), which was later filled in to make a huge oval mound (figure 6.9).[17] The sherds from the floor and the fill of the grave shafts and mound consistently date the whole complex as Middle Protogeometric, probably *c.* 1000–950 BC.

The Toumba burials are not just richer than the other 250 or so published tenth-century burials in central Greece: they are beyond all comparison. There are few traces of even simple grave markers at other sites before 900, but the Toumba mound would have required between 500 and 2,000 man-days of labor (Popham *et al.* 1993: 56). No building of comparable size is known in central Greece for the next 300 years. The Lefkandi structure covers more than twice the area of any other tenth-century building. The visual impact of this cemetery is equally unparalleled: the mound is at the top of the hill west of the Xeropolis settlement, with a commanding view over the Lelantine plain. After 950 the richest of Lefkandi's cemeteries formed around it. The only pre-seventh-century central Greek parallel for the horse sacrifices inside the apsidal building is Toumba gr. 68, right by the building's entrance. The excavators even suggest that "the unexpected presence of the knife with the female burial, its placing near the head and the apparently crossed position of hands and feet, which might have been bound, leave open the possibility at least of suttee" (Popham *et al.* 1993: 21).

This spectacular discovery is at odds with everything we thought we knew of tenth-century Greece, but discussion has focused more on its stratigraphic problems than its broader significance. The 1981 bulldozing damaged the layers above the burials. Mervyn Popham, the main excavator, believes that the burials came first, with the building erected

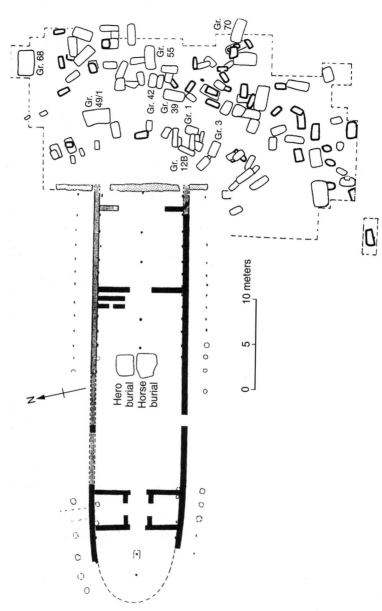

Figure 6.5 The Toumba apsidal building and cemetery at Lefkandi (based on Popham and Lemos 1996: plate 4)

Figure 6.6   The Toumba male cremation (photography courtesy of the Managing Committee of the British School at Athens)

over them as a shrine, and later filled in (Popham *et al.* 1993: 15, 99–100). Several critics argue that the building came first, probably being the dead man's home, and that the graves were dug through its floors, before the entire complex was buried under the mound (Calligas 1988; Crielaard and Driessen 1994; Antonaccio 1995: 236–41; Mazarakis Ainian 1997: 53–7). I side with the critics (I. Morris 1994), though the question is not crucial for my arguments here, and Popham is surely right that the state of the site "makes any interpretation difficult and appear extravagant, if not unlikely" (Popham *et al.* 1993: 101).

Fascination with the stratigraphic problems may explain why so few archaeologists have tried to put the building into some larger picture. The champions of the egalitarian, poor, and isolated Dark Age say little about the finds; while at the other extreme, Sarah Morris claims that "Recent archaeology on Euboia has dispelled Greece's 'Dark Age'" (1992b: 140), as if these two burials somehow overrule the rest of the evidence. Neither approach meets the interpretive challenge. We need an understanding of this period which can accommodate the Toumba discoveries *and* the rest of our finds, without ignoring any of the evidence.

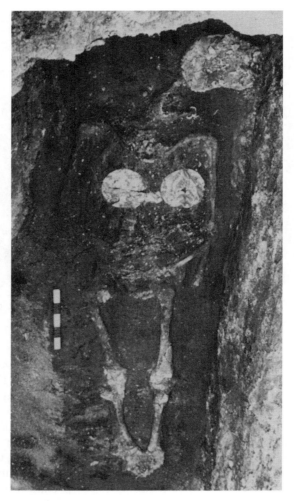

Figure 6.7 The Toumba female inhumation (photograph courtesy of the Managing Committee of the British School at Athens)

Thermon: A Parallel?

A second reason why so few archaeologists have taken a larger view may be that in the 1980s the Toumba complex seemed so different from other Iron Age finds that there were no comparanda. Petros Calligas (1988) suggested that tenth-century settlements consisted of

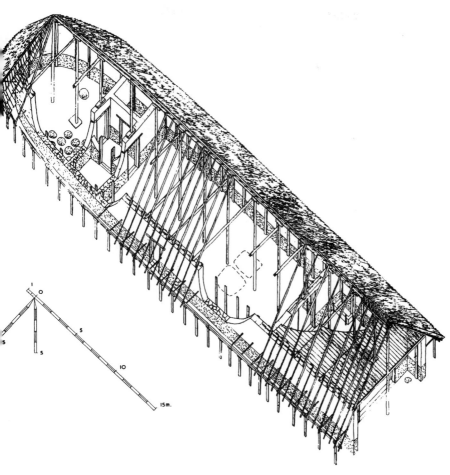

Figure 6.8 James Coulton's reconstruction of the Toumba apsidal building (based on Popham *et al.* 1993: plate 28)

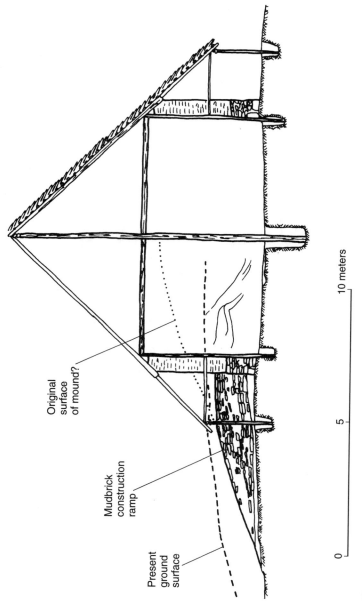

Figure 6.9 Reconstructed section through the building, showing the original mound surface (based on Popham *et al.* 1993: 54, fig. 1)

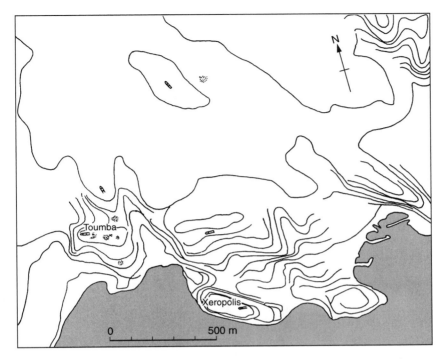

Figure 6.10 Petros Calligas' hypothetical map of the distribution of great houses at Lefkandi (based on Calligas 1984/5: 267, fig. 3)

up to half a dozen Lefkandi-type great houses scattered across neighboring hilltops, with the dwellings of lesser beings and the main cemeteries on the slopes of the hills (figure 6.10). He saw these houses as centers in new social structures emerging around 1000, focused on the *oikos* of a great man, as in Homer. In feasts at the great houses, he suggested, oral traditions developed about the leaders' ancestors. Eighth-century aristocrats were nostalgic for the earlier *oikos* society, and developed these songs into heroic epics. Dark Age elite culture may then have had much in common with Lévi-Strauss's model of "house societies" (Carsten and Hugh-Jones 1995), and Calligas' model is consistent with Whitley's (1991b) interpretation of settlement patterns.

We know so little about Iron Age settlements that there could well be more great houses waiting to be found, but for now it remains a hypothesis. However, since 1992, new digs at the old site of Thermon in Aetolia (figure 6.11) have uncovered parallels for some of the Lefkandi finds.[18] The first major building, apsidal Megaron A, was

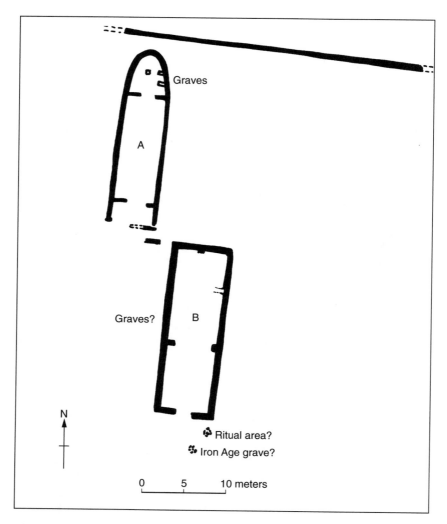

Figure 6.11 The Early Iron Age remains at Thermon (based on Mazarakis Ainian 1997: fig. 45a)

probably built around 1600. It stood for several centuries. Papapostolou discovered from unpublished letters that Sotiriadis found two groups of possible burials with Megaron A. The first consisted of two or three pits in the apse. Sotiriadis called them graves in an 1898 letter, saying that one contained human bones, charcoal, ash, sherds, fragments of bronze, and thin gold rings. The site report, however, spoke only of pits with animal bones. In front of Megaron A Sotiriadis found a single pit containing five iron swords and a fragmentary Geometric pot. Later, however, he suggested that at least one pit/grave was under the wall of Megaron A.[19] Mazarakis Ainian suggests that the only published pot from this part of the site, a Protogeometric mug, came from one of the pits. He puts all the burials in the Early Iron Age, arguing that Megaron A still stood well after 1200. Like Sotiriadis and Papapostolou, he sees the building being used in the eleventh or even the tenth century as a shrine for the people in the graves.[20]

Just south of Megaron A is the large rectangular Megaron B, now firmly dated to the Early Iron Age.[21] At 21.4 × 7.3 meters, it was almost half as big as the Lefkandi building. Just south of Megaron B, Papapostolou found a small pile of stones, earth, and ashes, 60 cm high, marked by a triangular slab. Among the stones was an iron knife. The stone pile was buried by accumulations when Megaron B was in use, but the triangular marker remained visible. Near this deposit was a group of three iron spearheads and an iron sickle knife, two round stone structures 80 cm. in diameter, and three small pits. One contained ash and an iron knife; the second, black earth, carbonized wood, and an Early Iron Age jug; and the third, lined with two stone slabs, held black earth, an iron spearhead, potsherds, and animal bones.[22] Stone circles are often associated with the cult of the dead (Hägg 1983a). Papapostolou sees some or all these deposits as human burials, suggesting that Megaron B, like Megaron A, was a shrine for worshipping the dead.[23]

A radiocarbon date from wood puts Megaron B's destruction around 830 BC.[24] Above its ruins Sotiriadis found a thick, late eighth-century black layer, full of bronzes. Above this was an apsidal peristyle of wooden columns on stone bases, replaced probably in the late seventh century by Temple C (Mazarakis Ainian 1997: 134–5). Megaron B probably had sacred associations right through the Iron Age, but in the eighth century, either these associations mutated from a cult of the dead to a cult of Apollo, or, if the area had always been dedicated to a god, the forms of cult activity changed dramatically.

At both Thermon and Lefkandi, we find large Early Iron Age buildings. Since Megaron B was destroyed around 830, it could be as old as the Lefkandi building, and could also continue a tradition going back to Megaron A. The Lefkandi building is definitely associated with a cremation, and Megara A and B may be associated with cremations (though there is no definite evidence for human burial, and in Megaron A the chronological relationships are unclear).

Despite the stratigraphic uncertainties at both sites, there are hints that the buriers drew on a shared cultural tradition. *If* the pits under Megaron A were human cremations, *if* there was continuity between Megara A and B, and *if* the pits near Megaron B were also burials, this tradition may go back some seven centuries, to the end of the Middle Bronze Age. Like the other apparent Middle Bronze Age continuities in Iron Age central Greece (p. 200 above), we might imagine it as a post-Mycenaean revival, or as being brought back to central Greece by new settlers. It involved cremation, often of men with weapons, in or near a large house. At Thermon, the house became a center for cult, then was destroyed in the late ninth century. In the eighth century the location was given over to sacrifices, and in the late seventh became a temple to Apollo. At Lefkandi, the house became a huge mound and the center for a cemetery. It fell out of use in the late ninth century; but then the whole Toumba site was abandoned.

Race of Heroes, Race of Iron

Calligas' model and the Thermon finds both provide an interpretive context for some features of Toumba, but by no means all. There may have been an Early Iron Age tradition from Aetolia to Euboea of cremating a great leader in or in front of the house which during the leader's lifetime had been the community's center, and which after his death became his shrine. But there is more to Toumba than just the scale of the house. We still face a bizarre contrast between what the Lefkandi buriers did and the other 250 or so tenth-century central Greek graves, which create an image of an austere, stable, and homogeneous elite turned in on itself, away from the past and the wider Mediterranean world. The burials under the apsidal building did not just break rules of scale: unlike the Thermon finds, they turned the spatial and temporal order on its head, linking the dead with the past and the east through spectacular imported heirlooms and the unique orientalizing tree-of-life motif on the krater (figure 6.12). We might see the antiques as a functional response to declining long-distance trade, the last resort of buriers who wanted to spend heavily but could not get hold of new oriental imports. But this would overlook their symbolic power. In Homer, nothing adds value to an object so effectively as a distinguished antiquity, allowing its owner (like the great men of Gawa, pp. 129–30 above) to list those who previously held it, going back ideally to a god. To someone used to elite funerals around 1000 BC, the behavior of the Lefkandi buriers would have been shocking. This funeral tore the fabric of time and space.

Figure 6.12   The krater marking the Toumba graves (based on Catling and Lemos 1990: plate 54)

Who could do such a thing? This, rather than whether we should call the tenth century a "Dark Age" or not, is the most important question which the Toumba graves raise. To answer it, we need to look beyond the physical remains. I suggest that the changes in death-rituals at the end of the eleventh century were part of a broader rethinking of identities, which transformed mythological, historical, and geographical categories. This left its traces on the earliest surviving Greek poetry, written down some 300 years later.

According to Hesiod's *Works and Days* (109–201), in the beginning, Kronos created a god-like race of golden men, who lived without toil or strife. Eventually the earth covered this race, who became kind spirits dwelling above the ground (*epichthonioi*). The gods then created a different and less noble silver race. Children lived with their mothers for a century, but adults neither restrained from wrongdoing nor sacrificed to the gods. So Zeus, who had by now succeeded Kronos as king of the gods, buried them beneath the earth, where they became underworld spirits (*hypochthonioi*). Zeus then made a third race of bronze, very unlike the silver men, terrible and strong. They were full of hubris, ate no bread, and loved war. "Their armor was bronze, their houses were bronze, and they worked with bronze," Hesiod tells us, "for there was no black iron" (150–1). They destroyed themselves and went down to Hades, without names. Zeus then made "a more just and better race, a god-like race of heroic men [*andron heroon theion genos*], who are called demigods [*hemitheoi*], the race before our own" (158–60). Some were killed fighting for Oedipus' flocks at Thebes, and others fighting for Helen at Troy. Others still Zeus sent away to the Isles of the Blessed, to live happily beyond the ends of the earth. "Thereafter," Hesiod concludes, "would that I were not among the men of the fifth race, but had either died before or been born after. For now is truly a race of iron [*genos sidereon*], and men never rest from labor and sorrow by day, and from perishing by night; and the gods shall lay sore trouble upon them" (*Works and Days* 176–80).

The heroes were important throughout antiquity. The demigods of the Trojan war were the quintessential heroes, but Greeks also promoted some contemporary men to heroic status at their deaths. Outstanding warriors, athletic victors, and the founders of new cities were the most likely to be so honored. In the most famous case, in 422, the people of Amphipolis mixed these two categories by deciding that the Spartan general Brasidas who had just been killed defending their city against Athens was their real founder, not the Athenian Hagnon, who had planted the settlement there just fifteen years before. Thucydides suggests that the Amphipolitans cynically manipulated heroization:

> The people of Amphipolis made an enclosure round [Brasidas'] tomb, and for the future they sacrificed to him as a hero and honored him by holding games and making annual offerings to him. They gave him the official title of founder of their colony, and demolished all the buildings of Hagnon, destroying everything that could possibly remind them of the fact that Hagnon had founded the place. It was Brasidas, they considered, who had been their preserver, and at the same time, because of their fear of Athens, they were exceedingly anxious to have the Spartan alliance. As for Hagnon, being at war with Athens, they could no longer honor him with the same profit as before, or with the same goodwill. (Thucydides 5.11)[25]

But we also hear of characters like Philippos of Croton, heroized because of his beauty, and Onesilos of Amathus, promoted after an oracle's interpretation of a strange omen (Herodotus 5.47, 114). In all cases, heroization came *at or after death*. Even in Homer's account of the Trojan War, the age when all living men could be called *heroes*, it was above all through a good death and funeral, commemorated by singers for all time to come, that a hero won true fame. Song and tomb (*sema*) were inseparable, and the grave mound was a metaphor for epic (Ford 1992: 158). A true hero had to die well, his body becoming more not less beautiful when torn apart by cruel bronze weapons. Vernant (1991: 50) notes that "As if it were an initiation, such a death endows the warrior with the set of qualities, honors, and values for which the elite, the *aristoi* [the "best men"], compete throughout their lives." A good death and the associated funeral and song raised a man to *truly* heroic status. Death rites made the hero, a god-like man who stood outside the flow of time, available to all through the mediation of an inspired poet.

In archaic and classical times, a living hero was a contradiction in terms. The line between mortals and demigods was permeable, and occasionally great deeds or an oracle's intervention showed that a man had lived up to the standards of the heroes. Once safely dead, he could be heroized, with a shrine at his tomb. The classical Greek countryside was dotted with these shrines, some of them for the panhellenic heroes famous from epic, others for heroes known only locally, or even without names (Farnell 1921; Brelich 1958; Kearns 1989). As Burkert sums up heroization, "Divine parentage is not a necessary precondition, however much the sons of gods are generally regarded as heroes. Even a criminal who has met a spectacular end may become a hero . . . It is some extraordinary quality that makes the hero; something unpredictable and uncanny is left behind and is always present." The result, Burkert suggests, was that "The gods are remote, the heroes are near at hand" (1985: 207–8).

I suggest that this distinctive Greek concept of the hero took shape at the end of the eleventh century. I argued in *Burial and Ancent Society* that the great changes in burial customs were part of the creation of a new elite; I now suggest that the new ruling class ended the symbolic chaos which began around 1100, the sense that everything was passing away but nothing was replacing it, and imposed order. In myth and death-ritual they proclaimed that Zeus had created a new world, a race of iron. Nothing could be more appropriate in the dark years around 1000, when central Greeks embraced iron so thoroughly in their burial symbolism. They fixed this world by pairing the race of iron with a second invention, an image of what they were not: the god-like race of heroic men, who were called demi-gods.

Archaeologists and historians commonly treat Greek ideas about the heroes as distorted memories of the Mycenaean past, a sort of bad history. But this is the one thing they were not. Eleventh-century central Greeks *created* the heroic race to give themselves a usable past, to make sense of the ruins and evident decline which surrounded them. Paul Veyne suggests that we should imagine ancient Greeks thinking of the distinction between their own time and the lost heroic world in much the same way that the horizon limits vision:

> mythic time had only a vague analogy with daily temporality . . . One does not perceive the limit of the centuries held in memory, any more than one perceives the line bounding the visual field. One does not see the obscure centuries stretching beyond this horizon. One simply stops seeing, and that is all. The heroic generations are found on the other side of this temporal horizon in another world. (Veyne 1988: 18)

To the people of the twelfth century who struggled to preserve Bronze Age ways, the Mycenaean world and its physical remains lay on the near side of the temporal horizon, in view, and worth holding onto. But by 1000 this past faded across the horizon and was mythologized, recreated in thought as the age of heroes. The race of iron could not be expected to build mighty palaces or to trade gifts with the kings of Egypt and Ugarit. Yet feeble as the race of iron might be, it was nonetheless part of Zeus's order, inseparable from its imagined past. Vernant captures the core idea of Hesiod's myth of the races in saying that "In mythical thought any genealogy is also at the same time the expression of a structure . . . The succession of the races in time reflects a permanent, hierarchical order in the universe" (1983: 5–6).

This makes more sense of our complex data than ignoring either the Lefkandi finds or the other 99 percent of the graves. Whatever the man buried under the Lefkandi apsidal building did, those who laid him there claimed that he surpassed the sadly fallen race of iron, breaking through from the degenerate present to a better world. The late eleventh-century reshaping of death-rituals was part of a larger intellectual revolution, coming to terms with the ruins filling the landscape and the steadily contracting horizons of the present. Whether invented out of nothing in the eleventh century, adapted from beliefs going back to the Middle Bronze Age, or reworked from a Near Eastern myth of declining races of gold, silver, and bronze, this was a classic foundation charter, naturalizing the evident decline in power and sophistication since Mycenaean times and promoting the stability of the new elites. There was no point struggling against the limitations on mortals, since they were Zeus's will. But the boundaries between past and present were nevertheless permeable. An outstanding man might transcend the present, as happened at Lefkandi. Instead of challenging the internal egalitarianism of the ruling class, his success reinforced it. Promoted on death (but not before) to parity with the heroes, he left the order of the age of iron intact.

But there are obvious problems in trying to link Lefkandi to the Hesiodic myth. The first literary attestation comes three centuries after the Toumba burials: was the tradition really so old in Hesiod's day? The lack of earlier written versions is, of course, no argument against a connection, since there *are* no literary sources from before 750. But we must still confront one of the major questions in scholarship on early Greek myth: "Are we entitled to believe that certain institutions or conventions existed before the first explicit mention is made of them in the documents we have? Can we extrapolate from the evidence available to us? Can we reconstruct backward?" (R. P. Martin 1993: 113).

The word *heros* probably had a long history before Homer and Hesiod. Two Linear B tablets mention the goddess Hera. In Thebes Of 28 she occurs alone, but Pylos Tn 316 also mentions Zeus, Hera's husband in Homer, and a goddess Diwija, not known in classical sources. Etymologically, Diwija should be the consort of Zeus (Diwios) (although Burkert (1985: 44) infers from the co-occurrence of Zeus and Hera on Tn 316 that they were already married in Bronze Age myth). Noting the variety of Hera's functions, Homer's habit of calling her *potnia* (mistress), and her tendency to have separate shrines from Zeus, Walter Pötscher (1961) suggested that in the Bronze Age Hera was a powerful nature goddess, with a consort named Heros. Some philologists link Hera, Heros, and Hora, "season," suggesting that "*Hêrâ* would have been the Mycenaean goddess of the spring . . . The [*hêrôs*] would have been 'he who belonged to the goddess of the seasons' . . . early Greeks would have understood the *hêrôs* as *Hêrâ*'s 'man of the season,' untimely in his early death" (O'Brien 1993: 117). Heros is not attested in the tablets, though *tiriseroe* may mean "thrice-hero" (Burkert 1985: 429 n. 2). On this theory, between 1200 and 700 Hera and Heros were separated, and Diwija disappeared. Hera entered an uncomfortable marriage with Zeus, and Heros, untimely in his early death, was generalized from the Mistress's consort into a word for a race of semi-divine men, equally untimely in their deaths, with Hera as their patron mother (O'Brien 1993: 156–66).

This rethinking could have happened at any time in the Iron Age, or gradually across it. But there are indications that the pairing of races of heroes and iron took place relatively abruptly. Myths of metallic races of declining virtue are known from several parts of the Middle East (West 1978: 174–7). All post-date Hesiod, but West (1997: 314–19)

shows that the details of Hesiod's myth have parallels going back
into the second millennium. He concludes that "Its very formalism is
un-Greek," and that "It seems necessary to postulate a common
source, dating from the earlier first millennium" (West 1997: 312, 319).
Similarly, Ludwig Koenen suspects that "the motifs of this story, as
well as the story itself, enjoyed a long life in Greece prior to Hesiod's
day," but he suspects that "naming the present-day age after iron . . .
seems scarcely possible before the 9th or even 8th century BC"
(Koenen 1994: 25 n. 59). Philology cannot resolve the question, but
archaeology suggests to me that central Greece between 1025 and 925,
when iron had most power as a symbol distancing the modern world
from the past, is the most likely context for the creation of something
like Hesiod's myth. I suggest that central Greeks added races of heroes
and iron to an older east Mediterranean tradition about three metallic
races to create a coherent genealogy.

This is not to say that concepts of the five races remained stable
from the Toumba burials to Hesiod. A hundred years ago, Erwin
Rohde (1966 [1890]) argued from Homer's use of *heros* that the word
was originally connected to ancestor worship, and West (1978: 370–3)
suggests that Hesiod drew together two distinct Iron Age senses of
the word. In the *Iliad*, *heros* simply meant "warrior," with no religious
overtones. Only once does Homer use the Hesiod-like expression
hemitheon genos andron, "race of semi-divine men" (*Iliad* 12.23). West
suggests that Homer drew on Ionian Greek stories about the Trojan
war, in which *heroes* were simply warriors who lived in the past, while
Hesiod came from a mainland tradition in which *heroes* had nothing
to do with the Trojan war, but were "the honoured dead and more
loosely terrestrial *numina* resident in a district" (1978: 373). West
argues that as Ionian heroic epics became popular on the mainland in
the eighth century, Hesiod or his source merged the two senses of
the word *heros*, equating local and epic *heroes*. Snodgrass (1988: 22)
suggests that the geographical distribution of archaeological evidence
for the veneration of Bronze Age remains in the eighth century supports West's thesis. Cult activity was concentrated on the mainland,
with just a few cases in the islands, and none in Ionia.

Linguists and literary critics have attacked West's etymologies and
his assumption that Hesiod was a simple peasant who could not handle
Ionian and Near Eastern mythology. Nagy observes that Homer
usually describes the fighters at Troy war from a perspective within
the story, speaking in persona as the Muses' mouthpiece. It would
therefore be inappropriate for him to give *heros* a religious sense. But
Iliad 12.23 "is one of those rare moments when the narrative of the
Iliad distances itself from the epic action . . . the perspective shifts from

the heroic past to the here-and-now of the Homeric audience" (Nagy 1979: 159), and it makes sense for Homer to call the heroes a "race of semi-divine men." Nagy sees not a geographical-chronological distinction but a generic one, and van Wees similarly concludes that "Homer *does* share Hesiod's view of the heroes as a distinct, extinct, and semi-divine race" (van Wees 1992: 8; emphasis added).

Since we lack evidence before 750, linguistic debates cannot be decisive. Linking later texts to Iron Age archaeology is fraught with dangers, but it does offer new possibilities. I suggest that something along the lines of the myth of the five races coalesced in the late eleventh century. The Mycenaean past was mythologized into a race of heroes, many of them sent to untimely deaths by Zeus. But the heroes were not gone forever: for the next millennium, oracles continuously announced that an odd assortment of men – from Brasidas to common criminals – had reached the standards of the lost race of heroes, and deserved religious honors.

The male burial at Lefkandi Toumba is the earliest known example of a ritual package which was to define heroic status for more than a millennium. By archaizing and orientalizing, buriers connected heroes to broader and more glorious lost worlds. Singers of tales and buriers of great men worked out a shared symbolic language. A great mound was part of the hero's due (*Iliad* 16.457, 671–5; 23.44–7; *Odyssey* 1.239–40; 14.366–71; 24.188–90), and a source of renewed honor for his descendants (*Iliad* 7.79–86; 23.245–58; *Odyssey* 5.311; 14.366–71; 24.93–5). The hero must be cremated and buried in a metal urn. Hector (*Iliad* 24.795) even had a gold urn, while Achilles and Patroclus shared another (*Iliad* 23.243; *Odyssey* 24.73–5). By the fifth century, urn, mound, and stele were metaphors for the hero in Athenian tragedy: the playwright had only to mention them for the audience to know that they were being carried into the presence of the great heroes of the Trojan war (e.g., Aeschylus, *Libation Bearers* 323–5, 351–3, 686–7, 722–4 (performed in 458)).

The similarities between the Toumba finds and Homer's account of Patroclus' funeral (*Iliad* 23.110–83) encouraged the excavators to call the male burial "the hero of Lefkandi" (Popham *et al.* 1982).[26] However, some critics note, archaic and classical hero cults sometimes produce clear evidence for sacrifices and feasts for the dead, as in the recently excavated example of a tumulus dating around 600 with offerings continuing till 200 BC at Orgame on the Black Sea coast (Lungu 1998). No such evidence was found at Lefkandi. Rather than being marked by a shrine, the mound became the center for a rich cemetery. Some of Popham's critics suggest that because there are no traces of worship, we cannot speak of hero cult. Carla Antonaccio, for example, concludes that "Though it has been termed a heroön and its male burial a hero, this is surely anachronistic" (1995: 243; cf. Mazarakis Ainian 1997: 57).

But the greatest danger of anachronism is the assumption that tenth-century hero cult will look the same as that of the fifth century. As we shall see in chapter 7, that is not true for the worship of the Olympian gods, whose cults changed massively in the eighth century. Robin Hägg (1987) shows that the pottery dedicated in archaic cults at Bronze Age tombs was much like that dedicated gods in the same period; the soundest method for deciding whether the absence of such finds at Lefkandi is a decisive argument against interpreting the burial as heroization ought then to be a comparison with other forms of tenth-century worship.

The worship of gods in tenth-century central Greece is archaeo-logically almost invisible. There seems to be continuous cult activity across the Iron Age at Kalapodi, on the edge of my central Greek area, and perhaps also at Ephesus; and we probably see worship at Isthmia and Asine around 1000 BC. Pottery dedications began on several Attic mountain tops by 900, and at new Cycladic sites like Koukounaries on Paros and Minoa on Amorgos, while finds at Iria on Naxos may go back further into the tenth century.[27] Older excavations may have missed tenth-century evidence, but even on the best digs, finds are meager. There are no buildings or distinctive altars, and usually just a few open clay vessels, probably refuse from meals rather than votive dedications. Even the ash deposits from the meals rarely amount to much. De Polignac (1995a: 16) speaks of "a relative lack of spatial determination, with no clear differentiation between sacred space and profane space." At several of these sites, archaeologists would not have known they were excavating Dark Age religious deposits had it not been for the distinctive archaic and classical remains above them. Some sites with Bronze Age as well as archaic religious activity, like Ayia Irini on Keos and Apollo Maleatas at Epidaurus, almost certainly remained sacred places across the Iron Age, even though no tenth-century finds are reported.[28]

Dark Age cult activity took varied forms, but they all have low visi-bility. If people worshipped the man under the Toumba mound from 950 till 825 (when the cemetery was abandoned) like they worshipped the gods, and particularly if they did so on top of the now badly eroded mound (see figure 6.9), it is no surprise that we have no evi-dence for it. All religious activity before about 750 BC has low archaeo-logical visibility, and we can infer little from the absence of clear evidence for worship at Lefkandi.

Buriers continued to draw on elements of the package of rites that we first see at Lefkandi until hellenistic times, whenever they wanted to establish heroic status for a dead man. This burial stands at the head of a millennium-long cultural tradition. The Lefkandians announced that the man under the mound was a hero, transcending the race of iron. They cremated him, put his bones in a bronze urn which had been handed down for two centuries, and perhaps killed his wife or courtesan and his horses. They laid the bodies alongside him, surrounded him with weapons and orientalizing and archaizing grave goods, and buried him and his apsidal building under a great mound.

Popham stresses the similarities with Patroclus' funeral, thinking it "likely that Homer is describing, and no doubt elaborating, the kind of funeral that a warrior or king of this period might be given" (Popham *et al.* 1993: 22). But when we look at the archaeological record as a whole, we see that the power of this burial was precisely that it was *not* the kind of funeral that a warrior or king of around 1000 BC might be given. It was part of the invention of a new tradition. The "heroic age" was not the Mycenaean age, and never had been; it was a creation of the final years of the eleventh century, a mirror in which the new elites defined themselves.

There is in the end no way to prove that this myth-complex took shape in the late eleventh century. This is mind-reading, not fact-grubbing. But the great merit of this model is that it makes sense of more of our data, literary and archaeological, than any other way of looking at them. Archaeologists have either ignored 99% of the known burials to emphasize Lefkandi, or have bracketed Toumba as an anomaly to the statistically dominant pattern. The interpretation I advance here does not require us to do either of these things.

But it also complicates our understanding of early Greek ideas about the past and the east, and through this process of complication offers new ways to grasp the origins of the archaic ideologies I discussed in chapter 5. By 1000, central Greek communities were dominated by elites which represented themselves as internally egalitarian. I argued in *Burial and Ancient Society* that they were defined largely by control of land and dependent labor. They turned their backs on the past and the wider world. But a few men showed that they preserved the qualities of the ancient heroes, seen as the occupants of the Mycenaean ruins. In the earliest such burial known, the mourners constructed a ritual package linking the dead with just that wider world which, under pressure of circumstances, they denied to themselves in their everyday lives. The scale of labor in the mound implies that someone, somehow, persuaded hundreds of people of the justness of this claim. The relationship between this burial and normative elite practices also suggests that people felt a sad decline from the race of heroes. The burdens Zeus inflicted on the race of iron isolated them from that past and from the wider world.

Half a millennium later, we find city-states dominated by internally egalitarian male citizen elites defined by descent and gender but not by wealth, and controlling excluded and fragmented groups of women and slaves (Part III). These citizens also turned their backs on the heroic past and the oriental world, but now from a sense of superiority. A narrower elite of wealth, birth, and education claimed to rise above these associations of peasants. Their ability to manipulate Lydian culture and act like heroes and even gods constituted, in their own eyes, proof of this.

Long-term continuities and abrupt discontinuities are both evident. Creating an internally egalitarian ruling class by rejecting the east and the past was not an invention of classical Athenians or even of Hesiod: it went back to the beginning of the Iron Age. But between the tenth century and the sixth something happened to turn the Dark Age elite into the classical community of middling citizens.

Redefining the Past and the East in the Ninth Century

The relationships established around 1000 BC between the locality and the east and the present and the past survived, in their main outlines, until the middle of the eighth century. But around 900 alternative visions challenged them. Tenth-century culture explained the Aegean's isolation and its decline from past glories, but by the century's end this isolation broke down. This is most obvious in the increase of grave goods, particularly gold. Coldstream (1977: 55–781) speaks of an "awakening in mid-ninth century" followed by a period of "consolidation," as grave goods escalated from 900 until 850, then declined until 750. This is important, but the statistical pattern again only reveals part of the story. Changes around 900 in the precise kinds of grave goods and monuments used were as significant as the quantitative increase. And while the distribution of grave goods remained relatively stable across the tenth and ninth centuries, there were important variations at the level of individual sites. To clarify this, I briefly summarize the seven major groups of burials in central Greece.

1. Euboea

A rich cemetery developed round the Toumba mound after 950.[29] Gr. 49/1, probably the first burial after the mound, already contained gold rings, gilt coils, and iron pins. A little before 900, gr. 39 contained 20 pots, an iron axe, dagger, spear butt, and fibula, 7 gold ornaments, a jug and fibula of bronze, and a pair of probably Cypriot bronze wheels. The faïence included a ring with a ram-headed god as a bezel, a couchant lion, 2 flasks, a duck-askos, and a necklace of 96 beads. Gr. 70, also late tenth-century, produced 6 bronze fibulas, a bronze jug, 9 gold rings, gilt hair coils, iron rings with crystal heads, and a remarkable engraved Near Eastern gilt bronze bowl. Gr. 42, soon after 900, included (in addition to a gold band and six attachments) 9,250 faïence beads and an imported Egyptian bronze situla; and gr. 55, of the same date, held 5 gold rings, 2 gold earrings, another embossed Syrian bronze bowl (figure 6.13), and 2 gilt pins, one with an extraordinary globe of crystal cones.

On present evidence, Lefkandians anticipated developments elsewhere in central Greece by a generation. By 850, graves with a dozen or more gold ornaments were common in the Toumba cemetery, and Skoubris gr. 59 parallels its wealth. But just as the graves' magnificence peaked around 850–825, all the cemeteries went out of use, and the settlement may have been destroyed.

There are few burials of this period elsewhere on Euboea. Disturbed graves have been found at Malakonda, but only pottery was reported. At Chalcis, a child grave around 1000 contained no metal, which is what we would expect, but the seven known graves dating 925–825 are also poor. Graves of Coldstream's consolidation phase are known only from Eretria. Two date 850–800. One contained only pottery, and the other an iron sword. Four more graves belong to the early eighth century. One, the inhumation of a young woman, held amber beads, and another, a primary cremation, a plain gold diadem.[30]

None of these graves is as rich as the mid-ninth-century examples from Lefkandi, and the contrasts between the ninth-century graves at sites so close together may be important. However, the samples outside Lefkandi are small, and it would be premature to build much on them.

2. Attica

Developments at Athens seem more hesitant than on Euboea. We see tentative challenges to Protogeometric austerity soon before 900. There were no graves with metal and imports like Lefkandi, but Kerameikos grs. PG 39, 40, and 48 held 22, 16, and 30 vases respectively, and two or three bronzes each. PG 48 is the first example of closing the mouth of the urn with a bronze bowl, which became

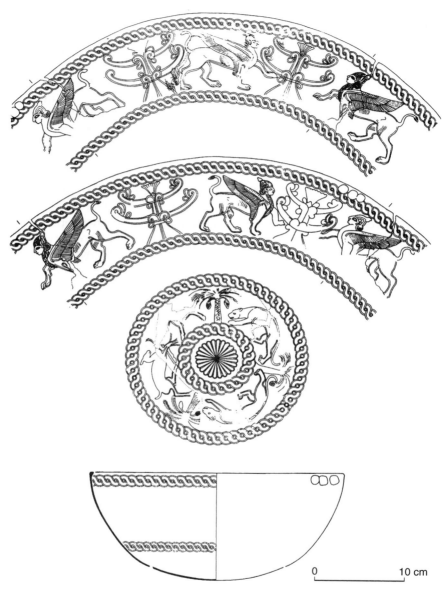

Figure 6.13 Engraved Near Eastern bronze bowl from Lefkandi Toumba gr. 55 (after Popham and Lemos 1996: pl. 133)

normal practice in the ninth century. It is as if the buriers were cautiously testing the limits of Protogeometric norms. After 900, their successors went further. A group of well-provided warrior burials (Kerameikos grs. G 2, 38; cf. G 7, with two gold rings) was dug next to PG 39, 40, and 48, followed around 850 by grs. G 41–3. These burials greatly surpassed the earlier experiments. G 41, for instance, contained 10 bronze fibulas, a bronze bowl, 2 gilt iron pins, 3 gold rings, and a small ivory duck, while the urn in G 42 was sealed by the first actual oriental import known from Athens, a Levantine bowl with an embossed hunting scene, a generation or so after the first such bowl at Lefkandi.[31]

By 850–825 graves with gold were no longer unusual. Ten meters west of the plot discussed in the last paragraph, gr. G 13 held two plain gold diadems and an iron sword and dagger; and 25 meters north, the unusual gr. hS 109 held an iron sword and spearhead and another gold diadem. Similar plots appeared all round Athens c. 850. On Kriezi St, grs. 1968/2, 7, and 14 all held gold bands; and in the later Agora, gr. H16:6, the richest known Athenian Iron Age burial, produced 29 vases, 3 bronze pins, 6 gold rings, a spectacular pair of gold earrings, 3 ivories, and a necklace of 17 glass and more than 1,000 faïence beads.[32] This necklace, like the bowl in Kerameikos G 42, was probably imported, and the earrings betray knowledge of Near Eastern skills. However, none of the gold diadems which are so common in mid-ninth-century graves had impressed orientalizing scenes; all were plain or decorated with meanders.

There was a general escalation in grave goods, with many plots boasting one or more rich burials (see Whitley 1991a: 133), and a trend toward more impressive pots as grave markers. At the same time, some grave plots emerged as distinctly richer, and only a few had actual oriental objects. This might point to variations in access to orientalia or uncertainty about the attractions of the east, but the general unwillingness to put overtly oriental decoration on pottery and metalwork favors the second possibility.

Grave goods began to decline at Athens before 800. There are no rich Middle Geometric II graves in the Kerameikos, though Barbara Bohen (1997) argues from the high-quality early eighth-century sherds in the fill of sixth-century Mound G that the builders of this monument destroyed the richest graves of this period. Elsewhere in Athens around 800, Aktaiou St gr. 1985/1 contained a gold band and two gold rings, Kavalotti St gr. B an ivory figurine of Isis, and Theophilopoulou St gr. 4 another gold band; a group of Middle Geometric II graves near the Kynosarges gymnasium produced 12 gold ornaments; and Kriezi St gr. 1968/12 held 3 more, and 4 bronze vessels.[33] These graves are not so rich as those of *c.* 850, but in the Attic countryside, the reverse is true. Coldstream (1977: 78) suggests that there was a "decentralization of wealth," with new, richer, settlements appearing along the coasts, siphoning luxurious grave goods away from Athens. Anavyssos gr. 1966/2 (*c.* 800) produced 7 gold ornaments and a faïence scarab, and the wealth of the Alpha and Isis graves at Eleusis has few parallels. Each of these and Anavyssos gr. 1966/51 held a pair of gold earrings rivaling those from Agora H16:6, and as well as a wealth of gold, silver, and bronze jewelry, the Isis grave held three faïence scarabs, necklaces of faïence and amber, and ivory figurines.[34]

3. The Argolid

Argos followed much the same pattern as Athens. Grave goods increased and diversified around 900. Hägg (1974: 30) dates gr. 3 at the Telephone Company (OTE) building, containing 2 gold spirals, and gr. 6, holding 2 gold bands, at the very end of the Protogeometric period. But these are the earliest rich grave goods, and Argives seem even more cautious about luxury than Athenians. Even by 850 the richest burials are Papanikolaou gr. 1, containing only 3 gold ornaments, and Makris gr. 2/1, with no gold, but 17 bronzes. No actual oriental imports have been found, although at Tiryns, Southwest Cemetery gr. 13 (probably Late Protogeometric) contained a faïence plaque; gr. 2, around 900, a pair of iron pins with ivory globes; and early ninth-century gr. 1972/6, a necklace of faïence and clay beads.

As at Athens, rich graves went out of fashion at Argos by 800. No Middle Geometric II grave contains gold. The most lavish offerings come in South Cemetery gr. 6/1, probably around 775 BC, with 25 bronzes and 6 iron pins; and in the Argive countryside a grave at Berbati, *c.* 825 BC, had 36 pots and 14 bronzes.[35]

4. Corinthia

Following a gap since Submycenaean, five Late Protogeometric graves have been found at Corinth. They are poor, as are most of the roughly twenty graves dated 900–750. One grave of around 900 held four bronzes, and another 32 pots. The evidence is consistent with the general picture of increasing wealth after 900, but is too meager for confidence. Later in the ninth century, a grave at Athikia produced 23 bronzes, and another at Klenia eight bronzes and two gilt bronze spirals.[36]

Table 6.5 Mean numbers of grave goods per adult burial at Akraiphia, *c.* 925–750 BC

	n	*Pots*	*Bronze*	*Iron*	*Glass*
Pre-825	5	3.4	5.2	1.0	0.2
825–750	5	4.6	4.2	0.8	0

Note: Pre-825 = grs. ΔΔ/151, Grava 2, ΓΗΠ/16, 30, and 31; 825–750 = grs. ΓΗΠ/19, 25, 27, 32, and 123. I have not included the robbed gr. ΓΗΠ/132.
Sources: Andreiomenou 1991; *Praktika* 1989: 127–32.

5. Boeotia

The earliest graves at Vranezi and Andikyra probably date a little before 900, but most of the excavated pots look ninth-century. The original reports mention bronze and gold ornaments, but there are no quantifiable data. Another early report says that a ninth-century grave at Orchomenos contained glass beads. Other than an urn cremation without grave goods of *c.* 900 at Tachi, the only early graves published in recent excavations are at Akraiphia, beginning *c.* 925. These were quite rich in bronzes, but contained no gold or imports. There was a slight decline in metal after 825, but the sample is small (table 6.5).[37]

6. The Dodecanese

In the small cemetery at Asarlik, tomb A, in use around 1000, contained only pots and iron weapons; while tomb C, in use in Geometric times (and certainly in the early eighth century) also held bronze and gold. The earliest known graves on Rhodes date soon before 900, with small groups of adult urn cremations and child inhumations. Three graves at Kameiros are Protogeometric and three Early or Middle Geometric. All are poor, though the number of pots increases sharply after 900 (table 6.6). At Ialysos, the four Protogeometric graves were also poor, but Early Geometric gr. 1936/43 produced bronzes and faïence, including an Egyptian statuette of Bes. Two of its pots were Cypriot imports.[38]

The limited evidence from Asarlik and Rhodes follows the same patterns as the mainland sites, but the larger cemeteries on Kos are more complex. About fifty graves dating *c.* 925–750 were dug into the

Table 6.6   Mean numbers of grave goods per burial on Rhodes, Late Protogeometric through Middle Geometric

| | | Mean number of objects per grave | | | |
Period	n	Pots	Bronze	Iron	Faïence
Ialysos, LPG	4	3.75	0	1.5	0
Ialysos, EG	1	12.0	8.0	1.0	3.0
Kameiros, LPG	3	3.0	0	0	0
Kameiros, EG/MG	3	7.3	0	0.3	0

Sources: Ialysos, *AD* 23:1 (1968) 82–3, gr. 98; *ClR* 3 (1929), gr. 470; 8 (1937) 7–207, grs. 44, 45 (all LPG); gr. 43 (EG). Kameiros, *ClR* 6/7 (1933) 7–219, grs. 43, 45, 84 (LPG), 39, 80, 83 (EG/MG).

ruins of the Bronze Age town on the edge of or within the contemporary Iron Age settlement (Kantzia 1988: 181). Since many of the graves contain no offerings there is uncertainty about dating, but between 1 and 15 adults belong to this period, and 73 children (table 6.7). Some of the Protogeometric child graves were rich. Seven contained 1–3 gold ornaments, and gr. 10 more than 1,000 faïence beads. And in contrast to the pattern in adult graves all over central Greece, the wealth of the child burials declined after 900. None of the adult Early and Middle Geometric graves with offerings contained gold, and there was little faïence (although Fadil gr. 1 held 13 bronzes).[39]

In 1984, a small excavation uncovered a Middle Geometric I urn cremation, in the manner favored on Rhodes for adults, along with a second pot, and bronze ornaments. This suggests that Kos had a separate, unexcavated, adult cemetery.[40]

7. The Aegean Islands

Few graves are known. Naxos is the only island with hints of continuous activity. Here a group of unusual graves goes back to *c.* 1000 (see p. 246). Syrivli gr. 2 on Skyros may date around 950, but otherwise no graves are earlier than 925–900. Their grave goods are like those from mainland regions (table 6.8), although there are not enough to make meaningful distinctions between those before and after 850. Skyros has the richest burials, very like those on Euboea. Three contained gold,

Table 6.7 Grave goods on Kos, Protogeometric through Middle
Geometric

Adult burials

Period	n	Pots	Gold	Silver	Bronze	Iron	Faïence
LPG-MG,							
maximum n	15	0.3	0	0	*c.* 0.6	0.3	0
minimum n	1	2.0	0	0	*c.* 2.0	0	0

Child burials

Period	n	Pots	Gold	Silver	Bronze	Iron	Faïence
LPG-EG,							
maximum n	63	2.7	0.2	0	0.7	0	50.9
minimum n	31	4.4	0.4	0	1.5	0.1	106.6
MG,							
maximum n	42	4.1	0	0	0.5	0	0.1
minimum n	10	14.5	0	0	2.0	0.1	0

Sources: ASAA 56 (1978) 9–427; *AD* 35:3 (1980) 552–3; 39:4 (1984) 331; 42:3
(1987) 625.

Table 6.8 Early and Middle Geometric grave goods in the Cyclades

	Graves	Pots	Bronzes	Iron	Gold
Number	29	129	23	5	8
Mean per grave	—	4.4	0.8	0.2	0.3

Sources: see p. 318, notes 41 and 42 below; Cambitoglou *et al.* 1971: 10 n. 15;
Cambitoglou 1981: 99–102.

and two faïence. Kardiani gr. 1 on Tinos had a little amber, and Minoa
gr. 3 on Amorgos, from the early eighth century, held 11 faïence beads.
The debris dumped on Rheneia when Delos was purified in 426 BC
contained fine pottery but no metalwork. The purifiers might have
stolen gold and silver, but surely not old iron and bronze.[41]

These sites fit Snodgrass' argument that the bronze shortage ended
around 900, and the revival of Phoenician commerce provides a

plausible context (p. 209). In the new international situation, it is no surprise that bronze, gold, and finished Near Eastern objects entered central Greece. Barrett (1994: 65) rightly criticizes prehistorians for assuming that such exotica *always* undermine symbolic systems; but in this case, these objects must have created problems for the ideology of the race of iron. This had made sense of a world where such objects and the easterners who carried them were a thing of the past; in a changed world, it no longer provided such a coherent vision. Ninth-century funerals questioned the verities of the old order.

The boundaries between the race of iron and the vanished heroes, so stark in the tenth century, now blurred, as redefinition of spatial relationships with the east stimulated rethinking of temporal relation-ships with the heroes. One of the most interesting finds comes from the main town on Naxos (figure 6.14). Five cist graves dating 925–900, four of them containing cremations, have been found in the Grotta area. All lay within a curved wall which partially reused the walls of a Mycenaean house, and gr. 5 had a twelfth-century pot on its cover slabs. These graves became the focus for cult activity around 900. Small altars were built over them for sacrifices or meals. Another excavation about 60 meters away, outside the Metropolis church, found graves going back to *c.* 1000. A tall stele marked a cist containing a crema-tion, dating shortly before 900. Early in the ninth century a small room was added to this marker. A series of ash deposits and altars began over the grave, accumulating to a depth of over a meter. No new burials were added after 900, but the complex was extended and several circular platforms added. Lambrinoudakis (1988: 239) points out that two of the features here – the raised plastered oval platform, and the mud-brick box containing ashes – closely parallel structures in the Lefkandi apsidal building; and in the eighth century the Naxians again followed the Lefkandians by burying the whole complex under a mudbrick mound, which was respected until Roman times.

Just ten kilometers away at Tsikalario, a group of more than twenty large mounds, some marked by huge stelai, and covering rich cremations, began around 850/825. Between the mounds were small rooms like those at Metropolis (figure 6.15). One contained a round stone altar, and a semicircular peribolos surrounded a stone offering table. And 20 kilometers east of Naxos on Donoussa is a contempo-rary group of small rooms, full of ash, signs of heavy burning, and pottery like that from Tsikalario. Coldstream (1977: 91) suggests that these resulted from the collapse of a tumulus, making them sound even more like Tsikalario.[42]

From the beginning of Protogeometric until shortly before its end, there was no middle ground between the rigid, inward-looking,

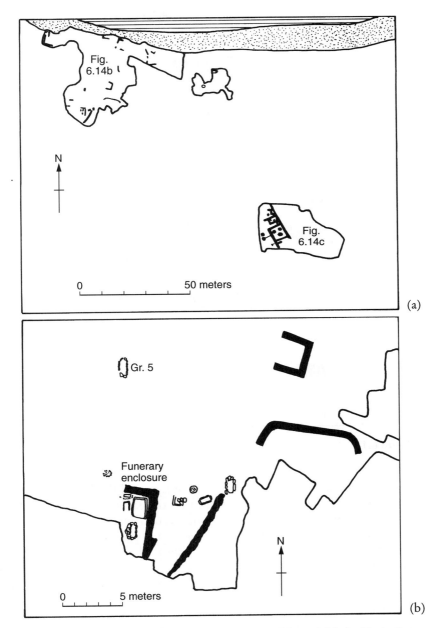

Figure 6.14 (a) The excavated areas at Grotta on Naxos; (b) the Early Iron Age remains near the sea; (c) the Metropolis area. (Based on Mazarakis Ainian 1997: figs. 330–3)

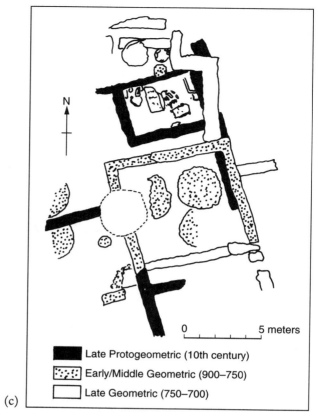

Figure 6.14 *Continued*

normative rites of the great majority of burials and their extraordinary inversion for the hero of Lefkandi. But by the early ninth century that was no longer the case. The symbolic system was being used more flexibly. In the three groups on Naxos, and perhaps on Donoussa too, buriers deployed elements of the Lefkandian heroic burial package – cremation, funerary buildings, clay boxes for ashes, and mounds – to claim similar status for their dead. Just as specialists disagree whether the Lefkandi apsidal building was a shrine or a house, there has been debate over whether the Cycladic sites are settlements or cemeteries (Themelis 1976). Lambrinoudakis (1988: 244) and Antonaccio (1995: 201–2) are probably right that the Naxian finds were family ancestor cults, while the scale of the Lefkandi complex

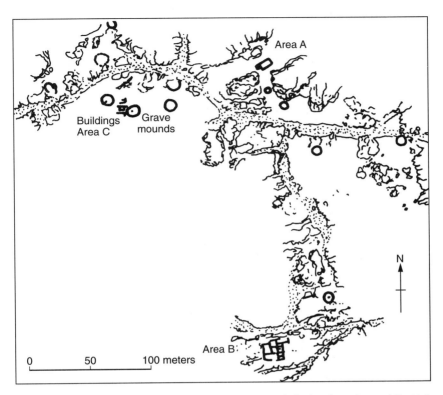

Figure 6.15   The ninth-century complex at Tsikalario (based on *AD* 21:3 (1966) 394)

indicates greater communal involvement. But even if the Naxians did not persuade so many people to believe them as the Lefkandians had managed, they were making similar claims for their dead as heroic beings whose achievements reached out beyond the contemporary world.

Bronze Age heirlooms appear in central Greek graves at just this moment. Other than the Lefkandi heroön burials, the only Middle Protogeometric grave with heirlooms is Toumba 12B, right outside the entrance to the apsidal building, containing two paste seals with thirteenth-century parallels. But the explicitly heroizing Toumba gr. 79 (875–850 BC), the only known ninth-century cremation with the ashes in a bronze urn, included (along with iron weapons and bronze ornaments) a north Syrian cylinder seal, dating about 1800 BC.

We find similar behavior all over central Greece in the early ninth century. I already mentioned the Mycenaean pot on the covers of Grotta gr. 5 on Naxos. Electran Gate gr. 2 at Thebes included another twelfth-century pot, while on Kos the rich child burial Serraglio gr. 10 held three. Some heirlooms were grander. Another Koan child burial, Sabrie gr. B, held a bronze javelin point. A Late Protogeometric warrior grave on Skyros contained Mycenaean gold rosettes and numerous faïence beads, and Tiryns gr. 1972/6 a group of Mycenaean carved gems. Mycenaean-style bronze swords turn up in ninth-century graves at two Boeotian sites. One is an unpublished grave at Orchomenos, while near Andikyra a sword was found in cist cremations directly above Mycenaen tombs, also including gold beads and earrings. There were no heirlooms at Vranezi, just five kilometers away, but a conical mound contained rich late tenth- and ninth-century cremations and inhumations.[43]

Archaeologists have not seen these finds as part of a coherent pattern. Popham and Lemos explain the Near Eastern pottery, Syrian cylinder seal, and iron weapons in Toumba gr. 79 by calling its occupant a "warrior trader,"[44] while Snodgrass (1971: 382–3) suggested that the ninth-century heirlooms at other sites were a last "hint of deprivation" after the years of isolation. He suggested that Thessalian customs influenced the Vranezi mounds (Snodgrass 1971: 159). Similarly, Coldstream (1977: 92) linked the Tsikalario mounds to Macedonia. But putting the new symbols within the tradition begun by the Lefkandi Toumba hero burials, we can link the increase in bronze, ivory, and gold with the interest in heirlooms and appearance of altars, tumuli, and in one case even a cremation in a bronze urn, as elements of a single process, symbolically restructuring the relationships between present and past and Greece and the east.

The most intriguing find of all is the famous clay model centaur from Lefkandi (figure 6.16). The head comes from Toumba gr. 1, and the body from gr. 3, both dating around 900. The model clearly shows a knee wound, and seven centuries later Apollodorus (2.85) described Chiron, the centaur who educated Achilles, as having just such a wound. The argument for long-term mythological continuities is strong. Just as we cannot assume that the first textual attestation of a myth coincides with its creation, so too this first artistic representation need not mean that the story of Achilles and Chiron was invented around 900. But it is striking that such an evocative object entered the record in just this period. Nor is it an isolated example. A similar centaur, but without the wound, comes from Fadil gr. 7 on Kos, also dating c. 900 BC, and the leg of another, of the same date, has been found on a house floor at Mende in Chalcidice.[45]

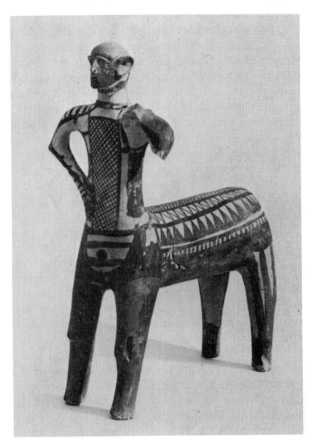

Figure 6.16 The Lefkandi centaur, found in Toumba grs. 1 and 3 (photography courtesy of the Managing Committee of the British School at Athens)

Discussion

The Phoenician penetration of the Aegean made access to Near Eastern goods easier than it had been for a century. We cannot know how individual Greeks felt about this, but as a general framework for thinking about the issues we might start from Curtin's (1984) and Appadurai's (1986) discussions of how people in other societies have dealt with similar episodes. Comparative reading does not prove anything about the Greek case, but it suggests something of the range of psychological, sociological, and cultural factors we need to keep in mind.

Early tenth-century rituals reserved a space for orientalia; their parsimonious use was one way in which buriers ascribed special status to the hero of Lefkandi. When these objects became more widely available, we can expect central Greeks to have reacted in varied ways, depending on frequency of contact with Phoenicians, local circumstances, personal attitudes, and family traditions. We might imagine a typology of responses. Conservatives could resist novelty, seeing it as corroding the moral order of the race of iron. Others might welcome the chance to express more complex and grander personas for dead relatives, while wanting to keep potentially disruptive forces under control. At Athens we see people selecting grave marker pots with human figures on them, but keeping the figures tucked away in the margins of the decoration, and burying gold bands, but decorating them with traditional meanders.

Others still perhaps leapt at the chance to create new identities, feeling the tenth-century ideologies as restrictive and old-fashioned, artificially enforcing much the same status on all members of the elite. It might have been possible to use new objects to reinforce the old system, but they also offered alternative sources of value, making access to gold and ivory, rather than performance on the battlefield, or whatever it was that won such honor for the hero of Lefkandi, the basis for worth. There would doubtless be disagreements within each community and even each family over what should be done, partially worked out in the rituals which produced the observed variations in metal use within cemeteries. According to the outcomes of these debates, different communities might embrace or recoil from the east. The people who used the Toumba cemetery for a century after the heroic burial were particularly enthusiastic about links with the east and the past, perhaps seeing it as only proper for the descendants of such a man (assuming that this was what they thought that they were) to set themselves apart from the common rabble; while on the present limited indications, nearby Chalcidians were not very interested in such displays at all. Phoenicians might have found Lefkandi a more welcoming port of call than Chalcis, and Athens more welcoming than Corinth or Argos, adding to the contrast between the communities, as well as giving Lefkandians and Athenians more incentive to strike out on voyages of their own to the Levant.

This simple model is speculative, based on my own perceptions of how people might react to changing circumstances and on my comparative reading about how people have reacted in other historical settings. But its advantage is that it lets us think about the data in terms of human dispositions and practices instead of reducing cultures to billiard balls, like the most influential approaches to Greek relations with the east (pp. 102–5). As more members of the elite buried their dead with at least a few trinkets hinting at a grander place in history than the old system had allowed, traditional ways came under increasing pressure. It was perhaps a short step from aping the finery of the east to other practices which breached the boundaries of time and space. Some buriers seized on "semi-heroic" symbolism, producing the finds from Naxos and Boeotia, even if they convinced few people outside their own families to share their high opinion of themselves. Others thought of still more ways to link present and past. At Athens, a new practice began around 900 of leaving a depression in the shaft of the grave for the descendants of the deceased to come back and make offerings, while at Argos there was a shift toward large cist tombs which remained in use for several generations.

Early ninth-century funerals were getting competitive. Some people used more valuable objects, fragmenting the equality of the dead, and symbolism linking the dead to wider horizons. This escalation is visible in many dimensions. Whitley suggests that some Athenians now chose the pottery they placed in graves more carefully, so that painted motifs amplified distinctions between the dead. For them, "stylistic emulation became a game of its own" (Whitley 1991a: 134–7). As members of the ninth-century elite asserted the prominence of their dead more aggressively, so too they defined membership of their group more rigorously. At Athens, the only site with reliable skeletal sexing, funerary distinctions between male and female are less obvious after 900, but those between adults and children are stronger, as the proportion of archaeologically visible sub-adult burials declined sharply (I. Morris 1987: 57–62). The few known child burials at Athens and Argos are relatively rich, reinforcing the impression that membership of the elite was now only being ascribed at death to the children of very special people. In the Toumba cemetery at Lefkandi, the unusually high proportion of children in the ninth century (40 percent of the total, as compared to 6–7 percent in Athens and Argos) may be related to the buriers' presumed claims of special status through descent from the hero. Members of other families had to reach adulthood to count as part of what Houby-Nielsen (1995: 145) calls the "burying family," but here the simple fact of being born was enough.

Consumption within elite funerals steadily escalated, and the boundaries between these elite burials and the disposal of the lower orders were reinforced. But the three-generation cycle of spiraling spending tailed off after 825. We should not exaggerate this, but at Athens and Argos, on Euboea and Skyros, and perhaps at Akraiphia there was a decline in the use of rich and eastern grave goods, and fewer archaizing/heroizing burials (though Tsikalario may be an exception).

Coldstream (1977: 103) sees in this "a curious stagnation in dealings with the Levant" – curious, because while oriental metalwork is again rare in central Greek graves by 800, Greek pots are common in the east Mediterranean. The major site is Al Mina in Syria, where Euboean and Attic pottery becomes so abundant that most archaeologists see it either as a Greek trading post or as a Syrian merchant town with special connections to Greece. The earliest levels with Greek pottery are usually dated around 800 by pendent semicircle skyphos sherds, but Rosamund Kearsley (1995) would down-date this whole class of pottery, arguing that Greek wares only became prominent around 750. Even if this is correct, however, Greek pottery is well represented at other Levantine sites from 900 on (see p. 316 n. 13).

The first Greek finds in the west Mediterranean – Euboean and Euboeanizing pots in graves in Sicily, Sardinia, Etruria, and Carthage, a more substantial deposit of Corinthian pottery at Otranto, and an Attic Middle Geometric II krater at Huelva, the port of Tartessos in Spain – begin around 800, or soon after (Shefton 1982; D'Andria 1982; Markoe 1992; Ridgway 1992: 26–9, 129–38; 1994; Docter and Niemeyer 1994). Greeks and Levantines were necessarily in frequent contact in the west; Italian metals attracted Phoenicians as well as Greeks, and there are grounds for thinking either that some of the Greek finds were carried west by Phoenicians, or that Greeks traveled in Phoenician ships (Markoe 1992; Ridgway 1994). Either way, the western evidence points to increasing not declining contact with the wider Mediterranean after 825. Funerary fashions changed: in the late ninth century burying orientalia with the dead went out of style.

I suggest that by 800 central Greeks had come to terms with the east. Even in the mid-ninth century, there was still a certain hesitancy about displays of orientalizing wealth. The east and the past were perhaps as much threatening as liberating. By the end of the century, central Greeks brought the larger world under control in their rituals, feeling little need to impress one another by piling up Syrian bowls or Egyptian figurines in their graves.

Conclusions

The east and the past were live issues in the Iron Age. Recent scholarship has done great things in forcing Hellenists to think about the east, but the frameworks that have been proposed are simplistic.

In the mid-1980s, it was a radical step to suggest that the Near East played a major role in the formation of Greek civilization, but the debate has not moved on much since then. Instead of returning to the same questions – was Greece part of an east Mediterranean cultural *koine*? If so, when? – we need to bring the tools of the cultural historian into play. Bits-and-pieces methods, taking the Lefkandi hero burials out of context and assuming that they do away with the need to study the rest of the evidence, get us nowhere. The archaic poetry which I discussed in chapter 5 shows that relationships with the Near East were important in Greek thought in the seventh and sixth centuries, and that there were huge differences of opinion over what they should be. We cannot assume that ninth-century Greece was such a simple place that everyone agreed on what the east meant. Given the complexity of the archaeological record and the background of renewed contacts after near-isolation in the tenth century, there is every reason to expect that there were sharp disagreements and heated debates; but not necessarily the same disagreements and debates as in the archaic period.

The first step is to define the appropriate analytical context. Ideas about the east were tied to those about the past. In the dark days around 1000 BC, death-rituals emphasized the isolation of the new elite. They belonged to a race of iron; the great ones whose ruins filled the countryside faded across the temporal horizon. No longer did the past provide a model for the good life, as it had for the twelfth-century aristocrats who built mansions in the Cyclades and redesigned Tiryns. It became the time of heroes, demigods destroyed at Troy and Thebes. The beauty of the race of heroes was that Zeus had not cut them off completely. Once in a while, a truly great man showed through his deeds that he too could be promoted in his funeral to membership of the *andron heroon theion genos*. As the twelfth century headed toward its violent end, would-be Mycenaeans sailed less and less to the Levant, and by the last years of the eleventh century, ships came no more from the east. In the tenth century, the east and the past blurred together to form the world of heroes, full of gold, ivory, and bronze, foreign, and wonderful. It was everything the present was not.

This, I suggest, was a useful way to think around 1000 BC. It made sense of the obvious historical decline in power and sophistication by explaining them as part of Zeus's plan. But by the end of the tenth century it no longer worked so well. As order returned to the Levant and Phoenicians began to use the Aegean as an occasional detour on their westward trips, the kinds of artifacts formerly associated with the vanished days proliferated. Perhaps if everyone in central Greece had fully internalized the idea of the races of heroes and iron, they would have been unresponsive, and the Levantines, judging the Aegean to be the home of unfriendly natives, would have avoided it. But that, of course, did not happen. Enough Greeks welcomed the new possibilities, and by the early ninth century Near Eastern objects were circulating in all the major towns of central Greece. Apparently they were not appropriate things to give to the gods, since hardly any are known from the simple shrines of the ninth century, but more and more families linked their dead relatives to the grander worlds that these objects evoked. By 850, some groups were spending heavily on grave goods, with orientalizing themes common, as well as generalizing the symbolism of heroic death by using grave mounds and Bronze Age heirlooms. But before 800 this process slowed down or even stopped.

You may or may not find this narrative persuasive. I doubt that my thinking would have gone this way were it not for the discovery of the Lefkandi heroon, and a single major new find may force me to abandon my model. But the most important point is that these are the *kind* of questions we must ask about the past and the east. Just talking about an abstract "Greek culture" and how "oriental" or "Myce-naean" it was is a 1990s version of culture history (pp. 18–20 above). The tools we need are those of the cultur*al* historian, sensitive to long-term continuities, abrupt changes, and competing constructions of meaning. I have suggested that some of the issues which obsessed the poets of the seventh and sixth centuries, and the speakers of the fifth and fourth, were very old indeed. Already by 1000 Greek communities were dominated by elite groups which defined them-selves against the past and the east. In classical Athens, we see a different kind of elite, the internally egalitarian male citizen body, which also defined itself against the past and the east. Here we have continuity across seven centuries, but borrowing Michel Vovelle's Annaliste terminology (1990: 8–9), I distinguish between long-term mentalities which saw the east as an exotic challenge (or threat) and the past as a world of heroes, and shorter-term ideologies, the political uses people made of shared beliefs. The elites of Dark Age central Greece and the citizen communities of archaic and classical central Greece were very different, even if they used some of the same ideas to draw lines around themselves. So too, ninth-century challenges to the Dark Age race of iron were radically different from those which archaic elitists made to the middling ideology in the seventh and sixth centuries. The fundamental question is what hap-pened in the eighth century.

7

Rethinking Time and Space

The Collapse of Distance

So much for the question; the answer, I suggest, is that central Greeks redrew the boundaries around their communities. In a sense, they had little choice in this. The Mediterranean was a smaller place in 700 than it had been in 800. Greeks were sailing from one end of the sea to the other, and from 750 on some of them made new homes in Sicily and Italy. Though there is plenty of room for argument over numbers, 10,000 or more Greeks may have moved to the colonies by 700. Most Greeks probably still lived their whole lives without ever going more than a few hours' walk from where they were born, but the more dynamic few who moved back and forth between the colonies, the Aegean, and the east, opened up new horizons. Judging from the prominence of Near Eastern pottery and Semitic graffiti, Pithekoussai, a Greek settlement founded off the coast of Italy around 750 (figure 7.1), was something of a cultural melting pot (Boardman 1994; Docter and Niemeyer 1994). The *Odyssey*, one of the foundations of Greek literature, can even be called the first ethnography (Hartog 1996: 11–45).

Thucydides says that

> The Corinthians are supposed to have been the first to adopt more or less modern methods in shipbuilding [*metacheirisai ta peri tas naus*], and it is said that the first triremes ever built in Greece were laid down in Corinth. Then there is the Corinthian shipwright, Ameinocles, who appears to have built four ships for the Samians. It is nearly 300 years ago (dating from the end of this present war [i.e., *c.* 704]) that Ameinocles went to Corinth. And the first naval battle on record is the one between the Corinthians and the Corcyreans: this was about 260 years ago [*c.* 660]. (Thucydides 1.13)

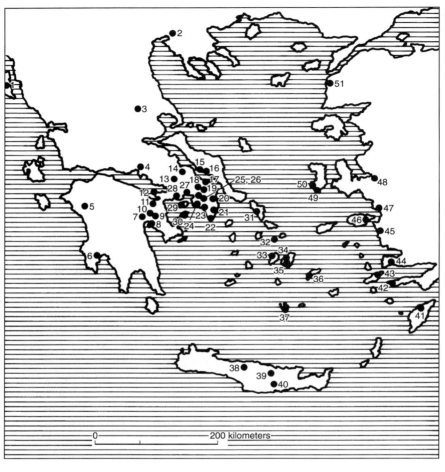

Figure 7.1 Sites mentioned in this chapter

1 Corcyra	14 Paralimni	27 Eleusis	40 Arkades
2 Thessaloniki	15 Lefkandi	28 Megara	41 Kameiros
3 Ayios Yeoryios Larisis	16 Eretria	29 Salamis	42 Knidos
4 Delphi	17 Oropos	30 Aegina	43 Kos
5 Olympia	18 Menidi	31 Zagora	44 Halicarnassus
6 Nichoria	19 Tourkovouni	32 Delos	45 Miletus
7 Argos	20 Marathon	33 Koukounaries	46 Samos
8 Asine	21 Sounion	34 Naxos	47 Ephesus
9 Heraion	22 Thorikos	35 Iria	48 Smyrna
10 Mycenae	23 Lathouriza	36 Minoa	49 Emborio
11 Corinth	24 Trachones	37 Thera	50 Kato Phana
12 Perachora	25 Athens	38 Eleutherna	51 Troy
13 Thebes	26 Mt. Imittos	39 Knossos	

This has generally been read as meaning that triremes, the fast and highly maneuverable triple-decked oared warships which dominated fifth-century seafaring, were brought to Corinth (perhaps from Phoenicia) in the eighth century, and that by 700 their use was spreading. Thucydides (1.14) goes on to say that even in the sixth century Greek navies "do not seem to have possessed many triremes, but to have still been composed, as in the old days, of long-boats and boats of fifty oars," but most historians have seen the late eighth century as a turning-point in Greek ship construction (Morrison and Williams 1968: 12–69; Casson 1971: 43–60, 71–6). More recently, H. T. Wallinga (1993) has argued that we should translate Thucydides' *metacheirisai ta peri tas naus* not as "shipbuilding" but as "the use of ships," meaning that the Corinthians created the first state fleet, rather than relying on contributions from private citizens, and that what made Ameinocles unusual was that he built four ships for the polis of Samos, not that he built four triremes. Wallinga holds that triremes only became common at the end of the sixth century. This would be consistent with some of Herodotus' comments (1.166; 3.39), though it strains the meaning of Thucydides' words. But however we interpret Thucydides, Wallinga suggests that Greek vase paintings and Phoenician reliefs show that new types of double-banked oared ships with raised benches appeared in the mid-eighth century, and concludes that "This epoch appears therefore to be of crucial importance for the development of Greek shipping" (1993: 45).

There were probably few differences between warships and merchant ships before about 525 BC, but in the late eighth century Phoenicians and Greeks developed faster and safer ships, some of which could carry large cargoes. These technical advances stimulated what Giddens (1981: 38) calls "time-space convergence": people, goods, and information could move with increasing speed and reliability across distances which had until recently seemed unimaginably vast. As Greek settlers spread around the shores of the Mediterranean, and mercenaries fought for Babylon and Egypt, the world of the exotic and adventurous was pushed steadily further away, until stories like Aristeas' had to be set far off in central Asia (p. 182).

At the same time, there may have been a trend within the old Greek world toward greater localism. Snodgrass (1980a: 35–7; 1987: 188–209) has argued that there was a partial shift from mobile pastoralism toward sedentary agriculture in the eighth century, and de Polignac (1995a: 38) builds on this to see the creation of a new sense of the countryside in this period, in which clearly defined boundaries and ownership of specific areas of land became critical. Similarly, Whitley (1991b) suggests that before the eighth century villages were short-lived, and communities would have moved repeatedly within an area of settlement, rather than developing a sense of being fixed to a specific place. Richard Bradley suggests that such mobile populations normally have a larger sense of the landscape than sedentary farmers. Whereas the latter think in terms of fixed plots of land, the former envisage more extensive networks of "paths, places and viewpoints" (Bradley 1997: 7).

We still know little about Dark Age subsistence practices and settlement dynamics, and these ideas are as yet no more than interesting hypotheses. But if they turn out to be well grounded, the eighth century saw diametrically opposed processes: on the one hand, an exploding sense of *space*, as the whole Mediterranean became (some of) the Greeks' backyard; and on the other, a contracting sense of *place*, as the countryside filled up, mobility declined, and boundaries hardened.

Harvey describes precisely this phenomenon as "space-time compression," meaning "processes that so revolutionize the objective qualities of space and time that we are forced to alter, sometimes in quite radical ways, how we represent the world to ourselves . . . so overcoming spatial barriers that the world sometimes seems to collapse inwards upon us." He suggests that "The experience of space-time compression is challenging, exciting, stressful, and sometimes deeply troubling, capable of sparking, therefore, a diversity of social, cultural, and political responses" (1989: 240). In modern times, he notes, "Working-class movements are . . . generally better at organizing in and dominating *place* than they are at commanding *space*" (1989: 236), and although much remains obscure about the organization of long-distance trade and travel in early Greece (Bravo 1977; 1984; Mele 1979; 1986), there is general agreement that the aristocracy dominated this sphere. Arguments from analogy prove nothing, but they raise possibilities: particularly in the light of the attitudes in archaic poetry (chapter 5), there is every reason to suspect that the compression of space (and perhaps place) in the eighth century was, as Harvey suggests, both exciting and deeply troubling.

Roughly one hundred years ago, new forms of transport and communication stimulated the most radical episode of spacetime compression the world had yet seen, transforming every kind of thought, from painting to militarism, and playing a large part in rushing the world to war in 1914 (Kern 1983). In the past twenty years, new technologies have stimulated ever more dizzying changes (Castells 1996). The forces at work in the Aegean around 700 BC were far weaker, but still potentially revolutionary. Nicholas Purcell has criticized historians for ignoring the importance of mobility in archaic Greece. He suggests (1990: 58) that we have been misled by the image of a "small Greece" which "was created during the late sixth and fifth centuries when the Greeks became self-conscious and xenophobic." But like the 1980s turn toward reconnecting Greek historiography with the east, Purcell promotes a single model, of mobile Greeks enjoying a larger world. We need different methods to make sense of the phenomenon. The expanding world was troubling as well as exciting. Throughout the archaic period, an elitist ideology emphasized the wonders of this new control of space, while a middling view stressed the strength of being rooted in place, tied to a self-sufficient locality.

Harvey suggests that

> Spatial and temporal practices are never neutral in social affairs. They always express some kind of class or other content, and are more often than not the focus of intense social struggle ... During phases of maximal change, the spatial and temporal bases for reproduction of the social order are subject to the severest disruption ... it is exactly at such moments that major shifts in systems of representation, cultural forms, and philosophical sentiment occur. (Harvey 1989: 239)

In this chapter I explore new senses of space and link them with novel techniques which compressed time, to argue that this episode of time-space convergence generated precisely the kind of results Harvey envisages. Central Greeks argued intensely over the boundaries of the good community and how to imagine its location in time and space. I trace these arguments in the remains of sanctuaries, settlements, and cemeteries, and conclude that between 750 and 700 Greeks revolutionized the belief systems they had inherited from the Dark Age. In this revolution, I argue, we can find the origins of the intellectual spectrum from middling to elitist ideologies.

Spacetime Compression

Writing the Poetry of the Past

In the eighth century, central Greeks started writing down heroic, theogonic, and probably genealogical poetry. This revolutionized their relationships with the past, circumscribing the oral poet's freedom to compose in performance.[1] West (1985: 164–71; cf. Farenga 1998) suggests that by 700 or 650, traveling poets had blended local mythologies into a single grand genealogy which "sprawled across a Panhellenic canvas." As we saw in chapter 5, there were debates over what this history meant. West (1985: 11) stresses that a poem like *The Catalog of Women* is not "what 'the Greeks' knew or believed about their past. It represents one particular construction made at a particular epoch from a particular vantage-point." Poets long tinkered with the details; but across the archaic period authoritative versions slowly drove out rival treatments.

Written texts gave new ways of reaching back through the ages, and there is every indication that writing was an ideologically charged technology. The alphabet was based directly on west Semitic consonantal scripts, probably Phoenician (figure 7.2). Some Greeks thought that writing had come from Egypt, and a few claimed it as an independent Greek invention; but these were minority positions (Powell 1991: 5–10). Greeks generally called letters *phoinikeia*, "Phoenician things," and papyrus rolls *bybloi*, after Byblos in Phoenicia; and in one Cretan inscription the official term for a scribe is *poinikastas*. Herodotus (5.58) says that Kadmos, a Phoenician who settled at Thebes in heroic times, introduced writing to Greece. Kadmos' descendants modified their script to suit the Greek language, and after further reforms by Ionians who then lived around Thebes, it became the modern (fifth-century) script.

The first evidence for the Greek alphabet may be four or five signs scratched on a flask in gr. 482/3 at Osteria dell' Osa in Italy, which can hardly be later than 800–775 (Bietti Sestieri 1992: 184–5). There is debate over whether the word is actually Greek, but inscriptions are known from at least a dozen sites by 700. Some Semiticists argue that although the oldest finds are eighth-century, the letter forms they use (especially the five-stroke *mu* and dotted *omicron*) are closest to Phoenician signs of the late eleventh century (Naveh 1982). This would mean that for 300 years writing was known in Greece but used in archaeologically invisible ways. The obvious analogy is Cyprus, where a syllabary is well documented from the eighth century on, but a bronze spit inscribed O-PE-LE-TA-U from a tomb at Paphos seems to date a little before 1000 (Karageorghis 1983: 411–15). There are some question about the context, but even if we down-date the Opheltas spit, the archaic Cypriot syllabary was nevertheless derived from the Cypro-Minoan script, which went out of use in the eleventh century. Ten generations of Cypriots knew of writing but left almost no traces. This need not be true of Greece, but a bronze bowl bearing a short Phoenician inscription found in a Knossian tomb dating about 900 (Sznycer 1979) shows that at least some Greeks knew the concept of writing.

But the argument from silence, that the Greek alphabet was created in the eighth century, still carries most weight. We know of fewer than

	Hypothetical Phoen. name	Hypothetical Phoen. sound	9th–8th cent. Phoen. shape	Selected Greek shapes from epichoric varieties 8th–5th cent. (all forms-right-to-left)	Greek sound	Greek name	Greek shape in 4th-cent. Koinē left-to-right	Modern printed Greek shape
	a.	b.	c.	d.	e.	f.	g.	e.
1	ʾalf	ʾˣ			a	ἄλφα	Α	A α
2	bēt	bˣ			b	βῆτα	Β	B β
3	gaml	gˣ			g	γάμμα / γέμμα	Γ	Γ γ
4	delt	dˣ			d	δέλτα	Δ	Δ δ
5	hē	hˣ			ĕ	εἶ, ἒ ψιλόν	E	E ε
6	wau	wˣ			w	ϝαῦ	–	–
7	zai	zˣ			dz, zd	ζῆτα (from sade?)	Ι Ζ	Z ζ
8	ḥēt	ḥˣ			h, ē	ῆτα	H	H η
9	ṭēt	ṭˣ			th	θῆτα	Θ Ο	Θ θ
10	yōd	yˣ			i	ἰῶτα	Ι	I ι
11	kaf	kˣ			k	κάππα	K	K κ
12	lamd	lˣ			l	λάμβδα	Λ	Λ λ
13	mēm	mˣ			m	μῦ, μῶ	M	M μ
14	nūn	nˣ			n	νῦ	N	N ν
15	semk	sˣ			ks	ξεῖ	Ξ Ξ	Ξ ξ
16	ʿain	ʿˣ			o	οὖ, ὂ μικρόν	O	O o
17	pē	pˣ			p	πεῖ	Π	Π π
18	ṣādē	tsˣ			s	σάν (from zai?)	–	–
19	qōf	qˣ			q	ϟόππα	Ϲ Ϙ	–
20	rōš	rˣ			r	ῥῶ	P	P ρ
21	šin	shˣ			s	σίγμα (from semk?)	Ϲ	Σ σ s
22	tau	tˣ			t	ταῦ	T	T τ
23	see wau above				u	ὓ	Y	Y υ
24	(? ϙ [qof] >)				ph	φεῖ	Φ	Φ φ
25	(? x, + [tau] >)				ks, kh	χεῖ	X	X χ
26	(? Ψ [kaf] >)				ps, kh	ψεῖ	Ψ	Ψ ψ
27	o [ὂ μικρόν] >				ō	ὦ, ὠ μέγα	Ω	Ω ω

Figure 7.2 The Greek and Phoenician scripts in the eighth century (based on Powell 1991: table II)

a dozen west Semitic inscriptions dating before 500 BC, which weakens arguments based solely on letter forms. But even if Naveh's high date is correct and some Greeks used writing in archaeologically invisible forms across the Dark Age, for my arguments here the most important point is still that the alphabet's uses changed radically after 750.

If it existed much before 750, it was only used on papyrus, parchment, skins, or wood; after 750 it was regularly scratched or painted onto pottery, metal, and stone. The frequency with which Late Geometric inscriptions are turning up in settlement excavations suggests that even if the alphabet was not invented in the eighth century, then at the very least its use was transformed.

The forms of the early inscriptions suggest that writing was central to the rethinking of cultural categories around 750. Unlike most ancient scripts, the earliest texts are not economic. Half a century ago H. T. Wade-Gery (1952: 12–14) pointed out that whereas Phoenician was a consonantal script, normally omitting vowels, all the Greek versions took the Phoenician symbols *alf*, *hê*, *yod*, and *ain* which Greek did not need and used them to represent the vowels *alpha*, *epsilon*, *iota*, and *omicron*. This was an unnecessary luxury for accounting. Signs showing the quantities of vowels are not strictly required for transcribing poetry either, but using them certainly made it easier to read verse accurately. Barry Powell (1991) shows that many inscriptions dating 750–650 are poetic, often written in hexameter, like epic verse. Giddens (1981: 39, 94–5) calls writing a technology for "stacking" the past, in the sense of making information from an earlier time available in the present. But eighth-century Greeks may have adapted writing to make the past present in an even more pronounced way: Wade-Gery and Powell argue that the alphabet was developed expressly to write down heroic epics. This poetry was probably the major technique available for bringing the past into the present during the Dark Age; writing fixed the relationships between the present and the past.

The most famous example is "Nestor's cup" from Pithekoussai gr. 168, a cremation of a boy aged 10–14. The burial held 27 pots and a silver fibula, all dating 725–700, and was part of a cluster of burials (grs. 159–68) distinguished by rich grave goods and Near Eastern pottery (Buchner and Ridgway 1993).

One of the 27 pots was a Rhodian kotyle, inscribed with three lines of retrograde writing:

> I am the cup of Nestor, a joy to drink from.
> Whoever drinks this cup, straightaway that man
> The desire of beautiful-crowned Aphrodite will seize.[2]

In the *Iliad*, Homer tells of

> a beautifully wrought cup which the old man [Nestor] brought with him from home. It was set with golden nails, and eared handles upon it

were four, and on either side there were fashioned two doves
of gold, feeding, and there were double bases beneath it.
Another man with great effort could lift it full from the table,
but Nestor, aged as he was, lifted it without strain.
(Homer, *Iliad* 11. 632–7)

The Pithekoussai clay cup is nothing like Homer's golden vessel, but
Powell (1991: 165) sees in it, as early as 725 BC and on the furthest
fringe of the Greek world, a humorous allusion to the *Iliad* in much
the form that we have it.

The themes of early central Greek inscriptions – the gods, beauty,
competition, dance, same-sex intercourse, the heroic age – parallel
those of archaic elitist poetry; and many texts are hexameter verses,
like the epics.[3] I give just a few examples (see Powell 1991: 119–86).
Many texts are dedicatory formulas on votives, of the form "so-and-
so dedicated me to X." But longer versions tend to be hexameters, like
the inscription on the thighs of a bronze statuette dedicated to Apollo
at Thebes around 700, "Mantiklos dedicated me to the far-shooter, him
of the silver bow, as a tenth part [of his spoils]. So do you, O Phoibos,
grant to me a pleasing gift in return." In describing the origins of the
alphabet, Herodotus (5.59–61) quotes three more dedicatory hexameter inscriptions in "Kadmean letters" which he saw in Apollo's temple
in Thebes.

One of the best-known early inscriptions, the Dipylon oinochoe
from Athens (figure 7.3), probably reads "Whoever of all the dancers
now dances most friskily / of him this . . . kmmnn." There is one
hexameter line and the beginning of a second, before the inscription
degenerates into an abecedarium, perhaps in a clumsier hand than the
first line. There are more hexameters among the erotic inscriptions
carved on rocks on Thera, also emphasizing dance and perhaps
competition: "Barbax dances well and he's given [me] pleasure." This
almost certainly alludes to sex between men, perhaps linked to
the male initiation rites of Apollo Karneios, celebrated somewhere
nearby. Another line says bluntly "Pheidippides got fucked [*oiphe*].
Timagoras and Empheres and I – we got fucked too."

The letters these inscriptions were written in were borrowed
directly (and probably recently) from the Near East, and most Greeks
were conscious of that. From the beginning, writing was most attractive within the elitist ideology, and it remained suspect in democratic
Athens (Steiner 1993). Writing allowed the fixation in script of a
particular aristocratic vision of the heroic age (see p. 173 above). Just
as when they dressed in Lydian headbands, those who invested the
material resources, time, and technology required to record 28,000

Figure 7.3   The Dipylon oinochoe from Athens (photograph courtesy of the German Archaeological Institute at Athens)

lines of Homeric poetry put themselves on a cultural level with the sophisticated ruling classes of the east, the masters of *phoinikeia*, "Phoenician things."⁴ And it may be no accident that so many of our early inscriptions come from Euboea, heavily involved in long-distance travel, and the western colonies. It was in just those places where spacetime compression was moving most rapidly that the new technology might be most appreciated; and such enthusiasm for writing could only further accelerate spacetime compression.

The people who began recording heroic poetry created monuments which borrowed from the east to dominate the past. Redfield (1973) suggests that once brought into being, the *Iliad* cast a shadow over Greek poetry. We cannot explain Monro's Law – the fact that the *Odyssey* never directly refers to any episode recounted in the *Iliad* – without assuming that the *Odyssey*-poet knew a fixed text more or less like our *Iliad*. For two centuries or more, varied oral tales about the heroes flourished in the Aegean, but more and more archaic poets became conscious of the monument, *the* poem, and of their inability to match its power and authority. There was little to do but become a reciter, a *rhapsoidos*, singing selections from Homer for discerning audiences.

Early Greek poetry is above all the poetry of the past, dominated by heroic epics, theogonies, and genealogies. I suggest that the alphabet and the fixation of historical poetry were responses of people of elitist sympathies in the face of traumatic shifts in popular consciousness at a time when everything they believed in was under threat but which also offered them unimagined new possibilities. An oriental technology allowing them to control the past, celebrate their own wit and beauty, and show everyone how close they were to the gods, and all while emulating the practices of the east, was a powerful thing indeed.

The Bodies of the Heroes

Nor was it the only new tool for crossing the centuries. Central Greece was honeycombed with Mycenaean tombs, and the handful of tenth- and ninth-century pots and even secondary burials found in these tombs show that Iron Age Greeks were aware of them (Antonaccio 1995: 19, 24–8, 44–6, 58–60, 77–9). But Antonaccio is surely right to conclude that "funerary and profane use of Bronze Age tombs implies a degree of familiarity, not of awe or the practice of worship" (1995: 141). The tombs may have attracted attention in much the same ways as Cornelius Holtorf suggests of German megaliths at certain phases in their history, as

> Fascinating curiosities in the landscape . . . Sometimes it may have been in a spirit of entertainment and adventure that people of later ages visited ancient monuments . . . Such fascination could have motivated people, perhaps especially children, to spend afternoons at megaliths, dig holes or explore animal burrows. (Holtorf 1998: 28)

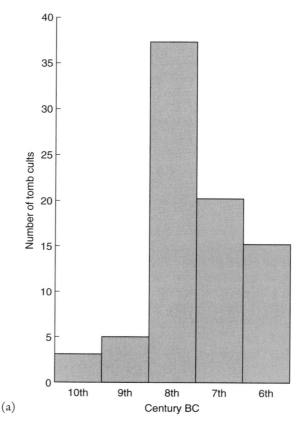

Figure 7.4 (a)   Numbers of Bronze Age tombs containing Iron Age objects

Whatever the appeal of Mycenaean tombs in the early Iron Age, Greeks began to treat them very differently after about 750. There is a sharp increase in the number of Bronze Age tombs containing Late Geometric and seventh-century objects (figure 7.4a). Some of these deposits may just be garbage dumps in convenient hollows created by the collapse of burial chambers. But some cases, like the substantial deposits spanning many years at Menidi or Prosymna, must be the results of religious activity. Even if we restrict ourselves to these definite cases, the increase in activity is striking (figure 7.4b).

There are three obvious interpretations. First, we might suggest that before 750 people had few strong feelings about Bronze Age tombs, but after 750 they began to care a great deal. Second, perhaps people

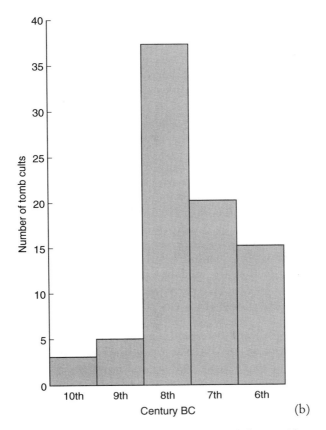

Figure 7.4 (b) Numbers of Bronze Age tombs with definite evidence of religious activity

took these tombs seriously all through the Iron Age, but began expressing their concern in new and archaeologically visible ways around 750. Or third, it may be that as Michèle Devillers (1988: 76) suggests happened at Thorikos, votive deposits were cleaned out, obscuring the earliest activity.

The third hypothesis seems least likely. At Prosymna, despite extensive excavation, no dumps of redeposited finds dating before 750 are reported;[5] and while it is possible that all around Greece people did major cleaning operations around 750 but thereafter disposed of old votives less thoroughly, the first two hypotheses seem more economical.

Returning to the second hypothesis: the worship of the Olympian gods took on new forms around 750, which suddenly made it far more visible to us than before. As noted on p. 236 above, Hägg (1987) has shown the similarities between the pots dedicated at Mycenaean tombs and those given to the gods. There is a recurring theme here, of low visibility. Whether we are looking for their houses, their graves, or their worship of the gods (and perhaps also their writing), the people of the tenth and ninth centuries are elusive. Dark Age mortals trod lightly on the landscape, *not* altering the earth. They were sad relics flitting through the shadows left behind by a great past, living out Zeus's plan, with little hope for a better future.

There is no obvious way to distinguish archaeologically between the first two hypotheses, but whichever we prefer, two conclusions are certain. First, Late Geometric Greeks became positively assertive, rapidly and decisively transforming the face of their world, and nowhere more so than in their relationships with Bronze Age tombs. Their material investment increased: as at sanctuaries of the gods, they drank and feasted at the ancient tombs, and gave gifts to the beings within. They did not behave as lavishly as in sanctuaries of the gods (pp. 273–80 below), but the forms of activity before and after 750 contrast sharply.

Second, they were interested above all in the *bodies* of the heroes. People were living at Mycenae and Troy, with Bronze Age ruins in clear sight: but we have no evidence that they paid these relics any particular attention, even when they reused them as foundations for their own houses.[6] But ancient bodies were a different matter. In the sixth century, finding the bones of a hero could have tremendous consequences (e.g., Herodotus 1.67–8); so too in the eighth century it was tombs, containing bodies, which fascinated people.

But whose bodies were they? In a classic article, Coldstream (1976) suggested that as knowledge of Homer spread, Greeks began to think of Mycenaean tombs as heroic, and to worship them. But as Snodgrass observes,

> the contrast between the cremation, covered by a tumulus, that Homer describes and the multiple inhumations in rock-cut chamber-tombs where most of the cults were instituted is so complete that it positively excludes familiarity with Homer – or, at least, identification of the object of the cult with a "Homeric hero." (Snodgrass 1987: 161)

Following West (1978: 186), Snodgrass (1987: 165; 1988) notes that Hesiod had called the Silver Race "the blessed dead beneath the ground (*hypochthonioi*)" (*Works and Days* 141). The Mycenaean dead might have been seen as the Silver Race; or perhaps, as West argued (1978: 373), there was a mainland tradition of anonymous, inhuming local heroes which was distinct from an Ionian/Homeric tradition of named, cremating heroes, and the two concepts merged around 700.

The basic similarities in tomb cults from Messenia to Attica encourage us to think of this as a single phenomenon. But the ambiguity of the literary sources (I. Morris 1988) and the differences in details of practice from one region to another (Whitley 1988) suggest that while there was a broad desire to make more direct contact with the past, there was little agreement on what it meant. The heroization of the recent dead points the same way.

As noted above (pp. 253–4), heroizing burials are less common after 850 or 825; but they return with a vengeance after 750. There are some spectacular examples, like the 19 graves of roughly 700 BC found near the West Gate of Eretria (Bérard 1970). Seven were cremations in bronze urns, in a rough semi-circle around gr. 6. In this central grave one bronze cauldron held the bones, with a second as the lid. The urns were wrapped in cloth inside a heavy stone box, closed by three stone slabs on top of each other, with mud bricks over them. The floor was a stone block 20 cm. thick, hollowed out so the urn would fit securely. The deceased was accompanied by a silver ring, burned bronze and iron ornaments, four iron swords (one of them "killed," i.e., heavily burned and twisted into a loop), four iron spearheads, a Levantine scarab in a gold mounting imitating an Egyptian design, and a Mycenaean bronze spearhead. The other graves included similar offerings. Above the graves was a massive stone triangle, each side measuring 9.2 meters. Next to this was a pit of debris from seventh-century meals. Shortly before 600 building O, probably a dining room, was set up over the monument. The whole complex was abandoned soon after.

The use of archaizing and orientalizing grave goods and cremation in a bronze urn links these graves to the older heroizing tradition. Bérard (1970: 28–32, 56–64) argued that the graves were not marked by a mound, which would set them apart from many Dark Age examples, but there are severe stratigraphical problems (R. Martin 1975; Bérard 1978). These cannot be resolved, but there is no good reason to doubt that these were heroic burials.

There are equally remarkable finds from the fringes of the Greek world. As Coldstream observes (1977: 349–50), the "royal" tombs at Salamis on Cyprus parallel Patroclus' funeral in uncanny detail. Tomb 1 contained a bronze urn wrapped in cloth, and tomb 79 held several chariots. The dromos of each tomb contained two or more horse skeletons, and that of tomb 2 a cattle bone from the funerary meal. Tomb 3 had a mound ten meters tall, and a skeleton in the dromos of tomb 2 had bound hands, possibly paralleling Achilles' sacrifice of a dozen Trojans at Patroclus' funeral (*Iliad* 23.175–82).[7] At the other edge of the Greeks' world, early excavations at the Eretrian colony[8] of Cumae in Italy found 15 cremations in bronze urns. Several were in stone boxes even grander than Eretria gr. 6. The richest burial, Fondo Artiaco gr. 104, contained iron weapons, silver ornaments, bronze vessels, horse bits, and perhaps even the remains of a wheeled vehicle. Another urn, looted from the site, may have been Urartian or north Syrian (Coldstream 1977: 231).[9]

Salamis, Eretria, and Cumae are the grandest heroizing burials since Lefkandi; and all over central Greece we see a revival of heroization. On Thera, two cremations were found in bronze urns, and two more tombs held bronze tripods, while at Athens there was a series of cremations in bronze urns, one on a tripod. These often had rich orientalizing grave goods, including impressed gold bands and imported ivory figurines, and marker pots with heroizing imagery. I discuss these finds in detail below. At Argos, three burials with bronze helmets (and in one case, a complete panoply) have been found, which may be attempts to heroize the dead.[10] Salamis tomb 1 probably dates slightly before 750; the last of the Eretria burials, perhaps slightly after 700. In central Greece and its Italian colonies, the horizon of heroizing burials falls entirely within this two-generation period. This is not the case outside central Greece, where the most "heroic" cemeteries (e.g., Ayios Yeoryios Larisis in Thessaly, Arkades on Crete) are archaic (I. Morris 1998b: 36–9, 52–5, 59–63).

Men continued to be heroized after 700, but this great cluster of archaeologically known examples thins out. Bérard (1982) and de Polignac (1995a: 129–33) suggest that the Late Geometric heroes were ambivalent figures, warriors standing at the boundary of two systems of politics and values: they were the last champions of the Dark Age aristocracy, and the first of a new civic order. At Eretria, Bérard believes that the heroes' descendants celebrated rites in building O throughout the seventh century, claiming special status from them; but by the early sixth century the heroes were fully communalized, as semidivine protectors of the entire polis. The logical next step was the heroization of the war dead as a whole. The remarkable tumulus and offering trenches over the casualties of the battle of Marathon in 490 perhaps represent an early stage of this, taking over for ordinary hoplites the heroizing imagery of the archaic Athenian aristocracy (Whitley 1994b).

Conclusion

In burials, tomb cult, and poetry (as well as in art, which I consider briefly below), the period 750–700 was a "heroizing horizon" of heightened interest in the past. We can be sure there were heroic poems and heroizing burials before 750, and there may have been writing and some kind of tomb cult; but in each case, the late eighth century saw a massive increase in energy expenditure. People were committing new levels of resources to creating *timemarks* (Chapman 1997), physically tangible monuments which brought the past into the present. As Snodgrass concludes (1980a: 77), "it begins to look as if this attitude of deference to the heroic past was an important element in the revolution that was sweeping through Greek life." This rethinking of time was inseparable from the rethinking of space, and permeated eighth-century culture. In the rest of this chapter I examine how the new ideas played out in the three major depositional contexts of sanctuaries, settlements, and cemeteries.

The Worship of the Gods[11]

We now have evidence for cult activity in the tenth or even eleventh century (p. 236), but there is no denying the scale of changes around 750. Stone altars appear at many sites, and signs of repeated animal sacrifice. Large deposits of ash formed, and whereas before 750 only a few objects can be associated with cult, after 750 regular votive offerings of pottery began. A group of 44 small pots in the upper part of a storage vessel at Asine dating around 1000 BC is one of the largest Dark Age religious deposits (p. 317 n. 27), but late eighth-century sanctuaries received offerings in quantities which leave excavators numb. Apart from the small deposit from Mt. Imittos, which increased from 69 Protogeometric pots to 116 Early and Middle Geometric to no less than 965 Late Geometric and seventh-century,[12] no one has even tried to quantify ceramic offerings. There are simply too many to count on most sites by 700.

In contrast to the earlier Iron Age, many sites had discrete cult spots after 750, often marked off by peribolos walls. There may have been cult buildings at Iria and Ephesus in the early eighth century, but around 750 most communities started to feel that the gods wanted

temples to house their images. Many of these were small, though by
the standards of the villages they were in, they were imposing. The
sanctuary of Athena at Koukounaries on Paros is typical. It stood
above a twelfth-century building, and piles of ash containing small
sherds from open vessels began to accumulate near the end of the
tenth century. These built up through the ninth and earlier eighth
centuries, then soon after 750 the whole area was replanned. By 700 it
had a stone altar, a stone enclosure wall, and an all-stone temple lined
with stone benches. Votive pottery, as distinct from vessels used in
sacrificial meals, came into use. Similarly, at Minoa on Amorgos, small
sacrifices and sherds in a cutting into bedrock in the lower town
date back to 900, but around 750 a stone temple was set up on the
acropolis, and several sacrificial pyres excavated around it turned out
to contain huge amounts of pottery and even some metal offerings.[13]
Worshippers at larger towns went much further, and the first
hekatompedon ("hundred-footer") known temple dates around 750,
at Eretria.[14]

There was an explosion of temple-building around 700. By 650
every hamlet seems to have a temple, and big sites had monumental
stone structures with clay roof tiles, architectural terracottas, and
pedimental sculptures. Some used blocks of stone weighing up to
twenty tons, as if to show the effort they felt they should expend to
honor the gods. Dedications also intensified. Even modest shrines now
often have metal offerings. Kato Phana on Chios, for example, yielded
gold, scarabs, two bronze cauldron attachments, and a miniature silver
tripod. Literally tons of pottery accumulated in the seventh century,
only to be swept into vast garbage pits.[15]

At major temples – and there were surprisingly many – the level of
seventh-century activity is breathtaking. At Ephesus, for example,
Artemis' peripteral apsidal temple was rebuilt in the early seventh
century as a bigger rectangular stone temple with a new altar, and
rebuilt again in the early sixth century; and another sequence of
temples culminated around 550 in a massive stone structure for which
Croesus of Lydia provided columns (Herodotus 1.26). The whole area
is strewn with rich offerings, including gold, ivory, electrum, Phoenician imports, and the earliest known Greek coins, probably deposited
between 650 and 625. At Samos, Hera's first *hekatompedon* was built
around 725; in the seventh century the sanctuary filled up with other
buildings, and by 600 a monumental paved Sacred Way linked it with
the town. Two more temples were built in the sixth century, and
Herodotus (3.60) says that the final version (109 × 55 m.) was the
biggest Greek temple he had ever seen. The dedications included
magnificent jewelry, a zoo of exotic animals, and at some point in the

late seventh century a complete ship.[16] Seventh-century archaeology is primarily the archaeology of sanctuaries.

Attica is something of an exception, with few seventh-century temples. The Sacred House at the Academy and "tholos" at Lathouriza have odd plans, and the sanctuary on Tourkovouni was very simple. Even the richest sanctuary, at Sounion, was poorer than a minor Chian shrine like Kato Phana. It seems that monumental religious architecture only appeared in Attica around 600, with a large stone altar on the acropolis, and the Old Temple of Athena perhaps in the 590s.[17]

In the 1970s, the major question was whether there had been religious continuity across the Dark Age. Recent finds raise new questions, and de Polignac suggests that

> What needs to be done is not to decide once and for all whether there was a general "break" or a general "continuity" in religious sites, practices, and architecture, but rather to try to see what part was played by both breaks and continuity in the history of each sanctuary and each cult, and to understand their implications in the history of the society concerned. (de Polignac 1995a: 29)

Eighth-century worship drew on traditions centuries old. But at a certain point, quantitative changes become qualitative, and the late eighth century saw a veritable revolution in religious practice. Rich votives, large temples, and walls marking off the *temenos* were not essential to Greek cult, which theoretically required no more than a rock, a tree, and water (though in practice an altar for sacrifice was also a core feature). But most seventh-century Greeks apparently felt so strongly about all these things that they directed more energy and wealth into them than had been seen since the Bronze Age palaces. Around 800, cult activity most often took place at a small fireplace, whether in the open air or, as Mazarakis Ainian (1997) argues, in a large house. A hundred years later, it was normally at a stone altar surrounded by thousands of pots and perhaps hundreds of bronzes which believers had given to the gods, before a substantial temple housing the god's image, and in a specialized precinct marked by a well-built wall.

We do not know who paid for the temples. Drawing on Homer and Herodotus, Burkert suggests that it was normally aristocrats or *basileis*, and that "war, victory and booty" were the major motivations (1996: 25). That is probably true of the great temples, but most examples are in villages of just a few dozen people. Possibly large land owners or military leaders wanted to display their piety in every hamlet in the land, but it seems more likely that most of the simple eighth- and seventh-century temples were communal, village-level efforts. A building like the temple of Athena at Koukounaries was far grander than the houses around it, and would have been a great drain on the villagers' resources; but there is no need to imagine a central- ized temple-building program coordinated by wealthy aristocrats. We do hear of rich men investing in village religion in later years, most famously Xenophon at Skillous (Xenophon, *Anabasis* 5.3.9). But like Morgan (1994: 140), I suggest that we should also imagine hundreds of local initiatives, which did not draw the attention of the text-producing classes. The eighth- and seventh-century religious revolution had a considerable popular component.

The new forms of worship offered an arena where competing visions of how mortals should relate to the gods – and therefore of the nature of humanity itself and the good society – were made explicit. One of the most striking developments in central Greece (but not in other regions: I. Morris 1997c) is the coincidence between a sudden boom in rich, often orientalizing, metal goods in sanctuaries and an equally sudden impoverishment of grave goods. Snodgrass calls this "a big social change with the redirection of attention towards the com- munal sanctuary and away from the individual grave" (1980a: 54). This is a compelling argument, but the literary sources suggest that there may be more to the story.

The change in depositional behavior was created through countless individual decisions. Helmut Kyrieleis (1979) argues that Near Eastern visitors to Greek sanctuaries dedicated most oriental votives, as in Herodotus' stories of Croesus, Alyattes, Necho, and Amasis (1.14, 25, 50–2, 69, 92; 2.159, 182; 3.47; 5.35), while Ingrid Strøm (1992) sug- gests that each temple sent out officials to obtain sets of orientalia for rituals. No theory of how the eastern objects got to Greek temples can be proven, but de Polignac (1992: 122–3) gives good reasons to think that at least some Near Eastern objects were deposited by Greeks. And in any case, actual oriental objects are outnumbered by oriental*izing* imitations of Near Eastern goods, which seem certain to have been offered by Greeks. The linked changes in dedicatory practices in funerals and worship need to be understood in central Greek terms.

There is no contemporary literary discussion to clarify matters. The most explicit analysis is Aristotle's account of *megaloprepeia*, or "magnificence," written four centuries later (see also p. 126 above). Aristotle anticipated the kind of approaches recommended by Chartier and Bourdieu: he insisted that the meanings of material culture were context-dependent and constructed by its users. The magnificent man was a master of the art of spending, and as such knew that "the same things are not appropriate for gods and for men, nor the same for the sacrifice and the funeral" (*Ethics* 1123a10). The most effective spending, that which was definitely called honorable, involved votives, sacrifices, and everything concerning the gods (1122b19–21), because "the magnificent man spends not for himself, but for the common good" (*ta koina*: 1123a4–5).

This part of Aristotle's argument is consistent with Snodgrass's interpretation of the shift from grave-goods to votives: religious dedications created a sense of community. But Aristotle went on to say that "A poor man [*penes*] cannot be magnificent." If such a man lavished gifts on the gods, he was just foolish, because it would have been out of proportion. "But," Aristotle continued, "such great spending is appropriate for those who have the resources from either their own labors or from their ancestors, as well as for the well-born and the famous, and such people; for all these qualities involve greatness and distinction" (1122b27–33). There would always be room for disagreement over whether a dedication fitted the status of the dedicator; and depending on how they handled these situations, individuals could improve or harm their standing. Public generosity to the gods was always ambiguous, working simultaneously for the common good, creating community, and for the individual, creating a hierarchy of honor.

No other text interprets votive practices in such detail, but several earlier authors seem to share Aristotle's assumptions. For Xenophon, Critoboulos' sacrifices both honored Athens and justified his position as a leading man. Socrates suggested that if Critoboulos stopped them, he would be in trouble with both mortals and immortals (Xenophon, *Estate Manager* 2.5; cf. 11.3). Kurke (1991: 167–9) argues that we see similar attitudes in Pindar, where spending on the games not only brings glory to the winner's household but also guides the polis as a whole. But different interpreters read actions in different ways, which was why poets were needed, to promote the right message. Much the same idea was already present in Homer, where no material *sema* was unambiguous. Meaning was created in the application of *noesis*, and some people were better interpreters than others (Nagy 1990: 202–20).

Difficult as it may be, we need to see the eighth-century cultural changes in these terms. From the point of view of a "middling" man, a character like Archilochus' carpenter Charon (p. 162 above), the fact that oriental luxury was only deployed in sanctuaries, not in other social contexts, might have seemed like a success for the community. But to someone steeped in the elitist vision, things might have looked very different. In Sappho's verses, generous gifts to the gods created a special relationship between the giver and the divine (p. 178 above).

Using oriental or orientalizing offerings added an extra layer of meaning: the dedicator evoked his or her privileged links to the east as well as to the gods, and indeed reperformed the actions of eastern potentates in giving such wealth at sanctuaries. A gift which evoked the heroic age as well as the east turned the offering into a virtual epiphany. From this perspective, restricting rich orientalizing and heroizing artifacts to a group of select sanctuaries looks less like a defeat for aristocrats and more like the creation of a coherent alternative belief system.

No gift can have been more powerful within this worldview than the bronze tripod-cauldrons which accumulated in huge numbers in the major sanctuaries in the eighth and seventh centuries. Morgan observes that "it would surely have taken a relatively wealthy man to afford one of the more elaborate tripods," and interprets their popularity as evidence for "increasing competition for status via the conspicuous consumption of wealth" (1990: 45). But a tripod was much more than its weight in bronze: its rich associations went far toward making it the ultimate gift. Hector Catling (1984) argues that no tripods were made in eleventh- and tenth-century Greece, but that twelfth-century Cypriot heirlooms had continued to circulate until production restarted after 900. These heirlooms were still prominent among the tripods in circulation in the eighth century. But Hartmut Matthäus (1988) thinks that tripods were in fact being made in Crete and the islands by the tenth century, but that they deliberately imitated much older Cypriot models. Either way, in the eighth century tripods were intimately linked with both the past and the east, and were established in Homer's vision as *the* gift of heroes. Examples dating from before c. 750 were made from almost pure copper, but in the second half of the century a new series appeared, imitating both the designs and the high tin content of eastern (probably north Syrian) tripods.[18] The new tripods simultaneously heroized and orientalized: all sources of external power flowed together in the act of giving a tripod to the gods.

Being seen by peers and the pious citizens of other poleis to make such offerings was perhaps the most potent use of material culture open to an elitist. It created an alternative reality which may have been even more exciting than the use of exotic grave goods had been in the ninth century, since it reached beyond the natural world as well as through time and space. Yet I suspect that we should nevertheless see this elitist interpretation largely as a reaction to the success of a middling ideology which excluded more overt statements of aristocratic power from arenas of display within the political space of the city-state. It is hard to imagine archaic nobles willingly deciding that it would be inappropriate to make similar offerings at the funerals of their relatives and friends. Sappho, Alcaeus, Alcman, and Anacreon evoke a world where gold and orientalia were regularly on display, but settlements have produced few archaeological traces of this. We cannot press the point, since few settlements are yet known in detail and bronze, silver, and gold could be endlessly recycled. However, if the wealthy did adorn their homes with rich orientalizing art we should expect to find *some* traces. Tripod fragments are distinctive, yet few are found on settlements.

There can be no proofs in empathetic arguments (Samuel's "mind-reading": see p. 13 above), but it seems best to interpret the simultaneous decline of rich and orientalizing grave goods and the increase in votives in central Greece as Snodgrass does – as pressure from the community as a whole, forcing elitists to accept that displaying these artifacts within the civic space was in bad taste, even hubristic, and was not the act of an eighth-century version of Aristotle's *megaloprepes*. The closest thing to direct evidence may be Herodotus' story (1.144) that "a long time ago" athletic victors at the Triopian sanctuary won bronze tripods, on condition that they dedicated them in the sanctuary. When Agasicles of Halicarnassus took his tripod home, the Rhodians, Coans, and Cnidians were so outraged that they banned Halicarnassians from the sanctuary.[19]

It would be in the elitists' interests to bring the forms of behavior appropriate in the liminal space of the sanctuary back into the heart of the polis; and the appeal of Alcaean poetry perhaps lay in this, as a paradigm of the struggle to recreate the once perfect but now sundered fellowship of true, noble friends. The man most responsible for subverting Alcaeus' fantasy world, Pittacus, was consistently associated in the legendary tradition with opposition to luxury in all forms, and most strikingly with attempts to ban eastern imports (Kurke 1994).

To the extent that individual poleis conformed to the pattern of rich, orientalizing offerings to the gods and poor, non-orentalizing offerings to the dead, they moved toward middling values. In Eretria, for example, rich graves disappeared by 700, while fabulously wealthy oriental and orientalizing votives escalated at the sanctuary of Apollo in the main town. In Argos and Corinth, on the other hand, few orientalizing votives were offered in the urban center, instead being deployed in rural sanctuaries. In the Argolid there were several such places, although the Heraion was the most important; while in Corinthia such gifts were largely limited to Perachora. At Kameiros, however, rich orientalizing metalwork was buried in a few graves in the seventh century, but on nowhere near the scale of votives in the local sanctuary. I would see Kameiros as a polis in which the middling ideology was less successful than in Argos or Eretria, although Kameiros clearly did shift far in that direction.

On most Aegean islands burials are poor, with little orientalizing art beyond painted amphoras serving as coffins for children; but votives on most islands are also poor. Middling values might have driven would-be elitists to leave the island altogether and go to Delos or Samos to indulge in such questionable behavior. Or maybe no self-respecting aristocrat would waste his or her time on wretched village shrines frequented only by peasants and farm animals – not at all the kind of place for an epiphany. Both views may be valid. Different people, at different times, would think about local sanctuaries in different ways. Some thought that Emborio and Kato Phana were sensible places for rich offerings, or perhaps that they were appropriate under certain circumstances. But most of the time, people interested in making lavish dedications crossed to Samos or went even further afield. Christopher Simon suggests that some sanctuaries were particularly good places for rite-of-passage dedications, such as the women's bronze girdles from Emborio; and east Greek sanctuaries generally have few tripods, suggesting either that easterners judged these objects less appealing to the gods than did mainlanders, or that easterners preferred to go to Delphi or Olympia to dedicate them (Simon 1986: 415–16, 165). Morgan (1994: 127) suggests a similar model for Corinthia, with Isthmia and Perachora serving different needs, with Olympia playing a part in any aristocrat's calculations.

Gender and Household Space[20]

In the single-room apsidal and oval houses characteristic of the Dark Age (p. 200 above), most activities – eating, sleeping, cooking, storage, stalling animals – must have gone on in the undivided main room or in the open air. But after 750, rectilinear houses replaced these simple structures on some sites. At first, these were also single-roomed or megaron houses with a small porch, like the earliest houses at Zagora (see figure 7.7a below). The best examples come from Syracuse, Naxos, and Megara Hyblaea on Sicily. Some oval houses were converted into rectangles by just adding corners, as at Pithekoussai on Ischia (figure 7.5), or the seventh-century House A at Miletus.[21] In the Roussos plot at Eretria, we see a clear progression during the eighth century from one-room oval huts, to larger apsidal mudbrick houses, and finally rectangular stone megara (I. Morris 1998b: figure 5). At Smyrna, on the other hand, the excavator identified a more complex

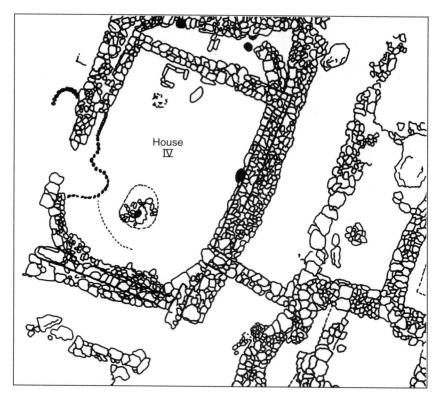

Figure 7.5 The rebuilding of Mazzola House IV, Pithekoussai (based on *AR* 1970/1: 65)

sequence, from a late tenth-century oval hut to a ninth-century multiroom rectilinear structure, only for apsidal houses to return around 750, then more multiroom rectilinear houses in the seventh century.[22]

By 700, we see more formal divisions of space. Cemeteries and sanctuaries are commonly marked off, and the edges of settlements are often bounded by defensive perimeter walls. Within settlements, more complex rectilinear houses gain popularity. Heinrich Drerup (1967: 11–12) and Clemens Krause (1977) see continuity from the earliest rectilinear houses to fourth-century *pastas*-houses, via archaic houses with two rooms opening off a frontal corridor. Development was uneven: two corridor houses on Aegina continued in use until about 500, while corridor-style House I at Corinth was modified substan-

Figure 7.6 Eighth- and seventh-century houses at Oropos, Attica (photograph courtesy of the Archaeological Society of Athens)

tially in the sixth century. At Koukounaries and Smyrna, much more complex houses were already normal by 650.[23]

The earliest documented developments are at Zagora. As early as 700 we can see courtyard houses of the kind Nevett (1995) identifies as underpinning classical concepts of space and gender, inward-turned and accessible only via a narrow door onto a street. Houses were built more sturdily, especially in the Cyclades, where all-stone construction was common. Flat roofs of thin slabs of stone supported by beams and sealed with clay were normal. Hearths were sometimes carefully constructed, with stone slabs around them, and drains became common. A bathtub built into a fortification wall at Miletus may date as early as 700.[24]

At most sites, the transition from one-room or megaron houses to courtyard houses took longer, and we see old and new styles in use alongside each other. At Miletus, one rectilinear house was built early enough to be destroyed by fire c. 750, and stretches of late eighth-century walls from the early excavations seem to belong to rectilinear houses. But oval huts were still being built in the seventh century, and the first definite courtyard house dates after 650, when an early seventh-century multiroom rectilinear house was replanned.[25] On Sicily, the simple rectangular houses of the first settlers at Naxos gave way to courtyard houses in the seventh century, perhaps even by 700, but at Megara Hyblaea, founded in 728, the shift was slow, proceeding unevenly across the whole seventh century. Only after 650 did the area round the agora look like late eighth-century Zagora, as the original plots of 100–120 m² filled with courtyard houses. On Ischia, even though curvilinear houses were being converted into rectilinear ones at Pithekoussai before 700, an oval house could still be built at Punta Chiarito well after 650.[26] By 600, the courtyard house was normal almost everywhere, though Attica was again an exception. A group of rectilinear rooms dating around 700 is known from Thorikos, but the two biggest groups of houses, at Lathouriza and Oropos, combine rectilinear and curvilinear styles in unusual ways (figure 7.6), and there is a report of an early archaic apsidal house at Eleusis. Some of these houses retained old-fashioned pitched thatch roofs. By the early sixth century, though, a group of houses and shops in Athens seems typical of the rest of central Greece.[27]

The symbolic association of the outer/public/light areas of a house with masculinity and the inner/private/dark areas with femininity, so fundamental to classical thought about gender, appears as early as Hesiod (*Works and Days* 519–25). Multiroom houses, and particularly the courtyard house which we first see on Zagora around 700, made this linkage possible. Before 750, most houses were flimsy, one-roomed, and open, without physical separators to break up the flow of activity.[28] People can develop complex spatial symbolism without solid physical boundaries (the contemporary Brazilian Mehinaku are a well-known case in point (Gregor 1977: 48–62)), but cross-cultural surveys do show correlations between rigid, hierarchical gender/age structures and subdivided domestic space (Lawrence and Low 1990; Kent 1990).

Checklist approaches are open to well-known criticisms, and concrete ethnographic studies always reveal more complexity than the macromodels. For example, Henrietta Moore notes that most 1970s Marakwet compounds in Kenya had two round huts. Informants said that "in the past" the husband lived in one hut and his wife in the other. There had been a shift toward using one hut for sleeping and the other for cooking; but, as Moore observes, "even when the houses are differentiated in this functional manner they are still thought to have a gender affiliation, partly because of the marked identification of a woman with her hearth, home and cooking activities" (1986: 48–9). In 1981, three Marakwet families built square houses, with mud and stone walls, tin roofs, and cement floors. They explicitly associated these with modernization and westernization. Westernizers, in all cases families with men in wage labor, replaced traditional goods with manufactured items, and the women abandoned many conventions about garbage disposal (1986: 145). The westernizers were more involved in complex, national market economies than traditionalists, but contrary to the cross-cultural models, in modernizing compounds "the wealth and progressiveness of the individual household form the focus of concern . . . The theme of spatial order is one of family unity and prosperity; conflicts and tension between the sexes do not appear to be represented spatially" (Moore 1986: 151–2).

The full westernizing package of square house and manufactured goods is expensive. Moore identifies eight other families who say they would live in square houses if they could afford them. Since they cannot, they pursue manufactured goods and arrange the interiors of their round houses to look like square houses (1986: 133).

Comparative cases have little probative value, but they suggest factors which we cannot observe in archaic literature or archaeological remains, but which must have applied in the eighth century. First, houses are expensive. It would be easier for Milesians to reconstruct identities by eating off orientalizing pottery or changing the family's burial place than by rebuilding Südschnitt House A as a rectangle or remodeling a Kalabaktepe house around a courtyard. We should expect house design to respond to new ideas more slowly than pottery design, metalwork, or burial, and for people caught in such a transition to create contingent, hybrid meanings for physical spaces which they inherited from the past but are transforming into a new future.

Second, a house is an emotional repository. A major change in house design like that around 700 is no small thing, if only we could read the historically specific symbolic language of space. Kent's cross-cultural survey shows that economically advanced societies, which segment the world through complex divisions of labor, do so partly by breaking up household space, assigning different values to functionally discrete rooms. But Moore's study shows how little cross-cultural regularities tell us about specific cases. Among the Marakwet, commitment to the market and the west can enrich the educated and link them to the state society, but the particular structures of modern capitalism also undermine traditional gender hierarchies, encouraging models of domestic space which mute male/female distinctions.

Without the kind of evidence ethnographers collect, interpreting space is highly conjectural. But the classical sources make it clear that few things were so charged with meaning as household space, and much of this meaning clustered around gender (p. 125 above). The slow changes between about 750 and 600 were one of the major cultural developments in archaic Greece. The best we can do is to thicken our descriptions, creating a microarchaeology of remodeling and the manipulation of household goods.

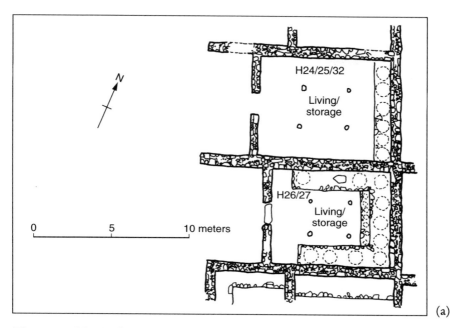

(a)

Figure 7.7 (a)   Units H 24/25/32 and H 26/27 at Zagora, *c.* 750–725 BC

The best evidence, from Zagora, is suggestive. Some house-owners broke the one-room houses and megara built between 775 and 725 into functionally specific multiroom structures after 725 (Cambitoglou *et al.* 1971; 1988). For example, between 750 and 725, unit H 24/25/32 was a simple megaron house (figure 7.7a). Sherds from the floors show that cooking, storage, eating, and drinking all went on in the one main room. By 700, though, the occupants divided this room into three smaller rooms (H24, H25, H32). Judging from the finds, all three were used solely for storage. The south wall of the old porch was extended 8 meters, and two new rooms, H40 and H41, built at its end (figure 7.7b). H40, with an unusually wide door, was probably an anteroom to H41, with a monumental stone hearth and many sherds from fine cups. The new house was reached from the courtyard now formed by the space between H32 and H40. Turning right, the visitor entered through the wide doorway into the public area of the house for feasting; turning left, to storerooms at the back. The house immediately to the south went through a similar transformation at just this time.

Attributing gender to excavated space is almost impossible, but I am not suggesting that men or women were restricted to particular

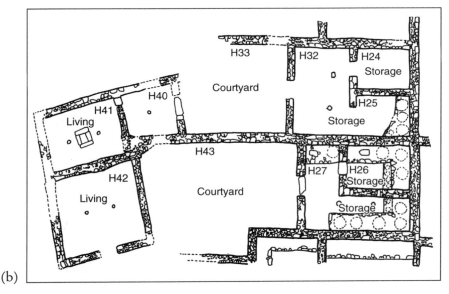

(b)

Figure 7.7 (b)   Units H 24/25/32/33/40/41 and H 26/27/42/43 at Zagora, *c.* 725–700 BC. (Based on Cambitoglou 1981: fig. 9)

parts of the house. Surely women often went into Zagora H40 and H41, and men into H24, H25, and H32. But I do want to suggest that the *ideas* about gendered space which we see in Hesiod and classical Athens began to take shape in the late eighth century.[29] The courtyard houses we see at Zagora by 700 and Miletus by 600 cut the individual *oikos* off from other units. The *oikos* was accessible only through a narrow door, guarded by its male *kyrios* or "master." Inside were his dependent women, children, relatives, and perhaps slaves, shielded from the world. Outside he related to other citizen *kyrioi* as an equal in open civic space.

   Classicists often suggest that Homeric notions of gender are less rigid than those in Hesiod and later authors (e.g., van Wees 1995: 154–63; Zeitlin 1996: 19–86). Possibly eleventh- through ninth-century Greeks did interpret their simple, open houses in much the same ways as the subdivided space of archaic and classical courtyard houses; but putting together the poetry and the transformation of house forms and activity areas between 750 and 600, the most economical theory is that gender ideologies changed in this period, in a general shift toward "middling" values.

Death, the Past, and the East

The number of burials increases sharply after 750. During the Dark Age, Athens, Corinth, Argos, other regions of central Greece each had their own burial customs, but within each area, customs were quite homogeneous. This changed after 750. New rites appeared, and variability increased everywhere. In Attica, virtually every village had its own twist on normative practices, and even within cemeteries, it was rare for two graves to be very similar. Some graves were now very rich, like the famous warrior burial (gr. 45) at Argos,[30] or had monumental markers. The explosion in the quantity and variety is most pronounced in Attica, Corinthia, the Argolid, Megara, Euboea, and the Dodecanese. In the Cyclades burials remain rare until 700, and in Ionia and Boeotia, until 550.[31]

Around 700, rich graves, especially warrior graves, disappeared. At Argos and Eretria the richest warrior burials date close to 700, but they had no successors. Variability declined. Most seventh-century cemeteries are monotonously normative – at Argos, inhumation in cylindrical pithoi; at Corinth and Megara, inhumation in simple stone sarcophagi; on Thera, small primary cremations in rock-cut pits.

The age structure changed dramatically. Before 725 there are few known child graves; after 725, they often make up roughly half our sample, just what we expect in an agrarian society. Sometimes children were buried with adults, and sometimes they had their own grave-yards. Intramural burial generally ended for adults before 700, and even child graves among houses were rare after 600. By 675 most main-land and island sites had large, homogeneous cemeteries along the roads away from town, without lavish monuments. Grave goods were poor; anything more than two or three pots is exciting in archaic funer-ary archaeology, and metal almost disappears. The Hospital and Gym-nasium cemeteries at Argos, the North Cemetery at Corinth, and the West Cemetery at Eretria are the best examples.

In *Burial and Ancient Society* (I. Morris 1987; cf. 1998b), I inter-preted this general move toward what I called "citizen cemeteries" as one dimension of the collapse of Dark Age forms of hierarchy, what I here describe as the first triumph of a middling ideology. I suggested in chapter 5 that archaic poleis were dominated by something like Dahl's Principle of Equal Consideration of Interests. In connecting archaeology with the literary sources, I inevitably constructed an ideal type of the overall tendency, but even the brief review of major sites I have offered in this chapter illustrates the fact that no two poleis were exactly the same. The model I have set out works best for places like

Table 7.1 Grave goods in Late Geometric and early archaic Rhodes

Adult burials

Period	n	Pots	Gold	Silver	Bronze	Iron	Faïence
LG	32	7.2	0.4	0.25	2.0	0.4	0
700–550	206	4.4	0.1	0.1	0.4	0.1	0.1

Child burials

Period	n	Pots	Gold	Silver	Bronze	Iron	Faïence
LG	3	3.3	0.3	0	0.3	0	0
700–550	124	2.4	0.1	0.1	0.6	0	0.3

Sources: ASAA 6/7 (1923/4) 83–341; *Clara Rhodos* 3 (1929); 4 (1931); 6/7 (1933) 7–219; 8 (1936) 7–207; *A Arch* 28 (1957) 1–192; *AD* 23:1 (1968) 77–98; 35:3 (1980) 547; Kinch 1914.

Corinth, Argos, Eretria, Megara, and the Aegean islands, though even within this group there is variation. For instance, on Thera we have substantial cemeteries of multiple burials from about 775 BC, which were replaced by individual burials after 700, though on Naxos and Paros major cemeteries only begin around 700. On Rhodes, seventh-century burials were definitely poorer than those of the eighth century, but still richer than those on the mainland (table 7.1). The settlements and sanctuaries of Ionia (including Samos and Chios) follow the general pattern, but there are few graves before 550. Boeotia is rather similar, though we know little about housing there.

    Some poleis moved further toward a "middling" material culture than others. I would suggest that Corinth, Argos, and the other cities listed above embraced the new ways most enthusiastically; Ionians and Boeotians perhaps rather less so; while Athens rejected the middle way altogether around 700. In the mid-eighth century, Athens was at the forefront of developments, but by 700 it was an exception to every generalization. Seventh-century Athenian adult cemeteries contain few graves, almost all of them under mounds; and Houby-Nielsen (1992; 1996) argues that their grave goods evoked heroic feasts. Athenians built no great temples until 600, and their votives were poor. The early seventh-century Velatouri houses at Thorikos seem to be going in the same direction as other central Greeks, but the larger areas of housing at Lathouriza and Oropos do not. Seventh-century Attica would have looked most peculiar to visitors from Thebes or Samos.

This variability is crucial. The world was being turned upside-down, and not everyone liked it. The values that some Greeks held most dear were set at naught by others, and dearly cherished principles defiled. We hear stories in Aristotle's *Politics* and other late sources about violence, redistribution of land, and struggles over the formalization of law. In some places, a new civic ideology was very successful; in others, moderately so; in Athens, it was blocked and then reversed. There was nothing inevitable about the upheavals of the late eighth century. Different communities moved in different directions because of the actions and attitudes of real people.

The unusual detail of the Kerameikos cemetery and a tight absolute chronology may allow us to follow the steps through which, in the space of a generation, Athenians turned away from the new mores sweeping through central Greece. This calls for a cultural microarchaeology of the kind I described in chapter 1. In *Burial and Ancient Society* I treated the details of Athenian burial – the form of the grave, disposal methods, pottery decoration, etc. – as formal attributes through which buriers expressed the structural principles of their view of the world. I did not worry too much about whether Athenians decorated pots with human figures or meanders, or whether they burned the dead or left them to rot. What mattered was that each period had a normative disposal form and variations on it. The form of the norm did not matter, but the structure behind it did (see p. 99 above).

This is a practical way to deal with burials, but it is only a convenient fiction. Tilley insists that "such a structuralist approach marks only the beginning of a fresh perspective on material culture studies: it is something to be transcended" (1990: 66). A cultural history of one of the most meaningful decisions for any buriers – how to dispose of the corpse – may provide a key to understanding the Athenian responses to the new intellectual currents of the eighth century. It is one of the truisms of functionalism that while the same symbol can express two different ideas in two different social systems, two different symbols can express the same idea within a single social system at different points in time. Yet it strains credibility to think that it meant nothing to Athenian buriers whether the custom of the day was to burn their dead relatives or to leave them to rot in the ground. Like most Greeks, Athenians inhumed their dead in chamber tombs in Mycenaean times. In the eleventh century, they switched to individual inhumation in cist graves; then around 1025 to cremation with the burned bones buried in an amphora for adults, and inhumation in a pit grave or pot for the young (though few children have been found).

Around 750 they reintroduced inhumation for adults, usually in pit graves (though there is much variety), only to switch to primary cremation (i.e., burning the body on a pyre in the grave itself) for adults again after 700. By 550 a slow move back to inhumation in pit graves was underway. Apart from the years 425–400, inhumation remained the norm throughout antiquity. This volatility contrasts with most of central Greece, where inhumation always dominated. I suggest it tells us something important about the construction of time and space in the late eighth century, and about why Athenian culture diverged from what we find in the rest of central Greece.

Burning and Rotting

John Cook (1953) suggested that Homer inspired the Athenians to adopt cremation around 700. But this runs into problems when we widen the context. If Athenians felt this way, why were few other Greeks so overcome by Homer that they switched to cremation (and why did Athenians not make their cremations *more* like Homer's)? Vidal-Naquet (1986: 139–40), by contrast, suggested that the cremation of adults and inhumation of children in the West Gate cemetery at Eretria around 700 reflects the opposition between culture and nature, with adults being burned, a cultural transformation of bodies into stable bones, while children, less domesticated beings, changed state through the natural process of rotting. But this faces the same problems. If burning adults and leaving children to rot reflects a nature/culture opposition rooted in human brain structures, why did Argives ignore it, inhuming all age groups? And why did the people of Anavyssos in Attica, only fifty miles from Eretria, inhume adults and cremate children? Burkert (1983: 12–29) suggests instead that cremation and sacrificial meals both go back to palaeolithic hunters. He starts from an old idea of early man as an inherently aggressive killer. Recent research suggests this is a fantasy (e.g., Isaac 1989: 312–25), but even ignoring this, if cremation linked Greeks with the dawn of man the hunter, why were seventh-century Athenians more in touch with their roots than Athenians of the eighth century? Or the sixth century? Or their neighbors in Corinth? Appealing to universal meanings obscures more than it reveals, and in the standard textbook on Greek burial, Kurtz and Boardman conclude from the variety of rites that "Cremation was nothing special" (1971: 329).

Yet there is more to it than this. In a famous passage, Herodotus tells a story that

Darius, during his own rule, called together some of the Greeks who were in attendance on him and asked them what they would take to eat their dead fathers. They said that no price in the world would make them do so. After that Darius summoned those of the Indians who are called Callatians, who *do* eat their parents, and, in the presence of the Greeks (who understood the conversation through an interpreter), asked them what price would make them burn their dead fathers with fire. They shouted aloud, "Don't mention such horrors!" These are matters of settled custom, and I think Pindar is right when he says, "Custom (*nomos*) is king of all." (Herodotus 3.38)

Herodotus knew that the form of the disposal of the dead mattered. But at the same time he saw *nomos* as inexplicable, locally generated and irreducible to any other factor. When his Greeks and Callatians burned or ate their dead they were saying more or less the same thing about them: these are our fathers. To understand the eighth century, we have to get inside its *nomoi*, but there are no methodological shortcuts.

Greek Fire

In seventh-century myth, fire mediated between gods and mortals and between mortals and animals, or, as Vidal-Naquet argues, between culture and nature. Fire transformed the raw grains of nature into bread, defining humans as the "bread-eating mortals" of epic poetry. In sacrifice it transformed animal bones into smoke for the gods, and animals' bloody flesh into cooked meat for humans; and it transformed the torn bodies of heroes into dry white bones for burial. The Athenians' adoption of cremation for adults around 700 has to be seen in this light.

The myth of Prometheus, formalized by the seventh century in Hesiod's *Works and Days* (42–89) and *Theogony* (507–616), connected the defining properties of fire. Prometheus' adventures mark "a place between the history of the gods and that of man" (Rudhardt 1981: 272). Back in the days when mortals and gods associated freely, Prometheus planned to deceive Zeus in a feast at Mekone. He gave the king of the gods a plate of bones covered by fat, while the mortals ate meat. Zeus saw through this, but accepted the portion of bones anyway. Angry, Zeus hid *bios*, the means of life, from man. *Bios* in *Works and Days* 42 and the *pyr*, fire, which Prometheus stole back in a fennel stalk in line 50, complementary: fire is the means of life. Zeus punished Prometheus' theft with a "gift," sending Pandora to earth as the source of evils and pains. These events established the need for labor and its sexual division. Men plowed the earth while women created the domestic sphere, including the use of fire in cooking. Mankind's place relative to the gods was also fixed, mediated through the use of fire in sacrifice as a constant attempt to recreate the intimacy enjoyed before Mekone. Hesiod says that "because of this the tribes of men on the earth burn white bones for the deathless gods on perfumed altars" (*Theogony* 556–7).

Burkert (1983: 48–58) shows how Hesiodic sacrifice and Homeric cremation of dead heroes functioned similarly, as ways of fixing the places of animals, men, the dead, and the gods. Although Vernant (1989: 38–41) notes certain differences – in sacrifice, bones are separated from flesh and then offered to the gods by being burned, while in cremation it is the burning which separates the bones – the mortality–agriculture–sex–work chain underpinning the cosmology of middling culture runs through early Greek literature, tied together by Prometheus and the use of burning in sacrifice, cooking, and the funeral.

The Meanings of Cremation in Archaic Athens

But how important would these connections have been for seventh-century Athenians watching a cremation? There must have been many uniquely Athenian traditions about fire, but at least by the sixth century the Homeric *Hymn to Demeter*, also dealing with mortality and the origins of agriculture, tied Attica into panhellenic myth. The homology between burning the dead and burning the bones of sacrificed victims was presumably fairly obvious, the kind of thing any competent person could be expected to grasp. Like other Greeks, Athenians had been making burned offerings to the gods since at least 900, and the sacrificial pyres from Tourkovouni, Mt. Imittos, and the Academy Sacred House show that the practice continued through the seventh century.

Houby-Nielsen (1996) points out that when seventh-century Athenians cremated men they usually left burned pottery in an offering trench east of the grave, placed just like an altar before a temple. She suggests that this ritual package blurred the boundaries between elite men and both heroes and gods. We might, then, follow Cook in linking seventh-century cremation with the heroic world, but without seeing it as a passive reponse to Homeric epic. But Houby-Nielsen also emphasizes (1992: 346–7) that seventh-century burial looks back *past* 750 BC to the cremations and vase types of earlier Geometric times. Some Athenians might have seen different historical references in the revival of cremation. I argued in *Burial and Ancient Society* that between 1050 and 750 and again between 700 and the late sixth century only about one-quarter of adults were buried in ways which show up in our archaeological record. In both periods, almost all known adult graves are cremations. When burning returned around 700, it had been only two generations since the end of its Dark Age vogue. Seventh-century cremation was different from Dark Age cremation – a point I return to below – but its return must surely have put some Athenians in the 690s in mind of the customs of their grandparents' days.

Athenians attending seventh-century funerals probably did not make either/or choices between references to the Dark Age or to the more distant heroic age.[32] Cremation could evoke sacrificial access to the gods, Prometheus' adventures and the definition of a stable world order, and the heroes. For all we know, these connections may never have been made explicit in speech. Some Athenians may have sensed all of them; others, a few, or even none. But the availability of these associations made cremation a good symbol for reasserting an Athenian order which once again drew sharp lines between the privileged and the unprivileged.

Body treatment had rich external references. Burning and rotting would have called for different responses in different contexts. A family inhuming a dead relative in Argos around 725, for example, may have known that they were paralleling the rites used in the ancient tombs at nearby Prosymna, where sacrifices were offered to a vanished race (p. 267 above); or they may have thought of inhumation as local practice for countless generations, simply what people in Argos had always done. Most likely the two ideas were inseparable. In Athens, things were different. Inhumation was a new rite in the late eighth century, returning to favor after ten generations of cremation. Athenians may have made connections between inhumation and the beings in the Bronze Age tombs at Menidi and Thorikos, but they may equally have felt their break with the past and movement toward the *nomoi* of neighboring city-states even more strongly. Opinions doubtless differed, and there is some evidence that the new rite was hotly debated.

The alternation between burning and rotting redefined symbolic relationships between Athenians and their neighbors as well as those between present and past. Around 750, when Athenians embraced inhumation as the normative adult rite, they were at the forefront of the great transformation in death-rituals. Grave goods escalated, numbers of burials increased, and inhumation almost completely replaced cremation. By 725 intramural cemeteries went out of style and rich grave goods lost favor at Athens itself, though they continued until 700 at some rural sites. Cemeteries were walled off, and simple temples appeared, with abundant cheap votives and a few more expensive ones.[33]

So far, the story at Athens was like that at Corinth or Argos. By adopting new forms of space, widening the burial family, and changing from cremation to inhumation, Athenians took part in a broadly central Greek phenomenon. But in the last decades of the eighth century something happened. The Athenians did not go on to elaborate the bipolar religious orientation which de Polignac (1995a: 81–8) takes as typical of archaic city-states, or to build monumental stone temples. Their votives, both within Attica and at panhellenic sanctuaries, grew poorer just as those of other Greeks escalated. Through most of the seventh century there is no evidence for Athenian involvement in panhellenic games, hoplite warfare, colonization, or other typically "Greek" activities. Attic sanctuaries and probably the city of Athens itself would have looked out of date to Corinthian or Argive visitors around 650; and so would Attic funerals. The reversion to cremation was a striking element in a visual system which looked back to the past, recalling the simpler religious practices and social relationships of the Dark Age. The Athenian elite cut themselves off from the growth of polis institutions, shutting out the middling ideas which were taking hold all around them, and obviating the need for some of the responses typical of the elitist worldview.

They did not, of course, succeed in turning the clock back. The developments of the mid-eighth century had set the limits of the possible for the reaction of the seventh. Athenian art was permanently changed in Late Geometric times by the admission of orientalizing motifs. Whitley (1994a) shows that seventh-century Athenians "rationed" these new forms to limit their disruptiveness, but Sub-Geometric styles still had to be used alongside a Protoattic tied to the exotic. Athenians continued the eighth-century practice of offering many cheap pots to the gods, but did not follow the Peloponnesians and islanders toward metal gifts and stone temples. Similarly, changes in burial in the seventh century were shaped by developments in the eighth.

Arguing Through the Dead

As noted on p. 287 throughout the Dark Age there was little variation in burial rites in Attica,[34] but after 750, every cemetery had its own peculiarities. In the Agora (figure 7.8), we find a mixture of shaft graves

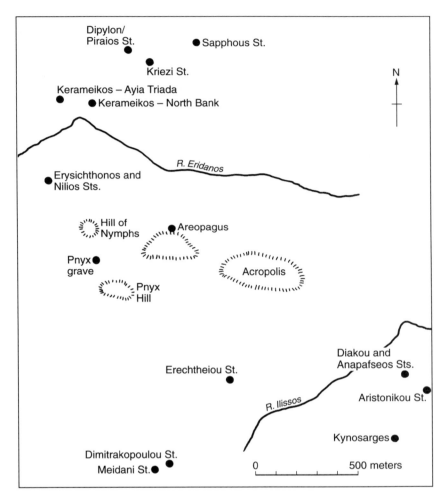

Figure 7.8   Sites in Athens mentioned in this chapter

and pit graves, all for inhumations; in the strange cemetery on Erysichthonos and Nilios Streets, we find T-shaped pits, with pyres and offerings in the end compartments. On Erechtheiou Street pit inhumations and primary and urn cremations coexisted. Outside Athens, there was still more variety. In the Eleusis West Cemetery, a few primary cremations appeared before 725. At the Academy, Trachones, and Anavyssos the Dark Age practice of cremations in amphoras continued briefly, although these were now laid on their sides. In the South Cemetery at Eleusis and at Thorikos we have as much variety as on Erechtheiou Street; but the most interesting case is Merenda. Here, a 1960 excavation uncovered 15 cremations, mostly late eighth-century. Some were in amphoras and some were primary cremations with vases in separate cuttings, like the seventh-century offering trenches. Less than 200 meters away, a 1967 dig found a mixed group of late eighth-century inhumations in pits and cists, and further work in 1972 uncovered primary cremations and inhumations. Even if we assume that some of the 1960 primary cremations date to the seventh century, we see remarkable variety, mixing old and new rites (references in I. Morris 1987: 222–33).

Attic burial customs were more diverse between 750 and 700 than at any time before or after, and no other contemporary polis has such variation within its territory. The most likely interpretation is that the adoption of inhumation around 750 was highly problematic, and that not all Athenians – and still less those in the Attic countryside – were equally enthusiastic about it. It must have had tremendous religious implications, which meant abandoning the recent past and assimilating to the *nomoi* of Athens' neighbors.

Theories like Cook's, Vidal-Naquet's, or Burkert's overlook the complexity of the ritual scene in the late eighth century. Cremation with the bones in amphoras continued in some parts of Athens, and we also find a few Late Geometric primary cremations. Heroizing cremations with the bones in bronze urns made its first appearance at Athens around 750.[35] Adult inhumations took two main forms, in shaft graves and in simpler pit graves. The shaft grave had Middle Geometric II antecedents, in amphora cremations with shelves down the long sides of the grave cutting to support cover slabs (e.g., Kerameikos grs. G 29 and 31). Dipylon gr. 3, probably the earliest cremation in a bronze urn (Late Geometric Ia), was also a shaft grave. By Late Geometric Ib (*c.* 750–735), however, shaft graves were established for inhumations. Pit graves were not necessarily poorer versions of shaft graves; right from the start of Late Geometric I we find "outsize" pit graves, substantially larger than the skeletons to be laid in them. At first these were rare. Dipylon grs. 1 and 3, some 2.95 and 3.1 meters long respectively, date to Late Geometric Ia; the biggest of all Geometric graves, Kerameikos hS 290 (3.9 m.) and 291 (4.3 m.), are Late Geometric Ib. In all, only five Late Geometric I graves were over 3 meters long, compared to ten Late Geometric II graves (735–700).[36] We see considerable variation and perhaps competition, but an overall trend toward greater elaboration, whether by using a bronze urn, digging an enormous grave pit, or offering large quantities of grave goods, is visible throughout Late Geometric I.

The best evidence for the charged nature of inhumation around 750 comes from the small Dipylon cemetery (figure 7.9), which was among the trend-setters in the mid-eighth century. At the start of Late Geometric I we see huge marker vases with elaborate paintings of funerals and battles, including many figures (figure 7.10). Marker vases go back to 900 over Kerameikos grs. G 1 and 2, and there is an example of about 850 from Kriezi Street gr. 1968/3,[37] but the concentration and magnificence of the Late Geometric I Dipylon finds have no parallels. About two-thirds of all known Geometric funeral scenes come from the Dipylon, and are the products of an artist conventionally known as the Dipylon Master and a small group of painters working in his style (Snodgrass 1987: 148–50).[38]

This concentration may be partly a result of postdepositional factors. Several Dipylon graves were preserved under the classical tumulus A, while the Kriezi cemetery is only known through salvage digs, that of 1968 conducted at night. These factors have skewed recovery toward the Dipylon, but cannot account for the whole pattern. Even before the 1871 excavation, remarkable figured scenes were known from the Dipylon, and while meticulous German digs in the Kerameikos recovered many fragments of destroyed grave markers, none compares with the Dipylon finds.[39]

There are two striking coincidences here. First, the Dipylon buriers chose funerals for the main scenes on many marker vases – the only monumental artform we know from eighth-century Athens – just as Athenians abandoned a three-century-old tradition of cremation. Second, a high proportion of the Greeks' earliest experiments with representational art come from this tiny area on the northwest edge of Athens, used by families who led the way in experiments with inhumation, cremation in bronze urns, and elaborate burial.

Jeffery Hurwit (1985: 65–70) divides explanations for the florescence of figured painting after 750 into two types, "tabula rasa" and "artistic precursor" theories. The former present representational art as a basic instinct, raising the question of why Greeks repressed that instinct between 1100 and 750. The latter assume that representational art is unusual, and ask what stimulated it after 750. Hurwit identifies two variants of precursor models, one looking to the past and the other to the east. The first holds that after 750 Greeks encountered Mycenaean pictorial art, and emulated it. The second sees Greek picture-painting as a response to Near Eastern representations. Both Bronze Age and west Asian influences are clear in Late Geometric art (e.g., Hurwit 1985: 53–202; S. P. Morris 1992b), but as so often, it may be wrong to make this an either/or question. Hurwit (1985: 69) notes that conventional theories "address the 'how' of the

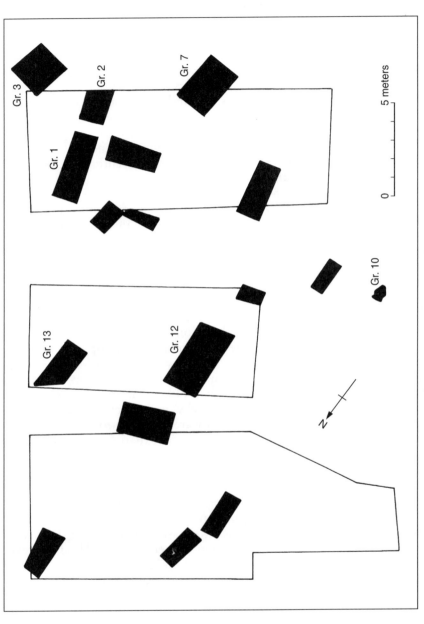

Figure 7.9 The Dipylon cemetery on Peiraos Street, Athens (based on *AM* 18 (1893) fig. 1)

Gr. 3

Gr. 2

Gr. 7

Gr. 1

Gr. 13

Gr. 12

Gr. 10

N

0   5 meters

Figure 7.10 A Late Geometric I battle scene from the Dipylon cemetery (Paris A 519; drawing based on Coldstream 1977: fig. 33b)

issue but not the 'why,' " and as we have seen, by 750 there was a long
tradition of merging the past and the east. Snodgrass in particular
(1980a: 65–78; 1987: 147–69; 1998b) argues that the Athenian painters
who combined Levantine and Bronze Age traditions with local
Geometric styles actively tried to blur distinctions between the
mid-eighth-century Athenians buried in the Dipylon, Kriezi, and
Kerameikos cemeteries, and great ancestors or even heroes from the
past. Their paintings represented neither the contemporary world nor
specific myths drawn from Homer; rather, they evoked a generalized
heroic atmosphere, imbuing the warriors and aristocrats whose graves
they honored with some of the aura of the heroic race.

But what the buriers put *in* the graves was often even more
remarkable than what they put on top of them. Whitley (1991a: 144)
notes that 24 of the 35 Late Geometric gold diadems known from
Athens come from this northwestern group of cemeteries. Of the
other eleven, three come from the Erysichthonos and Nilios Streets
cemetery, 300 meters southwest of the Kerameikos and possibly part
of the same group, where we also find oversize graves; and five
from the Kynosarges, one of the few sites in southern Athens with
monumental vases comparable to the northwest. The decoration of
gold diadems evolved rapidly, from plain or Geometric designs to
fluid, orientalizing styles. By Late Geometric Ib, figured scenes on
bands were more orientalizing than those on marker pots. Whitley
notes that by comparison "The resistance of the Athenian Geometric
[pottery] both to influences from the Orient and to fashions in other
media is notable" (1991a: 144).[40] The people buried in the Dipylon
and Kerameikos cemeteries had probably walked around wearing
orientalizing gold headbands, and their kin buried them with such
jewelry, as well as with such remarkable orientalia as the five nude
female Astarte-type ivory figurines from Dipylon gr. 13 (figure 7.11).
Robin Osborne (1996: 85) asks "How is it that the same person could
both choose pottery with geometric scenes, and gold bands with
these very different friezes? How are we to explain such cultural
schizophrenia?" He sees the answer in "A style war . . . eighth-
century-BC Athens witnessed the first debate in Greek history to
which we are privy over the role of the wealthy in society."

I see even more going on in this style war than debates over wealth.
It was also a debate over the place of the old, Dark Age elite in a world
which was making them irrelevant. Buriers needed to say where they
stood on their relationships to the heroes, on the wealth of the east
and the excitement of new horizons overseas, on the revolutions in
other central Greek city-states, and not least on the claims of the poor
in Athens itself. It is perhaps hardly surprising that the results confuse

Figure 7.11 Ivory figurines from Dipylon gr. 13 (photograph courtesy of the German Archaeological Institute at Athens)

us, but even after 27 centuries we can still see that the users of these northwest Athenian cemeteries drew attention to their own part in the switch to new burial rites, and all that went along with them. The funerary scenes on the marker vases emphasized the act of burial, and through their association with the new rite of inhumation looked away from the cremating past and toward neighboring cities. They made the graves they marked stand out from those of other Athenians who, while they adopted the new rites, did not draw such attention to the act of burial by displaying it in above-ground paintings for passers-by to see. Grand graves, cremation in bronze urns, representational painting, nude female ivory figurines, and flowing orientalizing scenes on gold bands, all spoke to different degrees the old language of heroization and orientalism, but did so in very new ways.

After just a decade or so (on Coldstream's dating) of experiments around 750 in the Dipylon, figured scenes spread through Athenian cemeteries, but changed in the process. The number of known laying-out scenes increased from 23 in Late Geometric I to 33 in Late Geometric II. The so-called "classical" workshops, descended from the Dipylon Master, relegated funerary scenes to subsidiary zones, while the painters in nonclassical workshops continued to put these scenes in more prominent places. Most of the funerary scenes cluster around 700 BC, when burial rites were again changing, and come from the Attic countryside; and some of the painters who produced them, such as the Thorikos Painter and Trachones Group, were probably based outside Athens (Rombos 1988: 77–91, 357–68). After 700, funerary scenes again virtually disappear, only to return when burial customs shifted again in the mid-sixth century.

The meanings of funerary symbolism seem chaotically open in the later eighth century. One response was to orient rituals toward the new ideas of the citizen which had been forming since the early eighth century, with inhumation as one of several symbols of membership in a community of city-states. Another was what we might expect from archaic elitist poetry, with people putting on diadems and claiming to share in the splendors of the east. But by 700 Athenians found another way still, drawing on the rich traditions of their past, turning away from all these dangerous ideas to reinvent an older system involving a distinct elite and a dependent peasantry. Most likely everyone in the Athenian upper classes tried different things at different moments, but overall we see a distinct trend among the users of the northwest cemeteries. Cremation was an excellent symbol for those who leaned toward the third response, creating a warm glow of nostalgia by mixing the piety of sacrifice with a general sense of the age of heroes and the Athenians' own past – if indeed these categories were actually separated. Such an attitude might work well, absorbing a range of threatening new tendencies into a peculiarly Athenian reaction. For instance, the decline in the use of grave goods in most poleis around 700 could be seen as an egalitarian, middling process (p. 278 above), but careful choice of grave goods was also a Dark Age tradition. In Athens, poor seventh-century offerings could be seen as returning to the good old days after the excesses of giant graves, marker pots, and gold in the late eighth, rather than as a sign of a citizen state. There is no point privileging one group of readings over another when analyzing particular excavated graves; considering the number of people who attended funerals or looked at the Dipylon grave markers between 750 and 700, we should assume that all these points of view, and who knows how many others, had their adherents. Yet by the early seventh century, the Athenian elite had defeated the middling ideology.

Relatively few adult graves from the crucial years around 700 have been excavated, but by then the users of the Dipylon cemetery no longer set the cultural tone the way they had done with their ostentatious spending two generations earlier. Parts of the area from the Kerameikos to modern Sapphous Street along the northwest edge of Athens, including the Dipylon, became child cemeteries in Late Geometric IIb. Only five of the Dipylon graves from the nineteenth-century excavations date between 720 and 680, and three of these (grs. 9, 10, 19) are definitely children. Gr. 18 was probably an adult inhumation, but was destroyed. Gr. 8 was the only intact adult burial, a male inhumation. The offerings were poor by Late Geometric I standards, with just seven pots, none of them over 25 cm. tall; but by now even these few vases constituted a generous assemblage. The grave itself was also big, at 2.55 × 1.05 meters. This would have been unremarkable in Late Geometric I, and would not have aroused comment in Late Geometric II cemeteries outside Athens; but it was considerably larger than contemporary inhumations in the Kerameikos, which led the way in changes at the end of the eighth century. The impression of the Dipylon cemetery as being unfashionable by 700 is perhaps reinforced by the area's apparent abandonment from about 675 until the late sixth century.[41]

The Kerameikos led the way in the transition to seventh-century practices, particularly the poorly preserved area on the north bank of the River Eridanos (figure 7.12). As in the Dipylon, large graves predominate in Late Geometric I. Gr. G 89, dating 775–750 and still using cremation with the ashes in a clay amphora, was 2 meters long; the six adult graves dated Late Geometric I–IIa (760–720) had an average length of over 2.25 meters, even though two of them (grs. G 71 and 72) only needed to be big enough to hold a bronze urn. Excluding for a moment the Rundbau plot, the four Late Geometric IIb adult graves here averaged under 2 meters in length. The eight adults dated Late Geometric I–IIa had 31 pots, a mean figure of 3.9 per grave; the four Late Geometric IIb adults had only 9 pots, or 2.25 per grave. By Late Geometric IIb a shift was under way toward smaller, simpler graves. The plain pit graves of the end of the eighth century form an intermediate stage between the grand burials of the 750s through 720s and the seventh-century primary cremations. When the users of this cemetery decided to adopt cremation, they did so within the constraints of current practices, in a period when simplicity was valued over display and variety. Primary cremation was more complex and expensive than inhumation in a plain pit, but given the decision to burn the body, this was the simplest way to do it, cutting out the second stage of collecting and wrapping the bones and putting them in the

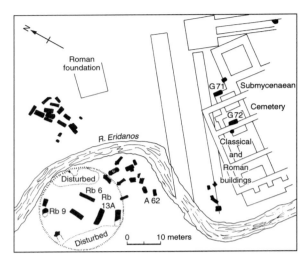

Figure 7.12   The cemetery on the north bank of the Eridanos river, Athens

urn. The poor pit graves of the last twenty years of the eighth century may already have been saying many of the same things about the dead that seventh-century cremations were to say, in reaction to the overblown display of the graves in other parts of Athens. Switching to burning the body in the grave instead of leaving it to rot added an extra layer of sophistication and power to the claims of social superiority that this plot's users made.

As happened around 750, some Athenians were less eager to change than others, and resisted the trend toward simplicity, even in the Kerameikos itself. The remarkable gr. A 62, probably from the first decade of the seventh century, was a pit 2.1 × 0.7 meters, containing a bronze urn plugged by a smaller bronze bowl, and nine vases. Inside the urn were the ashes of three men. Nearby was the still more remarkable Rundbau plot. The earliest two burials here, around 700 (grs. Rb 5 and 6), were adult inhumations in narrow pits 3.9 and 4.0 meters long respectively. Soon after, a mound 21 meters across was heaped up over these graves, at a time when other mounds in the Kerameikos were much smaller; and cut into the mound around 650 were grs. Rb 13A, an inhumation pit 4 meters long, containing four bronzes, and Rb 9, the burial of a horse.[42] For fifty years, the Rundbau buriers ignored the trend toward simplicity and homogeneity, and for some graves even ignored the switch to cremation. Most known early seventh-century burials have low mounds, and contain no grave goods. The displays of wealth in the Rundbau hark back to the mid-eighth-century tradition.

Despite the resistance of the Rundbau users, shortly after 700 a new, stable elite funerary system of simple primary cremations marked by low mounds took shape. There were minor variations, such as putting vases into the graves themselves at Anavyssos, Tavros, and Vari, or cutting child amphora burials into the fill of the adult graves in the Late Geometric IIb style as in the Bau Z area of the Kerameikos,[43] but there was remarkable uniformity. In the late eighth century we see a movement away from large pit graves or shaft graves with lavish grave goods and sometimes monumental marker pots toward simpler and smaller inhumation graves. This was a reaction against the Late Geometric symbolism which tied Athens to a wider central Greek cultural system, abandoning local Dark Age traditions.

Around 700 the users of prestigious plots like the Eridanos north bank went further, reintroducing cremation. They did not simply revert to the pre-750 practice of placing the burned bones in pottery amphoras, which was still in use in some parts of Athens, and was the general custom at a few rural sites until 700.[44] Doing this would have surrendered the right to define symbolism; and if anything is clear about Athens in the last decades of the eighth century, it is that the "correct" form of burial was hotly disputed. Even adopting as a normative rite the heroizing and showy Late Geometric fashion of using a bronze urn was unacceptable, because it negated the now-ingrained principle of simplicity. By 675 the Athenians were having their cake and eating it, partially heroizing but also holding to the traditions of restraint which had characterized the Dark Age race of iron. By attaching new values to primary cremation rather than simply reverting to urn cremation, those who would be the cultural elite in Athens around 700 not only turned away from the symbolism which characterized other Greek city-states – run on lines which did not much appeal to them – toward the heroic and specifically Athenian past, but also maintained their claims to be the ones who dictated standards.

Conclusion

Every dimension of eighth-century life seems filled with these debates over the location of the good society. This spatial metaphor, of communities arguing over where to place themselves, accords with the Greeks' own perceptions; the image of the male citizen community as the center of the universe with other groups arranged around it recurs from Anaximander to Aristotle (Hedrick 1994).

As new developments in shipbuilding and perhaps also the consequences of Assyrian imperialism in western Asia made the Mediterranean seem smaller, central Greeks experienced period rapid spacetime compression. In reordering their sanctuaries and cemeteries, they fixed the gods and the dead ancestors at safe distances, and in writing down their traditions about the age of heroes and in visiting the tombs which housed the bodies of the ancient dead, they created new structures for controlling the distant past. At just the same time they began reorganizing domestic space in ways that facilitated stronger gender distinctions.

There is nothing in the archaeological data themselves to tell us just how these negotiations worked out, but treating the archaic literary record as what Andrén calls a "contemporary analogy," I suggest that it was in these great upheavals that Dark Age beliefs about the importance of the east and the past were reworked into the core features of the middling and elitist ideologies which I described in Part III. I argued in this chapter that this was a messy process, generating different outcomes in each part of central Greece, and in the case of Athens diverted completely around 700. But overall, male citizen communities distanced themselves from external sources of authority. The gods were safely set apart in their sanctuaries, and the dead in their cemeteries. The cosmos was discontinuous. Great gulfs separated a polis from the heroic past, the exotic east, and the gods on Olympus. And within the community, attacks on distinctions among local-born males went hand-in-hand with ever more rigid boundaries between this group, women, and imported chattel slaves. Thus was the distinctive culture of the classical city-state created.

Part V

8

Conclusions

In this book I have argued for a particular approach to archaeology, seeing it as cultural history. I suggested that such a historical view of the field is best developed through very concrete empirical work rather than abstract theorizing. In trying to work out an archaeology of this kind I have developed a new interpretation of Iron Age Greek male egalitarianism.

One of the core questions I kept returning to was what kind of stories we can and should tell about the past from its material remains. I see two ways to think about this question. The first, which archaeology shares fully with all forms of cultural history, is about how we prefigure the field of study. It involves asking why anyone should spend years researching and teaching about a particular piece of the past – in my case, Iron Age Greece; and why we should study it in one particular way – as cultural history – rather than in some other form. My responses, concentrated in Part II, are unashamedly presentist. These are the most fundamental questions any historian or archaeologist can ask, and we can only answer them by reflecting on our own positions, and on who might be interested in a particular story about a specific past time and place. I devote so much space to institutional history and broad intellectual trends because I want to understand why histories of ancient Greece have the peculiar power they do in contemporary America and Europe.

I suggested in Parts II and III that approaching historical archaeology in this way encourages us to think about teleology and metanarratives. Both are bad words in the lexicon of the new humanities and social sciences. But as the critics of poststructuralist historiography regularly point out, claims to dissolve the past into a mosaic of discontinuous spaces tend to produce not history without foundations but simply a different set of teleologies and metanarratives. I argue that one of the things which makes Iron Age Greece interesting is the

creation there of social systems which restricted the power of wealth
and delivered unheard-of freedoms to ordinary male citizens, while
simultaneously buttressing gender, ethnic, and cosmological boundaries. When I confront the Greek material from the perspective of
modern concerns about egalitarianism, I find it challenging and
provocative. Even more to the point, I find that it fails to fit the frameworks conventionally adopted by archaeologists and many kinds of
historians. That makes a cultural history of Greek equality interesting,
even important.

But deciding *what* kind of stories we are interested in only responds
to one part of the question: we also need to decide *how* we can tell our
stories. In Part IV, I wrote a cultural history of Iron Age Greece in the
terms I set up in Part I, as an event-oriented archaeological narrative.
My story looks very different not only from the long-term histories
of neolithic Europe which postprocessualists have written (e.g.,
Hodder 1990; Barrett 1994; Thomas 1996; Tilley 1996; Bradley 1998),
but also from the stories which early-modern historical archaeologists
tell (e.g., McGuire and Paynter 1991; Johnson 1996; Praetzellis and
Praetzellis 1998). The reason for this is simple: our storytelling is necessarily constrained by our data, and different kinds of evidence call
for different kinds of stories.

There is no single, all-best structure for an archaeological narrative.
Shanks (1992) and Tilley (1993) suggest that archaeologists might
experiment with nonlinear narratives, abandoning the "tree-like"
stories historians conventionally tell for less linear accounts which
might be better suited to writing about artifacts. But in chapter 1 I
defended the value of chronologically tight, sequential stories,
and in Part IV I tried to show that in the case of Iron Age Greece we
really can write cultural history on something approaching a human
timescale. While wanting to embed my narrative in longer-term histories drawing on structural, sociological thinking, I also emphasized
the humanistic basis of cultural history, and the centrality of the event
as an analytical category. I suggested that the best place to begin developing such archaeological narratives is in cases like Iron Age Greece,
with surviving texts and a tight archaeological absolute chronology.
The vast increase in all kinds of evidence since AD 1500 means that
early-modern archaeologies may produce even more interesting
results. But as Andrén (1998: 122–6) suggests, in most parts of the
world it is protohistorical periods, where texts exist but are too few
to provide anything like a coherent narrative, where archaeologists
move most quickly to try to integrate words and things. The problems protohistorians face in integrating these two categories of
evidence do not apply directly to prehistorians, but the principles
involved – of how to weave a rich and compelling narrative from

the material record – are much the same whether we are looking at Çatalhöyük or Annapolis.

A generation ago, Geertz commented about cultural anthropology that

> If one looks for systematic treatises in the field, one is soon disappointed, the more so if one finds any . . . The major theoretical contributions not only lie in specific studies – that is true in almost any field – but they are very difficult to abstract from such studies and integrate into anything one might call "culture theory" as such. Theoretical formulations hover so low over the interpretations they govern that they don't make much sense or hold much interest apart from them. This is so, not because they are not general (if they are not general, they are not theoretical), but because, stated independently of their applications, they seem either commonplace or vacant. (Geertz 1973: 25)

This is every bit as true of historiography. Rather than formulating abstract rules describing archaeology as cultural history, in Parts III and IV I tried to demonstrate my points through a concrete study. I moved away from the "social history of culture" approach which had dominated my earlier work on this period toward a cultural history of society, or, as Samuel (1992) puts it, from fact-grubbing toward mind-reading. I focused on the creation of a peculiar set of ideas about the middling man in central Greece, and argued that the egalitarian spacetime forged by 500 BC made a strong principle of equality and the Greek version of democracy thinkable. I identified a half-millennium-long tradition of concern with the community's boundaries in time and space. I suggested that this cannot be reduced to a single narrative of the triumphal march of freedom and equality; but it can be usefully modeled in terms of the history of a spectrum of attitudes.

I argued that by 1000 BC in central Greece the glories of the Mycenaean past and the kingdoms of the east Mediterranean had blurred into the notion of a mythical race of heroes. This historical model played an important part in the worldviews of a newly forming elite, which was inward-turned, present-oriented, and internally homogeneous. We might even call them self-effacing, in that they did little to alter the earth around them in any permanent way, except for erecting occasional great monuments (we know of only one, at Lefkandi) for men who linked present and past, place and space, and mortals and immortals through actions so wondrous that they could, in death, be promoted to kinship with the heroes of the past. The existence of the race of heroes helped define the present as a race of iron, sadly fallen.

This was a good way to make sense of the world around 1000, when Mycenaean ruins filled the countryside and overseas contacts had shriveled almost to nonexistence. But with every passing year the physical presence of the past diminished, and before 900, a great transformation in long-distance trade had begun. The driving force was probably political and economic changes in the Levant. The Aegean was linked to a larger world, undermining its insularity. The more this happened, the less well the ideology of rigidly opposed races of iron and heroes worked, and the less it explained.

In the ninth century, the worship of the gods took on more archaeologically visible forms, and the wealth of grave goods spiraled. Eastern materials and imports were now popular gifts for the dead, and there is evidence that heroizing, archaizing, and orientalizing rites spread through society. The escalation of spending perhaps came under control by 800, but by 750 it seems that all the norms of the Dark Age were open to challenge and redefinition. Eighth-century central Greece was a contentious and exciting place.

To some extent, new forms of technology which collapsed time and space drove the cultural revolution: new ships made travel faster, safer, and easier; writing and pictorial art allowed Greeks to freeze particular visions of the heroic past. But underlying these intellectual shifts we can see population growth, pressure on resources, more intense warfare, and political centralization, which affected every part of the Mediterranean after 750. To understand properly what happened in Greece between 750 and 600 we need a genuinely Mediterranean-wide history, of how each region responded in its own ways to shared problems and opportunities.

But even within the small world of the Aegean, there was tremendous variation from place to place. Crete, northern Greece, and western Greece all reacted differently from the area I am calling central Greece; and within central Greece, the Athenians departed drastically from the general trend after 700 (I. Morris 1997c; 1998b). Old debates about relationships to the past, the east, and the gods were recast in the new circumstances, and out of these conflicts the middling and elitist ideologies took shape.

The preconditions of Athenian male democracy were created in this middling culture; so too the structural need for mass slavery. The freedom of the male citizen came hand-in-hand with harsh misogyny. Middling beliefs generated fierce resistance from some of the rich, who offered an alternative of a sophisticated and beautiful literary culture, exquisite artwork, and contempt for the common man. For all the naiveté of tracing a line of power from Athens to us, Iron Age Greeks created a cultural cauldron which remains good to think with. It inspires and appalls in equal measure.

Notes

Chapter 1: Archaeology as Cultural History

1 See the papers in Friedlander 1992, and *History and Theory* 32 (1993) to 34 (1995).
2 Trigger (1978: 75–95) suggests that Europeans and Americans had different attitudes toward their pasts, the former seeing continuities which made archaeology the study of early history, the latter seeing 1492 as a rupture which made archaeology the study of savages – the past tense of anthropology. But this oversimplifies the European situation. In the most careful study, Marchand (1996: 152–87) shows that through much of the nineteenth century, German officials denigrated prehistory to claim special German connections with the classical world, only for prehistorians to exploit new conceptions of Germanness after the 1890s to take revenge on the formerly privileged classicists.
3 See Hodder 1992, bringing together essays from the 1980s.

Chapter 2: Archaeologies of Greece

1 There is a new trend away from this: see Marchand 1996; Schnapp 1996; Shanks 1996; Dyson 1998. The new *Encyclopedia of the History of Classical Archaeology* (de Grummond 1996) is an important work of reference for the issues discussed in Part II.
2 Graves-Brown *et al.* 1996 discuss Continentalist archaeologies; Hamilakis and Yalouri (1996) examine Greek nationalist attempts to use the past.
3 "Romanticism" is notoriously difficult to define. In 1948, one literary critic counted 11,396 different definitions (Cuddon 1979: 586).
4 Historians have studied German education in detail. I have found Bruford 1975, Müller 1987, and Ringer 1979a, b most useful.
5 There are many excellent studies of nineteenth-century travelers and archaeologists. I have found Bracken 1975, St. Clair 1983, and Eisner 1991 most useful.

6 Näf 1986, Schlesier 1994, and Marchand 1996 review German developments in detail.

Chapter 3: Inventing a Dark Age

1 *JHS* 2 (1881) 7–43; 3 (1882) 69–80, 185–217, 264–82; 4 (1883) 73–85, 142–55, 281–304; 5 (1884) 185–94; 7 (1886) 170–88.
2 Robert Cook, pers. comm., May 1995.
3 *BSA* 33 (1932/3) 22–65; 35 (1934/5) 45–68; 39 (1938/9) 1–51; 44 (1949) 307–32; 48 (1953) 255–60.
4 Chester Starr, pers. comm., May 1995.

Chapter 4: Equality for Men

1 See Hansen (1991) on constitutional details.
2 The story is not above question. Plutarch wrote half a millennium after Pericles' day, and rarely cited sources. He read fifth-century authors who are now lost, but his methodological statements (e.g., *Alexander* 1) inspire little confidence. Hansen (1991: 15) suggests that Plutarch may "tell us more about the Roman Empire at the time of Trajan than about the Athenian constitution 500 years earlier."
3 Themistocles' temple has perhaps been found: *AD* 19:1 (1964) 26–36.
4 Some papers in Gilmore (1987b) stress a similar range; and Davis (1977: 90–2) mentions exceptions to his Mediterranean model.
5 Correcting Bowman's (1985) calculations, which produced even higher scores ($G = .74$ to $.82$).

Chapter 5: Antithetical Cultures

1 Archilochus 13, 14; Mimnermus 6 (= Theognis 793–800), 7, 15, 16; Phocylides 6; Theognis 367–70.
2 Xenophanes 1, 22; Archilochus 124b; Theognis 469–98, 503–10, 837–44; Phocylides 11; cf. Anacreon 356.
3 Theognis 335; cf. 219–20, 331–2, 401–6, 543–6, 693–4, 719–28 (= Solon 24).
4 *Iliad* 1.1–7; 2.484–92; 11.218–30; 14.508; 16.113–14; *Odyssey* 1.1–10; 8.73, 479–81, 488; 22.346–8.
5 E.g., Sappho 2.14; 30.4–5; 44.8–10; 46; 81; 92; 94.12–22; 98; 192; Alcman 1.64–8; 3.77; 56.3; 91; 117; Alcaeus 130B.17–20; Anacreon 388.10–12; 481; with Kurke 1992: 93–9.
6 E.g., Sappho 39; 132.3; Alcman 1.64–5; 13c; 16; cf. Alcaeus 94.5; 69.1–6; Anacreon 481; elegy 3; Alcman 13d.
7 The only better comparison than Lydian women was Helen, and fragment 16 began with her story.

8   Xenophanes 18; 34; Archilochus 16; 130; Semonides 1; Solon 13.65–74
    (= Theognis 585–90); 16; Theognis 133–42, 155–60, 557–60, 1075–8.
9   See also Hipponax 32, 38, 42, 72.7, 79, 125.
10 Robinson (1997: 126–7) suggests democracy was well established by 550,
    but the evidence for the early cases is particularly problematic.
11 Pindar, *Olympian* 5.16; 7.89–90; 31.2–3; *Pythian* 2.81–2; 4.295–7;
    11.28–30; *Nemean* 7.65–7; 8.38–9; 11.17; *Isthmian* 1.50–1; 2.37–8; 3.1–3;
    fragment 109.
12 Pindar, *Olympian* 2.95; 11.7–8; *Pythian* 2.89–92; 7.18–19; *Nemean*
    8.21–3; *Isthmian* 2.43; Bacchylides, *Ode* 13.199–203.
13 Pindar, *Olympian* 7.90–2; *Pythian* 4.284–5; 8.8–20; 11.54–6; *Nemean*
    7.65–7; *Isthmian* 3.1–3; fr. 180.3; Bacchylides, *Ode* 13.44–5.
14 Pindar, *Olympian* 7.20–4; 10.16–19, 43–77, 102–5; *Pythian* 4.253; 9.39–42;
    10.1–3, 49–53; *Isthmian* 5.26–7; 6.19.
15 Pindar, *Pythian* 9.93; cf. *Olympian* 5.4; 7.93–4; 9.19–22; *Nemean* 2.8;
    Bacchylides, *Ode* 6.15–16; 13.77–83.
16 Pindar, *Nemean* 1.31–3; *Isthmian* 1.67–8; 4.29; Bacchylides, *Ode* 3.13–14;
    see Kurke 1991: 225–9.
17 Pindar, *Olympian* 6.39–40, 104–5; 8.51; 9.32–3. 13.65–6; *Pythian* 1.1–2;
    3.9–10, 89–90, 93–5; 4.53–4, 178; 5.9, 104; 9.6, 9, 56, 59, 109; *Nemean*
    5.2–4; 6.37–8; 7.77–9; *Isthmian* 1.1; 2.1–2, 26; 4.60; 6.75; 8.6–7; *Paean* 6.1;
    fragments 29.1, 3; 30.1–2, 6; 75.14; 139.1, 9; 195; Bacchylides, *Ode* 9.1,
    100; 11.4, 37–8, 49; 13. 194–5; *Dithyramb* 3.34–6; 5.22; fragment 15.12;
    Simonides, fragment 577.
18 Pindar, *Olympian* 7.64; *Pythian* 4.232; 10.40; *Nemean* 8.27; *Isthmian*
    6.19; fr. 166.3; Bacchylides, *Dithyramb* 1.4.
19 Pindar, *Olympian* 8.67; *Pythian* 8.76–8; 12.29–30; *Nemean* 10.29–30;
    Isthmian 3.4–6; 5.52–3; Bacchylides, *Dithyramb* 3.117–18; fragment 24;
    Simonides 526.
20 Pindar, *Olympian* 5.23–4; *Pythian* 2.49–53, 88–9; 3.59–62; 10.21–9;
    Nemean 7.55–6; 11.13–16; *Isthmian* 3.17–18; 5.14–16; Bacchylides, *Ode*
    5.94–6.
21 Robinson (1997: 73–8, 108–11) discusses Achaea and Elis, outside central
    Greece. The Achaean case depends on Polybius, writing 400 years later,
    and the evidence for Elean democracy is fifth-century.

Chapter 6: The Past, the East, and the Hero of Lefkandi

1   *AA* 1978: 449–70; 1979: 379–411; 1981: 149–94; 1982: 393–430; 1983:
    277–328.
2   Tiryns, *AA* 1981: 151–3; 1988: 106–7. Lefkandi, Popham and Sackett
    1968: 14, 22. Cycladic sites: Barber 1987.
3   Corinth, *Hesperia* 48 (1979) 383–4; Rutter 1981. Mycenae, Mountjoy
    1986: 194. Tiryns, *AA* 1988: 240. Asine, Frizell 1986.
4   Salamis, *AM* 35 (1910) 17–36; *Op Ath* 4 (1954) 103–23. Pompeion,
    Kraiker 1939; *Hesperia* 30 (1961) 174–7; *AM* 78 (1963) 148–53, and now
    AR 1994/5: 4, transitional to EPG.

5   Vassilisis Sophias, *AD* 38:2 (1983) 23–5. Kriezi St., *AD* 22:2 (1967) 92–6;
    23:2 (1968) 67; *AAA* 1 (1968) 20–7. Drakou St., *AD* 32:2 (1977) 18–20.
    Erechtheiou St., *AD* 23:2 (1968) 55–7; *BSA* 75 (1980) 13–31.
6   Deiras, Deshayes 1966. Kourou plot, *AD* 18:2 (1963) 60–2; *AAA* 8 (1975)
    259–75. Thebes, *AD* 3 (1917) 25–31; 29:3 (1973/4) 439; and 2 EPG graves
    in *Praktika* 1989: 254–6. Lefkandi, Popham *et al.* 1980: 109–41.
7   *AD* 36:2 (1981) 200; *AAA* 19 (1986) 35–6.
8   Kerameikos gr. SM 108, Kraiker 1939; Rendi St. gr. 8, *AD* 34:2 (1979)
    16–17; Skoubris gr. 38, Popham *et al.* 1980: 122–3; Tiryns gr. 1957/28,
    AM 78 (1963) 10–24.
9   Amphikleia, *AD* 26:2 (1971) 231–2. Elateia, *AD* 40:2 (1985) 171; 43:2
    (1988) 229–32; 44:2 (1989) 175; 45:2 (1990) 183–4; 46:2 (1991) 196–8; 47:2
    (1992) 207; Dakoronia 1993.
10 Kerameikos and Salamis, n. 4 above; Deiras, n. 6 above; Perati, Iakovidis
    1969.
11 Lefkandi, Popham and Sackett 1968: 14; Tiryns, *AA* 1979: 386–8; 1982:
    396; 1983: 289.
12 *BSA* 68 (1973) 100.
13 I draw here on Aubet 1993, Bikai 1987, Coldstream 1982, 1988, Hoffman
    1997, Kourou 1990/91, and reports in *Hesperia* 62 (1993) 95–113;
    BASOR 293 (1994) 57. The unpublished Amuq finds are in the Oriental
    Institute at the University of Chicago.
14 E.g., EPG: at Athens, Kerameikos gr. N 113 (*Hesperia* 30 (1961) 174–7)
    and Nymphaeum gr. XLII (*AD* 28:1 (1973) 34–5); at Lefkandi, Skoubris
    grs. 10 and 16 (Popham *et al.* 1980: 112–15). LPG: Athens, Kerameikos
    PG 39, 40, and 48 (Kübler 1943); at Tiryns, grs. 1957/VI, VII, and XVIII
    (*AM* 78 (1963) 27–30, 35); at Lefkandi, Palia Perivolia gr. 22 and Toumba
    grs. 39, 44, and 70 (Popham *et al.* 1980; Popham and Lemos 1996); on
    Skyros, Ayia Anna gr. A and some of the graves from the earlier digs
    (*AAA* 19 (1986) 38–9; see also p. 318 n. 41 below).
15 E.g., Konstandopoulos gr. 1 at Argos, with 2 bronze pins and a bronze
    ring (*AE* 1977: 172–6); Erechtheiou St gr. 1955/I at Athens, with 2 bronze
    pins, a bronze ring, and 5 iron rings (*BSA* 75 (1980) 24), both Middle
    Protogeometric.
16 *AD* 24:2 (1969) 104.
17 Alexandra Coucouzeli (1998) suggests that the building was never
    completed, and that the deposits which the excavators interpreted as
    evidence of deliberate infilling in fact belong to the construction
    phase. The published account of the ramps and fill (Popham *et al.* 1993:
    29–31, 52–6, 97–8, plate 37) seem more consistent with the infilling
    theory, but we must await her detailed presentation of this important
    argument.
18 Sotiriadis excavated Thermon between 1898 and 1908 (*AE* 1900: 171–212;
    1903: 75; *Praktika* 1906: 136–9; 1908: 95–8; Sotiriadis 1909), then
    Rhomaios between 1912 and 1932 (*AD* 1 (1915) 225–79; 2 (1916)
    179–85; 6 (1920/1) 168; 9 (1924/5) Parartema 4; *Praktika* 1931: 64;
    1932: 55). Papapostolou resumed excavations in 1992 (*Praktika* 1992:

88–128; 1993: 73–110; 1994: 101–16; *Ergon* 1995: 36–42; 1996: 57–61; 1997: 51–4).

19 Letters, *AE* 1990: 197–9. Site report, *AE* 1900: 178–9. Wall, *Praktika* 1908: 96.

20 Mazarakis Ainian 1997: 133. Shrine: Sotiriadis 1909: 19–20; *Praktika* 1908: 96–8; *AE* 1990: 199. The 1997 excavation (*Ergon* 1997: 54) showed that Megaron A definitely went out of use before Megaron B was built.

21 *Praktika* 1992: 127–8; 1993: 101–2.

22 *Praktika* 1993: 73–85; 1994: 101–12; *Ergon* 1995: 40–2; 1996: 57–61.

23 *Ergon* 1993: 56.

24 *Ergon* 1995: 42.

25 The tomb of Brasidas has perhaps been found: *AD* 31:3 (1976) 307; 32:3 (1977) 253–4; 33:3 (1978) 293–5; 41:2 (1986) 177.

26 Papapostolou makes the same claim for Thermon (*Ergon* 1994: 46), but the similarities are less striking there.

27 Kalapodi, Felsch 1996. Ephesus, *ÖJh* 38 (1988) 1–23, Beiblatt 1–38; 63 (1994) 30–9. Isthmia, *Hesperia* 61 (1992) 6–22; Morgan 1994: 113–24. Asine, Wells 1983: 29, 34, 160, 279–82. Attica, D'Onofrio 1995. Koukounaries, Schilardi 1988; *Praktika* 1987: 227–36; 1988: 202–7; 1989: 257–61. Minoa, reports in *Ergon* and *Praktika* most years since 1985. Iria, *AE* 1992: 201–16. Heraion, Waldstein 1902–5. Generally, Mazarakis Ainian 1997.

28 Ayia Irini, Caskey 1981. Epidaurus, Lambrinoudakis 1981. De Polignac (1995a: 27) exaggerates in saying that "virtually all the sanctuaries... were... built on the top of ruins from the Bronze Age."

29 Popham *et al.* 1980; Popham and Lemos 1996; *BSA* 77 (1982) 213–48; *OJA* 14 (1995) 103–7, 151–7.

30 Malakonda, *AAA* 17 (1984) 115–17. Chalcis, *BCH* 110 (1986) 89–120. Eretria, *Praktika* 1976: 75–6; *AntK* 24 (1981) 83; 36 (1993) 122, 130–1; *ASAA* 59 (1981) 192–6.

31 Kübler 1943: 39–42, 44–6; 1954: 209–12, 214–25, 234–9.

32 Kübler 1954: 218–20; *AM* 81 (1966) 7–8; *AAA* 1 (1968) 20–30; *Hesperia* 37 (1968) 77–116.

33 Aktaiou St, *AD* 40:2 (1985) 25–7. Kavalotti St, *AD* 20:2 (1965) 75–80. Theophilopoulou St, *AD* 27:2 (1972) 62. Kynosarges, *AD* 27:2 (1972) 93–6; *AAA* 5 (1972) 165–76. Kriezi St, *AAA* 1 (1968) 20–30.

34 Anavyssos, *AD* 21:2 (1966) 97–8. Eleusis, *EA* 1898: 106–10, with Coldstream 1977: 78–80.

35 OTE grave, *AD* 21:2 (1966) 126–7. Papanikolaou, *AD* 27:2 (1972) 192. Makris, *AD* 18:2 (1963) 58–9. Tiryns, Müller and Oelmann 1912; *AAA* 7 (1974) 24. The brief report in *AD* 35:2 (1980) 124 on a new group of 46 SM-LG graves mentions gold, but no imports. South Cemetery, Courbin 1974: 14–22. Berbati, Säflund 1965: 37, 81–90.

36 Corinth, Weinberg 1943: 9–19, 28–9; *Hesperia* 17 (1948) 204–6; 39 (1970) 16–20; 42 (1973) 4–6. Coldstream (1968: 92) suggests that the grave with 32 pots may really be three separate grave groups. Athikia, *Hesperia* 33 (1964) 91–3. Klenia, *AJA* 59 (1955) 125–8.

37 Vranezi and Andikyra, *Praktika* 1904: 39–40; 1907: 108–12; *AE* 1985: 57–84. Orchomenos, Bülle 1907: 83. Tachi, *AE* 1976: Chronika 12. Akraiphia, *Praktika* 1989: 127–34; Andreiomenou 1991.
38 Asarlik, *JHS* 8 (1887) 67–72. Kameiros, grs. 1933/43, 45, 84 (PG); 39, 80, 83 (EG/MG), in *ClR* 6/7 (1933) 7–219. Ialysos, grs. 1929/470, 1936/44, 45, 1968/98 (PG); 1936/43 (EG), in *ClR* 3 (1929); 8 (1936) 7–207; *AD* 23:1 (1968) 82–3.
39 *ASAA* 56 (1978) 9–427; *AD* 38:3 (1983) 396; 42:3 (1987) 624. *Praktika* 1959: 195 refers to more graves.
40 *AD* 39:2 (1984) 331.
41 Naxos, Lambrinoudakis 1988; for Tsikalario, see n. 42 below. Skyros, *BSA* 11 (1904/5) 78–80; *AD* 4 (1918) Parartema 43–4; *AA* (1936) 228; *AAA* 19 (1986) 37–44. Tinos, *ASAA* 8/9 (1925/6) 203–34; Desborough 1952: 149; *Praktika* 1955: 260–1; (1979) 232–3. Amorgos, *Praktika* 1993: 204–8. Rheneia, Dugas and Rhomaios 1934; Dugas 1935; Coldstream 1968: 149.
42 Neither site is fully published. Tsikalario, *AD* 18:3 (1963) 279–81; 20:4 (1965) 515–22; 21:3 (1966) 391–6, with Themelis 1976: 24–5. Donoussa, *AD* 22:3 (1967) 467; 24:3 (1969) 390–3; 25:3 (1970) 426–8; 26:3 (1971) 465–7; 28:3 (1973) 544–7; *AAA* 4 (1971) 210–16; 6 (1973) 256–9.
43 Lefkandi, Popham *et al.* 1980: 174, 225; *OJA* 14 (1995) 151–7. Thebes, *AD* 3 (1917) 25–6. Kos, *ASAA* 50/51 (1978) 85–8, 370. Skyros, *AA* 1936, 228–34. Tiryns, *AAA* 7 (1974) 24. Andikyra and Vranezi, see n. 37 above. Orchomenos, Snodgrass 1971: 241.
44 *OJA* 14 (1995) 156.
45 Lefkandi, Popham *et al.* 1980: 168–9, 344–5; *BSA* 65 (1970) 21–30. Kos, *ASAA* 56 (1978) 351. Mende, *AEMTh* 2 (1988) 332.

Chapter 7: Rethinking Time and Space

1 Nagy's evolutionary model of text fixation (1996: 29–112) puts less emphasis on written texts before the sixth century. I follow many of his arguments (chapter 5 above), but retain a focus on writing (cf. Janko 1998). But as Nagy points out (1992: 52), the two approaches are not incompatible.
2 All epigraphic translations from Powell 1991.
3 Cretans used writing differently, particularly for law codes. Whitley (1997b) shows how this may relate to differences in social structures.
4 Most scholars put Homer in the late eighth century, but the evidence is poor. See Janko 1982; Ruijgh 1995.
5 *AE* 1937: 377–90.
6 The evidence from Mycenae is poor, and the silence of the site reports may mean little, but the negative evidence from new excavations at Troy is more significant (e.g., *Studia Troica* 3 (1993) 108).
7 *AA* 1963: 126–207; Karageorghis 1967; 1973; Rupp 1988. There is also evidence for human sacrifice in a cremation of around 700 at Eleutherna on Crete (Stampolidis 1995).

8   Livy 8.22; Dionysius of Halicarnassus 7.3; Strabo C243.
9   *Mon Ant* 13 (1903) 201–94; 22 (1913) 5–447.
10 Thera: urns, *AM* 28 (1903) gr. 3; Dragendorff 1903: gr. 17; tripods: *Prak-tika* 1974: 196–9; 1976: 332. Athens, see below; tripod grave, *AM* 18 (1893) 414–15. Argos, *BCH* 81 (1957) 322–84; *AD* 26:2 (1971) 81–2; 28:2 (1973) 97–9.
11 Mazarakis Ainian 1997 and Østby 1993 catalog the sites.
12 On the standard absolute chronology, from .6 to .8 to 7.7 pots per annum.
13 Iria and Ephesus, p. 317 n. 27 above. Koukounaries, Schilardi 1988; *Praktika* 1986: 182–7; 1987: 227–36; 1988: 202–7; 1989: 257–61; Minoa, *Praktika* 1985: 187–96; 1986: 212–18; 1989: 268–73, 277–80; 1990: 257–64; 1991: 282–92; 1992: 197.
14 Eretria, Auberson 1968; *AntK* 39 (1987) 10–14, with references; 34 (1991) 127–31; 36 (1993) 122–4. For the dating *c*. 750, *Praktika* 1981: 144–6. The temple of Hera Akraia at Perachora may also date 800–750, but the evidence is unclear (Mazarakis Ainain 1997: 63–4).
15 Kato Phana, *AD* 1 (1915) 64–93; 2 (1916) 190–212; *AntJ* 39 (1959) 170–89; *BSA* 35 (1934/5) 138–64; 56 (1961) 105–6.
16 Ephesus, Hogarth 1908; Bammer 1984; *Anat St* 35 (1985) 103–8; 40 (1990) 137–60; *ÖJh* 56 (1985) 39–58; 58 (1988) 1–23, Beiblatt 1–31; 61 (1991/2) 18–54; 62 (1993) 120–67; *RA* 1991: 63–83; *AJA* 99 (1995) 239; D. Williams 1991/3. Samos, Kyrieleis 1993, with references; on the date of the first temple, *AA* 1981: 624–33.
17 Generally, D'Onofrio 1995 and Langdon 1976 on peak sanctuaries. Sacred House, *Praktika* 1958: 6–8; 1960: 322; 1961: 8–10; 1962: 5–8. Lathouriza, *AA* 1936: 178–9; Lauter 1985a; Mazarakis Ainian 1994; 1995. Tourkovouni, Lauter 1985b. Sounion, *AE* 1917: 168–213. Athens, *JHS* 80 (1960) 127–59. See Mazarakis Ainian (1997: 48, 87–9, 106, 116–19, 144–5, 150–3, 235–9) on the first three sites.
18 *BCH* 107 (1983) 111–32; 110 (1986) 121–36.
19 Herodotus tells another story (4.79) about Skyles, a prince of Scythia who greatly admired Greek customs. He built a rich house in Borysthenes, surrounding it with white stone griffins and sphinxes. Zeus destroyed it with a thunderbolt, but Herodotus does not say whether this was because of Skyles' hubris or was just another example of his bad luck.
20 Catalog in Mazarakis Ainian 1997.
21 Zagora, Cambitoglou *et al.* 1988. Sicilian Naxos, *ASAA* 59 (1981) 297. Syracuse, *ASAA* 60 (1982) 119–34. Megara Hyblaea, Vallet and Villard 1976. Pithekoussai, *AR* 1970/1: 63–7; *Expedition* 14 (1971) 34–9. The Pithekoussai houses are often interpreted as a metalworking district. Until they are fully published, this is hard to assess, but there are traces of metalworking in most early Greek houses. Miletus, *IM* 23/24 (1973/4) 68–85; 29 (1979) 115–23. Mazarakis Ainian (1997: 47) also notes this kind of rebuilding at Paralimni in Boeotia.
22 Eretria, *AntK* 30 (1987) 4. Smyrna, Akurgal 1983. There may be stratigraphic problems at Smyrna. Akurgal (1983: 23) dated the ninth-century

phase by pottery found 30 cm. below the foundations of room 41, so the rectilinear houses may be later; but there are also ninth-century rectilinear houses at Thorikos (Bingen 1967a), and Smyrnaeans may have used the "half-cellar" design popular in the Cyclades, with the floor dug beneath the level of the foundations to give more head room.

23 Aegina, *Praktika* 1894: 17–18; *EA* 1895: 238–42; *AA* 1925: 5–9. Corinth, *Hesperia* 40 (1971) 5–9, 26–34; 41 (1972) 145–8; 42 (1973) 12. Koukounaries, *Praktika* 1982: 235, 248–50; 1983: 282–6; 1984: 276–85; 1986: 172–6; 1987: 220–6; 1988: 197–200. Smyrna, Akurgal 1983; *BSA* 53/54 (1958/9) 55, 58, 66, 75–87, 91–4.

24 Zagora, Cambitoglou *et al.* 1971; 1988; Cambitoglou 1981. Drains: e.g., Koukounaries, *Praktika* 1985: 121–6; 1986: 179; 1987: 228–31; Miletus, *IM* 16 (1966) 21–2. Bathtub, von Gerkan 1925: 29–30; cf. Akurgal 1983: 36, for a bathroom in a seventh-century house at Smyrna.

25 Early rectilinear house, *IM* 9/10 (1959/60) 38–40, 57–8, with comments of Snodgrass 1971: 430; Coldstream 1977: 270 n. 53. Late eighth-century houses, von Gerkan 1925: 8–9. Seventh-century oval houses, *IM* 16 (1966) 21–2. Courtyard house, *IM* 40 (1990) 44–8; 41 (1991) 127–33; 42 (1992) 100–4.

26 Naxos, *BdA* 57 (1972) 211–19; *ASAA* 59 (1981) 299–301; *Kokalos* 30/31 (1984/5) 809–38. Megara Hyblaea, Fusaro 1982: 15–26; cf. De Angelis 1994. Punta Chiarito, Gialanella 1994. Di Vita (1990) suggests that most colonies went through a two-stage process, with major changes in plan once the community was properly established, two or three generations after its foundation.

27 Thorikos, Bingen 1967b. Lathouriza, p. 319 n. 17 above. Oropos, *Ergon* 1996: 27–38; 1997: 24–34; Mazarakis Ainian 1997: 47–8, 100–2, 115–16. Eleusis, *AD* 46:2 (1991) 38–9. Athens, *Hesperia* 23 (1954) 36; 25 (1956) 48.

28 This is obviously not true of the Lefkandi Toumba house (pp. 219–21 above), or of large apsidal houses outside central Greece at Thessaloniki Toumba (*AEMTh* 6 (1991) 209–218; 7 (1992) 259–72; 8 (1993) 220–6) and Units IV-1 and IV-5 at Nichoria in Messenia (MacDonald *et al.* 1983: 19–42, 47–53; *Op Ath* 17 (1988) 33–50; 19 (1992) 75–84). At Thessaloniki, there is some evidence that in the twelfth century storage was concentrated in a group of rectilinear rooms southeast of the apsidal structure, though this is less clear by 1000 BC. At Nichoria, storage may have been concentrated in the apses.

29 Fusaro (1982: 13–15) draws a similar conclusion. Houby-Nielsen (1992; 1995), D'Onofrio (1993), and Whitley (forthcoming) suggest that Athenian graves also reveal a shift toward more rigid gender categories after 700.

30 *BCH* 81 (1957) 322–84; cf. *AD* 26:2 (1971) 81–2; 28:2 (1973) 97–9.

31 Snodgrass 1971: 147–64 and Coldstream 1977 describe the eighth-century evidence. For Attica, add I. Morris 1987; 1998c; Whitley 1991a; Houby-Nielsen 1992; 1995; D'Onofrio 1993. Corinthia, add Dickey

1995. Argolid, add Hägg 1974; A. Foley 1988. Other regions are less systematically studied; see I. Morris 1998b: nn. 17–18, 23–5 for references for areas mentioned in this and the next three paragraphs.

32 Antonaccio (1995: 222) even suggests that ninth-century Athenian cremations in clay amphoras evoked heroic ideas.

33 For the acropolis bronzes, see *AM* 87 (1972) 57–72; 89 (1974) 27–46.

34 The main exceptions are the LPG and EG graves at Tsami on Salamis (*AD* 46:2 (1991) 71), including cist- and pit-inhumations as well as amphora-cremations, and two cist-inhumations at Marathon (PG grave, *AD* 34:2 (1979) 90–1; *AR* 1984/5: 11. MG grave: *AD* 40:1 (1985) 207–28. The MG cist inhumation mentioned in *AD* 47:2 (1992) 57 is so small that it probably belongs to a child).

35 The earliest primary cremations are Kerameikos grs. PG 10 and 42, around 925–900 (Kübler 1943), but the only Dark Age cemeteries where primary cremations are common is the odd Areopagus North Slope Cemetery (*Hesperia* 43 (1974) 329–65) and the Eleusis West Cemetery in its LG phase (Mylonas 1975). The earliest bronze urn cremations are Kriezi St. gr. 1967/26 (*AD* 22:2 (1967) 92–6) and Dipylon gr. 3 (*AM* 18 (1893) 104–6), around 750.

36 LG I: Dipylon grs. 1, 3 (*AM* 18 (1893) 101–6); Kerameikos grs. hS 290, 291 (*AD* 18:2 (1963) 29–30; Diakou and Anapafseos St. gr. 2 (*AD* 18:2 (1963) 37–8). LG II: Erysichthonos and Nilios Sts. grs. 6–9, 11 (*AD* 22:2 (1967) 79–83); Kerameikos grs. G 14, 51, 53 (Kübler 1954), Rb 6 (Knigge 1980); Aristonikou St. gr. 2 (*AD* 29:2 (1973/4) 84). This represents 8 percent of the LG I adult graves and 20 percent of the LG II.

37 *AD* 23:2 (1968) 67; *AAA* 1 (1968) 20–30.

38 Coldstream 1968: 29–33 and Ahlberg 1971a, b present the material.

39 Bohen (1997) discusses the fragmentary kraters.

40 Though Osborne (1996: 84) exaggerates in saying that the LG pottery "owed everything to the Attic ceramic tradition and nothing to any outside influence."

41 The 1967 Peiraios Street excavation (*AD* 23:2 (1968) 82) also found graves. Gr. 15 was probably an adult inhumation containing four pots and about 1.4 m. long, although it was disturbed by gr. 37. Gr. 18 was a child burial dated 700–675. The abandonment of the area is explicitly mentioned in *AM* 18 (1893) 78, although some seventh-century graves were found nearby in pipe-laying operations in 1961 (*AD* 17:2 (1961/2) 22–3). On both Kriezi and Sapphous Streets only one child inhumation in an amphora and one probable adult cremation date to the seventh century (Kriezi grs. 1968/4, 1967/P3; Sapphous grs. 1968/14, 1977/7: *AD* 22:2 (1967) 92–6; 23:2 (1968) 67, 89–92; 32:2 (1977) 27–8). With the decline in numbers of graves in the early seventh century all Athenian cemeteries contracted, and the only good evidence comes from the Kerameikos itself.

42 Gr. Rb 6A in Knigge's (1980) terminology is the same as Kübler's (1954) gr. G 98, and Knigge's Rb 13A the same as Kübler's (1959) gr. A 74.

43 Anavyssos, *Praktika* 1911: 110–31; *AD* 39:2 (1984) 43–5; Tavros, *AE* 1975:
    102–14; Vari, *AD* 18:1 (1963) 11–32; Bau Z, *AA* 1983: 221; 1984: 27–35.
44 In Athens, e.g., Diakou and Anapafseos Streets gr. 1, Dimitrakopoulou
    Street gr. 18, possibly a disturbed grave on Dimitrakopoulou and
    Aglavrou Streets, Erechtheiou Street gr. 1968/4, and Meidani Street gr. 3
    (*AD* 18:2 (1963) 37–8; 25:2 (1970) 55–8; 36:2 (1981) 19; 23:2 (1968) 55–6;
    19:2 (1964) 60). Outside Athens, p. 295 above.

References

Note that a list of journal abbreviations is printed at the front of this book.

Abercrombie, N., S. Hill, and B. S. Turner. 1980. *The Dominant Ideology Thesis*. London.

——, ——, and ——, eds. 1990. *Dominant Ideologies*. London.

Adkins, A. 1960. *Merit and Responsibility*. Oxford.

——, trs. 1986. "The *Apology*." In Adkins and White 1986: 181–206.

Adkins, A., and P. White, eds. 1986. *The Greek Polis*. Chicago.

Ahlberg, G. 1971a. *Fighting on Land and Sea in Greek Geometric Art*. Stockholm.

——. 1971b. *Prothesis and Ekphora in Greek Geometric Art*. Göteborg.

Akurgal, E. 1983. *Alt-Smyrna* I. Ankara.

Alcock, S. 1993. *Graecia Capta*. Cambridge.

Alcock, S., and R. Osborne, eds. 1994. *Placing the Gods*. Oxford.

Allsebrook, M. 1992. *Born to Rebel: The Life of Harriet Boyd Hawes*. Oxford.

Amandry, P. 1992. "Fouilles de Delphes et raisins de Corinthe." In *La redé-couverte de Delphes*: 77–128. Paris.

Andreiomenou, A. 1989. "Böotien in der Zeit von 1050–800 v. Chr." In H. Beister, ed., *Boiotika*: 253–63. Munich.

——. 1991. "Paratiriseis sti Mesi Geometriki periodo tis Akraiphias." In Musti *et al.* 1991: 451–64.

Andrén, A. 1998. *Between Artifacts and Texts: Historical Archaeology in Global Perspective*. Trs. A. Crozier. New York.

Annales. 1988. "Histoire et sciences sociales. Un tournant critique?" *Annales ESC* 43: 291–3.

——. 1989. "Tentons l'expérience." *Annales ESC* 44: 1317–23.

Antonaccio, C. 1995. *An Archaeology of Ancestors*. Lanham, MD.

Appadurai, A. 1981. "The Past as a Scarce Resource." *Man* 16: 201–19.

——. 1986. "Introduction." In A. Appadurai, ed., *The Social Life of Things*: 3–63. Cambridge.

Appleby, J., L. Hunt, and M. Jacob. 1994. *Telling the Truth About History*. New York.

Arthur, M. 1973. "Early Greece: The Origins of the Western Attitude toward Women." *Arethusa* 6: 7–58.

Aston, T. H., and C. H. E. Philpin, eds. 1985. *The Brenner Debate.* Cambridge.

Atkinson, J. A., I. Banks, and J. O'Sullivan, eds. 1996. *Nationalism and Archaeology.* Glasgow.

Auberson, P. 1968. *Eretria* I. Bern.

Aubet, M. E. 1993. *The Phoenicians and the West.* Trs. M. Turton. Cambridge.

Austin, D. 1990. "The 'Proper Study' of Medieval Archaeology." In D. Austin and L. Alcock, eds., *From the Black Sea to the Baltic*: 9–42. London.

Bagnall, R. 1992. "Landholding in Late Roman Egypt." *JRS* 82: 128–49.

Baillie, G. 1995. *A Slice Through Time.* London.

Bammer, A. 1984. *Das Heiligtum des Artemis von Ephesos.* Graz.

———. 1994. "Natur und Ruine in Ephesos." *ÖJh* 64: 97–116.

Barber, R. 1987. *The Cyclades in the Bronze Age.* London.

Barkay, G. 1992. "The Iron Age II–III." In A. Ben-Tor, ed., *The Archaeology of Ancient Israel*: 302–73. New Haven.

Barnes, B., and D. Bloor. 1982. "Relativism, rationalism and the sociology of knowledge." In M. Hollis and S. Lukes, eds., *Rationalism and Relativism.* Oxford.

Barrett, J. 1994. *Fragments from Antiquity.* Oxford.

Barstad, H. 1996. *The Myth of the Empty Land.* Oslo: *Symbolae Osloenses* supp. vol. 28.

Beazley, J. 1918. *Attic Red-Figured Vases in American Museums.* Cambridge, MA.

———. 1956. *Attic Black-Figure Vase Painters.* Oxford.

———. 1963. *Attic Red-Figure Vase Painters.* 2nd ed. 2 vols. Oxford.

———. 1971. *Paralipomena.* Oxford.

———. 1989. *Greek Vases: Lectures by J. D. Beazley.* Ed. D. C. Kurtz. Oxford.

———, and D. S. Robertson. 1926. "Early Greek Art." *CAH* IV: 579–610. Cambridge.

Bennet, J. 1997. "Homer and the Bronze Age." In Morris and Powell 1997: 511–34.

Bérard, C. 1970. *Eretria* III. Bern.

———. 1978. "Topographie et urbanisme de l'Erétrie archaïque." In *Eretria* VI: 89–95. Bern.

———. 1982. "Récuperer la mort du prince." In G. Gnoli and J.-P. Vernant, eds., *La mort, les morts, dans les sociétés antiques*: 89–105. Cambridge.

———, ed. 1989. *A City of Images.* Trs. D. Lyons. Princeton.

Berkhofer, R. 1988. "The Challenge of Poetics to (Normal) Historical Practice." *Poetics Today* 9: 435–52.

Bernal, M. 1987. *Black Athena* I. New Brunswick, NJ.

Berquist, J. 1995. *Judaism in Persia's Shadow.* Philadelphia.

Beyerchen, A. 1992. "What We Now Know about Nazi Science." *Social Research* 59: 615–41.

Bietti Sestieri, A. M. 1992. *The Iron Age Community of Osteria dell'Osa.* Cambridge.

Bikai, P. 1987. "Trade Networks in the Early Iron Age." In D. Rupp, ed., *Western Cyprus: Connections*: 125–8. Göteborg.

Binford, L. R. 1972. *An Archaeological Perspective*. New York.

———. 1977. "Historical Archaeology: Is It Historical or Archaeological?" In L. Ferguson, ed., *Historical Archaeology and the Importance of Material Things*: 13–22. Tucson.

Bingen, J. 1967a. "L'établissement du IXe siècle et les nécropoles du secteur ouest 4." *Thorikos II, 1964*: 25–46. Brussels.

———. 1967b. "L'établissement géométrique et la nécropole ouest." *Thorikos III, 1965*: 31–56. Brussels.

Bintliff, J., ed. 1991. *The Annales School and Archaeology*. Leicester.

Blackie, J. S. 1866. *Homer and the Iliad* I. Edinburgh.

Black-Michaud, J. 1975. *Feuding Societies*. Oxford.

Boardman, J. 1982. "The Geometric Culture of Greece." *CAH* III.1: 779–93. 2nd ed. Cambridge.

———. 1990. "Symposion Furniture." In Murray 1990b: 122–31.

———. 1994. "Orientalia and Orientals on Ischia." *AION* n.s. 1: 95–100.

Bohen, B. 1997. "Aspects of Athenian Grave Cult in the Age of Homer." In Langdon 1997: 44–55.

Bolger, D. 1994. "Ladies of the Expedition." In C. Claasen, ed., *Women in Archaeology*: 41–50. Philadelphia.

Botsford, G. W. 1924. *Hellenic History*. New York.

Bourdieu, P. 1977. *Outline of a Theory of Practice*. Trs. R. Nice. Cambridge.

———. 1984. *Distinction*. Trs. R. Nice. Cambridge, MA.

———. 1988. *Homo Academicus*. Trs. P. Collier. Stanford.

Bourriot, F. 1976. *Recherches sur la nature du génos*. 2 vols. Paris.

Bowen, J. 1989. "Education, Ideology and the Ruling Class." In G. W. Clarke, ed., *Rediscovering Hellenism*: 161–86. Cambridge.

Bowman, A. 1985. "Landholding in the Hermopolite Nome in the Fourth Century AD." *JRS* 75: 137–63.

Boyd Hawes, H. 1901. "Excavations at Kavousi, Crete." *AJA* 5: 125–57.

———. 1908. *Gournia, Vasilika, and Other Prehistoric Sites on the Isthmus of Hierapetra, Crete*. Philadelphia.

Bracken, C. P. 1975. *Antiquities Acquired*. North Pomfret, VT.

Bradley, R. 1993. *Altering the Earth*. Edinburgh.

———. 1997. *Rock Art and the Prehistory of Atlantic Europe*. London.

———. 1998. *The Significance of Monuments*. London.

Brandes, S. 1980. *Metaphors of Manhood*. Philadelphia.

Braudel, F. 1972 [1949]. *The Mediterranean and the Mediterranean World in the Age of Philip II*. 2 vols. Trs. S. Reynolds. Glasgow.

———. 1980 [1958]. *On History*. Trs. L. Cochrane. Chicago.

Bravo, B. 1977. "Remarques sue les assises sociales, les formes de l'organisation et la terminologie du commerce maritime grecque à l'époque archaïque." *DHA* 3: 1–59.

———. 1984. "Commerce et noblesse en Grèce archaïque." *DHA* 10: 99–160.

Brelich, A. 1958. *Gli eroi greci*. Rome.

Brenner, R. 1985. "Agrarian Class Structure and Economic Development in Pre-industrial Europe." In Aston and Philpin 1985: 10–63.

Bruford, W. H. 1975. *The German Tradition of Self-Cultivation*. Cambridge.

Buchner, G., and D. Ridgway. 1993. *Pithekoussai* I. 2 vols. Rome: *Monumenti Antichi* supp. vol. n.s. 2.

Bülle, H. 1907. *Orchomenos* I. Munich.

Burford, A. 1993. *Land and Labor in Ancient Greece*. Baltimore.

Burguière, A. 1995. "Le changement sociale: brève histoire d'un concept." In Lepetit 1995b: 253–72.

Burkert, W. 1983. *Homo Necans*. Berkeley.

——. 1985. *Greek Religion*. Trs. J. Raffan. Cambridge, MA.

——. 1991. "Oriental Symposia: Contrasts and Parallels." In W. Slater, ed., *Dining in a Clssical Context*: 7–24. Ann Arbor, MI.

——. 1992 [1984]. *The Orientalizing Revolution*. Trs. W. Burkert and M. Pinder. Cambridge, MA.

——. 1996. "Greek Temple-Builders: Who, Where and Why?" In Hägg 1996: 21–9.

Burnett, A. 1983. *Three Archaic Poets*. Chicago.

Bury, J. B. 1900. *A History of Greece*. 1st ed. London.

——. 1913. *A History of Greece*. 2nd ed. London.

——. 1924. "Homer." *Cambridge Ancient History* II: 498–517. 1st ed. Cambridge.

Cairns, D. 1993. *Aidos*. Oxford.

Calligas, P. 1988. "Hero-cult in Early Iron Age Greece." In Hägg *et al.* 1988: 229–34.

Callinicos, A. 1990. "Reactionary Postmodernism?" In R. Boyne and A. Rattansi, eds., *Postmodernism and Society*: 97–118. New York.

Cambitoglou, A. 1981. *Archaeological Museum of Andros*. Athens.

Cambitoglou, A., J. J. Couton, J. Birmingham, and J. R. Green. 1971. *Zagora* I. Sydney.

——, ——, ——, and ——. 1988. *Zagora* II. Athens.

Carlier, P. 1984. *La royauté grecque avant d'Alexandre*. Strasbourg.

——. 1991. "La procédure de décision politique, du monde mycénien à l' époque archaïque." In Musti *et al.* 1991: 85–95.

Carpenter, M. 1983. "Ki-ti-me-na and ke-ke-me-na at Pylos." *Minos* 18: 81–8.

Carson, A. 1990. "Putting Her in Her Place: Woman, Dirt, and Desire." In D. Halperin, J. Winkler, and F. Zeitlin, eds., *Before Sexuality*: 135–69. Princeton.

Carsten, J., and S. Hugh-Jones. 1995. "Introduction." In J. Carsten and S. Hugh-Jones, eds., *About the House: Lévi-Strauss and Beyond*: 1–46. Cambridge.

Cartledge, P. 1985. "Rebels and Sambos in Classical Greece." In P. Cartledge and F. D. Harvey, eds., *Crux*: 16–46. Exeter.

——. 1993. *The Greeks*. Oxford.

Caskey, M. 1981. "Ayia Irini, Kea: The Terracotta Statues and the Cult in the Temple." In Hägg and Marinatos 1981: 127–35.

Casson, L. 1971. *Ships and Seamanship in the Ancient World*. Princeton.

Castells, M. 1996. *The Information Age: Economy, Society and Culture.* Oxford.

Catling, H. 1984. "Workshop and Heirloom: Prehistoric Bronze Stands in the East Mediterranean." *RDAC* 1984: 69–91.

——, and E. Catling. 1980. "Objects of Bronze, Iron and Lead." In Popham *et al.* 1980: 231–64.

Catling, R., and I. Lemos. 1990. *Lefkandi* II.1. London.

Cavanagh, W. 1996. "The Burial Customs." In Coldstream and Catling 1996: 651–75.

Ceccarelli, P. 1993. "Sans thalassocratie, pas de démocratie? La rapport entre thalassocratie et démocratie à Athènes dans la discussion du Ve et IVe siècle av. J.-C." *Historia* 42: 444–70.

Cerutti, S. 1995. "Normes et pratiques, ou de la légitimé de leur opposition." In Lepetit 1995b: 127–49.

——. 1997. "Le linguistic turn en Angleterre." *Enquête* 5: 125–40.

Chapman, J. 1997. "Places as Timemarks – The Social Construction of Prehistoric Landscapes in Eastern Hungary." In G. Nash, ed., *Semiotics of Landscape*: 31–45. Oxford: *BAR* International Series 661.

Chartier, R. 1988. *Cultural History: Between Practices and Representations.* Trs. L. Cochrane. Ithaca, NY.

——. 1993. *The Cultural Origins of the French Revolution.* Trs. L. Cochrane. Durham, NC.

——. 1994. "The Chimera of the Origin: Archaeology, Cultural History, and the French Revolution." Trs. L. Cochrane. In J. Goldstein, ed., *Foucault and the Writing of History*: 167–86. Oxford.

Childe, V. G. 1929. *The Danube in Prehistory.* Oxford.

Clarke, D. L. 1973. "Archaeology: The Loss of Innocence." *Antiquity* 47: 6–18.

Clavier, M. 1809. *Histoire des premiers temps de la Grèce.* Paris.

Cohen, D. 1991. *Law, Sexuality, and Society.* Cambridge.

——. 1995. *Law, Violence, and Community in Classical Athens.* Cambridge.

Cohen, E. E. 1992. *Athenian Economy and Society.* Princeton.

——. Forthcoming. *The Athenian Nation.* Princeton.

Cohen, R. 1939. *La Grèce et l'hellénisation du monde antique.* 2nd ed. Paris.

——, and M. Roth, eds. 1995. *History and . . . Histories Within the Human Sciences.* Charlottesville, VA.

Coldstream, J. N. 1968. *Greek Geometric Pottery.* London.

——. 1976. "Hero-cults in the Age of Homer." *JHS* 96: 8–17.

——. 1977. *Geometric Greece.* London.

——. 1982. "Greeks and Phoenicians in the Aegean." In Niemeyer 1982: 261–75.

——. 1988. "Early Greek Pottery in Tyre and Cyprus." *RDAC* 1988: 35–44.

Coldstream, J.N., and H.W. Catling, eds. 1996. *Knossos North Cemetery.* 4 vols. London. *BSA* supp. vol. 28.

Collingwood, R. 1946. *The Idea of History.* Oxford.

Connor, W. R. 1989. "The New Classical Humanities and the Old." In Culham *et al.* 1989: 25–38.

———. 1991. "The Other 399." In *Georgica*: 49–56. London: *BICS* supp. vol. 58.

Constantine, D. 1984. *Early Greek Travellers and the Hellenic Ideal.* Cambridge.

Cook, J. M. 1953. "The Cult of Agamemnon at Mycenae." In *Geras Antoniou Keramopoullou*: 112–18. Athens.

Coucouzeli, A. 1998. "Architecture, Power, and Ideology in Dark Age Greece." In Docter and Moormann 1998: 34–5.

Courbin, P. 1966. *La céramique géométrique de l'Argolide.* Paris.

———. 1974. *Tombes géométriques d'Argos* I. Paris.

Cowan, M., ed. 1963. *An Anthology of the Writings of Wilhelm von Humboldt.* Detroit.

Crane, G. 1993. "The Politics of the Carpet Scene in the *Agamemnon.*" *CP* 88: 117–36.

Cribb, R. 1991. *Nomads in Archaeology.* Cambridge.

Crielaard, J. P., ed. 1995. *Homeric Questions.* Amsterdam.

Crielaard, J. P., and J. Driessen. 1994. "The Hero's Home." *Topoi* 4: 251–70.

Cuddon, J. A. 1979. *A Dictionary of Literary Terms.* Rev. ed. Harmondsworth.

Culham, P., L. Edmunds, and A. Smith, eds. 1989. *Classics: A Discipline and Profession in Crisis?* Lanham, MD.

Curtin, P. 1984. *Cross-Cultural Trade in World History.* Cambridge.

Dahl, R. 1989. *Democracy and its Critics.* New Haven, CT.

Dakoronia, F. 1987. *Marmara.* Athens.

———. 1993. "Elateia." *Phokika Chronika* 5: 25–39.

D'Andria, F. 1982. "Il Salento nell' VIII e VII sec. a. C." *ASAA* 60: 101–16.

Darnton, R. 1984. *The Great Cat Massacre and Other Episodes in French Cultural History.* New York.

Davidson, J. 1997. *Courtesans and Fishcakes.* New York.

Davies, J. K. 1971. *Athenian Propertied Families.* Oxford.

———. 1977/8. "Athenian Citizenship: The Descent Group and the Alternatives." *CJ* 73: 105–21.

———. 1981. *Wealth and the Power of Wealth in Classical Athens.* New York.

Davies, P. R. 1992. *In Search of "Ancient Israel."* Sheffield.

———, ed. 1996. *The Prophets.* Sheffield.

Davis, J. 1977. *People of the Mediterranean.* London.

Deagan, K. 1988. "Neither History nor Prehistory: The Questions that Count in Historical Archaeology." *Historical Archaeology* 22: 7–12.

De Angelis, F. 1994. "The Foundation of Selinous." In Tsetskhladze and De Angelis 1994: 87–110.

Deger-Jalkotzy, S., ed. 1983. *Griechenland, die Ägäis und die Levante wahrend die "Dark Ages."* Vienna.

De Grummond, N., ed. 1996. *Encyclopedia of the History of Classical Archaeology.* Westport, CT.

De Jong, I. 1987. "The Voice of Anonymity: *Tis* Speeches in the *Iliad.*" *Eranos* 85: 69–84.

Dentzer, J.-M. 1982. *Le motif du banquet couché dans le Proche-Orient et le monde grec du VIIème au IVème siècle avant J.-C.* Paris.

de Polignac, François. 1984. *La naissance de la cité grecque*. Paris.

———. 1992. "Influence extérieure ou évolution interne?" In Kopcke and Tokumaru 1992: 114–27.

———. 1994. "Mediation, Competition, and Sovereignty." In Alcock and Osborne 1994: 3–18.

———. 1995a. *Cults, Territory, and the Origins of the Greek City-State*. Trs. J. Lloyd. Chicago.

———. 1995b. "Repenser 'la cité'?" In M. Hansen and K. Raaflaub, eds., *Studies in the Ancient Greek Polis*: 7–19. Stuttgart: *Historia* Einzelschrift 95.

———. 1997. "Anthropologie du politique en Grèce ancienne." *Annales Histoire, Sciences Sociales* 52: 31–9.

Desborough, V. R. 1952. *Protogeometric Pottery*. Oxford.

———. 1964. *The Last Mycenaeans and Their Successors*. Oxford.

———. 1972. *The Greek Dark Ages*. London.

Deshayes, J. 1966. *Argos: Les fouilles de la Deiras*. Paris: *Études péloponnésiennes* 4.

Detienne, M. 1977. *The Gardens of Adonis*. Trs. J. Lloyd. Baltimore.

———. 1996. *The Masters of Truth in Archaic Greece*. Trs. J. Lloyd. New York.

Devillers, M. 1988. *An Archaic and Classical Votive Deposit from a Mycenaean Tomb at Thorikos*. Ghent.

Díaz-Andreu, M., and T. Champion, eds. 1996. *Nationalism and Archaeology in Europe*. London.

Dickey, K. 1992. "Corinthian Burial Customs *ca*. 1100–550 BC." Unpublished Ph.D. thesis, Bryn Mawr College.

Diels, H., and W. Kranz. 1956. *Die Fragmente der Vorsokratiker*. 8th ed. Berlin.

Di Vita, A. 1990. "Town Planning in the Greek Colonies of Sicily from the Time of Their Foundation to the Punic Wars." In J.-P. Descouedres, ed., *Greek Colonists and Native Populations*: 343–63. Oxford.

Dobbs, B. J. T. 1991. *The Janus Face of Genius*. Cambridge.

Docter, R., and E. Moormann, eds. 1998. *XVth International Congress of Classical Archaeology – Abstracts*. Amsterdam.

Docter, R., and H. D. Niemeyer. 1994. "Pithekoussai: The Carthaginian Connection." *AION* n.s. 1: 101–15.

Donlan, Walter. 1970. "Changes and Shifts in the Meaning of *Demos* in the Literature of the Archaic Period." *Parola del Passato* 135: 391–5.

———. 1980. *The Aristocratic Ideal in Ancient Greece*. Lawrence, KA.

———. 1997. "The Homeric Economy." In Morris and Powell 1997: 649–67.

D'Onofrio, A. M. 1993. "Le trasformazione del costume funerario ateniese nella necropoli pre-soloniana del Kerameikos." *AION* 15: 143–71.

———. 1995. "Santuari 'rurali' e dinamiche insediative in Attica tra il Protogeometrico e l'Orientalizzante (1050–600 a.C.)." *AION* n.s. 2: 57–88.

Donohue, A. 1985. "One Hundred Years of the *American Journal of Archaeology*." *AJA* 89: 3–30.

Dort, A. V. 1954. "The Archaeological Institute of America – Early Days." *Archaeology* 7: 195–201.

Dragendorff, H. 1903. *Thera* II. Berlin.

Drerup, H. 1969. *Griechische Baukunst in geometrischer Zeit.* Göttingen (*Archaeologia Homerica* O).

DuBois, P. 1988. *Sowing the Body.* Chicago.

———. 1995. *Sappho is Burning.* Chicago.

Dugas, C. 1935. *Délos* XVII: *Les vases orientalisantes de style non mélien.* Paris.

Dugas, C., and C. Rhomaios. 1934. *Délos* XV: *Les vases préhelléniques et géométriques.* Paris.

Duncan-Jones, R. 1990. *Structure and Scale in the Roman Economy.* Cambridge.

Duruy, V. 1887. *Histoire des grecs.* 3 vols. Paris.

Dyson, S. L. 1989. "Complacency and Crisis in Late Twentieth Century Classical Archaeology." In Culham *et al.* 1989: 211–20.

———. 1998. *Ancient Marbles to American Shores.* Philadelphia.

Eagleton, T. 1996. *The Illusions of Postmodernism.* Oxford.

Eisner, R. 1991. *Travelers to an Antique Land.* Ann Arbor, MI.

Engels, F. 1972 [1884]. *Origins of the Family, Private Property, and the State.* Trs. A. West. London.

Fallmereyer, J. P. 1830. *Geschichte der Halbinsel Morea während des Mittelalters* I. Stuttgart.

Farenga, V. 1998. "Narrative and Community in Dark Age Greece." *Arethusa* 31: 179–206.

Farnell, L. 1921. *Greek Hero-Cults and Ideas of Immortality.* Oxford.

Fehr, B. 1971. *Orientalischer und griechische Gelage.* Bonn.

Felsch, R., ed. 1996. *Kalapodi* I. Mainz.

Finley, M. I. 1952. *Studies in Land and Credit in Ancient Athens.* New Brunswick, NJ.

———. 1954. *The World of Odysseus.* 1st ed. New York.

———. 1970. *Early Greece: The Bronze and Archaic Ages.* 1st ed. London.

———. 1979. *The World of Odysseus.* 2nd ed. New York.

———. 1981 [1953–77]. *Economy and Society in Ancient Greece*, eds. B. Shaw and R. Saller. London.

———. 1983. *Politics in the Ancient World.* Cambridge.

———. 1985. *Ancient History: Evidence and Models.* London.

———, J. L. Caskey, G. S. Kirk, and D. L. Page. 1964. "The Trojan War." *JHS* 84: 1–20.

Fisher, N. R. E. 1992. *Hybris.* Warminster.

Fisher, N. R. E., and H. van Wees, eds. 1998. *Archaic Greece.* London.

Foley, A. 1988. *The Argolid 800–600 BC. An Archaeological Survey.* Göteborg.

Foley, H. 1982. "The 'Female Intruder' Reconsidered: Women in Aristophanes' *Lysistrata* and *Ecclesiazousae*." *CP* 77: 1–24.

Ford, A. 1992. *Homer: The Poetry of the Past.* Ithaca, NY.

Fornara, C. 1983. *Translated Documents of Greece and Rome* I. 2nd ed. Cambridge.

Foucault, M. 1985. *The Use of Pleasure.* Trs. R. Hurley. New York.

Foxhall, L. 1992. "The Control of the Attic Landscape." In Wells 1992: 155–9.

———. 1997. "A View from the Top: Evaluating the Solonian Property Classes." In Mitchell and Rhodes 1997: 113–36.

———. 1998. "Cargoes of the Heart's Desire." In Fisher and van Wees 1998: 295–309.

Francotte, H. 1922. *Histoire politique de la Grèce ancienne.* Brussels.

Fränkel, H. 1975. *Early Greek Poetry and Philosophy.* Trs. M. Hadas and J. Willis. Oxford.

Friedlander, S., ed. 1992. *Probing the Limits of Representation.* Cambridge, MA.

Frizell, B. 1986. *Asine II.3.* Stockholm.

Frodin, O., and A. Persson. 1938. *Asine I.* Stockholm.

Fukuyama, F. 1992. *The End of History and the Last Man.* Boston.

Fumagalli, V. 1994. *Landscapes of Fear.* Trs. S. Mitchell. Oxford.

Furtwängler, A. 1879. "Die Bronzefunde aus Olympia und deren kunstgeschichtliche Stellung." *Abhandlungen der Preussischen Akademie der Wissenschaft*: 3–106.

———. 1885. *Königliche Museen der Berlin: Beschreibung der Vasensammlung im Antiquarium.* 2 vols. Berlin.

———. 1886. *Mykenische Vasen.* Berlin.

Furtwängler, A., and G. Löschke. 1879. *Mykenische Tongefässe.* Berlin.

Furumark, A. 1941. *The Mycenaean Pottery.* 2 vols. Stockholm.

Fusaro, D. 1982. "Note di architettura domestica greca nel periodo tardogeometrico e arcaico." *Dialoghi di Archeologia* 4: 5–30.

Fustel de Coulanges, N. D. 1864. *La cité antique.* Paris.

Gabrielsen, V. 1994. *Financing the Athenian Fleet.* Baltimore.

Gallant, T. 1991. *Risk and Survival in Ancient Greece.* Stanford.

Gallet de Santerre, H. 1958. *Délos primitive et archaïque.* Paris.

Garlan, Y. 1988. *Slavery in Ancient Greece.* Trs. J. Lloyd. Ithaca, NY.

Garland, R. 1984. *The Greek Way of Death.* London.

Garnsey, P. 1996. *Ideas of Slavery from Aristotle to Augustine.* Cambridge.

Geddes, W. 1878. *The Problem of the Homeric Poems.* London.

Geertz, C. 1973. *The Interpretation of Cultures.* New York.

———. 1983. *Local Knowledge.* New York.

Gehrke, H.-J. 1985. *Stasis. Untersuchungen zu den inneren Kriegen in den griechischen Staaten des 5. und 4. Jhs. vor Chr.* Munich (*Vestigia* 35).

Gellner, E. 1985. *Relativism in the Social Sciences.* Cambridge.

———, and J. Waterbury, eds. 1977. *Patrons and Clients in Mediterranean Societies.* London.

Genovese, E. 1969. *The World the Slaveholders Made.* Middletown, CT.

Gentili, B. 1988. *Poetry and Its Public in Ancient Greece.* Trs. T. Cole. Baltimore.

Gercke, P., W. Gercke, and G. Hiesel. 1975. "Tiryns-Stadt 1971: Graben H." In *Tiryns* VIII: 7–36. Mainz.

Gialanella, C. 1994. "Pithecusa: Gli Insediamenti di Punta Chariato." *Annali di Archeologia e Storia Antica*, n.s. 1: 169–204.

Giddens, Anthony. 1979. *Central Problems in Social Theory.* Cambridge.

——. 1981. *A Contemporary Critique of Historical Materialism*. Stanford.

Gilmore, D. 1982. "Anthropology of the Mediterranean area." *Ann Rev Anth* 11: 175–205.

——. 1987a. *Aggression and Community*. New Haven, CT.

——, ed. 1987b. *Honor and Shame*. Washington, DC.

Gitlin, S., A. Amizar, and E. Stern, eds. 1998. *Mediterranean Peoples in Transition, 13th to Early 10th Centuries BCE*. Jerusalem.

Gladstone, W. 1857. "On the Place of Homer in Classical Education and in Historical Inquiry." In *Oxford Essays*: 1–56. Oxford.

Goldberg, S. 1990. "Goldberg Appointed New Editor of *TAPA*." *American Philological Association Newsletter* 13.3: 1–2.

Goldhill, S., and R. Osborne, eds. 1994. *Art and Text in Greek Culture*. Cambridge.

Goody, J. 1993. *The Culture of Flowers*. Cambridge.

Grafton, A. 1991. *Defenders of the Text*. Cambridge, MA.

Grafton, A., G. Most, and J. Zetzel. 1985. "Introduction." In Wolf 1985: 3–35.

Graves-Brown, P., S. Jones, and C. Gamble, eds. 1996. *Cultural Identity and Archaeology: The Construction of European Communities*. London.

Gray, C., trs. 1986. "The Old Oligarch." In Adkins and White 1986: 47–56.

Gray, D. 1954. "Homer and the Archaeologists." In M. Platnauer, ed., *Fifty Years of Classical Scholarship*: 24–31. Oxford.

Gregor, T. 1977. *Mehinaku*. Chicago.

Grene, D., trs. 1986. *Herodotus: The Histories*. Chicago.

Grenier, J.-Y. 1995. "Expliquer et comprendre. La construction du temps de l'histoire économique." In Lepetit 1995b: 227–52.

Grote, G. 1826. "Fasti hellenici." *Westminster Review* 5: 269–331.

——. 1843. "Grecian Legends and Early History." *Westminster Review* 39: 285–328.

——. 1846a. *A History of Greece* I. London.

——. 1846b. *A History of Greece* II. London.

Gupta, A., and J. Ferguson. 1997. "Culture, Power, Place." In A. Gupta and J. Ferguson, eds., *Culture, Power, Place*: 1–29. Durham, NC.

Guthrie, W. K. C., trs. 1956. *Protagoras and Meno*. Harmondsworth.

Habermas, J. 1984. *Theory of Communicative Action* I. Cambridge, MA.

Hägg, R. 1974. *Die Gräber der Argolis* I. Uppsala.

——, ed. 1983a. *The Greek Renaissance of the Eighth Century B.C.* Stockholm.

——. 1983b. "Funerary Meals in the Geometric Necropolis at Asine?" In Hägg 1983a: 189–93.

——. 1987. "Gifts to the Heroes in Geometric and Archaic Greece." In T. Linders and G. Nordquist, eds., *Gifts to the Gods*: 93–9. Uppsala.

——, ed. 1996. *The Role of Religion in the Early Greek Polis*. Stockholm.

——, and N. Marinatos, eds. 1981. *Sanctuaries and Cult in the Aegean Bronze Age*. Stockholm.

Hall, E. 1914. "Excavations in Eastern Crete, Vrokastro." *University of Pennsylvania, The Museum Anthropological Publications* 3: 79–185.

Hall, E. 1989. *Inventing the Barbarian*. Oxford.

Hall, J. 1997. *Ethnic Identity in Greek Antiquity*. Cambridge.

Halperin, D. 1990. *One Hundred Years of Homosexuality*. London.

Hamilakis, Y., and E. Yalouri. 1996. "Antiquities as Symbolic Capital in Modern Greek Society." *Antiquity* 70: 117–29.

Hansen, M. H. 1991. *The Athenian Democracy in the Age of Demosthenes*. Trs. J. Crook. Oxford.

Hanson, V. D. 1995. *The Other Greeks*. New York.

Hanson, V. D., and J. Heath. 1998. *Who Killed Homer?* New York.

Harris, D. 1995. *The Treasures of the Parthenon and Erechtheion*. Oxford.

Harris, E. 1992. "Women and Lending in Athenian Society." *Phoenix* 46: 309–21.

Harrison, J. E. 1903. *Prolegomena to the Study of Greek Religion*. Cambridge.

———. 1912. *Themis*. Cambridge.

———. 1965. "Reminiscences of a Student's Life." *Arion* 4: 312–46.

Hartog, F. 1988. *The Mirror of Herodotus*, trs. J. Lloyd. Chicago.

———. 1996. *Mémoire d'Ulysse*. Paris.

Harvey, D. 1989. *The Condition of Postmodernity*. Oxford.

Harvey, F. D. 1965. "Two Kinds of Equality." *CM* 26: 101–46.

Hedrick, C. 1994. "The Zero Degree of Society: Aristotle and the Athenian Citizen." In J. P. Euben, J. Wallach, and J. Ober, eds., *Athenian Political Thought and the Reconstruction of American Democracy*: 289–318. Ithaca, NY.

Herman, G. 1987. *Ritualised Friendship and the Greek City*. Cambridge.

———. 1993. "Tribal and Civic Codes of Behaviour in Lysias 1." *CQ* 43: 406–19.

———. 1994. "How Violent was Athenian Society?" In R. Osborne and S. Hornblower, eds., *Ritual, Finance, Politics*: 99–117. Oxford.

———. 1998. "Reciprocity, Altruism, and the Prisoner's Dilemma." In C. Gill, N. Postlethwaite, and R. Seaford, eds., *Reciprocity in Ancient Greece*: 199–225. Oxford.

Herzfeld, M. 1980. "Honour and Shame." *Man* 15: 339–51.

———. 1984. "The Horns of the Mediterraneanist Dilemma." *American Ethnologist* 11: 439–54.

———. 1985. *The Poetics of Manhood*. Princeton.

———. 1987. *Anthropology Through the Looking Glass*. Cambridge.

Heyck, T. 1982. *The Transformation of Intellectual Life in Victorian England*. New York.

Hinsley, C. 1985. "From Shell-Heaps to Stelae: Early Anthopology in the Peabody Museum." In G. Stocking, ed., *Objects and Others*: 49–74. Madison, WI.

Hodder, I. 1982. *The Present Past*. London.

———. 1986. *Reading the Past*. Cambridge.

———. 1987a. "The Contribution of the Long Term." In I. Hodder, ed., *Archaeology as Long-Term History*: 1–8. Cambridge.

———. 1987b. "The Contextual Analysis of Symbolic Meanings." In I. Hodder, ed., *The Archaeology of Contextual Meanings*: 1–10. Cambridge.

———. 1992. *Theory and Practice in Archaeology*. London.

Hodder, I., M. Shanks, A. Alexandri, V. Buchli, J. Carman, J. Last, and G. Lucas. 1995. *Interpreting Archaeology.* London.

Hoffman, G. 1997. *Imports and Immigrants.* Ann Arbor, MI.

Hogarth, D. G. 1908. *The Archaic Artemision.* London.

Holtorf, C. 1998. "The Life-Histories of Megaliths in Mecklenburg-Vorpommern (Germany)." *WA* 30: 23–38.

Houby-Nielsen, S. 1992. "Interaction between Chieftains and Citizens?" *Acta Hyperborea* 4: 343–74.

———. 1995. "'Burial Language' in Archaic and Classical Kerameikos." *Proceedings of the Danish Institute at Athens* 1: 129–91.

———. 1996. "The Archaeology of Ideology in the Kerameikos: New Interpretations of the Opferrinnen." In Hägg 1996: 41–54.

Hugo, H. E., ed. 1957. *The Portable Romantic Reader.* New York.

Humphreys, S. C. 1993. *The Family, Women and Death.* 2nd ed. Ann Arbor, MI.

Hunt, L., ed. 1989. *The New Cultural History.* Berkeley.

Hunter, V. 1994. *Policing Athens.* Princeton.

Hurwit, J. 1985. *The Art and Culture of Early Greece.* Ithaca, NY.

Iakovidis, S. 1969. *Perati: To Nekrotapheion.* 3 vols. Athens.

Iatrides, J., and L. Wrigley, eds. 1995. *Greece at the Crossroads.* University Park, PA.

Isaac, G. 1989. *The Archaeology of Human Origins.* Cambridge.

Isham, N. M. 1898. *The Homeric Palace.* Baltimore.

Jameson, F. 1989. "Marxism and Postmodernism." *New Left Review* 176: 31–45.

Jameson, M. H. 1977/8. "Agriculture and Slavery in Classical Athens." *CJ* 73: 122–45.

———. 1988. "Sacrifice and Animal Husbandry in Classical Greece." In C. R. Whittaker, ed., *Pastoral Economies in Classical Antiquity*: 87–119. Cambridge: Cambridge Philological Society supp. vol. 14.

———. 1992. "Agricultural Labor in Ancient Greece." In Wells 1992: 135–46.

Janko, R. 1982. *Homer, Hesiod and the Hymns.* Cambridge.

———. 1998. "The Homeric Poems as Oral Dictated Texts." *CQ* 48: 135–67.

Jebb, R. C. 1887. *Homer. An Introduction to the Iliad and Odyssey.* Boston.

———. 1907. *Essays and Addresses.* Cambridge.

Jencks, C. 1991. "Postmodern vs. Late-Modern." In I. Hoesterey, ed., *Zeitgeist in Babel*: 4–21. Bloomington, IN.

Jenkins, K., ed. 1997. *The Postmodern History Reader.* London.

Johnson, M. 1996. *An Archaeology of Capitalism.* Oxford.

Johnstone, S. 1994. "Virtuous Work, Vicious Toil." *CP* 89: 219–40.

———. 1998. "Cracking the Code of Silence." In S. Murnaghan and S. Joshel, eds., *Women and Slaves in Greco-Roman Culture*: 221–35. New York.

Jones, R. E. 1980. "Analyses of Bronze and Other Base Metal Objects from the Cemeteries." In Popham *et al.* 1980: 447–60.

Jones, S. 1997. *The Archaeology of Ethnicity.* London.

Joyce, P. 1998. "The Return of History: Postmodernism and The Politics of Academic History in Britain." *Past and Present* 158: 207–35.

Kantzia, Ch. 1988. "Recent Archaeological Finds from Kos." In S. Dietz and I. Papachristodoulou, eds., *Archaeology in the Dodecanese*: 175–83. Copenhagen.

Karageorghis, V. G. 1967. *Salamis* I. Konstanz.

———. 1973. *Salamis* III. Konstanz.

———. 1983. *Alt-Paphos* III. Mainz.

Kardulias, P. N. 1994. "Archaeology in Modern Greece: Bureaucracy, Politics, and Science." In P. N. Kardulias, ed., *Beyond the Site: Regional Studies in the Aegean Area*: 373–87. Lanham, MD.

Kearns, R. 1989. *The Heroes of Attica*. London: *BICS* supp. vol. 57.

Kearsley, R. 1995. "The Greek Geometric Wares from Al Mina Levels 10-8." *Mediterranean Archaeology* 8: 7–81.

Kent, S. 1990. "A Cross-Cultural Study of Segmentation, Architecture, and the Use of Space." In S. Kent, ed., *Domestic Architecture and the Use of Space*: 127–52. Cambridge.

Kepecs, S., and M. Kolb, eds. 1997. *Journal of Archaeological Method and Theory* 4.3/4. New York.

Kern, S. 1983. *The Culture of Time and Space 1880–1918*. Cambridge, MA.

Kirk, G. S. 1975 [1964]. "The Homeric poems as history." *CAH* II.2: 820–50. 2nd ed. Cambridge.

Kitchen, K. 1986. *The Third Intermediate Period in Egypt (ca. 1100–650 BC)*. 2nd ed. Warminster.

Kleiner, G. 1966. *Alt-Milet*. Frankfurt.

Knapp, B., ed. 1992. *Archeology, Annales, and Ethnohistory*. Cambridge.

Knigge, U. 1976. *Kerameikos* XII. Berlin.

———. 1980. *Kerameikos* XII: *Rundbauten*. Berlin.

Koenen, L. 1994. "Greece, the Near East, and Egypt: Cyclic Destruction in Hesiod and the *Catalogue of Women*." *TAPA* 124: 1–34.

Kohl, P., and C. Fawcett, eds. 1995. *Nationalism, Politics, and the Practice of Archaeology*. Cambridge.

Kondoleon, N. 1964. "Archilochos und Paros." In *Archiloque*: 39–73. Geneva (*Entretiens Fondation Hardt* 10).

Kopcke, G., and I. Tokumaru, eds. 1992. *Greece Between East and West, 10th–8th Centuries BC*. Mainz.

Kopytoff, I. 1982. "Slavery." *Ann Rev Anth* 11: 207–30.

Kotsakis, K. 1991. "The Powerful Past: Theoretical Trends in Greek Archaeology." In I. Hodder, ed., *Archaeological Theory in Europe*: 65–90. London.

Kraiker, W. 1939. "Die Nekropole nördlich des Eridanos." In W. Kraiker and K. Kübler, *Kerameikos* I: 1–177. Berlin.

Krause, C. 1977. "Grundformen des griechische Pastashauses." *AA* 1977: 164–77.

Krause, G. 1975. *Untersuchngen zu den ältesten Nekropolen am Eridanos in Athen*. Hamburg: *Hamburger Beiträge für Archäologie* III.

Kroeber, A. L., and Clyde Kluckhohn. 1952. *Culture – A Critical Review of Concepts and Definitions*. Cambridge, MA.

Kübler, K. 1943. *Kerameikos* IV. Berlin.

———. 1954. *Kerameikos* V.1. Berlin.

——. 1959. *Kerameikos* VI.1. Berlin.

Kuklick, B. 1996. *Puritans in Babylon*. Princeton.

Kuniholm, P. 1996. "The Prehistoric Aegean: Dendrochronological Progress as of 1995." *AArch* 67: 327–35.

Kurke, L. 1991. *The Traffic in Praise*. Ithaca, NY.

——. 1992. "The Politics of *Habrosyne* in Archaic Greece." *CA* 11: 91–120.

——. 1994. "Crisis and Decorum in Sixth-Century Lesbos." *QUCC* 47: 67–92.

——. 1999. *Coins, Bodies, Games, and Gold*. Princeton.

Kurtz, D. 1983. "Gorgos' Cup." *JHS* 103: 68–86.

——, ed. 1985. *Beazley and Oxford*. Oxford.

——, and J. Boardman. 1971. *Greek Burial Customs*. London.

Kyrieleis, H. 1969. *Throne und Klinen: Studien zum Formgeschichte altorientalischer und griechischer Sitz- und Liegemöbel vorhellenistische Zeit*. Berlin.

——. 1979. "Babylonische Bronzen im Heraion von Samos." *JdI* 94: 32–48.

——. 1993. "The Heraion at Samos." In Hägg and Marinatos 1993: 125–53.

Lambert, S. 1993. *The Attic Phratry*. Ann Arbor, MI.

Lambrinoudakis, V. G. 1981. "Remains of the Mycenaean Period in the Sanctuary of Apollon Maleatas." In Hägg and Marinatos 1981: 59–65.

——. 1988. "Veneration of Ancestors on Geometric Naxos." In Hägg *et al.* 1988: 235–45.

Lang, A. 1906. *Homer and His Age*. London.

——. 1910. *The World of Homer*. London.

Langdon, M. 1976. *A Sanctuary of Zeus on Mt. Hymettos*. Princeton: *Hesperia* supp. vol. 16.

Langdon, S., ed. 1997. *New Light on a Dark Age*. Columbia, MO.

Lateiner, D. 1995. *Sardonic Smile: Nonverbal Behavior in Homeric Epic*. Ann Arbor, MI.

Lattimore, R., trs. 1951. *The Iliad*. Chicago.

——, trs. 1965. *The Odyssey*. Chicago.

Lauter, H. 1985a. *Lathuresa*. Mainz.

——. 1985b. *Die Kultplatz auf dem Turkovuni*. Berlin: *AM* Beiheft 12.

Lawrence, D., and S. Low. 1990. "The Built Environment and Spatial Form." *Ann Rev Anth* 19: 453–505.

Leaf, W. 1915. *Homer and History*. London.

Lepetit, B. 1995a. "Histoire des pratiques, pratique de l'histoire." In Lepetit 1995b: 9–22.

——. 1995b, ed. *Les formes de l'expérience*. Paris.

Le Roy Ladurie, E. 1974. *The Peasants of Languedoc*. Trs. J. Day. Urbana, IL.

Lewis, D. M. 1981. *Inscriptiones Graecae* I. 3rd ed. Berlin.

Lewis, S. 1996. *News and Society in the Greek Polis*. London.

Lichtheim, M., trs. 1973–80. *Ancient Egyptian Literature*. 3 vols. Berkeley.

Link, S. 1991. *Landverteilung und socialer Frieden im archäischen Griechenland*. Stuttgart (*Historia* Einzelschrift 69).

Lobel, E., and D. L. Page. 1962. *Poetarum Lesbiorum Fragmenta*. Oxford.

Loraux, N. 1986. *The Invention of Athens*. Trs. A. Sheridan. Cambridge, MA.

——. 1991. "Reflections of the Greek City on Unity and Division." In A. Molho, K. Raaflaub, and J. Emmen, eds., *City States in Classical Antiquity and Medieval Italy*: 33–51. Stuttgart.

——. 1993. *The Children of Athena*. Trs. C. Levine. Princeton.

Lord, A. B. 1960. *The Singer of Tales*. Cambridge, MA.

Lord, L. 1947. *A History of the American School of Classical Studies at Athens, 1882–1942*. Cambridge, MA.

Lorimer, H. L. 1950. *Homer and the Monuments*. London.

Lungu, V. 1998. "*To heroon*: Architecture and Signification in the Greek Colonial Milieu." In Docter and Moormann 1998: 89–90.

Lyman, R. L., M. J. O'Brien, and R. C. Dunnell. 1997. *The Rise and Fall of Culture History*. New York.

Lyotard, J.-F. 1984. *The Postmodern Condition*. Minneapolis.

MacDonald, W. A., W. D. E. Coulson, and J. J. Rosser. 1983. *Excavations at Nichoria in Southwest Greece III: Dark Age and Byzantine Occupation*. Minneapolis.

Mackie, H. 1996. *Talking Trojan*. Lanham, MD.

Macmillan, G. A. 1911. "A Short History of the British School at Athens, 1886–1911." *BSA* 17: ix–xxxviii.

Maehler, H. 1989. *Pindari Carmina cum Fragmentis* II. Leipzig.

Mahaffy, J. P. 1890. "A Critical Introduction." In V. Duruy, *History of Greece* (trs. M. M. Ripley): 1–119. Boston.

Manning, S. 1998. "From Process to People: Longue Durée to History." In E. Cline and D. Harris-Cline, eds., *The Aegean and the Orient in the Second Millennium*: 311–27. Liège: *Aegaeum* 18.

Marchand, S. 1996. *Down From Olympus*. Princeton.

Markoe, G. 1992. "In Pursuit of Metal: Phoenicians and Greeks in Italy." In Kopcke and Tokumaru 1992: 61–84.

Martin, R. 1975. "Problèmes de topographie et d'évolution urbaine." In *Contribution à l'étude de la société et de la colonisation eubéennes*: 48–52. Naples: *Cahiers du centre Jean Bérard 2*.

Martin, R. P. 1984. "Hesiod, Odysseus, and the Instruction of Princes." *TAPA* 114: 29–48.

——. 1992. "Hesiod's Metanastic Poetics." *Ramus* 21: 11–33.

——. 1993. "The Seven Sages as Performers of Wisdom." In C. Dougherty and L. Kurke, eds., *Cultural Poetics in Archaic Greece*: 108–28. Cambridge.

Marx, K. 1977a [1859]. "Preface to *A Critique of Political Economy*." In McLellan 1977: 388–92.

——. 1977b [1852]. "The Eighteenth Brumaire of Louis Bonaparte." In McLellan 1977: 300–25.

——, and F. Engels. 1977 [1848]. "The Communist Manifesto." In McLellan 1977: 221–47.

Matthäus, H. 1988. "Heirloom or Tradition?" In E. French and K. Wardle, eds., *Problems in Greek Prehistory*: 285–300. Bristol.

Matthews, W., C. French, T. Lawrence, D. Cutler, and M. Jones. 1997. "Microstratigraphic Traces of Site Formation Processes and Human Activities." *WA* 29: 281–308.

Mazarakis Ainian, A. 1989. "Late Bronze Age Apsidal and Oval Buildings in Greece and Adjacent Areas." *BSA* 84: 269–88.

———. 1994. "Lathouriza: mia agrotiki katastasi ton proimon istorikon chronon sti Vari Attikis." In P. Doukellis and L. Mendoni, eds., *Structures rurales et sociétés antiques*: 65–80. Paris: *Annales littéraires de l'Université de Besançon* 508.

———. 1995. "New Evidence for the Study of the Late Geometric-Archaic Settlement at Lathouriza in Attica." In C. Morris, ed., *Klados: Essays in Honour of J. N. Coldstream*: 143–55. London: *BICS* supp. vol. 63.

———. 1997. *From Rulers' Dwellings to Temples*. Jonsered.

McCullagh, C. B. 1998. *The Truth of History*. London.

McDonald, T. J., ed. 1996. *The Historic Turn in the Human Sciences*. Ann Arbor, MI.

McLellan, D., ed. 1977. *Karl Marx: Selected Writings*. Oxford.

Meiggs, R., and D. Lewis. 1969. *A Selection of Greek Historical Inscriptions*. Oxford.

Mele, A. 1979. *Il commercio greco arcaico*. Naples.

———. 1986. "Pirateria, commercio e aristocrazia." *DHA* 12: 67–109.

Merkelbach, R., and M. L. West. 1967. *Fragmenta Hesiodea*. Oxford.

Merkouri, M. 1982. "Anaskaphes xenon archaiologikon idrymaton pou leitourgon stin Ellada." Athens: Circular 4833, Ministry of Culture and Science, 7/21/82.

Meskell, L. 1996. "The Somatization of Archaeology." *NAR* 29: 1–16.

Miller, M. 1997. *Athens and Persia in the Fifth Century BC*. Cambridge.

Millett, P. 1989. "Patronage and its Avoidance in Classical Athens." In A. Wallace-Hadrill, ed., *Patronage in Ancient Societies*: 15–48. London.

Miralles, C., and J. Pòrtulas. 1983. *Archilochus and the Iambic Poetry*. Rome.

Mitchell, L., and P. Rhodes, eds. 1997. *The Development of the Polis in Archaic Greece*. London.

Mitford, W. 1784. *The History of Greece* I. London.

Momigliano, A. 1952. *George Grote and the Study of Greek History*. London.

Moore, H. 1986. *Space, Text and Gender*. Cambridge.

Morgan, C. 1990. *Athletes and Oracles*. Cambridge.

———. 1994. "The Evolution of a Sacral 'Landscape.'" In Alcock and Osborne 1994: 105–42.

Morris, I. 1986. "The Use and Abuse of Homer." *CA* 5: 81–138.

———. 1987. *Burial and Ancient Society*. Cambridge.

———. 1988. "Tomb Cult and the 'Greek Renaissance.'" *Antiquity* 62: 750–61.

———. 1991. "The Early Polis as City and State." In Rich and Wallace-Hadrill 1991: 24–57.

———. 1992. *Death-Ritual and Social Structure in Classical Antiquity*. Cambridge.

———. 1993a. "Geometric Greece." *Colloquenda Mediterranea* 3.A.1: 29–38.

———. 1993b. "The Kerameikos Stratigraphy and the Character of the Greek Iron Age." *JMA* 6: 207–21.

———. 1994. Review of Popham *et al.* 1993. *AJA* 98: 570–1.

———. 1996. "The Absolute Chronology of the Greek Colonies in Sicily." *AArch* 67: 51–9.

———. 1997a. "Archaeology as a Kind of Anthropology." In Morris and Raaflaub 1997: 229–39.

———. 1997b. "Homer and the Iron Age." In Morris and Powell 1997: 535–59.

———. 1997c. "The Art of Citizenship." In Langdon 1997: 9–43.

———. 1998a. "Remaining Invisible." In S. Murnaghan and S. Joshel, eds., *Women and Slaves in Greco-Roman Culture*: 193–220. New York.

———. 1998b. "Archaeology and Archaic Greek History." In Fisher and van Wees 1991: 1–91.

———. 1998c. "*Burial and Ancient Society* After Ten Years." In S. Marchegay, M-T. Le Dinahet, and J-F. Salles, eds., *Nécropoles et pouvoir*: 21–36. Paris.

———, and B. Powell, eds. 1997. *A New Companion to Homer*. Leiden.

———, and K. Raaflaub, eds. 1997. *Democracy 2500?* Dubuque, IA.

Morris, S. P. 1992a. "Introduction." In Kopcke and Tokumaru 1992: xiii–xviii.

———. 1992b. *Daidalos and the Origins of Greek Art*. Princeton.

———. 1995. "From Modernism to Manure." *Antiquity* 69: 182–5.

Morrison, J., and R. Williams. 1968. *Greek Oared Ships*. Cambridge.

Most, G. 1985. *The Measures of Praise*. Göttingen.

———. 1997. "The Fire Next Time. Cosmology, Allegoresis, and Salvation in the Derveni Papyrus." *JHS* 117: 117–35.

Mountjoy, P. 1986. *Mycenaean Decorated Pottery*. Göteborg.

Mullen, E. T. 1997. *Ethnic Myths and Pentateuchal Foundations*. Atlanta.

Müller, D. K. 1987. "The Process of Systematization." In D. K. Müller, F. Ringer, and B. Simon, eds., *The Rise of the Modern Educational System*: 16–52. Cambridge.

Müller, W., and F. Oelmann. 1912. "Die 'geometrische' Nekropole." In G. Karo, ed., *Tiryns* I: 125–67. Berlin.

Munn, N. 1983. "Gawan Kula: Spatiotemporal Control and the Symbolism of Influence." In J. Leach and E. Leach, eds., *The Kula*: 277–308. Cambridge.

———. 1986. *The Fame of Gawa*. Cambridge.

Murray, G. 1907. *The Rise of the Greek Epic*. Oxford.

Murray, O. 1980. *Early Greece*. 1st ed. Glasgow.

———. 1990a. "Sympotic history." In Murray 1990b: 3–13.

———, ed., 1990b. *Sympotica*. Oxford.

Musti, D., A. Sacconi, L. Rocchetti, M. Rocchi, E. Scafa, L. Sportiello, and M. E. Giannotta, eds. 1991. *La transizione dal miceneo all' alto arcaismo*. Rome.

Mylonas, G. 1975. *To Dytikon Nekrotapheion tis Elefsinos*. 3 vols. Athens.

Myres, J. L., and D. Gray. 1958. *Homer and His Critics*. London.

Näf, B. 1986. *Vom Pericles zu Hitler?* Bern.

Nagy, G. 1979. *The Best of the Achaeans*. Baltimore.

———. 1985. "Theognis and Megara." In T. Figueira and G. Nagy, eds., *Theognis of Megara*: 22–81. Baltimore.

———. 1990. *Greek Mythology and Poetics*. Ithaca, NY.

———. 1992. "Homeric questions." *TAPA* 122: 15–60.

———. 1996. *Homeric Questions*. Austin, TX.

Naveh, J. 1982. *Early History of the Alphabet*. Jerusalem.

Neer, R. 1997. "Beazley and the Language of Connoisseurship." *Hephaistos* 15: 7–30.

Nevett, L. 1994. "Separation or Seclusion?" In M. Parker Pearson and C. Richards, eds., *Architecture and Order*: 98–112. London.

——. 1995. "Gender Relations in the Classical Greek Household." *BSA* 90: 363–81.

Niemeyer, H. G., ed. 1982. *Phönizier im Westen*. Mainz.

Niethammer, L. 1993. *Posthistoire*. Trs. P. Camiller. New York.

Nightingale, A. 1995. *Genres in Dialogue*. Cambridge.

——. 1996. "Aristotle on the 'Liberal' and 'Illiberal' Arts." *Proceedings of the Boston Area Colloquium in Ancient Philosophy* 12: 29–38.

Nilsson, M. 1933. *Homer and Mycenae*. London.

North, H. 1966. *Sophrosyne*. Ithaca, NY.

Norton, C. 1900. "The Progress of the Archaeological Institute of America." *AJA* 4: 1–16.

Novick, P. 1988. *That Noble Dream: The "Objectivity Question" and the American Historical Profession*. Cambridge.

Oakley, J. 1998. "Why Study a Greek Vase-Painter?" *Antiquity* 72: 209–13.

Ober, J. 1989. *Mass and Elite in Democratic Athens*. Princeton.

——. 1991. "Aristotle's Political Sociology." In C. Lord and D. O'Connor, eds., *Essays on the Foundations of Aristotelian Political Science*: 112–35. Berkeley.

——. 1996. *The Athenian Revolution*. Princeton.

——. 1998. *Political Dissent in Classical Athens*. Princeton.

O'Brien, J. 1993. *The Tranformation of Hera*. Lanham, MD.

Oldroyd, D. 1984. "How did Darwin Arrive at his Theory?" *History of Science* 22: 325–74.

Orser, C. 1996a. *A Historical Archaeology of the Modern World*. New York.

——, ed. 1996b. *Images of the Recent Past*. New York.

Osborne, M. J. 1981–3. *Naturalization in Athens*. 4 vols. Brussels.

Osborne, R. 1988. "Social and Economic Implications of the Leasing of Land and Property in Classical and Hellenistic Greece." *Chiron* 18: 279–323.

——. 1991. "Pride and Prejudice, Sense and Subsistence." In Rich and Wallace-Hadrill 1991: 119–46.

——. 1992. "'Is it a Farm?' The Definition of Agricultural Sites and Settlements in Ancient Greece." In Wells 1992: 21–7.

——. 1996. *Greece in the Making 1200–479 BC*. London.

Ostwald, M. 1969. *Nomos and the Beginnings of the Athenian Democracy*. Oxford.

Page, D. L. 1955. *Sappho and Alcaeus*. Oxford.

——. 1962. *Poetae Melici Graeci*. Oxford.

Papadopoulos, J. 1993. "To Kill a Cemetery: The Athenian Kerameikos and the Early Iron Age in the Aegean." *JMA* 6: 175–206.

Parker, D., trs. 1969. *Aristophanes: Three Comedies*. Ann Arbor, MI.

Parry, J., and M. Bloch. 1989. "Introduction." In J. Parry and M. Bloch, eds., *Money and the Morality of Exchange*: 1–32. Cambridge.

Parry, M. 1971 [1928–37]. *The Making of Homeric Verse*, ed. by A. Parry. Oxford.

Patterson, C. 1986. "*Hai Attikai.*" *Helios* 13: 49–67.

Patterson, O. 1982. *Slavery and Social Death*. Cambridge, MA.

Patterson, T. 1995. *Toward a Social History of Archaeology in the United States*. Orlando, FL.

Petrakos, V. 1987. *I en Athinais Archaiologikis Etairea: I Istoria ton 150 Chronon tis 1837–1987*. Athens.

Plassart, A. 1973. "Un siècle de fouilles à Délos." In *Études déliennes*: 5–16. Paris: *Bulletin de correspondance hellénique* supp. vol. 1.

Pomeroy, S. 1994. *Xenophon, Oeconomicus*. Oxford.

Popham, M. R. 1994. "Precolonisation: Early Greek Contact with the East." In Tsetskhladze and De Angelis 1994: 11–34.

Popham, M. R., P. G. Calligas, and L. H. Sackett. 1993. *Lefkandi* II.2. Athens: British School at Athens supp. vol. 23.

Popham, M. R., and I. Lemos. 1996. *Lefkandi* III: *Plates*. Athens: British School at Athens supp. vol. 29.

Popham, M. R., and L. H. Sackett. 1968. *Excavations at Lefkandi, Euboea, 1964–66*. London: British School at Athens supp. paper.

Popham, M. R., L. H. Sackett, and P. G. Themelis. 1980. *Lefkandi* I. London: British School at Athens supp. vol. 11.

Popham, M. R., E. Touloupa, and L. H. Sackett. 1982. "The Hero of Lefkandi." *Antiquity* 56: 169–74.

Poulsen, F. 1905. *Die Dipylongräber und die Dipylonvasen*. Leipzig.

Powell, B. 1991. *Homer and the Origin of the Greek Alphabet*. Cambridge.

Praetzellis, A., and M. Praetzellis, eds. 1998. *Archaeologists as Storytellers*. Tucson: *Historical Archaeology* 32.1.

Preucel, R., ed. 1991. *Processual and Postprocessual Archaeologies*. Carbondale, IL.

Pritchard, J. B. 1955. *Ancient Near Eastern Texts Relating to the Old Testament*. Princeton.

Purcell, N. 1990. "Mobility and the Polis." In O. Murray and S. Price, eds., *The Greek City*: 29–58. Oxford.

Raaflaub, K. 1985. *Die Entdeckung der Freiheit*. Munich: *Vestigia* 37.

———. 1989. "Contemporary Perceptions of Democracy in Fifth-Century Athens." *CM* 40: 33–70.

———. 1997. "Soldiers, Citizens, and the Evolution of the Early Greek Polis." In Mitchell and Rhodes 1997: 49–59.

———. 1998. "A Historian's Headache: How to Read 'Homeric Society'?" In Fisher and van Wees 1998: 169–93.

Radet, G. 1901. *L'histoire et l'oeuvre de l'Ecole française d'Athènes*. Paris.

Radt, S., B. Snell, and R. Kannicht, eds. 1977. *Tragicorum Graecorum Fragmenta* I. Göttingen.

Ravn, M., and R. Britton, eds. 1997. *Archaeological Review from Cambridge* 14.1. Cambridge.

Reber, K. 1991. *Untersuchungen zur handgemachten Keramik Griechenlands in der submykenischen, protogeometrischen und geometrischen Zeit.* Jonsered.

Redfield, James. 1973. "The making of the *Odyssey.*" In A. Yu, ed., *Parnassus Revisited*: 141–54. Chicago.

———. 1975. *Nature and Culture in the Iliad.* Chicago.

———. 1991. "Classics and Anthropology." *Arion* 3rd ser. 1: 5–23.

Renfrew, C. 1972. *The Emergence of Civilisation.* London.

———. 1973. *Before Civilisation.* London.

———. 1980. "The Great Tradition Versus the Great Divide." *AJA* 84: 287–98.

Rhodes, P. J., trs. 1984. *Aristotle, the Athenian Constitution.* Harmondsworth.

Rich, J., and A. Wallace-Hadrill, eds. 1991. *City and Country in the Ancient World.* London.

Ridgeway, W. 1908. "The Relationship of Anthropology to Clasical Studies." *Journal of the Royal Anthropological Institute* 39: 10–25.

Ridgway, D. 1992. *The First Western Greeks.* Cambridge.

———. 1994. "Phoenicians and Greeks in the West." In Tsetskhladze and De Angelis 1994: 35–46.

Ringer, F. 1979a. "The German Academic Community." In A. Oleson and J. Voss, eds., *The Organization of Knowledge in Modern America, 1860–1920*: 409–29. Baltimore.

———. 1979b. *Education and Society in Modern Europe.* Bloomington, IN.

Roberts, J. T. 1993. *Athens on Trial.* Princeton.

Robertson, M. 1985. "Beazley and Attic Vase Painting." In D. Kurtz, ed., *Beazley and Oxford*: 19–30. Oxford.

———. 1991. "Adopting an Approach." In T. Rasmussen and N. Spivey, eds., *Looking at Greek Vases*: 1–12. Cambridge.

Robinson, E. 1997. *The First Democracies.* Stuttgart: *Historia* Einzelschrift 107.

Rohde, E. 1966 [1890]. *Psyche.* Trs. W. B. Hillis. New York.

Rombos, T. 1988. *The Iconography of Attic Late Geometric II Pottery.* Jonsered.

Rose, P. 1988. "Thersites and the Plural Voices of Homer." *Arethusa* 21: 5–25.

———. 1992. *Sons of the Gods, Children of the Earth.* Ithaca, NY.

———. 1997. "Ideology in the *Iliad.*" *Arethusa* 30: 151–99.

Rosen, R. 1988a. *Old Comedy and the Iambographic Tradition.* Atlanta.

———. 1988b. "Hipponax, Boupalos, and the Conventions of the *Psogos.*" *TAPA* 118: 29–41.

———. 1990. "Poetry and Sailing in Hesiod's *Works and Days.*" *CA* 9: 99–113.

———. 1997. "Homer and Hesiod." In Morris and Powell 1997: 463–88.

Rosenmeyer, P. 1992. *The Poetics of Imitation.* Cambridge.

Rosivach, V. 1985. "Manning the Athenian Fleet, 433–426 BC." *American Journal of Ancient History* 10: 41–66.

Rouse, I. 1953. "The Strategy of Culture History." In S. Tax, ed., *Anthropology Today. Selections*: 84–103. Chicago.

Roussel, D. 1976. *Tribu et cité.* Lille.

Rudhardt, J. 1981. "Le mythe hésiodique des races et celui de Prométhée." *Revue européene des sciences sociales* 19, no. 58: 245–81.

Ruijgh, C. J. 1995. "D'Homère aux origines proto-mycéniennes de la tradition épique." In Crielaard 1995: 1–96.

Rupp, D. 1988. "The 'Royal Tombs' at Salamis (Cyprus)." *JMA* 1: 111–39.

Rutter, J. 1981. "A Plea for the Abandonment of the Term 'Submycenaean.'" *Temple University Aegean Symposium* 3: 58–65.

———. 1990. "Some Comments on Interpreting the Dark-Surfaced Handmade Burnished Pottery of the 13th and 12th Centuries." *JMA* 3: 29–49.

———. 1992. "Cultural Novelties in the Post-Palatial Aegean World: Indices of Vitality or Decline?" In Ward and Joukowsky 1992: 61–78.

Sabloff, J. and G. Willey. 1967. "The Collapse of Maya Civilization in the Southern Lowlands: A Consideration of History and Process." *Southwestern Journal of Anthropology* 23: 311–36.

Säflund, G. 1965. *Excavations at Berbati, 1936–1937.* Stockholm.

Sahlins, M. 1985. *Islands of History.* Chicago.

Said, E. 1978. *Orientalism.* New York.

St. Clair, W. 1983. *Lord Elgin and the Marbles.* 2nd ed. Oxford.

Ste. Croix, G. E. M. de. 1966. "The Estate of Phainippos (Ps.-Dem., xlii)." In E. Badian, ed., *Ancient Society and Institutions*: 109–14. Oxford.

———. 1981. *The Class Struggle in the Ancient Greek World.* London.

Sakellariou, M. 1980. *Les proto-grecs.* Athens.

Sallares, R. 1991. *The Ecology of Ancient Greece.* Ithaca, NY.

Samuel, R. 1992. "Reading the Signs: Part II. Fact-Grubbers and Mind-Readers." *HWJ* 33: 220–51.

Sartori, G. 1973. *Democratic Theory.* Westport, CT.

Schilardi, D. 1984. "The LH IIIC Period at the Koukounaries Acropolis." In J. A. MacGillivray and R. Barber, eds., *The Prehistoric Cyclades*: 184–206. Edinburgh.

———. 1988. "The Temple of Athena at Koukounaries on Paros." In Hägg *et al.* 1988: 41–8.

Schlesier, R. 1994. *Kulte, Mythen und Gelehrte: Anthropologie der Antike seit 1800.* Frankfurt.

Schmaus, W., U. Segerstrale, and D. Jesseph. 1992. "Hard Program: A Manifesto." *Social Epistemology* 6: 243–65.

Schnapp, A. 1996. *The Discovery of the Past.* Trs. I. Kinnes and G. Varndell. London.

Schuchhardt, C. 1891. *Schliemann's Excavations.* London.

Schweitzer, A. 1917. "Untersuchungen zur Chronologie und Geschichte der geometrischen Stile in Griechenland I." *AM* 43: 1–152.

Semple, S. 1998. "A Fear of the Past: The Place of the Prehistoric Burial Mound in the Ideology of Middle and Later Anglo-Saxon England." *WA* 30: 109–26.

Sen, A. 1992. *Inequality Reexamined.* Cambridge, MA.

Sewell, W. 1996. "Three Temporalities: Toward an Eventful Sociology." In McDonald 1996: 245–80.

Seybold, K., and J. von Ungern-Sternberg. 1993. "Amos und Hesiod." In K. Raaflaub and E. Müller-Luckner, eds., *Anfänge politischen Denkens in der Antike*: 215–40. Munich.

Shanks, M. 1992. *Experiencing the Past.* London.

——. 1996. *Classical Archaeology of Greece*. London.

——. 1999. *Art and the Early Greek City-State*. Cambridge.

Shanks, M., and C. Tilley. 1987a. *Re-Constructing Archaeology*. Cambridge.

——. 1987b. *Social Theory and Archaeology*. Albuquerque, NM.

——. 1989. "Archaeology into the 1990s." *NAR* 22: 1–14.

Shear, T. L., Sr. 1938. "The Campaign of 1937." *Hesperia* 7: 311–62.

Sheftel, P. S. 1979. "The Archaeological Institute of America, 1879–1979." *AJA* 83: 3–17.

Shefton, B. 1982. "Greeks and Greek Imports in the South of the Iberian Peninsula." In Niemeyer 1982: 337–70.

Shorey, P. 1919. "Fifty Years of Classical Scholarship." *TAPA* 50: 33–61.

Simmel, G. 1968 [1911]. "The Ruin." Trs. D. Kettler. In K. Wolff, ed., *Georg Simmel, 1858–1918*: 259–66. Columbus, OH.

Simon, C. 1986. "The Archaic Votive Offerings and Cults of Ionia." Unpublished Ph.D. dissertation, Berkeley.

Sipsie-Eschbach, E. 1991. *Protogeometrische Keramik aus Iolkos in Thessalien*. Berlin.

Small, D. 1990. "Handmade Burnished Ware and Prehistoric Aegean Economics." *JMA* 3: 3–25.

——. 1997. "An Archaeology of Democracy?" In Morris and Raaflaub 1997: 217–27.

Snell, B., and H. Maehler. 1970. *Bacchylides Carmina cum Fragmentis*. Leipzig.

Snodgrass, A. M. 1964. *Early Greek Armour and Weapons*. Edinburgh.

——. 1965. "The Hoplite Reform and History." *JHS* 85: 110–22.

——. 1971. *The Dark Age of Greece*. Edinburgh.

——. 1974. "An Historical Homeric Society?" *JHS* 94: 114–25.

——. 1977. *Archaeology and the Rise of the Greek State*. Cambridge.

——. 1980a. *Archaic Greece*. London.

——. 1980b. "Iron and Early Metallurgy in the Mediterranean." In Wertime and Muhly 1980: 335–74.

——. 1987. *An Archaeology of Greece*. Berkeley.

——. 1988. "The Archaeology of the Hero." *AION* 10: 19–26.

——. 1993. "The Rise of the Polis." In M. Hansen, ed., *The Ancient Greek City-State*: 30–40. Copenhagen.

——. 1994. "The Euboeans in Macedonia." *AION* n.s. 1: 87–93.

——. 1998a. "A Liberating Event." *Cambridge Archaeological Journal* 8: 132–4.

——. 1998b. *Homer and the Artists*. Cambridge.

Sørenson, M. L. S., and R. Thomas, eds. 1989a. *The Bronze Age-Iron Age Transition in Europe*. Oxford: *BAR* S 483.

——. 1989b. "Introduction." In Sørenson and Thomas 1989a: 1–21.

Sotiriadis, G. 1909. *Ta Elleipsoeidi Ktismata tou Thermou*. Athens.

Spahn, P. 1977. *Mittelschicht und Polisbildung*. Frankfurt.

Stampolidis, N. 1995. "Homer and the Cremation Burials of Eleutherna." In Crielaard 1995: 289–308.

Stanyan, T. 1739. *The Grecian History*. London.

Starr, C. G. 1961. *The Origins of Greek Civilization*. New York.

———. 1974. Review of Desborough 1972. *American Journal of Philology* 95: 114–16.

———. 1977. *Economic and Social Growth of Early Greece*. Oxford.

Stedman Jones, G. 1983. *Languages of Class*. Cambridge.

———. 1996. "The Determinist Fix." *HWJ* 42: 19–35.

———. 1998. "Une autre histoire sociale?" *Annales Histoires Sciences Sociales* 53: 383–94.

Stehle, E. 1990. "Sappho's Gaze." *differences* 2: 88–125.

Steiner, D. T. 1993. *The Tyrant's Writ*. Princeton.

Stein-Hölkeskamp, E. 1989. *Adelskultur und Polisgesellschaft*. Stuttgart.

———. 1997. "Adel und Volk bei Theognis." In W. Eder and K-J. Hölkeskamp, eds., *Volk und Verfassung im vorhellenistischen Griechenland*: 21–35. Stuttgart.

Stocking, G., ed. 1996. *Volksgeist as Method and Ethic*. Madison, WI.

Strauss, B. 1997. "Genealogy, Ideology, and Society in Democratic Athens." In Morris and Raaflaub 1997: 141–54.

Strøm, I. 1992. "Evidence from the Sanctuaries." In Kopcke and Tokumaru 1992: 46–60.

Styrenius, C. G. 1967. *Submycenaean Studies*. Lund.

Szegedy-Maszak, A. 1978. "Legends of the Greek Lawgivers." *Greek, Roman and Byzantine Studies* 19: 199–209.

Sznycer, M. 1979. "L'inscription phénicienne de Tekke, près de Cnossus." *Kadmos* 18: 89–93.

Tandy, D. 1997. *Warriors into Traders*. Berkeley.

Taylor, W. 1948. *A Study of Archaeology*. Menasha, WI: *Memoirs of the American Anthropological Association* 69.

Thalmann, W. 1988. "Thersites: Comedy, Scapegoats, and Heroic Ideology in the *Iliad*." *TAPA* 118: 1–28.

Themelis, P., and Y. Touratsoglou. 1997. *Oi Taphoi tou Derveniou*. Athens.

Themelis, P. G. 1976. *Frühgriechische Grabbauten*. Mainz.

Thirlwall, C. 1835. *History of Greece* I. London.

Thomas, J. 1996. *Time, Culture and Identity*. London.

Thompson, E. P. 1978. *The Poverty of Theory and Other Essays*. London.

———. 1991. *Customs in Common*. New York.

Tilley, C. 1990. "Claude Lévi-Strauss: Structuralism and Beyond." In C. Tilley, ed., *Reading Material Culture*: 3–81. Oxford.

———. 1993. "Introduction." In C. Tilley, ed., *Interpretative Archaeology*: 1–27. New York.

———. 1996. *An Ethnography of the Neolithic*. Cambridge.

Trigger, B. 1978. *Time and Traditions*. Edinburgh.

———. 1984. "Alternative Archaeologies: Nationalist, Colonialist, Imperialist." *Man* 19: 355–70.

———. 1989. *A History of Archaeological Thought*. Cambridge.

Tsetskhladze, G., and F. De Angelis. 1994. *The Archaeology of Greek Colonisation*. Oxford.

Turner, F. M. 1981. *The Greek Heritage in Victorian Britain*. New Haven, CT.
——. 1997. "The Homeric Question." In Morris and Powell 1997: 123–45.
Vallet, G., and F. Villard. 1976. *Mégara Hyblaea* I. Paris.
van Effenterre, H. 1985. *La cité grecque*. Paris.
Vanschoonwinkel, J. 1991. *L'Égée et la méditerranée orientale à la fin du IIe millénaire*. Louvain-la-Neuve and Providence, RI: *Archaeologia Transatlantica* 9.
van Seters, J. 1983. *In Search of History: Historiography in the Ancient World and the Origins of Biblical History*. New Haven, CT.
van Wees, H. 1992. *Status Warriors*. Amsterdam.
——. 1995. "Princes at Dinner." In Crielaard 1995: 147–82.
——. 1996. "Heroes, Knights and Nutters." In A. Lloyd, ed., *Battle in Antiquity*: 1–86. London.
——. 1997. "Homeric Warfare." In Morris and Powell 1997: 668–93.
Verdelis, N. 1958. *O Protogeometrikos Rythmos en Thessalia*. Athens.
Vernant, J.-P. 1980. *Myth and Society in Ancient Greece*. Trs. J. Lloyd. Brighton.
——. 1983. *Myth and Thought Among the Greeks*. London.
——. 1989. "At Man's Table." In M. Detienne and J.-P. Vernant, eds., *The Cuisine of Sacrifice Among the Greeks*. Trs. P. Wissing. Chicago.
——. 1991. *Mortals and Immortals*. Trs. F. Zeitlin, A. Szegedy-Maszak, and D. Lyons. Princeton.
Veyne, P. 1988. *Did the Greeks Believe in Their Myths?* Trs. P. Wissig. Chicago.
Vidal-Naquet, P. 1986. *The Black Hunter*. Trs. A. Szegedy-Maszak. Baltimore.
——. 1995. *Politics Ancient and Modern*. Trs. J. Lloyd. Cambridge.
von Bothmer, D. 1987. "Greek Vase Painting: 200 Years of Connoiseurship." In D. von Bothmer, ed., *Papers on the Amasis Painter and His World*: 184–204. Malibu, CA.
von Gerkan, A. 1925. *Milet* I.8. Berlin.
Vovelle, M. 1990. *Ideologies and Mentalities*, trs. E. O'Flaherty. Chicago.
Wace, A., and F. Stubbings, eds. 1962. *A Companion to Homer*. London.
Wade-Gery, H. T. 1952. *The Poet of the Iliad*. Cambridge.
Walcot, P. 1962. "Hesiod and the Instructions of 'Onchsheshonqy.'" *Journal of Near Eastern Studies* 21: 215–19.
——. 1966. *Hesiod and the Near East*. Cardiff.
Waldstein, C. 1902–5. *The Argive Heraeum*. 2 vols. Boston.
Waley, D. 1968. *The Italian City-Republics*. London.
Wallinga, H. T. 1993. *Ships and Sea-Power Before the Great Persian War*. Leiden.
Walzer, M. 1983. *Spheres of Justice*. New York.
Ward, W., and M. S. Joukowsky, eds. 1992. *The Crisis Years: The Twelfth Century* BC. Dubuque, IA.
Warner, R., trs. 1954. *The Peloponnesian War*. Harmondsworth.
Weber, M. 1949. *The Methodology of the Social Sciences*. Trs. E. Shils and H. Finch. Glencoe, IL.

———. 1968. *Economy and Society.* 2 vols. Trs. G. Roth and C. Wittich. New York.

———. 1976 [1896]. *The Agrarian Sociology of Ancient Civilizations.* Trs. R. Hilty. London.

Weinberg, S. 1943. *Corinth* VII.1. Princeton.

Wells, B. 1976. *Asine* II.4.1. Stockholm.

———. 1983. *Asine* II.4.2–3. Stockholm.

———, ed. 1992. *Agriculture in Ancient Greece.* Stockholm.

Wertime, T., and J. Muhly, eds. 1980. *The Coming of the Age of Iron.* New Haven, CT.

West, M. L. 1966. *Hesiod. Theogony.* Oxford.

———. 1974. *Studies in Greek Elegy and Iambus.* Berlin.

———. 1978. *Hesiod, Works and Days.* Oxford.

———. 1985. *The Hesiodic Catalogie of Women.* Oxford.

———. 1991/2. *Iambi et Elegi Graeci.* 2 vols. 2nd ed. Oxford.

———. 1997. *The East Face of Helicon.* Oxford.

White, H. 1973. *Metahistory.* Baltimore.

———. 1987. *The Content of the Form.* Baltimore.

———. 1992. "Historical Emplotment and the Problem of Truth." In S. Friedlander, ed., *Probing the Limits of Representation*: 37–53. Cambridge, MA.

Whitehead, D. 1977. *The Ideology of the Athenian Metic.* Cambridge: Cambridge Philological Society supp. vol. 4.

———. 1986. *The Demes of Attica.* Princeton.

Whitley, J. 1988. "Early States and Hero Cults." *JHS* 108: 173–82.

———. 1991a. *Style and Society in Dark Age Greece.* Cambridge.

———. 1991b. "Social Diversity in Dark Age Greece." *BSA* 86: 341–65.

———. 1994a. "Protoattic Pottery: A Contextual Approach." In I. Morris, ed., *Classical Greece*: 51–70. Cambridge.

———. 1994b. "The Monuments that Stood Before Marathon." *AJA* 90: 213–30.

———. 1997a. "Beazley as Theorist." *Antiquity* 71: 40–7.

———. 1997b. "Cretan Laws and Literacy." *AJA* 93: 635–61.

———. Forthcoming. "Gender and Hierarchy in Early Athens." Forthcoming in *Métis.*

Williams, D. 1991/93. "The 'Pot-Hoard' Pot from the Archaic Artemision at Ephesus." *BICS* 38: 98–103.

Willis, P. 1977. *Learning to Labour.* London.

Winckelmann, J. J. 1968 [1764]. *History of Ancient Art.* 2 vols. Trs. J. Ungar. New York.

Winkler, J. 1990. *The Constraints of Desire.* London.

Winter, I. 1995. "Homer's Phoenicians." In J. Carter and S. P. Morris, eds., *The Ages of Homer*: 247–71. Austin, TX.

Wiseman, J. 1980. "Archaeology in the Future." *AJA* 84: 279–85.

———. 1989. "Archaeology Today: From the Field to the Classroom and Beyond." *American Journal of Archaeology* 93: 437–44.

Wolf, F. A. 1985 [1795]. *Prolegomena to Homer.* Eds. A. Grafton, G. Most, and J. Zetzel. Princeton.

Wolpert, A. 1995. "Rebuilding the Walls of Athens." Unpublished Ph.D. dissertation, University of Chicago.

Wood, E. M. 1988. *Peasant-Citizen and Slave*. London.

Woodhead, G., ed. 1967. *Supplementum Epigraphicum Graecum* 22. Leiden.

Wright, J. H. 1897. "Editorial Announcement." *AJA* n.s. 1: 1–4.

Yoffee, N., and A. Sherratt, eds. 1993. *Archaeological Theory: Who Sets the Agenda?* Cambridge.

Zaimis, A., and Petridis, P. 1928. "Peri tropou ekteleseos archaiologikon anaskaphon." Athens: Presidential Decree FEK/6/1929/tA'.

——. 1932. "Peri archaiotiton." People's Law 5351. Athens.

Zeitlin, F. 1986. "Thebes: Theater of Self and Society in Athenian Drama." In J. P. Euben, ed., *Greek Tragedy and Political Theory*: 101–41. Berkeley.

——. 1996. *Playing the Other*. Chicago.

Index

Mimnermus, 177
Minoa (Amorgos), 236, 274
misogyny, 155, 181, 312
Mitford, W., 55, 80–3
Mittelschicht, 161–2, 190
Mnesiepes, 159
model building, 112–13, 159–61,
 252–3; *see also* Mediterranean
 models
Moore, H. L., 283–4
Morgan, C., 110, 276, 278, 280
Morris, S. P., 101–3
Most, G., 188
Mount Imittos, 273, 292
Munn, N., 129–30, 153
Murray, G., 89–90
Murray, O., 78, 97, 183
Muses, 164
museums, 53–4, 55, 58, 60, 62–3
music, 189
Mycenae, 50, 198, 199, 210
myth of races, 229–30, 270–1

Nagy, G., 97, 157, 166, 169, 172–3,
 175, 234–5, 318 n. 1
Napoleon, 44, 46
narrative, 6, 52–3, 69
nationalism, 37–8, 43, 47–9, 51–2,
 57, 60, 65, 82, and chapter 2
 passim
Naveh, J., 262–3
navy, Athenian, 143, 162
Naxos, 186, 244, 246–9, 250, 288
Naxos (Sicily), 280–3
Near East, 102–5, 128–9, 167–8,
 178–85, 208–10, 232–4, 239–46,
 254–6, 265, 272, 274–9
Neoboule, 159
"Nestor's Cup," 264
Nevett, L., 149, 282
Newton, C., 53–4, 85
Nicias, 122
Nicomachus, 127
Niebuhr, B., 51
Niethammer, L., 109
Nilsson, M., 89
nomads, 200, 259–60

nomos, 166, 290
Norton, C., 57–8, 60

Ober, J., 114, 119, 131, 132
oikos, 184, 286; *oikos* society, 225
Old Oligarch, 127, 132, 136
Olympia, 50, 52, 89
Onqsheshonquy, Instructions of, 167
Opheltas spit, 262
oracles, 126
Orchomenos, 243, 250
Orgame, 235
orientalism, 45–8
orientalizing styles, 182, 184, 228,
 241, 276–80, 294, 297, 300
Oropos, 283, 288
Orphics, 26
Osborne, R., 140–1, 142, 300
Osteria dell' Osa, 262
ostracism, 138
Ostwald, M., 166
Otanes, 186
Otranto, 254
Oxford University, 65

Page, D., 177
Pandora, 164, 170, 291–2
Panhellenism, 97, 157, 190, 261–2
Papadopoulos, J., 226–7
Paphos, 262
paradigm shifts, 97
Paros, 283; *see also* Koukounaries
Parry, J., 133
Parry, M., 90–1
Pasion, 152
PASOK, 65
pastoralism, 96, 259–60
Patroclus, 235, 237, 271–2, 317 n. 26
patronage, 139–44
Patterson, C., 145
Patterson, O., 150
Patterson, T., 71
Perachora, 279
Perati, 198, 202, 204
perfume, 178, 180–1, 182, 189; *see
 also* cosmetics
Pericles, 120, 124, 143